FIFTY
FIFTY

FIFTY
FIFTY

CARCANET'S JUBILEE IN LETTERS

with an introduction and interjections by
Michael Schmidt

edited by
Robyn Marsack

CARCANET

First published in Great Britain in 2019 by
Carcanet
Alliance House, 30 Cross Street
Manchester M2 7AQ
www.carcanet.co.uk

A CIP catalogue record for this book is
available from the British Library.
ISBN 978 1 78410 878 6

Book design by Andrew Latimer
Printed in Great Britain by SRP Ltd, Exeter, Devon

The publisher acknowledges financial
assistance from Arts Council England.

CONTENTS

For Kate Gavron

EDITOR'S NOTE

My own connection with Carcanet Press began in 1981, when I approached Michael Schmidt with the suggestion that Carcanet re-publish the poems of Edmund Blunden. He said they had been wanting to do so and asked me to make a selection. When I delivered it to him in Manchester, I was enthralled by the nature of the operation in the small Corn Exchange office. Michael forgave me for tripping over a cord and wrenching a plug from the wall, which erased his morning's typesetting – and in 1982 I joined the firm as a novice sales and marketing understudy, while hankering to be an editor. I worked out of Helen Lefroy's spare room in London, had a spell at the Corn Exchange when Peter Jones was away in India, and then moved to premises in Southwark when Bob Gavron acquired Carcanet. The Folio Society kindly gave us an office in the corner of their building: my own desk at last, and a phone, and access to all sorts of publishing experience in kind colleagues there... My connection with Carcanet continues, and so does the education in poetry it provides.

Mark Fisher's 20th anniversary compilation, *Letters to an Editor* (Carcanet, 1989), proceeded along different lines from the current one, with 328 letters, several from the same writers over the years, no notes, and introductions to each locale – Oxford, Cheadle Hulme, Manchester – of the Press that are shrewdly informative. I was amused to read some of the reactions to the request for permissions to publish those letters, including this one from Patricia Beer (21 January 1989):

I am fascinated by the idea of an anthology of letters to Carcanet and in principle I am delighted with the possibility of being included in it. I'm fairly certain that I haven't said anything indiscreet in mine (though of course I shall be glad to be shown that I haven't) but I do wonder if I've said anything interesting – lapidary comments or good jokes or anything like that – and I shall be glad to be shown that I have.

[…] is there anything else I can do? Shall I write a bestseller?[1]

James Atlas, nine of whose letters were included in the compilation, wrote to MNS on 16 May 1989:

I have just spent the morning reading through these letters; what a strange experience! I feel paralyzed with self-consciousness as I sit down to write to you now: to think that one actually writes about oneself, and leaves a public record even in private correspondence. Of course, no one will ever write my biography; but as I read these letters, I had many tumultuous thoughts: that I've had an interesting life; that I did actually possess a certain degree of self-knowledge, though not enough to prevent me from doing things I shouldn't have done; that I'm only slightly different now than I was twenty years ago; and that these letters, I'm glad to say, might be of some slight interest to people interested in literature […] illuminate a little corner of literary life. It was fun reading them, remembering how happy and unhappy I've been.[2]

Living authors have mostly been very obliging about allowing publication in this volume, even if they have had misgivings about their younger selves and opinions; we are very grateful to them, and also to authors' executors/estates.

It has not always been easy to match correspondents with years: some correspondents would have provided letters of interest for every year; others, who have been really important to the Press, are nevertheless not represented here. As Stella

Halkyard observed to me: 'it's so interesting to see how significant numbers of writers seem to store up their best/ most lively writing for the work and seem not to want to waste it on mere letters, whilst for others their letters are all of a piece with the work'.

In the present compilation I have tried to suggest, through the footnotes, the wider context of the letters, and the connections between writers and publications – even so, not all the authors connected with the Press are mentioned. The bibliography, valiantly undertaken by Stella Halkyard, at least gives a sense of the range of each year's publications.

I have standardised dating, references to *PN Review* and book titles within letters. Omissions or occasional emendations are indicated by square brackets. Michael Schmidt is referred to as MNS.

NOTES

1. Patricia Beer (1924–99) was brought back into circulation by Carcanet, starting with her *Collected Poems* (1988) and then her fiction and non-fiction in the 1990s.

2. James Atlas (1949-2019) was at Oxford on a scholarship exchange from Harvard when MNS and Peter Jones were setting up Carcanet. He went on to become a notable editor (at the *New York Times*), critic and biographer, first of Delmore Schwartz and later of Saul Bellow. His *Shadow in the Garden: a biographer's trail* was published in 2017.

INTRODUCTION

I.

Memory, over time, becomes more and more a collaboration between actual events, accretions and imagination. There are gaps which imagination plausibly bridges or supplies from hearsay. The main problem with my memory, apart from its increasingly tenuous hold on some parts of the past, is that it has very little sense of chronology. Before and after are reversed and therefore, sometimes, effect and cause. One thing is unarguably true: the world into which Carcanet Press edged uncertainly in 1969 is so remote from the present-day reality of poetry publishing as to seem a foreign country and, despite its technological poverty, in many ways more amenable to the innocent prospector than the present republic of poetry. We did things differently there.

As an undergraduate at Wadham College, Oxford, and then for just a year as a graduate student, I experienced a curriculum remote from modern curricula. To be admitted to Oxford in 1967, one was required to know Latin, both to read it and in a rudimentary way to compose. Undergraduates spent the first year re-reading Virgil. Like most English writers and readers for generations before ours, from richer and poorer backgrounds, we knew something not only of Virgil but also of Horace, Catullus, Ovid, Caesar (*Gallia est omnis*...), Cicero, and we had been exposed to the historians, Tacitus in particular. If we hadn't read Martial, Juvenal, Propertius *et al*, we expected to make their acquaintance in due course.

We had to study Old and Middle English, reading the whole of *Beowulf,* much of the Anglo-Saxon poetic canon, and Chaucer, a substantial amount of Gower, Langland, *Gawain, Pearl* and then the Scottish Chaucerians (as we were taught not to call them) – Dunbar, Henryson and Gavin Douglas. Our main concern – certainly mine – was the primary texts, not the critical literature.

At the same time we were reading the English canon from the sixteenth through to the early twentieth century. All of us reading English spent our first term on Milton, conning the poetry and some of the prose, and applying to it what theory was about at the time (mainly classical theories of rhetoric and genre). Thus all undergraduates had a common grounding. We then progressed rapidly, more or less chronologically, from Wyatt and Surrey up to – if I'm not mistaken – D.H. Lawrence. Contemporary literature, being contemporary, we could tackle on our own.

Each week we wrote an essay for our medieval course and an essay for our modern course. Essays averaged 3,000 words. Each week we had a shared tutorial (usually two students) with our medieval tutor (in my case, Alan Ward) and with our modern tutor (in my case, Ian Donaldson in my first year and subsequently Terry Eagleton, fresh from Cambridge). There were lectures, too. Some of them were shrill and mannered and quite famous, like David Cecil's. The lectures I best remember were occasional, by Christopher Ricks, and by Roy Fuller when he was Professor of Poetry. The course lectures were not compulsory and, not being compelled, my attendance was irregular.

Terms were short – eight weeks of intensive study – with long breaks for reading and for travel, and for travail, as I began with friends to put Carcanet Press together.

The nature of the Oxford curriculum had a considerable impact on Carcanet. I loved the structure of the course and the way it gave me and my contemporaries a strong sense of continuities and developments, of the generic and thematic connections between works remote in tone and time. As the curricula changed, one of my missions as a publisher was to try to provide some texts a new reader might miss – hence an accessible Gower or Henryson, a Surrey, a Smart – reminders, signals of the primary wealth that is there, giving off its energies. And there were the neglected figures, neglected even by our teachers: Gascoigne, say, and the great Sermon writers, and Chatterton who seemed to us much more than a footnote, and Aphra Behn, the Rossettis. Carcanet's Fyfield Books (now the Carcanet Classics) were a response to a growing sense that the tradition, and not only the minor but key figures in it, were being allowed to drift off, or were being consciously sloughed, when they should remain current resources for poetry writers and readers.

We did not at the time seem troubled by the lack of choice in the curriculum, though we sometimes complained about omissions. We thought we would learn to choose our own ways in due course, which of course we did. My friends and I in establishing Carcanet thought we were publishing for writer-readers like ourselves. The *lecteur* was our *semblable* and *frère* and not yet an *hypocrite*. We learned to be ironists after the die was cast.

Had I not had a kind of phobia of libraries, I might not have become involved in publishing. Until my third year at Oxford, libraries struck me as picturesque but insanitary places. I would no more share a book (except with a friend) than I would a toothbrush. I did not like to read among other readers, their different degrees and intensities of concentration were a distraction, their physical presence a provocation. I liked to sit back comfortably and privately, indoors or out, to read, not bend forward in study mode. I must have been more of a reader than a student even then.

I bought books, especially second-hand books, which as soon as I acquired them seemed to be purged of pestilence. I became obsessed with editions published by Jacob Tonson (1655–1736) and down the years I acquired several. I developed a substantial personal library of old and new books that became an almost intolerable burden when changing domicile and city, and requiring miles of shelving. And now on my computer I have a good quarter of those expansive editions contained in no space at all. That's one of the most radical changes that half a century has wrought: to read widely we no longer need books.

Which is sad news for a publisher.

II.

It would be disingenuous of me not to mention one particular book which was formative and certainly had an impact on my editorial discriminations and set me at odds, from time to time, with writers I valued deeply – Edwin Morgan, Donald Davie, Laura Riding Jackson. I still think *Understanding Poetry* is a wonderful point of departure for a reader and writer, but one that needs to be left behind at a certain point. That point for me was when I encountered the poetry of C.H. Sisson in 1971 and realised that the furrow I was beginning to plough needed to be wider. There was much that I had to learn, and part of that learning entailed self-contradiction. Whitman's

Do I contradict myself?
Very well then I contradict myself,
(I am large, I contain multitudes.)

is a proper legend for the tombstone of a servant of any modern Muse. It is as well to remember that in Whitman's poem these words are uttered by a book. The book that speaks to us is the book we are reading, *Song of Myself*.

In the 1960s, and for three decades before and as many as three decades after, *Understanding Poetry: an anthology for college students*, edited by Cleanth Brooks and Robert Penn Warren, was the staple expository anthology for poetry-reading seniors in many American schools, and for university undergraduates. There was a companion volume about fiction.*

Understanding Poetry was first published in 1938, and after the war it gained ground, becoming *the* anthology of choice for teaching purposes in the United States. It went through three revisions, the first in 1950, by which time its use was widespread and its perceived defects needed remedying. There was the 1960 edition, with further improvements, the edition I used at school. The most recent revision to the book occurred in 1976. It had a run of almost half a century, adjusting New Critical ideas to a changing world. The changes in the anthology, of inclusion and exclusion, of critical extension and contraction, were in the interests of making the anthology's approach incontestable.

The book came out of the very milieu that helped to form Randall Jarrell, Robert Lowell, John Berryman and (to a lesser extent) Elizabeth Bishop; it is a book familiar to almost every American poet born between 1930 and 1970. Its effect was to clarify and to simplify; it homogenised readership. We – my classmates and I, my American generation – knew what

---

* I wonder if this is the specific book Thom Gunn had in mind when he called the anthology 'a pernicious modern nuisance which keeps readers away from *books* of poetry'.

poems are. There were right answers, there were acceptable procedures of reading and interpretation. Certain canonical poems responded well to the New Critical approach. They were foregrounded; poems that failed to respond were not included. Lyric and narrative were privileged and certain poetic procedures came to seem inevitable. Ron Silliman, who like many of us has had a struggle escaping the book's gravitational pull, describes it as 'hegemonic'. The contemporary reader brought up with it had specific expectations and recognised 'real poetry' and 'fake poetry' a mile off. Silliman's mature poetry wouldn't have stood a chance.

The introduction to *Understanding Poetry* lists general mistakes people make with poetry. Soon we are put right, we make no more mistakes; our career as contemporary readers is off to a confident start. We read well in ways we have been trained to do. A habit of mind is created: readers need explanation and direction; there is an authority and that authority is not generally challenged; the more a reader – student or teacher – instinctively performs the reading function promoted by the book, almost as a reflex, the better. The first step is to step back, create distance: we come to the perimeters of the poem not receptive and self-effacing, but with fixed expectations. We sneer at pretension and distrust experiment.

In the original prefatory 'Letter to the Teacher' the principles of the anthology are established.

This book has been conceived on the assumption that if poetry is worth teaching at all it is worth teaching as poetry. The temptation to make a substitute for the poem as the object of study is usually overpowering. The substitutes are various, but the most common ones are:

1. Paraphrase of logical and narrative content;
2. Study of biographical and historical materials;
3. Inspirational and didactic interpretation.

Of course, paraphrase may be necessary as a preliminary step in the reading of a poem, and a study of the biographical and historical background may do much to clarify interpretation; but these things should be considered as means and not as ends. And though one may consider a poem as an instance of historical or ethical documentation, the poem in itself, if literature is to be studied as literature, remains finally the object for study. Moreover, even if the interest is in the poem as a historical or ethical document, there is a prior consideration: one must grasp the poem as a literary construct before it can offer any real illumination as a document.

By this series of prescriptions, the poem should be sufficient in itself. We experience the poem by *reading*: it is textual, whatever its aural properties, and the strategies for understanding it start always in its textuality.

This book gave the American poet coming of age between 1940 and 1980 (at least) a substantial, stable and more or less constant 'contemporary reader' to address or affront, to beguile or *épater*. Poets had a clear choice: they could go along with it (they might be quite comfortable with it, as I was), or they could kick against it. Ginsberg, Creeley, Duncan, Snyder, Plath, Rich, Levertov, Baraka, Koch and Ashbery, Bernstein, Hejinian and Antin all had experience, direct or indirect, of the book and the people of the book and this experience was part of their formative environment.

A stable readership is a convenience. For publishers, the risk of selection is minimised. Teachers know what they are doing, examiners too. When decorums are rigorous, young writers have to be plucky to challenge them. Deviants are instantly recognised. No wonder reaction, when it came, was powerful, and diverse; no single party emerged but a number of different deniers. The independent imagination, once liberated, would neither accept the old confines nor subject itself to new – at least, for a time.

III.

It was also important in the formation of the Press that my close friends and colleagues, though we had a substantial shared culture, were profoundly engaged with certain poets and poetries. Gareth Reeves, whose father worked with Robert Graves and Laura Riding and who had spent childhood holidays in Mallorca in the company of the Graves establishment, was a gentle but firm editor in his own right; he and I spent – it sometimes seemed – all our waking hours talking about poetry, and his edition of George Herbert, produced shortly after we left Oxford, was a book that had a big impact on me.

Peter Jones, my closest friend and collaborator in establishing Carcanet, was passionate about Pound and was soon editing the *Penguin Book of Imagist Verse*. He was also writing *Fifty American Poets* and we read together, puzzling over some of those writers who would not fit the Procrustean bed of *Understanding Poetry* and who seemed especially difficult in an English context. Grevel Lindop was passionate about Yeats, and specifically about elements in Yeats, the mythologies, which I found and still find rebarbative. He was also reading Northrop Frye. There was continual, committed conversation; and other writers, too, played into this discourse.

Some of them were established writers. Peter Jones gave me the first *Collected Poems* of Elizabeth Jennings in 1967. I went to meet her, forming a close and durable friendship, though her own concerns did not intersect with mine, particularly, at the time. Anne Ridler was among the first poets I met and from whom I sought advice. It was either Donald Davie (who had come to know her work by way of Yvor Winters) or Roy Fuller (due to his fascination with syllabics and the prosodies it made possible), who suggested I go to meet Elizabeth

Daryush at Stockwell, the home her father, the poet laureate Robert Bridges, had built for her on Boar's Hill. I wrote a poem about her: she seemed so singular and exemplary to me at the time (even more so now). It included the lines:

> You evolved a mystic disregard for commerce,
> For war, assassination; instead adhered
> To what does not change, is not destroyed,
> What you share with Sumer, Greece and Alexandria,
> With Amherst, Weimar. Hampton Court,
> Curious territory no single map contains,
> A *Geist* without race, which cannot be annexed,
> Enjoined, perverted, a refinement
> Hungry for forms and the few sharp timeless truths.

Nothing could have been more remote from the poetics of modernism that enthralled my friends and me at the time, or the Poundian aesthetics of Donald Davie, and yet her poems appealed despite their remoteness from speech, the time-bound timelessness of their diction, their rhyme, their insistent otherness:

> Old hunter for youth's head,
>   These are your old decoys –
> A matron diamonded,
>   A man with golden toys;
>
> And these, too, long ago,
>   Were children that you charmed –
> This lad who failed to grow,
>   This girl still empty-armed

Even her syllabics, which are clearly spoken poems, come from a realm remote from the present. If syllabics were intended to bring the language closer to that of speech, her speech was from another age and realm.

There were other poets whose writing, if not lives, were as rooted as Elizabeth Daryush's, among them the ubiquitous, witty Sally Purcell, whose translations *Provençal Poems* (1970) was among our first crop of seven pamphlets, and who edited George Peele's poems for our Fyfield Books series. The Jesuit priest Peter Levi and the poet John Fuller – his Sycamore Press active producing hand-printed broadsheets and pamphlets – were also presences, but we were not so close to them. While I was an undergraduate, John's father Roy was elected Professor of Poetry. Though I campaigned against his candidacy, he was of a forgiving nature. Having pointed me in the direction of Elizabeth Daryush, he wrote the preface to her *Verses: Seventh Book* (1971), our first of her collections. He also urged me to read the poems of Marianne Moore. He was drawn to her syllabics, a form she articulated in the same year as Elizabeth Daryush did, and by her tone and manner, remote from the sometimes archaic feel of Daryush's.

IV.

I was in the habit of writing letters to people early on. Going away to school at the age of fourteen, I wrote almost daily to my mother; and as friendships developed there were always the long gaps of holidays when the only way of keeping in touch was writing. An epistolary habit is hard to shake, even when e-mail comes along. Indeed, e-mail can make the habit an addiction. Though the medium is treacherous and reductive, and one revises less than one should on a computer, still, it facilitates rather than inhibits the letter-writer.

Oxford and the wider literary environs, when my friends and I were undergraduates, were full of people who had served in the Second World War and quite a few from the First and those who had participated in the Spanish Civil War. Many not very much older adults had been children during the Second World War and history felt close. Peter Jones, born in 1927, was from Walsall and could remember the bombing of Coventry and the immediate post-war years.

For my own part I was a runaway from the Vietnam War, having won the draft lottery and renounced my American citizenship in 1968. I stress the feeling for continuities and for living – or survived – history because it was part of the sense of place we had, a place (and, in retrospect, a time) we were fortunate to occupy. It also entailed a strong belief in the centrality of politics, political ideas and debates, and of the literature to those ideas and debates, from the beginning but especially as exemplified in Milton, the great pamphlet tradition and the later engagements of Romanticism. Left and right had not polarised to the extent that they have today and, while the Entitled Tory was already a figure of caricature, the genuine conservative could be understood, the principles of permanence had not yet been discredited, and the fourth estate fulfilled its democratic function with relative care and tact. We were all sceptics but had not developed the cynicism that has become pervasive.

One final sub-set of observations, before we start reading the letters that my long-term comrade Robyn Marsack has chosen for this compendium.

When Carcanet began, the floor and the ceiling of the literary world were much closer together than they are now. I wrote a letter to Sir Basil Blackwell, one of the great booksellers of the age, and after a few days I had a reply. He invited me to tea, we had a lively exchange, and we remained in touch after that. He invited me to put little racks with Carcanet's pamphlet publications in his Broad Street shop (his office was just above the shop) and those racks survived for two decades, though they were used for other publishers' produce later on. A tiny publisher and a great bookseller were on the same side, as it were, and they met, despite the substantial gulf of years and experience between them, almost as equals. It was not impossible, in fact, for a tiny publisher to sell books to W.H. Smith, and when Elizabeth Jennings's *Collected Poems* received the W.H. Smith Award in 1987, we disposed of over 40,000 copies through that most commercial of marketplaces. Beyond W.H. Smith, there were few chains, and it was possible to meet the independent bookseller face to face with, or sometimes without, an appointment, and not always in a pub.

On a similar note, I wrote to Peter du Sautoy, Managing Director of Faber and Faber, for advice. He replied, we met, we became friendly, and he nominated me for the Arts Council's Literature Panel as a junior member. In those days the different art forms had committees of specialists (for literature the committee consisted of publishers, writers, librarians and broadcasters). On this panel I met C.B. Cox, editor of *Critical Quarterly* and Professor of English at the University of Manchester, and this indirectly paved the way for Carcanet to move to Manchester in 1972. Peter du Sautoy's successor Charles Monteith, then editorial director at Faber, was a friend and patron. There was a strong sense of common purpose rather than competition between established independent imprints and the poetry start-ups which, around that time, included Fulcrum Press (1965–74), Anvil (1968–2016), Carcanet and (a decade later) Bloodaxe (1978).

Despite my personal, early, and now overcome aversion to them, the public and academic libraries of the 1960s and 1970s were crucial for publishers of all kinds. More than a quarter of our early turnover went through major library suppliers. That is one of the elements in the commercial equation that has most sadly mutated in half a century: library sales meant books reached a wide variety of readers for whom access through bookshops was not an option. The decline in the libraries inevitably contributes to a decline in readership.

v.

The first meeting I attended when I went up to Oxford as an undergraduate in 1967 was that of the Oxford University Poetry Society. Its president was Roger Garfitt, subsequently a Carcanet poet and in the early years a close collaborator. I seem to remember him on that occasion wrapped in a kind of wizard's gown and with the inclusive, friendly, smoky vagueness that accompanied many young cultural people in the evenings of the late 1960s. He declared that the Oxford-Cambridge literary magazine Carcanet was up for grabs and if anyone was interested they should see him after the meeting. I did so and came away with the prize.

We ran Carcanet as a magazine for two years, then decided that as a swan song, since we were all graduating in 1969 and the journal had run its fitful course, we would produce some pamphlets of key poets from our brief editorship. The decision was catalysed by the suicide of Robert Needham, a brilliant young man who was translating the poems of Celan well before Celan was on the English map. His tiny posthumous pamphlet was our first publication, entitled *Blind Openings*. There were six further pamphlets, two of translations. We sold them by subscription in advance. They were widely and positively reviewed and did so well we decided on a second and then a third series. That was where the history of Carcanet began, though after the third series we had turned to book publications.

The Oxford University Poetry Society was crucial in the development of Carcanet. I became its president in due course and was able to invite poets I wanted to hear. Basil Bunting declined (we offered expenses and no fees), declaring, 'You don't invite a fiddler to play and offer him his expenses.' I got to know a number of writers I liked, came to admire and, in some instances, to publish.

In 1967 the Poetry Society invited Anthony Rudolf to read his Yves Bonnefoy translations. Various seeds were planted on that fateful evening. Rudolf urged me to invite Elaine Feinstein and Daniel Weissbort to read, and both became close friends and key figures in the development of Carcanet. We published an early pamphlet and then books of Rudolf's poems and translations. He was the catalyst for our three substantial volumes of Bonnefoy. A dear friend now, in 1967 he was fresh-faced and as innocent of the ways of the reading circuit and the poetry game as I was. He likes the Yiddish saying, 'one word is not enough; two words are too many'. I will risk quoting him to himself, lines from a poem he later abandoned (in his own parentheses from his 1971 pamphlet):

(Loping in old trousers
From poem to crisis, he survives
Like the feather on his mantelpiece.)

1969

Anne Ridler (1912–2001), poet and verse dramatist, was an editor at Faber and Faber. Her husband, the printer and typographer Vivian Ridler, printed her first volume for OUP, but the whole stock was lost in a bombing raid in 1940. Carcanet published her *Collected Poems* in 1994. Grevel Lindop, who interviewed her that year, wrote: 'She was also a fine, understated raconteuse, with a perfect ear for dialogue and a neat sense of comic self-deprecation, whether recalling the contorted scrupulousness of Eliot's response when she dared to show him her earliest work, or confessing to the illicit delights of translating an opera libretto ("When you hear it sung, you get this marvellous delusion that you've written the whole thing yourself!").'[1]

FROM ANNE RIDLER
Oxford
9 December 1969

Dear Mr Schmidt,

Thank you for your letter about the new Carcanet venture. I shall be interested to see the first pamphlets, and I enclose my two-guinea subscription. Why should you want to codify yourselves with a group name? I hope you won't – and certainly not as *vividist*.

I was sorry not to get to any of the meetings this term. I fully intended to, but something always cropped up on a Tuesday to prevent me.

I think Kathleen Raine is always interested in new poetry, though I don't know how much money she can spare for subscriptions of this kind.[2] You also ask about my verse plays: they are published by Faber, and I think *Henry Bly and other plays* would be the one to interest you. One which I wrote about Cranmer, commissioned for the fourth centenary of his death and broadcast and acted* at the time, is now out of print, I believe.

All good wishes,
Yours sincerely,
Anne Ridler

*in the University Church, with Frank Windsor and Derek Hart, then little-known actors, in the cast.[3]

FROM ANNE RIDLER
Oxford
11 May 1989

Dear Michael,

Many thanks for the copy* of my letter which Mark Fisher proposes to use in the Twentieth Anniversary book. What a noble record you have to show! I am proud that my two-guinea subscription earns me a connexion, however small.

My first thought was that of course you should print the letter as it stands. My second is that if you don't mind, I'd prefer you to delete, in the third paragraph, the rest of the sentence after 'new poetry'. I ask this because I have found that allusions to want of money tend to annoy Kathleen, even though she makes them herself. (For instance, 'Wearing anxiety about money like a hair shirt', or something to that effect.) Now will this go into the archive for the <u>next</u> twenty years??

I have just had offprints of the article on Marriage in Literature in which we used Joy Scovell's poem, and I've sent one to her.[4] She was here to tea last week, and mentioned that she had not seen the review of her book in the *Times Lit. Supp.* – all too brief I thought, but at least she did get a review, whereas this time they have ignored my book completely. If there is a cutting in the office, perhaps you could send her one? I didn't keep it myself.

Cordial good wishes,
Yours ever,
Anne

*This is written with the same Royal table-model typewriter, slung out by OUP & bought for a song. We bought an electric one, but I can't get used to it.

*

Anne Ridler was among the many poets I wrote to soliciting a subscription for our first series of pamphlets. I typed each letter of solicitation on my huge Adler manual typewriter, one of the prime acquisitions of my second undergraduate year. A good typewriter was then as important as a good laptop is today. The letters I wrote were not personalised but personal. I did not keep copies of these bespoke ingratiations, but whatever they said, they did the trick. We had over 160 subscribers to the first series of seven pamphlets, which could be acquired for seven shillings and sixpence unsigned or one guinea signed and numbered.

Peter Jones had started work on his *Penguin Book of Imagist Verse* and he, Gareth Reeves, Grevel Lindop and I were casting about for a label or brand to distinguish the work we were doing. In writing to a poet who had been T.S. Eliot's secretary and editorial assistant, it seemed appropriate to seek her advice on 'vividist', our then preferred epithet, and she advised in no uncertain terms.

Later on, some friends and I decided the most beautiful word in the English language was 'numb' and we joked about starting a 'numb school' of poetry. When I was typing *Notebook* for Robert Lowell I induced him to introduce the word 'numb' into one of the sonnets (I am not sure it survived the final cut), so we were able to claim Lowell as a marginal member of the 'numb school'.

NOTES

1. See https://www.theguardian.com/news/2001/oct/16/guardianobituaries.books (accessed 5 June 2019).

2. Kathleen Raine (1908–2003), poet and scholar of Blake and Yeats; there is a particularly fine photograph of her by Christopher Barker in *Portraits of Poets* (Carcanet, 1986), alongside many poets from the Carcanet list, including Ridler. The editor of this book has taken the decision to over-ride Anne Ridler's request; she doubts that Raine's shade will be troubled by the mention of lack of money.

3. The British actor Frank Windsor (b.1927) was famous for his part in the TV series *Softly Softly* and *Z Cars* in the 1970s, as well as roles in films and on stage; Derek Hart (1925–86), actor and broadcaster, was well-known for his appearances in the BBC's *Tonight* programme.

4. Joy Scovell (1907–99), poet and translator, had published collections in the 1940s–50s; Geoffrey Grigson described her as 'a poet less concerned with celebrity and self-importance than with being alive and in love […] The purest woman poet of our time.' Carcanet published her *Collected Poems* in 1988, and a *Selected* in 1991.

THE YEAR IN BOOKS

Peter Jones, *Rain*
Ishan Kapur, *Tomorrow's Dark Sun*
Grevel Lindop, *Against the Sea*
Robert Needham, *Blind Openings*

1970

Elizabeth Bishop (1911–79), who published 101 poems in her lifetime, was not as famous in the 1970s as she is now. In the UK, Chatto & Windus published an abridged edition of her *Poems* in 1956, and *Selected Poems* in 1967; *The Complete Poems* was published by Farrar, Straus (NY) in 1969. Carcanet published the UK editions of Bishop's *Exchanging Hats: paintings* (ed. William Benton) in 1997, and of *Edgar Allan Poe & the Juke-Box: uncollected poems, drafts and fragments* (ed. Alice Quinn) in 2006. Her name recurs in Carcanet correspondence; for example, writing to Val Warner in 1998, MNS admits: 'I continue to adore Bishop, probably disproportionately. Poets that one can teach and actually convey one's enthusiasm for are few. I manage it sometimes with [W.S.] Graham, usually with [Eavan] Boland, and almost always with Bishop.'

FROM ELIZABETH BISHOP
Harvard University, Cambridge, Mass.
16 October 1970

Dear Mr. Schmidt,

Your letter was forwarded to me by my publisher and I just received it two days ago. I think if I could receive such a letter once a month, say, life would be greatly improved; you probably can have no idea how cheering I found it. Thank you very much. I am touched by your going to all that trouble to find my poems, and buy them.

Of course I'll be happy to have you use the lines from 'Varick Street' and 'Questions of Travel'. I'm curious to see which lines. Please be sure to send me your book, won't you – I rather hope that Faber takes it because they print the best-looking commercial books, don't you think? Your own Carcanet Press may do even better – I wonder what that name comes from – but I suppose it is more helpful to be published by one of the big recognised houses.[1]

The idea of a dedication seems almost too much – but of course I'd be awfully flattered. I am eager to see *Desert of the Lions* – perhaps you could send it to me, but only if you have extra copies…

Robert Lowell is an old friend and has always been very kind about my work and has helped me innumerable times, in many ways.[2] We met about the time we published our first books – or rather it was really his second: *Lord Weary's Castle*. I have had two letters from him recently and he sounds much better, and was about to start teaching at Essex when he wrote the last one. I am here for this semester, teaching the two seminars he taught here for six years, I think. I am not really a teacher; I've done it only once before, and of course it is impossible to take his place. However, I am hoping the novelty of my amateurishness and the change of sex, etc., may help out – the students have been very nice to me so far.

This will be my address until Christmas, at least. As Cal may have told you, I live mostly in Brazil and have for many years – so I was interested to hear that you apparently make Mexico your home and also live in Egypt. Perhaps we share a geographical obsession?

Faithfully yours,
Elizabeth Bishop

*

Ian Hamilton, editor of *the review*, had given me Elizabeth Bishop's *Selected Poems* to write about and I had been astonished by them. In part it was the varied and inventive formalism, the understatement, and the clarity of them, in part the variety of geographies, which seemed to take in my own Latin America in ways I'd not seen in verse before. Originally Hamilton had offered the book to Charles Tomlinson, but he had declined to write about it. I worked on my review essay for a couple of months, sent it to Hamilton who, at the time, I much admired. He never responded at all and the piece did not appear.

When Robert Lowell came to All Souls, his British publisher Charles Monteith arranged that I meet him. It had been my hope to study with him at Harvard, but when I went up he was ill and William Alfred had taken over his poetry course. I did not meet him in the States but at Oxford he was larger than life. Monteith had hoped he might become Professor of Poetry but Edmund Blunden had pipped him at the post, largely on the strength of the anti-American vote, it seemed to most of us.

I discovered Lowell, when I first went to meet him, in great distress, rather like Laocoön tangled in his typewriter ribbon, which he had tried to change but unavailingly. I extricated him, changed the ribbon for him and soon had agreed to type for him, working in particular on the final typescript of *Notebook*. He agreed to read for the Poetry Society. We met regularly, both in his rooms and on occasion at Pin Farm where Carcanet was taking shape. It was there that Peter Jones and I introduced Lowell to Ian Hamilton, who came to tea with his beautiful wife Gisela. What I best remember is that she was wearing a lovely slanting beige summer hat, said nothing, and charmed Lowell.

My main interest in Lowell was to find out from him about Elizabeth Bishop. He must have tired of my continual inquiries, but he mentioned me to her, and he encouraged me to write to her. I dedicated my second book of poems to her.

NOTES

1. The Carcanet website explains: Shakespeare calls holidays 'captain jewels in a carcanet'. A carcanet (pronounced KAR-ka-nett) is a 'jewelled necklace' with an etymological skeleton in its cupboard. Its ancestor is the Old French *carcan*, 'a slave's halter'.

2. Robert Lowell (1917–77), known as 'Cal' to his friends, moved from New York to England in 1970; he was a visiting fellow at All Souls 1970-76, and taught at the University of Essex for two years. His *Life Studies*, which won the 1960 National Book Award, has been called 'perhaps the most influential book of modern verse since *The Waste Land*'. Farrar, Straus published the third edition of his *Notebook* in 1970; in the UK, Faber and Faber had published his *Selected Poems* in 1965.

THE YEAR IN BOOKS

Guillaume Apollinaire, *Hunting Horns*, translated by Barry Morse

John Balaban, *Vietnam Poems*

George Buchanan, *Annotations*

Marcus Cumberlege, *Poems for Quena and Tabla*

Roger Garfitt, *Caught on Blue*

Peter Jones, *Seagarden for Julius*

Sally Purcell (ed and tr), *Provençal Poems*

Gareth Reeves, *Pilgrims*

Michael Schmidt, *Bedlam & the Oakwood*

Michael Schmidt, *Black Building*

Alexandra Seddon, *Sparrows*

Robert B. Shaw, *Curious Questions*

Adrian Wright, *Waiting for Helen*

1971

Scotland's first official Makar in modern times, Edwin Morgan (1920–2010), was endlessly inventive, inquiring, energetic, internationalist and deeply committed to his home city of Glasgow. The first of his books to be published by Carcanet was a collection of translations of V.V. Mayakovsky's poems into Scots, *Wi' the Haill Voice* (1971). Thereafter Carcanet was his principal publisher for poetry, essays and drama.[1] His letters were both business-like and playful, and his own immaculate archive of copies and replies was drawn on to compile *The Midnight Letterbox: selected correspondence 1950–2010*, edited by James McGonigal and John Coyle (2015). His presence on the list attracted other Scottish poets, of his own generation and younger. He wrote to the young man he had fallen in love with at seventy-eight: 'Sailing into calmer waters, writing *Tempests*, composing last quartets, taking a deckchair into the garden – no, that doesn't seem to be me.'[2] Two years later, in 2000, the year that saw the publication of his *New Selected Poems*, the performance and publication of *A.D. a trilogy on the life of Jesus Christ*, and his translation of *Jean Racine's Phaedra*, he received the Queen's Gold Medal for Poetry.

FROM MICHAEL SCHMIDT
18 November 1971

Dear Mr Morgan,

Your essay came today – many, many thanks. It is the only essay I have received for the book which I find exactly as I would have wished – it is <u>exciting</u> to read, larded with excellent quotation, and in every way my sort of essay.[3] I only wish you had planted yourself in the landscape you so beautifully conjure. We'll have you later writ large.

The rest of the book is almost complete excepting two essays still tardy, so you were not last. I feel the book is attaining a completeness at long last and pray it will be ready for Herr Printer on December 15th. Which is two months later than I'd hoped, but the span of time was painfully short, wasn't it.

You will, in the book, especially like Anne Cluysenaar's piece about Steiner and the poets who refute him in practice; and Terry Eagleton's piece on myth and legend.[4] Jon Silkin's piece on Geoff Hill is a little heavy going but very good, I think. I am not too keen on a piece we have about Bunting – but then, I am not at ALL keen on Bunting, which may help explain things.

I was stunned by the MacCaig you quoted.[5] What a superb poem. I will have to go back to him again. I liked but forgot him, which was silly. Scotland is producing exciting things. More so than any other 'region'.

Mr Garioch has ordered *Wi' the Haill Voice* today.[6] I think we must try to arrange a feature in *The Scotsman* about it, if only we knew whom to contact. They've always been warm about our books. Do you know the editor? Would Mr Garioch be a good person to ask about this?

My goodness we are working hard. And yet I did today finally manage to find or make time to get a poem down. And it was good! It's a relief that the service of letters has not lamed me for lettering!

Again, a multitude of thanks for your excellent piece and for – believe it or not – your comparative promptness!

Ever,
Michael

Did I send you the catalogue? It is quite impressive – if you haven't seen it I'll send it.

FROM EDWIN MORGAN
Glasgow
20 November 1971

Dear Michael,

Needless to say I am enormously pleased that the article was on time and acceptable. Even not being last of all – well now. I shall look forward to reading the pieces you mention. Bunting is also not one of my absolute favourites, though I can see he has a gluey music all his own – but I like a verse that <u>moves</u>.[7] It is not enough to have images, fine though many of them certainly are. On the other hand, his quirky crabbitness is also a 'northernness' and in some moods this attracts just because at least it is not smooth.

How nice of Robert Garioch to order a Mayakovsky already. I would undoubtedly value his opinion on it eventually. But if you were to try to ask him to review it this might be taken as backscratching since we are both editorial advisors on *Scottish International*. If he reviews it somewhere unasked, fine. The *Scotsman* idea is worth pursuing. Probably you should write to Robert Nye, who is the literary editor.[8] He is not himself Scotch, but is well-disposed to Scottish poetry (and I believe to Carcanet) and might well be interested in a feature of some kind.

I have a promise of a review in *Soviet Studies* (a quarterly edited from Glasgow University) if you will send a copy when the time comes to Dr Alan Ross, Department of International Economic Studies, University of Glasgow.

Could you please make two small changes in my typescript of the Scottish Poetry essay: Page 7 line 20 – for <u>vehement</u> read <u>forceful</u>, and page 9 line 13 for <u>period</u> read <u>decade</u>.

From my window I am watching the snow flittering down past the orange streetlamps like – like – come on Bunting – like

doom-grated
orange-peel
purified through
fine fans
etc.

Yours ever
Edwin
(do please drop the Mr!)

P.S. I nearly forgot: yes, thanks, I did receive your fine catalogue!

FROM EDWIN MORGAN
Glasgow
4 December 1971

Dear Michael,

Thank you very much for page proofs and two letters. On going through the proofs I found a fair number of corrections and I'm enclosing the relevant sheets – I hope there will still be time to make these changes as some of them are quite bad – especially the <u>contents</u> page – whatever happened there?

I'd like to have the next Karcanet batch and enclose my cheque for the paperback edition. For consistency I should have written chekue. Two possible subscribers (unless you already have them) might be my two co-editors of *Scottish Poetry* – George Bruce (Fellow in Creative Writing, Glasgow University) and Maurice Lindsay [address]…[9]

Yes, I wish I could have seen the Amalrik plays – perhaps you can tell me what they are like in due course.[10] On Tuesday I hope to go to a massive Stockhausen jamboree which the university music department are sponsoring. Perhaps you saw the article in today's *Times* about violence and crime in Glasgow – not untrue, of course, but I can't help feeling that the headline STOCKHAUSEN CONCERT A SELLOUT IN GLASGOW UNIVERSITY'S HUGE BUTE HALL is unlikely to make the English papers though it is also true and might help to alter our – what is the word, oh yes, image.

Best as ever,
Edwin

*

I must have come across Edwin Morgan, as I did so many poets and translators in the early years, by the kind agency of Daniel Weissbort, the founder-editor with Ted Hughes of *Modern Poetry in Translation*, with whom I had undertaken to edit the Carcanet modern translations list. He no doubt had Morgan's implausible translations of Mayakovsky into Scots, one of the earliest of our translation titles, along with Danny's own versions of Natalia Gorbanevskaya, *Poems, the Trial, Prison*. Gorbanevskaya was a dissident poet held in a Soviet prison mental hospital, her poems and a transcript of her trial having been spirited out of the country. Mayakovsky was quite another kettle of fish. When we published *Wi' the Haill Voice*, C.P. Snow noted in the *Financial Times* that he found the translations 'marginally more difficult than the Russian originals'.

Morgan when I first knew him was a committed avoider of the conventional. He had radical energy, an instinct for using language as subversion, keeping readers on their toes formally and semantically, teasing them with etymology, sound properties, echoes, and with unexpected formal resources. His commitment to European rather than Anglo-American modernisms set him apart not only from his British contemporaries but also from Scottish predecessors except for MacDiarmid, whom he respected, and W.S. Graham and Burns Singer.

We had a cheerful and open friendship, exchanging dozens of letters and even collaborating on what we called 'Dovetails' but were published as *Grafts* (Mariscat, 1984). When they were published, in a note Edwin explicitly rejected the term 'collaboration': 'These poems are based on fragments from abandoned poems by Michael Schmidt. They grew round the fragments, which were kept intact but might appear in any part of the completed poem. There was no collaboration; I merely used the alien material as if the lines (as often happens) had suddenly floated into my head.'

His discomfort with the idea of collaborating with me had a specific origin. When I became friends with Donald Davie and C.H. Sisson and my close association with C.B. Cox and the University of Manchester were known, this strong English, Modernist and in various ways conservative association put my relations with Edwin, as with Douglas Dunn and other close early contacts, under strain. Edwin did not contribute to *PN Review* until 1998. The bulk of his contributions, the 'Translator's Notebook' series, edited by James McGonigal, appeared well after his death. Yet we remained regular correspondents and friends at one remove, as it were, and Carcanet published more than a score of his books of poems, plays, essays and translations, with thirteen of them still in print.

NOTES

1. On 29 December 1971, MNS wrote to Morgan: 'Just a note at the year's turning to wish you a happy new one, and to thank you for the very beautiful card and the very wonderful poem it contained. It was a superb poem, and it suddenly dawned on me that I don't know your work except in anthology. Do you have any copies, or can you tell me where I can get copies, of your books? Who "does" you?' Morgan had published with a variety of small presses at this stage; his breakthrough volume *A Second Life* (1968) had been published by Edinburgh University Press.

2. Letter quoted in James McGonigal, *Beyond the Last Dragon: a life of Edwin Morgan* (Sandstone Press, 2010), p.370.

3. The essay referred to here, 'Scottish Poetry in the 1960s' was published in *British Poetry Since 1960: a critical survey* (eds Grevel Lindop and Michael Schmidt, Carcanet, 1972).

4. Anne Cluysenaar (1936–2014) was a Belgian-born poet and teacher, who lived much of her life in the UK, latterly in Wales. Carcanet published two collections of her poems, *Double Helix* (1982) and *Timeslips: new and selected poems* (1997).

5. Norman MacCaig (1910–96), Scottish poet, of whom Morgan wrote: 'Short on alienation, but surprising, accurate, and well turned, his poetry offers many pleasures. Its urbanity is by no means unable to get under the skin…' ('Scottish Poetry in the 1960s', *Essays*, 1974, p.181).

6. Robert Garioch (1909–81), poet and translator, edited the anthology of contemporary Scottish poetry *Made in Scotland* for Carcanet (1974) and Carcanet reissued his *Collected Poems* in 1980.

7. Basil Bunting (1900–85), a modernist poet whose high reputation was established with the publication of *Briggflatts* in 1966. Morgan wrote a playful elegy for him, 'A Trace of Wings' (*Themes on a Variation*, 1988).

8. Robert Nye (1939-2016), poet, novelist and critic, edited selections of poems by William Barnes and Laura Riding for Carcanet, as well as *English Sermons 1750-1850* (1976). Carcanet published Nye's *Collected Poems* in 1998.

9. George Bruce (1909-2002), Scottish poet and BBC radio producer; Maurice Lindsay (1918-2009), Scottish poet, broadcaster and cultural historian, who edited the landmark anthology *Modern Scottish Poetry: An Anthology of the Scottish Renaissance, 1920-1945* (Faber and Faber, 1946). Carcanet published a much-revised edition in 1976.

10. Andrei Amalrik (1938–80), Soviet dissident dramatist, who was at this time serving a prison sentence in a labour camp in Kolyma. He was famous in the West for his essay *Will the Soviet Union Survive Until 1984?* and his account of his first exile, *Involuntary Journey to Siberia*, published abroad in 1970.

THE YEAR IN BOOKS

Michael Cayley, *Moorings*

Elizabeth Daryush, *Verses: Seventh Book,* preface by Roy Fuller

H.D. (Hilda Doolittle), *Tribute to Freud,* introduction by Peter Jones

Margaret Newlin, *The Fragile Immigrants*

Anthony Rudolf, *The Manifold Circle*

Val Warner, *These Yellow Photos*

Daniel Weissbort, *The Leaseholder*

1972

Charles Tomlinson (1927–2015), poet, critic and translator, was born in Stoke-on-Trent. He read English at Cambridge where he was tutored by Donald Davie, who later became a close friend. He taught at the University of Bristol, retiring in 1992 as Emeritus Professor of Poetry. His colleague Professor David Hopkins wrote: 'One sometimes forgot that one had someone so famous in one's midst. The inevitably rather trivial and myopic business of department meetings was, however, always freshened with a new blast of reality when one realised that across the table was someone who had met Ezra Pound, had read *The Waste Land* aloud in the presence of T.S. Eliot's widow [...]'.[1]

Tomlinson's poetry was published by Oxford University Press until the Press closed its poetry list. Carcanet then became his publisher, his work having often appeared in *PN Review*. His *New Collected Poems* came out in 2009, and *Swimming Chenango Lake: Selected Poems* (ed. David Morley) as a Carcanet Classic in 2018.

FROM CHARLES TOMLINSON
Ozleworth
11 October 1972

Dear Michael,

Your most generous letter has strengthened me against whatever the reviewers make or don't make of that book of mine. I have felt for a <u>long</u> time that, really, very few people (certainly not my colleagues – the 'experts') have any inkling of the level at which I have been and am working. It was typical that nothing of mine should appear in the Porter-Thwaite programme and that somebody like Enright should carry the preference there.[2] It struck me – just this one instance, and I have done moaning – that but for you and Calvin Bedient I could very well have been missing from *British Poetry Since 1960*![3] It takes a couple of furriners to see the point! But I was, indeed, very moved by what you say – the first reaction of any sort I've had to the book. You are probably right about 'Mackinnon's Boat'. It leaves me dissatisfied and yet it seemed a pity to scrap it altogether. Nice that you liked the shorter pieces – I had great difficulty in placing many of these: 'Urlicht' came back regularly, 'Juliet's Garden' also. Yes A.A. is Alvarez and I think it's time we gave that wilful self-regard, posing as toughness, a shove over the edge.[4] I had a row with a *Manchester Guardian* correspondent at a dinner in Budapest, who said what a good influence A.A. was, that <u>these</u> people (the poor Huns) could understand the kind of language he speaks. I don't know why I was so angry – probably unbalanced by the tokay – but I heard a deathly voice say out of me: 'And what's wrong with the truth as a good influence? What have "these people" done to deserve these blatant simplifications?' My wife trod on my foot under the table and I subsided into the goulash or whatever. Rather funny in retrospect.

Yes, I want Wordsworth and Marvell <u>together</u>. Wordsworth still seems to me our greatest since Shakespeare.

Your mentioning Adrian Stokes *re* my pictures makes me want to kick myself – I'd intended to tell him of the show, since I use a quote from him in one of the pictures, then I didn't do anything about it.[5] Stupid of me. I think he's extraordinarily interesting.

Yes, I too approve of what Bill did with those Modern Town minors, but I still think him unfair to Bunting. In *British Poetry Since 1960* the three essays on figures are all very fine, Eagleton is very subtle too, and Garfitt very good on Porter. I thought Hamilton glumly destructive on The Movement – I did a take-to-pieces myself in *Essays in Criticism* c.1956 or 7, 'The Middlebrow Muse' – much jollier altogether. The trouble with Ian (of course I am prejudiced since he takes a blind swipe at each book I publish) is that his intelligence is essentially reductive even at best.[6]

The bookshops in London those Americans deal through had ordered *British Poetry Since 1960*, so it looks as though they're going ahead after all with buying them. Thanks for the forms anyhow.

I've just read through your letter once more and greater perspicacity on the part of a reader – all you say of the role of time and the comparison of self to self, object to object – a writer could hardly ask for. [*in the margin*: horrid sentence] In one sense, I cannot regret the passage of time because it has forced me to see things more coherently. I am weary of 'attitudes' to time, from Proust onwards…

We shall be meeting not too far ahead and I am greatly looking forward to that.

Shantih,
Charles

FROM CHARLES TOMLINSON
Ozleworth
9 November 1972

Dear Michael,

I was delighted to hear that you'll meet us. There will be lots of time for a chat* [*chat, not discussion!] – train from Stoke (where we break our journey and pause to prop up the family) arrives on the Saturday at Piccadilly at 5.11. We return to Stoke at 11.3 (God help us) from Oxford Road.

I'd asked Professor Cox where we should come to, but now you'll be able to tell us... There will, I hope, be a lectern and a glass of water...?

Yes, I feel very close to Donald (you may have seen his note in the *Collected* to 'To a Brother in the Mystery'). He is the one Englishman to have seen consistently and from the start what I was at. Without his support I should have foundered or grown bitterer than sometimes I fear myself becoming, at the minuscule recognition of twenty years' work. But I mustn't go on.

I have done and am doing some poems I hope will be worthy of the magazine. I look to it as a real new hope and have now a poem as long as 'Prometheus', Donald's favourite, which I am keeping for you. It is about the demolition of cities – based in part on Bristol, in part on London. I think I may read it at Manchester. I dislike Larkin because (tho' as Donald says in his brilliant book, his landscapes are the landscapes we all recognise) I want something more – and something less redolent of British films.[7] I want nobility – of the kind one finds in Baudelaire's 'Le Cygne' or 'Les Petites Vieilles' and I am trying now, in a full look at the city, to get that, in attitude of mind and in diction. I believe I have achieved this in the new poem I've spoken of – 'The Way In'.[8] Wandering round

London, Bristol, Stoke of late, and driving so often through Birmingham, I see Larkin's subject matter everywhere, but I want a bigger containing vision, a felt sense of what civilisation is or can be. So I am putting nature by for a bit. It is a return to roots. Hang it, I was born in the fumes of the biggest steel works in the Midlands!

I do regret not to see you here but we both look forward to seeing you there.

An excellent collaborator on French lit. for the mag would be Michael Edwards (he does most of the *TLS* reviews of Frrrrrrench poetry).

Very best,
Charles

*

I remember one of Charles Tomlinson's early visits to our offices in the Corn Exchange. It was cold out but the office was piping hot. Arriving, he removed his coat and folded it carefully. Then he removed the coat's lining and folded it, equally carefully, and set it down beside the coat. Fastidious, but also wry. Elegant, but also frugal and, well, threadbare. We visited the City Art Gallery and, among many moments of insight he shared with me, there was an exchange about William Etty's nudes. They often stand – certainly the City Art Gallery ones do – in darkening water, surrounded by foliage and ruins, with a sunset, usually rosy, effulgence glowing upwards, illuminating their shadowy undercarriages. 'One might write a PhD on "Etty's Pudenda",' he said.

I often liked the idea of Charles Tomlinson's poems better than I liked the poems themselves. They were pretexts. I loved the man, his conversation, his correspondence, his company, his essays. I like the 'civic' poems, the French Revolution poems, best of all. And he clarified something that his poems have which his British and American contemporaries lack. He suggested a playfulness in the language of his poems – 'an element of epistemological comedy' – which reviewers in a hurry and solemn readers do not hear. This playfulness can provide glimpses, gaps through, into a world of latent meanings. It becomes an orienting feature of *tone*, and if it is missed, a key element in the poem's delivery is missed as well.

This sense of 'epistemological comedy' is remote from conventional English irony, both in the possibilities of tone it provides and in the effects it achieves. English irony draws attention, self-diminishing attention, to the poet as speaker; it is an element in the transactions both with the subject matter of the poem and, primarily, with the reader. Tomlinson's other *kind* of comedy focuses on the subject, focuses the subject. It is not coyly about the poet's place in the poem or vis-à-vis the reader. The poet is not *in* the poem in that sense. I loved the poem 'Hyphens':

> 'The country's love-
> liness,' it said:
> what I read was
> 'the country's love-
> lines' – the unnec-
> essary 's'
> passed over by
> the mind's blind-
> ly discriminating eye:
> but what I saw
> was a whole scene
> restored: the love-
> lines drawing
> together the list
> 'loveliness' capped
> and yet left

vague, unloved;
lawns, gardens, houses,
the encircling trees.

The first book by Tomlinson that Carcanet published was a book of his strange surrealising images, with an introduction by Octavio Paz. It was called *In Black and White*. John Berger, reviewing the book in the *New Statesman* in 1976, said, 'It touches upon, lays its touch upon, the profoundly totalizing experience of the visible.' Is that not one of the things the poems do?

The first poem in the first issue of *Poetry Nation* was 'The Way In', his answer to Larkin's 'The Whitsun Weddings'.

NOTES

1.   David Hopkins also noted that Tomlinson was 'one of the first English men of letters to appreciate the great achievements of the American poets of the mid-20th century, particularly the work of William Carlos Williams, Marianne Moore, Yvor Winters, Louis Zukofsky and George Oppen – all of whom he came to know personally – and his poetry showed from the start, particularly in its versification, a strong American influence' (published on the University of Bristol's website, 25 August 2015).

2.   D.J. Enright (1920–2002), academic, poet and critic, was Professor of English at the University of Singapore 1960-70, and received the Queen's Gold Medal for Poetry in 1981. Carcanet published his poetry when it took over the OUP poetry list. BBC Genome does not list a Peter Porter-Anthony Thwaite programme for autumn 1972, although both men appear often in connection with poetry programmes. They were described as 'mid-career poets' in the listing for their 26-programme series 'The English Poets from Chaucer to Yeats' which started in September 1971 on Radio 4. A 50th

birthday celebration, 'Poems for the BBC', broadcast on Radio 3 on 13 November 1972, included W.H. Auden, Porter and Thwaite reading their own poems, with Seamus Heaney and Edwin Morgan representing Northern Ireland and Scotland.

3. The American academic and poet Calvin Bedient wrote the essay 'On Charles Tomlinson' in *British Poetry Since 1960*. Other essays referred to by Tomlinson in this letter are 'Poetry in the North East' by W.E. Parkinson, Roger Garfitt on 'The Group', Terry Eagleton on 'Myth and History in Recent Poetry' and Ian Hamilton on 'The Making of the Movement'.

4. Al Alvarez (1929–2019), poet and critic, was an influential poetry editor, both at *The Observer* (1956–66) and as an anthologist of *The New Poetry*, published by Penguin in 1962 (revised 1966), with his controversial introduction 'The New Poetry *or* Beyond the Gentility Principle'. The anthology includes five poems by Tomlinson.

5. Adrian Stokes (1902–72), art critic, whose study of the painting and sculpture of the early Renaissance led him to appreciate the sculpture of Hepworth and Moore. He lived in St Ives for some years, helping to make it a recognised centre for art; in the 1930s he was in analysis with Melanie Klein, after which he also began to paint. His poetry was first collected in Penguin Modern Poets 23 (posthumously, 1973), and he was happily corresponding with MNS about further publication the year he died. Eric Rhode collected his papers on psychoanalysis, politics, philosophy, aesthetics and ethics as *A Game that Must be Lost* (Carcanet, 1973), and Peter Robinson edited *With All the Views: collected poems* (Carcanet, 1981).

6. Ian Hamilton (1938–2001), poet and critic, founder editor of the noted poetry magazine *The Review* (1962–72), succeeded by *The New Review* (1974-79). His first collection of poems was *The Visit* (Faber and Faber, 1970). His magazines were often the subject of negative comments from various Carcanet correspondents.

7. Philip Larkin (1922–85), poet and librarian, recommended that the John Rylands Library in Manchester acquire the Carcanet archive as an important primary resource, which it did. Donald Davie's *Thomas Hardy and English Poetry*, first published in 1972, was reissued by Carcanet in *With the Grain: essays on Thomas Hardy and modern British poetry* (ed. Clive Wilmer, 1998). Wilmer writes about 'To a Brother in the Mystery' (published in 1960) in his introduction, p.xiii.

8. Tomlinson's *The Way In and other poems* was published by OUP in 1974.

THE YEAR IN BOOKS

George Buchanan, *Minute-book of a City*

Paul Celan, *Nineteen Poems*, translated by Michael Hamburger

Thomas Chatterton, *Selected Poems*, selection and introduction by Grevel Lindop

Richard Crashaw, *Selected Poems*, selection and introduction by Michael Cayley

Elizabeth Daryush, *Selected Poems (from Verses 1-VI)*, preface by Roy Fuller

H.D. (Hilda Doolittle), *Hermetic Definition*

Natalya Gorbanevskaya, *Poems: The Trial, Prison: Selected Poems*, translated by Daniel Weissbort

Nâzim Hikmet, *The Day before Tomorrow*, translated by Taner Baybars

Peter Jones, *The Peace and the Hook*

Vladimir Mayakovsky, *Wi' the Haill Voice*, translated by Edwin Morgan

George Peele, *Selected Works*, selection and introduction by Sally Purcell

Fernando Pessoa, *Fernando Pessoa I–IV*, translated by Jonathan Griffin

Michael Schmidt and Grevel Lindop (eds), *British Poetry Since 1960: a critical survey*

Michael Schmidt, *Desert of the Lions*
Christopher Smart, *The Religious Poetry of Christopher Smart*,
    selection and introduction by Marcus Walsh
Daniel Weissbort, *In an Emergency*
Adrian Wright, *The Shrinking Map*

1973

Donald Davie (1922–95), poet and critic, was one of the tutelary spirits of Carcanet Press and particularly of *PN Review*; MNS's letters often refer to his judgements of the latter's contents. At this period he was teaching at Stanford University; he returned to England permanently in 1988. Carcanet published his *Selected Poems* in the 'Poetry Signature' series in 1985, and went on to publish his extensive *Collected Works* over the next decades, both poetry and prose. Michael Wood, in his review of *Essays in Dissent* (1995), remarked that 'It's true that [Davie] placed "sourness and spite [...] among the legitimate pleasures of pedantry", and said he had made "a comfortable career" out of the jeremiad', but that while Wood 'often felt daunted by him', he 'never met him without feeling better for the meeting'. Wood suggested that Davie 'would have been the Empson or Eliot of his generation, if his generation had not largely failed to need him, as it largely failed to need either poetry or criticism in anything other than easy doses.'[1]

FROM DONALD DAVIE
Tours, France
12 January 1973

Dear Michael,

When I was in Liverpool after Christmas I bought both *Bedlam & the Oakwood* and *Desert of the Lions*, and I had hoped to write to you about your poems at the same time as I answered your two letters about my Hardy book.[2] But I haven't been able to achieve the secure leisure for reading poetry so as to do it justice, and I'm feeling guilty about leaving your good letters unacknowledged, so I have decided to write now, if only as an interim measure.

In fact there is not much that I can say, or need to say, about *Thomas Hardy and British Poetry*, except to thank you for liking the book and being, as you profess, stimulated by it. As you acknowledge in effect, where you differ from me is about tactics: I have spent 30 years maintaining the apolitical or suprapolitical position that you now expound, and I believe that it is the only right and secure position; but at 50 I begin to feel the sands running out, with all the 'passionate intensity' still a perquisite of the partisan and over-simplified positions, and so I have taken the admittedly risky step of trying to answer our enemies in their own terms, strike back at them with their own weapons. You are young, so you can afford to be both more sanguine and more patient than I can be.

I wonder whether there isn't after all a more substantial difference between us. For I've a hunch that you don't share to the full my admiration for Ezra Pound. Why should you? Yet I suspect that your blessedly right and timely and well-informed exasperation with the self-congratulating permissiveness of the American poetic scene may have blinded you to the authentically heroic passion of Pound and some other Americans of the Poundian persuasion, such as George Oppen;[3] and to the woeful and conspicuous lack of just that passion among their British contemporaries. To bring it really home, I suggest that when *Poetry Nation* makes its case for the British poets it admires (Hill, Tomlinson, Silkin) the case should be made – not just for tactical reasons, but in mere justice – on the grounds of greater passion and intensity, a passion which, once it is recognised, makes the intensity of Hughes seem what you rightly see it as being – merely rhetorical.[4] No other argument will really force into a corner what I see as the most resourceful and remorseless opposition that you'll have to deal with – the world-weary urbanity of a Peter Porter.[5] Tomlinson is a patriot, he wants to do something for England and to be acknowledged by the English – this is the passion in and behind his writing, no one has yet acknowledged it, and until it is acknowledged, endless things about him (e.g. his animosity to Larkin) cannot fall into place. It is lack of that sort of passion in Hardy for which I repeatedly castigate him, in a way you don't much like.

Please keep me regularly posted about how preparations for *Poetry Nation* go forward. I have received, and I read with relish, the collection of East German Poetry in translation.[6] (Room for an essay there – but let it pass.) I don't yet have Peter Jones.[7]

All good wishes,
Donald

FROM MICHAEL SCHMIDT
24 March 1973

Dear Donald,

You may like to know that *Poetry Nation* is slowly maturing – it is going to be a rather fine issue, I think.

I'm writing now to ask if we can commission (we = Carcanet) an essay from you for our new Irish Writing book which is coming out in October 1974, God and the National Westminster Bank willing. We will pay each of the twelve essayists, if we can get the correct subsidy, £50 for the essays. I hoped you might be able to write a general piece on Austin Clarke – between 3,000 and 7,000 words.[8] I know this is a tall order, especially since the deadline would be October 31st of this year (though of course a little flexible).

If you could countenance this task, could you let me know you agree in principle, and then I can hurry the application through the Irish Arts Council for the whole book. We hope to receive a grant towards the essayists' fees, not towards production. The book follows in the footsteps of the *British Poetry* book and the forthcoming *American Poetry* which I hope you'll enjoy – it is somewhat less 'committed' than our volume.

Charles Tomlinson and I are discussing the possibility of a collection of his paintings being 'booked' – a nice idea. With a text, of course. His new poems are excellent. You will, I hope, be pleasantly surprised at the high quality of the new poets we are including in *PN*.

Could you let me know about the Clarke possibility as soon as convenient? We seem to have chosen (yet again!) a cramped deadline.

All good wishes,
Michael

FROM DONALD DAVIE

Tours

29 March 1973

Dear Michael,

I have just got my hands on a book by Sisson (*Metamorphoses*) and hasten to say how right you are about him. He is certainly one of the elect. I thought at first he was a sort of elderly Thom Gunn, but as I read on I saw that his language, spare as it is, has the sort of proper luxuries that Thom regrettably denies himself. In this collection his writing in metre sometimes goes wooden and mechanical as to rhythm, and I think he is more sure-footed in free verse, but many of his metrical pieces are admirable too. Undoubtedly he should be singled out from the ruck.

October 31st is without doubt an uncomfortably close deadline, but still – yes, I'll be glad to write something for your *New Irish Writing*. And it shall be on Clarke if you want it that way, though I'm afraid all my Clarke books are in California, so you'll have to send them to me here. I wonder if you are taking account of Padraic Fallon, a poet a little younger than Clarke, uneven but at his best very good and never yet sufficiently recognised.[9] I am in touch with him and would write on him if you could get someone else to deal with Clarke. (For instance a man called Augustine Martin, of the Department of English, University College Dublin, would do a good essay on Clarke I think.) This is only an idea, and perhaps you haven't left yourself enough time to approach new contributors, so (to repeat) I <u>will</u> take care of Clarke for you if you wish. However, I hope Paddy Fallon won't go unnoticed…

Can you send me your *C[ritical] Q[uarterly]* article on the grrreat Davie in typescript?[10] Never mind if you can't or don't want to.

You are right about the reviews of the Hardy book. I explicitly say (p.130) that I'm <u>not</u> doing the usual source-and-influence job, that I'm concerned for (as you say very exactly) a 'presiding spirit'. What angers me most is to have people say, 'What's all this about Roy Fisher not being recognised?'[11] However, in general the reviews haven't angered me – chiefly because I'm pretty well indifferent about that book, as compared with the *Collected Poems*. It's a very good thing that they didn't come out together, because if and when they are reviewed together it's the poems that suffer.

My thoughts return to Sisson – he nags so steadily at the one or two ultimately important questions that I feel many of my poems are unimportant and marginal by comparison.[12]

Good luck from this ghost that you are struggling to exorcise!

Donald

I saw a nice poem of yours the other day – was it in the *TLS*?

*

Of all the relationships I forged over the years with other writers, those with Donald Davie and C.H. Sisson were the most complex and durable, and their impact persists. I worked relatively closely with both of them on *Poetry Nation* and then *PN Review*. Sisson was and remains my favourite Carcanet poet and, with Idris Parry, my favourite Carcanet critic, in part because neither was deeply afflicted by the academy, whereas Donald Davie was caught in the thick of the academic world. His passion for poetry was expressed in study, analysis and theory as well as practice, whereas the strict particularism of both Sisson and Parry (Sisson's rooted in the traditions of English conservatism, Parry's in a Welsh temperament and a European vocation) was proof against some of the more emphatic stringencies and occasional distortions of Davie.

Both Davie and Sisson wrote about Pound and knew that important things began with him, were shaped by him, and ultimately were distorted by the historical directions he took. Sisson's interest in Pound was temperate and critical. Davie's was much more an article of faith. For him Pound was uniquely important.

Davie contacted me in the wake of a review I wrote for *Poetry* in which I praised Charles Tomlinson and Geoffrey Hill (and, incidentally, Jon Silkin), though I was less generous to George MacBeth. I can date our first meeting precisely to 3 November 1972: when we met, Donald gave me a copy of *Thomas Hardy and British Poetry*, more or less hot off the Oxford University press. He corrected an error in the blurb, 'irrelevent' had somehow got through. We met, as I recall, in Manchester. In Manchester his presence remains strong. When he left Vanderbilt University, he was presented with a portrait bust of himself in bronze. This accompanied him back to England, but when he died the family did not know what to do with it. It's not a very good likeness, more like the cast of a clay maquette than a considered portrait bust. They gave it to me and it watches me as I work, occasionally functioning as a hat rack. It will, I am sure, end up on a ledge in the Rylands Library, a vague, ironic smile playing on its knobby features.

NOTES

1. Michael Wood, 'In Love', *London Review of Books* Vol. 18 no. 2 (26 January 1996).

2. *Thomas Hardy and British Poetry* was published in 1972/3 (New York: OUP/London: Routledge & Kegan Paul). It is included in *With the Grain: essays on Thomas Hardy and modern British poetry* (Carcanet, 1998), edited by Clive Wilmer. The book opens with Davie's contention that in the previous fifty years of British (not American) poetry, 'the most far-reaching influence, for good and ill, has been not Yeats, still less Eliot or Pound, not Lawrence, but *Hardy*'. As Wilmer writes in his introduction, the sentence enacts 'a sense of having surprised himself' with his own proposition.

3. Davie's allegiance lay with Ezra Pound, his modernism and his European cast of mind; he wrote two full-length studies, *Ezra Pound: Poet as Sculptor* (1965; reprinted in Davie's *Studies in Ezra Pound*, 1991) and *Pound* (1975). He wrote about the American Objectivist George Oppen (1908–84) in his essay 'English and American in *Briggflatts*' (*PN Review* 5), reprinted in *With the Grain*. Carcanet published Oppen's *New Collected Poems* in 2003.

4. For Charles Tomlinson, see above. Geoffrey Hill (1932–2016), 'arguably our greatest post-war poet' (*Daily Telegraph*) contributed poems to *Poetry Nation* 3 in 1974 and a knotty article the following year, '"Perplexed Persistence" – the exemplary failure of T.H. Green'. His third (and final) article for *PN Review* was on the poetry of F.T. Prince (*PNR* 147,

September–October 2002). Jon Silkin (1930–97), poet, critic and founder of the literary magazine *Stand*. In 1973 he published his collection *Air that Pricks the Earth* and his influential study of WWI poets, *Out of Battle*, as well as the anthology he edited for Penguin, *Poetry of the Committed Individual*. Carcanet published his *Complete Poems* in 2015. Ted Hughes (1930–98) had published *Crow* at the beginning of this decade, confirming his position as Britain's best-known and widely acclaimed poet, becoming the Poet Laureate in 1984. He contributed occasionally to *PN Review* in the 1970s and '80s, and had a cordial professional relationship with MNS.

5.   Peter Porter (1929–2010), an Australian-born poet who had lived in England since 1951, was a freelance writer and broadcaster, and poetry critic for the *Observer*. He had poems published in *Poetry Nation* 4 and 5; his only other contribution was an essay, 'The Messiness of Life' (*PN Review* 99, September–October 1994) on the poetry of John Ashbery, in which he wrote:

> It lives in a world I recognize; it knows how to go out of doors into the town, to turn on the TV, to read books, look at pictures, have opinions, play word games, and make art face the difficult opportunities of daily discourse. Ashbery has the Browningesque gift of wresting truth and consequence from some very impure prospects. To risk my bias showing, I will add that his work seems uninterested in foxes in the damp ground, Carpathian fables, childhood sensitivity and bathroom confessional.

6.   *East German Poetry: an anthology*, translated from the German by Michael Hamburger (Carcanet, 1973). Michael Hamburger (1924–2007), poet and translator, published the first of many books of poetry and criticism with Carcanet in 1971, his translation of *Nineteen Poems* by Paul Celan. His family had left Berlin for London in 1933, and he went to Oxford and

served in the army. His translations opened up German poetry to post-war Anglophone readers. When several major firms stopped publishing poetry in the early 1970s, Carcanet was the beneficiary – Hamburger and Middleton, also Elizabeth Jennings, came to the press at this time. Relations between Hamburger and MNS were often difficult, but they had great respect for each other, and he was a valued advisor to Carcanet on German-language literature.

7. Peter Jones (b. 1929) was one of the co-founders of Carcanet Press, sharing 'the labour and the risks', as Mark Fisher writes in *Letters to an Editor*. After 1972, Jones and MNS themselves set the majority of Carcanet's books and *PN Review* for the first ten years or so of the press's existence. He had been teaching English and Classics at Christ's Hospital, where MNS met him during his time at that school. *The Peace and the Hook*, published by Carcanet in 1972, was his third collection of poetry. The same year saw his anthology of *Imagist Poetry* published by Penguin; it was reprinted as a Penguin Classic in 2001 and remains in print. Writing to MNS on 30 March, Davie commends the collection and also remarks on 'an inexcusably brutal review [of *Imagist Poetry*] in the *TLS*, which seems to have recruited lately an extremely intransigent and vicious anti-Poundian – I suspect a very senior Gravesian, if not indeed Robert Graves himself.' Jones retired from Carcanet in 1984.

8. Davie contributed a long essay on Austin Clarke (1896–1974) and Padriac Fallon (1905-74) to *Poetry Nation* 3 (1974). *Two Decades of Irish Writing: a critical survey*, edited by Douglas Dunn, was published by Carcanet in 1976.

9. In 1990 Carcanet co-published the *Collected Poems* of Padraic Fallon with Gallery Press, edited by Brian Fallon and with an introduction by Seamus Heaney.

10. Brian Cox sent proof sheets of the review to Davie, and Davie was 'very grateful indeed for the trouble you have

taken' although he went on to defend his Poundian principles at some length (*Letters to an Editor*, letter 31). C.B. Cox (1928–2008) edited *Critical Quarterly*, which he founded with A.E. Dyson in 1958, for thirty years. Often controversial in its editorial positions, *CQ* was also a notable publisher of contemporary poetry. Cox taught at the University of Manchester and was instrumental in bringing Carcanet Press to that city.

11. Chapter 7 of *Thomas Hardy* was 'Roy Fisher: an appreciation'. Fisher (1930–2017), poet and jazz musician, published one collection with Carcanet, *The Thing About Joe Sullivan*, in 1978, but took up OUP's offer for a *Collected Poems* (1980). It was a disappointment to MNS, as he wrote to Davie; he had seen Carcanet as a 'leaping-off point' but by now regarded it as a 'home' for good poets. See *Letters to an Editor*, pp.56–7.

12. In a letter to MNS (1 December 1973), Davie wrote:

> Very important to keep the poetry section up to the standard of *PN* 1, where it was, as the *TLS* said, quite exceptionally good. One could read through all those pages with steady and secure enjoyment. [But how could the *TLS* reviewer] overlook the powerfully harrowing and utterly characteristic 'Usk' by Sisson? […] Charles's poems are the best he's written for a very long time; I think he knows it too, and accordingly reserved them for you – which was generous of him.

THE YEAR IN BOOKS

James Atlas (ed), *Ten American Poets: an anthology*
William Barnes, *Selected Poems*, edited by Robert Nye
Glen Cavaliero, *The Ancient People*
Michael Cayley, *The Spider's Touch*
Sergei Esenin, *Confessions of a Hooligan*, translated by Geoffrey Thurley
Michael Hamburger (ed and tr), *East German Poetry: an anthology*

Michael Hamburger, *A Mug's Game: Intermittent Memoirs*

Michael Hamburger, *Ownerless Earth: new and selected poems*

W.J. Harvey, *Descartes' Dream*, preface by Seamus Heaney

Dawson Jackson, *Ice and the Orchard*

Attila József, *Selected Poems and Texts*, translated by John Bátki, edited by James Atlas and George Gömöri

Takagi Kyozo, *Selected Poems*, translation and introduction by James Kirkup and Michio Nakano

Paris Leary, *The Snake at Saffron Walden*

Edwin Morgan, *From Glasgow to Saturn*

Margaret Newlin, *Day of Sirens*

Charles of Orleans, *Charles of Orleans*, selection and introduction by Sally Purcell

Sally Purcell (ed), *Monarchs and the Muse: poems by monarchs and princes of England, Scotland and Wales*, introduction by C.V. Wedgwood

Laurence Sterne, *Sermons of Mr Yorick*, selection and introduction by Marjorie David

Adrian Stokes, *A Game That Must be Lost: uncollected papers*, introduction by Eric Rhode

Val Warner, *Under the Penthouse*

1974

Sylvia Townsend Warner (1893–1978), novelist, story-writer and poet, was one of Carcanet's early 'patrons'. Her first book of poems came out in 1925; when interviewed by MNS and Val Warner in 1975 and asked whether she still wrote poems, she answered 'Oh yes, usually just when I'm about to pack or catch a train or have someone to stay. Always at inconvenient moments like that. And I revise them endlessly, endlessly. I revise everything that I do.'[1] The same year she wrote to MNS, 'I am not ungrateful for your suggestion of a Selected Poems (I have written some which are much better than those of *The Espalier* and *T[ime] I[mportuned]*). But I must seriously warn you that I DO NOT SELL. I doubt if even your two new machines could overcome that bleak fact.' In 1978 she wrote to him presciently: 'I propose to be a posthumous poet!' Claire Harman edited her *Collected Poems* (1982), followed by a *Selected Poems* (1985).

FROM SYLVIA TOWNSEND WARNER
Lower Frome, Vauchurch, Dorchester
26 November 1974

Dear Mr Schmidt,

Both book parcels have come. Thank you very much for the Edgell. I am delighted to have it; it will be rational reading through the irrational days to come.[2] Please give him my regards, and tell him how happy I am to be recalled to the days of my youth – and often to essays of his which I read in the *New Statesman* and still remember because they helped me to make up my mind about the literature of that time; or introduced me to writers like Corbière.

You have made a handsome book of it. I have grown to look with great esteem at your Cat.[3] She represents discrimination.

Here are three books of my poetry. *Opus 7* I have several copies of – so if you care to, please keep it.

With best wishes,
Sylvia Townsend Warner

FROM SYLVIA TOWNSEND WARNER
Lower Frome Vauchurch, Dorchester
21 December 1974

Dear Michael,

Thank you for the Corbière.[4] Thank you for the Sisson. Corbière doing the splits enchants me. Low be it spoken, I think he does *le poète maudit* better than Verlaine. His litter-bin abundance is so entirely himself; he has an immediacy that Verlaine forfeits by being too technically scrupulous. And I admire Val Warner's repertory of language. He [*sic*] matches Corbière even when he misunderstands him: to my mind, at least, misunderstands. Surely the name on the collar (in Sir Bob, p.13) should be Hers, to continue the capitalised She?

As for the Ste-Anne de la Palud – I have never read it before, and I am bowled over by it. You have given me a treasure.

I have been too be-Christmassed to read Sisson properly. What I have read impresses me a great deal. He is obviously 'a learned poet', like those in the Byrd madrigal.[5] Learned, as Jonson was – not just scholarly.

Thank you again. See you in the New Year.

Ever, Sylvia

*

Sylvia Townsend Warner became the subject of a poem I published in *The Love of Strangers* (1989) and I can reconstruct a kind of chronology from our first epistolary encounters in 1973/4, possibly at the instigation of Edgell Rickword, and her death in 1978 in Maiden Newton, Devon. Val Warner and I trudged up to her flat in Churton Place, London, to interview her in 1975, the piece finally appearing in *PN Review* 23 (1982). Later on, my quondam student and friend Nicholas Rhodes and I travelled to Maiden Newton and made the wonderful recording of her reading her poems, in particular 'Gloriana Dying', which remains my favourite. My poem remembers the occasion: 'Late winter, pitch dark at five, thorned boughs across the door– /And caught your rusty voice doing 'Gloriana/ Dying', with you dying...' When Claire Harman was working on her biography of the poet, I was surprised to see the volume of self-revelation that was available to her. There were other specific recollections:

> You called me a rogue, your rogue cat liked me,
> Sat on my lap, stitched me gently with his claws,
> Needling, needling, hinting what he might do.
> Was his name Tib, or Titus? Is he still alive,
> Bleached by years, as you were: white witch, white cat ...

In the end we published her *Collected Poems* and in 2008 a much fuller edition, both edited by Claire Harman; and the same year we published the poetry of Warner's long-time partner Valentine Ackland, *Journey from Winter: selected poems*, edited by Frances Bingham.

NOTES

1. Interview in *PN Review* 23 (January–February 1982). This issue had a section celebrating STW, edited by Claire Harman. She is the author of *Sylvia Townsend Warner – a biography* (Chatto & Windus, 1989) and the editor of *The Diaries of Sylvia Townsend Warner* (Chatto & Windus, 1994).

2. Alan Young brought the work of Edgell Rickword to Carcanet's attention, and edited his *Essays and Opinions 1921–1931* (1974). See below, pp.210 ff.

3. The outlined, bewhiskered cat, making a 'c' shape with its arched back and tail curled under, was the colophon of the Press for many years. It was designed by Priscilla Eckhard – who designed many of the early Carcanet covers – for the cover for *The Religious Poems* of Christopher Smart, edited by Marcus Walsh (1972). Eckhard was the second wife of the poet Roger Garfitt (b. 1944); his latest collection, *The Action*, was published by Carcanet in 2019.

4. *The Centenary Corbière*, a bilingual edition of poems and prose translated by Val Warner, was published in 1974 to mark the centenary of the French poet's death. STW refers here to the poem 'La Rapsode Foraine et le Pardon de Sainte-Anne' (pp. 71-93). Carcanet published several volumes of Val Warner's poetry, also her edition of *The Collected Poems and Prose of Charlotte Mew* (1981), encouraging the revival of interest in that author.

5. STW probably refers to the 1974 publication of Charles Sisson's *In the Trojan Ditch: collected poems and selected translations*. In the 1920s she was part of the committee producing the monumental edition of *Tudor Church Music* published by Oxford University Press at the end of the decade, including the works of William Byrd. It has been suggested that, after Milton, Ben Jonson (1572–1637) was the most learned of English poets.

THE YEAR IN BOOKS

Sam Adams (ed), *Ten Anglo-Welsh Poets*

Robert Bridges, *Selected Poems of Robert Bridges*, edited by Donald Stanford

Tristan Corbière *The Centenary Corbière: Poems and Prose*, translation and introduction by Val Warner

Mahmoud Darwish, *Selected Poems*, translated by Ian Wedde and Fawwaz Tuqan

H.D. (Hilda Doolittle), *Trilogy*, foreword by Norman Holmes Pearson

Colin Falck, *Backwards Into the Smoke*

Robert Garioch (ed), *Made in Scotland: an anthology of fourteen Scottish poets*

Peter Huchel, *Selected Poems*, translated by Michael Hamburger

Dan Pagis, *Selected Poems*, translated by Stephen Mitchell

Edgell Rickword, *Essays and Opinions 1921–1931*, edited by Alan Young

John Wilmot, Earl of Rochester, *The Debt to Pleasure: John Wilmot, Earl of Rochester, in the Eyes of his Contemporaries and in his Own Poetry and Prose*, edited by John Adlard

Robert B. Shaw (ed), *American Poetry Since 1960: some critical perspectives*

Jon Silkin, *The Principle of Water*

C.H. Sisson, *In the Trojan Ditch: collected poems and selected translations*

Derek Stanford (ed), *Three Poets of the Rhymers Club: Ernest Dowson, Lionel Johnson, John Davidson*

Arthur Symons, *Selected Writings*, edited by Roger Holdsworth

1975

C.H. Sisson (1914–2003) was a civil servant, poet and translator, whose poetry, essays, translations and novels were at the centre of Carcanet's twentieth-century list. He also had a determining influence on *PN Review*, and was responsible for the addition of several authors to the list, including Ford Madox Ford, Wyndham Lewis and David Wright. Michael Schmidt's seventieth birthday tribute records his encounter with Sisson's work at the age of twenty-five, when he was planning the first issue of *PN*: 'Sisson's submission of poems knocked Carcanet off the rather predictable course it had embarked on, changing my expectations as reader and editor. [...] For me, Sisson's work was a slow imaginative earthquake. [...] It was intellectually and spiritually ambitious, and it pursued its subjects without looking over its shoulder at the reader.'[1]

FROM C.H. SISSON

Langport

14 July 1975

Dear Michael,

I have now read most of *PN* IV, which seems to me a very good number, particularly as to prose. May I offer a few reflections, not so much by way of critique of IV as in relation to later issues? I need hardly say, you do not have to agree, or even justify any alternatives.

I thought Geoffrey Hill's article ["'Perplexed Persistence":
The Exemplary Failure of T.H. Green'] a useful departure
from the pattern established by the first numbers. I don't say
that its rather painful worrying over the reflection of Oxford
academics is a model in all ways, but I think that a magazine
of this size can stand one article of that difficulty, which will
no doubt be appreciated by a number of your tougher readers.
I think that extending the range of articles beyond the merely
literary/poetic is a good thing, and necessary if *PN* is to become
solidly influential. In this case you have every justification for
the departure, because it is obviously of interest – or ought
to be of interest – to readers of G. Hill to learn a little more
about the sort of mind he has and how he uses it. There would
be room for other articles which gave a similar glimpse of the
preoccupations of other poets: and while it would I think be a
mistake – even if your terms of reference allowed it – to have
merely technical articles on specialised subjects, it seems to me
that to allow a little more general intellectual exercise in your
pages could do nothing but good.

I have always had a hankering for a new version of *The
Criterion* – tho' obviously any such thing would have to be
much less lavish – and this deforms my vision to some extent.[2]

Still the real point is that even a magazine devoted to
poetry should, for the health of poetry, do something to avoid
the impression that The Poet is interested in poetry, literary
criticism and literary politics: full stop. I endorse strongly the
paragraph beginning 'For I suppose' on p. 122 of his article.

Incidentally, I find it difficult, this time, to know exactly
what Donald Davie is on about ['Ezra Pound Abandons the
English']. I never knew anyone put out by the alleged anti-
Englishness or anti-Britishness of Pound's squibs; indeed
never thought of him that way before. To be pro-English in
any way is generally thought much more odd and sinister. Of
course what Pound is mainly saying is (1) our civilisation begins

in the Mediterranean and (2) Eliot and himself were the best English poets of their generation, which they were. Can't say I ever knew any Englishman, anyhow, who was seriously put out by what any Yank had to say about this country.

Yours,
Charles

FROM C.H. SISSON
Langport
1 November 1975

Dear Michael,

I have been wondering whether some re-vamping of the title of *PN*, so as to indicate the wider scope without losing the familiar ring of the old title, would not be desirable. I suppose one could do as you suggest or possibly have a joint title *Poetry Nation and The English Magazine*: But what that would mean I am not too sure.[3] An 'English interest' could be dangerous ground, too near to a half-baked intervention in practical politics; my own conception – fleeting – of a magazine was too personal to survive the diffused direction of four editors. How would it apply to such an article as Munton's on Lewis?[4] Munton is visibly toying with some more or less Marxist thoughts, and I fell over backwards not to take exception to some expression on those grounds. It might be better to avoid any title or sub-title which would strike people as partisan, unless the partisanship were on behalf of good writing, and *The Intelligence* – a faint ghost enough, but it means something to say, for example, that silly or mis-stated notions should not be immune from attack on grounds of political pre-conceptions. I suppose so far as one looks to the concrete and meaningful – which is also the viable, so far as the poet/writer is concerned – one brings everything to a test of reality in geographical and historical terms, which for us is England. Obscure and inadequate adumbrations! I don't know a lot about Brian Cox, but Donald Davie is a self-confessed man of ideas, see the notes to the *Collected Poems*. Anyway, he says he wants to have a preliminary talk about *PN* when he comes here, on 9 November, and this will help clear the air. But I have the feeling that if we four try to botch up too much in the way of agreed principles the whole thing will burst explosively in a very short time. So we must be content to be largely exploratory. I will let you know if anything becomes clear when I have seen Donald.

I do not think we need to take exception to the excellent name of Schmidt, nor to the sombrero which must be supposed to shade his eyes from the dazzle of the Mexican sun, it being rather a principle of the enterprise – I should have hoped – that no one ever got anything, intellectually, by concealing his origins. Big words, big words.

Yours,
Charles

*

In April 2017 a conference 'Revisiting C.H. Sisson: Modernist, Classicist, Translator' was co-sponsored in London by King's College, London, and Brigham Young University. I was asked to provide an opening lecture. Relevant to Sisson's place in this book, and in Carcanet's history, was my opening declaration: 'At the heart of my editorial life, of my writing life, and dare I say even of my civic and spiritual life, C.H. Sisson occupies a central position. I would say, even after the forty-five years since he first wrote to me, it is *the* central position.' I was not given a title for my lecture. The freedom this gave me was rather unfocusing. I provided 'a series of tangents in search of a circle'. Here are three tangents that touch on the themes of this book that I would like to quote here:

1.

His 'Metamorphoses' ends with the incarnation, having run through a gamut of tones and transformations. In short, unlike any of the Modernists except Eliot, Sisson has at the core of his imagination a Christian hope, sometimes a Christian belief, specifically and rootedly Anglican. And that core is not so much of doctrine – the doctrine is given – as of culture, a liturgical, biblical, hymn culture, a culture of sermons and essays and poems, which he more than any other poet I have met took to heart. It is the constitutive element of his imagination, and its weakening hold on his wider culture was the great elegiac occasion of his later poems, which came with such unexpected fluency in the years after his retirement from the Civil Service, which more or less coincided with his becoming a Carcanet and *PN Review* author. Indeed his loss of certainty and confidence coincides with the radical changes in liturgy which he, and a large group of us, protested in *PN Review 13: Crisis for Cranmer and King James*.

2.

My library is an echo of his, I adopted many of his enthusiasms and followed many of his leads. He was keen for us to publish Hugh MacDiarmid; he brought the poems of Ian McMillan to my attention. Many of our translations, from Bove to Botho Straus, were down to him. The volumes of *The English Sermon* we published were a joint project of his and mine. His prints are all over Carcanet in its first thirty years, and he remains a – the – presiding tutelary spirit.

3.

Sisson's dislikes the modern insistence on poets' posturing, demonstrating their ideological *bona fides*, especially to their peers, and demanding from their peers a reflecting demonstration. Such poets generally remain aloof from engagement. Hill, while not quite this kind of poet himself, marks a transition from the engagement and resistance that illuminatingly (some would say fatally) trammel writers as different in aspect as MacDiarmid and Pound, Eliot and David Jones, Auden and Roy Campbell, whose hands got dirty and whose art was in part nourished by that dirt, and the contemporary poets whose ideological purity and the self-regard of that purity ('the poet's own heroism') makes it hard for them to understand the constituency whose interests they believe they represent, those, in short, who reside in the 'outside world'. Their incredulity at the Brexit vote, or in the United States at the outcome of the recent Presidential election, reveals how remote they have grown from the life of their nations as that life is lived not in academic quarantine, and how helpless they are to address it in their essays or their art.

NOTES

1. *Times Higher Education Supplement*, 23 March 1984.

2. *The Criterion* (1922–39), a journal founded and edited by T.S. Eliot. Although in a letter to a friend in 1935 George Orwell had said 'for pure snootiness it beats anything I have ever seen', writing in 1944 he referred to it as 'possibly the best literary paper we have ever had'. Discussions of what kind of journal *PN* should be constantly recur in the editors' letters, and are well described in Mark Fisher's introduction to 'The Corn Exchange (1975–1981)' in *Letters to an Editor*.

3. *The English Magazine* was the title Sisson played with for a periodical of his own, written mostly by himself: 'a kind of powder magazine, aimed at blowing up sundry foolish notions by its own energies', as he wrote to MNS on 6 January 1975. In the same letter, he asked, 'Did I ever tell you that the people who ran *The New English Weekly* once thought of offering me the editorship, and did not do so only because Philip Mairet, who was giving it up, advised that I might accept and so ruin my family and myself by leaving the Civil Service?'

4. Alan Munton was awarded a PhD by Cambridge University in 1976 for a thesis on Wyndham Lewis and with C.H. Sisson

was editing the *Collected Poems and Plays of Wyndham Lewis* for publication by Carcanet (1979; reissued in the Fyfield series, 2003). His article 'The Politics of Wyndham Lewis' was published in *PN Review* 1 (October–December 1977).

THE YEAR IN BOOKS

David Day, *Brass Rubbings*

Hugh Franks, *I'm sorry to Have to Tell You: How to Drive*, illustrations by ffolkes, foreword by O.F. Lambert

Roger Garfitt, *West of Elm*

Michael Hamburger, *Art as Second Nature: occasional pieces 1950–1975*

Michael Hamburger, *Hugo von Hofmannsthal: three essays*

Horace, *The Poetic Art: a Translation of Horace's Ars Poetica*, translated by C.H. Sisson

Elizabeth Jennings, *Growing Points: new poems*

George Kendrick, *Bicycle Tyre in a Tall Tree*

Maurice Lindsay, Alexander Scott, Roderick Watson (eds), *Scottish Poetry 8*

Lucretius, *The Nature of Things*, translated by C. H. Sisson

Christopher Middleton, *The Lonely Suppers of W.V. Balloon*

Edwin Morgan, *Essays*

Michael Schmidt, *My Brother Gloucester*

James Simmons (ed), *Ten Irish Poets*

C.H. Sisson, *Christopher Homm*

John Cargill Thompson, *The Boys' Dumas, G.A. Henty: aspects of Victorian publishing*

Alexander Tvardovsky, *Tyorkin and the Stovemakers: poetry and prose*, translated by Anthony Rudolf, introduction by C.P. Snow

Dudley Young, *Out of Ireland: The Poetry of W.B. Yeats*

Edward Young, *Selected Poems*, edited by Brian Hepworth

1976

Thom Gunn (1929–2004) was educated at Cambridge, and left England shortly after the publication of his first collection of poems, *Fighting Terms* (Faber and Faber, 1954). He moved to California to be with Mike Kitay (with whom he lived until his death) and to study poetry with Yvor Winters, whom he described as 'the most exciting teacher I ever had'.[1] In a *PN Review* interview (70, November-December 1989), Gunn said that he didn't think about his audience when he was writing, and that when he came across a reference to himself as 'an Anglo-American poet' he thought '"Yes, that's what I am I'm an Anglo-American poet." So that resolves that question! I don't think of the audiences as being that different.' *Jack Straw's Castle* was published in 1976.

FROM MICHAEL SCHMIDT
Manchester
7 June 1976

Dear Thom Gunn

Charles Monteith gave me your address.[2] I am now editing, with Brian Cox, Donald Davie and C.H. Sisson, a magazine – shortly to become quarterly – called *Poetry Nation Review*. Up to now it has been twice-yearly.

I have also recently been finding some poets whose work seems to me to share a debt to your poems and to Winters's. They are Cambridge people – Dick Davis, Clive Wilmer, and

– especially – Robert Wells.[3] He seems to me better than just good, and I plan to publish him wherever I can. There are a few others who might, similarly, be seen as having certain debts to you – especially in your 'middle period' (that period must seem to be moving further and further forward in time!).

My plan is to have three of these poets write in *Poetry Nation Review* brief essays on *Jack Straw's Castle*. I was wondering whether there was any chance of you considering writing a piece for us on what Winters continues to mean, in view of some of your formal (and vital) experiments and developments?

The magazine, I should hasten to add, is <u>not</u> a Wintersian Journal. You know Donald's ambivalent respect; mine is less ambivalent but also less instructed (I love the poems but find the critic hard to deal with).

If you were in a position to write anything for us, I'd be grateful. Especially on a Wintersian theme. My hope is to give the magazine a kind of depth by, in verse, publishing no fewer than four poems at a time by any poet; and, in the prose, a balance achieved through juxtaposition and contrast (though, alas and woe, the magazine has a somewhat consistent polemic).

Thanks in any case for your attention.

Sincerely,

Michael Schmidt

FROM THOM GUNN
San Francisco
16 June 1976

Dear Michael Schmidt,

Thank you very much for your letter, which I have been thinking about for the last week. I have known about Davis, Wilmer and

Wells since the publication of their joint book *Shade Mariners* about six years ago.[4] And I have liked their work a lot. In fact I just wrote, a few weeks ago, a reviews of Davis's book, *In the Distance*, which I think will be in the next issue of *Thames Poetry*. Much as I like to think of them writing about me – I am very flattered – perhaps it would not be a good idea to ask him. Him reviewing me and me reviewing him within just a few months would look a bit like back scratching.

There are difficulties about the piece on Winters, all of them in my own head. I do want to write something about him one day, partly to get everything straight for my own benefit.[5] But I don't see it very clearly yet. You speak about your ambivalence with Winters: it could not be greater than my own. There was the personal *sweetness* of the man, and then the public ferocity, and then again the disastrous tendency to confuse a man's personal worth with his poetic worth. Also though there is much I admire about his criticism – and much I have learned from it – it excludes a tremendous amount of what I consider to be indispensable poetry. His own poetry was fantastic, I agree, and there seems to me no question at all that he was one of the abidingly good poets of the century. Ultimately, I suppose, my problem with him was this, and still is: learned and wise as he was, beautiful poet as he was, he felt a distaste for the multitudinous particularity of life, there was a fastidiousness, ultimately perhaps a fear for all the careless thriving *detail* of everything, a strong tendency – increasing as he got older – to exclude all that could not be transformed to principle. Perhaps the main reason, after all, why he couldn't stand such an obviously great poet as Whitman, was because Whitman was one of the great enjoyers – and in the end I have to admit that because his sympathies were wider than Winters's his understanding was wider too.

But I'm not sure how to go about writing this for a year or two, if ever. Maybe the way to go about it would be to make it an entirely personal and chronological account. But I'll postpone it for now. Meanwhile I thank you very much for asking me, and I will send you some stuff some time (I had already promised D[onald] D[avie] I would). I'm having a peculiarly infertile summer, but I might be able to send you something in time for the issue you speak of if you give me the deadline. (This is more of a hope than a promise.)

Best,
Thom Gunn

FROM MICHAEL SCHMIDT
Manchester
24 June 1976

Dear Mr Gunn,

Warm thanks for your letter of 16 June. I half-expected that your reply to the Winters letter would be tentative, but I'm very glad to know that if thoughts take a prose form you will let us see them! I thought the letter itself expressed – very clearly – the nature of the predicament. I find it helpful, in any event, and am grateful for it.

The problem of an excluding art is one which worries me a great deal. In a sense, it is this very element that draws me to Winters. The terms in which the excluding works tend, sometimes, in the best poems, to suggest what tensions are being excluded. The very act implies their presence. But a kind of desiccation (especially in the critical approach) may follow.

You might like to know that Clive Wilmer, after I had been urged to read the poems by my colleague Gareth Reeves (he met you briefly during his long stay at Stanford), sent me the poems – all of them – of Edgar Bowers.[6] I was a little disappointed with the first book, but the second book and the five new poems interested me tremendously – especially that Autumn sequence and a few of the short poems. I am asking Clive to try to secure for Carcanet Press rights to publish a Collected Poems for England. Bowers is the sort of poet (I'm sorry for that phrase!) I would most like to publish. My problem is that I have had considerable difficulties with Godine in Boston, and I have vowed never to deal with them again. We printed Middleton's last book for them. So I am praying that Bowers is contractually bound to Swallow rather than Godine and that he may be willing to contemplate publication by a small press here.[7] We now have the largest poetry list (especially new poetry and translations) in England (I mean, we produce a wider range of new titles than any of the larger houses). However, since we do only poetry and related work, we don't have any money. We are good at getting the books around. I hope *something* will come of this.

I hope that you – who seem to be featuring rather prominently in *PNR* as it develops because the new poets I most admire seem to have learned a great deal from you – will be able to send us work for *PNR* when your lean period is over.[8] I eagerly look forward to *Jack Straw's Castle*. I confessed to Clive Wilmer that I was, in the Gunn oeuvre, keenest on *Touch* and *Moly* (*Moly* fared so ill with the critics I hardly dared mention my enthusiasm). Clive waxed exceeding eloquent on the subject. Brian Cox and I have been teaching *Moly* in our seminars. Teaching. Well… reading.

[the document ends here]

*

Thom Gunn was a frequent contributor to *PN Review* (getting on for thirty poems between 1979 and 1999, some of them shared with *Threepenny Review*) as well as reviews and some substantial essays. There was always a certain edge in his relations with the magazine and with the Press. It related sometimes to questions of tone which are, after all, an aspect of substance and Gunn had to call me out from time to time. As with most of my correspondents, an actual dialogue was in progress, an engagement over issues which mattered deeply to us, in different ways. Thus relations with Gunn were complicated by the close presence within *PN Review* of Donald Davie, a committed but critical advocate who knew Gunn's Wintersian roots almost as well as Gunn himself; and while Gunn remained deeply in Winters's debt he also came to find the Winters coterie narrow and narrowing. He also wanted to go part way with Davie on Pound but, as we have seen in Davie's own letters, part way wasn't quite far enough. He never engaged with Sisson's work, distrusting a politics he erroneously presumed.

About his own severe and generous politics, which evolved so exemplarily over time, there is little doubt. In 1994 he contributed a quatrain to *PN Review* called 'Eastern Europe' and dated *February, 1990*':

'The iron doors of history' give at last,
And we walk through them from a rigid past.
Free! free! we can do anything we choose
– Eat at McDonald's, persecute the Jews.

He added a telling note: '"Eastern Europe" is purely cerebral. Of course, people hate ideas without imagery these days, and I notice that by consequence epigrams are found repellent. But the Romans valued them, and so did Ben Jonson, and we should keep the form around for joking and cleverness and also for those occasions when pointed rudeness is appropriate.' In a later note he chides himself for having 'slipped into expressing the intentions I wanted to avoid'.

NOTES

1. Yvor Winters (1900–68), American poet and literary critic, was Professor of English at Stanford University. In his first critical volume, *Primitivism and Decadence* (1937), Winters concluded that 'experimental meter loses the rational frame which alone gives its variations the precision of true perception', and in the foreword to *In Defence of Reason*, he defined a poem as 'a statement in words about a human experience'. His award-winning *Collected Poems* was published in 1952. Carcanet published his *Collected Poems* in 1978, introduced by Davie.

2. Charles Monteith (1921–95) was a Director of Faber and Faber from 1954 to 1974.

3. Dick Davis (b. 1945), poet, critic and translator, contributed regularly to *PN Review* for several years, and translated works by Natalia Ginzburg for Carcanet. He moved to Iran in 1970, but had to leave after the revolution in 1978. He is Emeritus Professor of Persian at Ohio State University. Clive Wilmer (b. 1945), poet, critic and lecturer, contributed poetry, articles and reviews regularly to *PN Review* from 1975 onwards. Carcanet published his *New & Collected Poems* in 2012, including a selection of his translations from several languages, notably Hungarian. He edited and annotated Thom Gunn's *Selected Poems* (Faber and Faber, 2017). Robert Wells first approached Schmidt about his poems in 1976. See below, [p.239.]

4. *Shade Mariners* (1970) was published by Gregory Spiro in Cambridge, with an introduction by Tony Tanner. Dick Davis's first collection, *In the Distance*, was published by Anvil Press in 1975. Carcanet published his collected poems and selected translations, *Love in Another Language*, in 2017.

5. Gunn did write about Winters in the 1980s, and his account of their relationship is collected in 'On a Drying Hill: Yvor Winters' in *Shelf Life: Essays, Memoirs and an Interview*, which is dedicated to Clive Wilmer (University of Michigan Press, 1995; Faber and Faber, 1996).

6. Gareth Reeves (b.1947), poet and critic, worked closely with Carcanet in its early years as one of the founders of the press, along with Schmidt and Peter Jones. He spent some time at Stanford University on a Wallace Stegner Writing Fellowship. His first collection, *Real Stories*, was published by Carcanet in 1984; *To Hell with Paradise: new and selected poems* in 2012, and most recently *Nuncle Music* in 2013.

7. Edgar Bowers (1924–2000) studied with Winters at Stanford. He published five collections of poetry in his lifetime and his *Collected Poems* was published in 1997 by Knopf; he was openly gay but this was not a focus of his poems. Some poems were published in *PN Review* in the 1980–90s, and his work was reviewed there. *Living Together: new and selected poems* appeared on the Carcanet list in 1977. David R. Godine (a distinguished Boston publisher) published Bowers's third collection in 1973, and the two previous books were published by Alan Swallow (1915–66), whose Swallow Press in Colorado published authors including Allen Tate and Yvor Winters.

8. Gunn contributed poems to nine issues of *PN Review* over the 1980s–90s; his first appearance was in *PN Review* 8 (July–September 1979). Concerns raised by two letters from 1981 that take issue with the attitude of the journal to homosexuality must have been satisfactorily answered. See *Letters to an Editor*, nos 189, 191.

THE YEAR IN BOOKS

John Adlard (ed), *The Fruit of that Forbidden Tree: Restoration poems, songs and jests on the subject of sensual love*

Cliff Ashby, *The Dogs of Dewsbury: new poems*

Thomas Lovell Beddoes, *Selected Poems*, edited by Judith Higgens

Anne, Charlotte and Emily Brontë, *Selected Poems*, edited by Stevie Davies

George Buchanan, *Inside Traffic: new poems*

Thomas Campion, *Ayres and Observations: selected poems*, edited by
Joan Hart

John Cornford, *Understand the Weapon, Understand the Wound:
selected writings of John Cornford with some letters of Frances
Cornford*, edited by Jonathan Galassi

Thomas Crawford (ed), *Love, Labour and Liberty: the eighteenth
century Scottish lyric*

Elizabeth Daryush, *Collected Poems*, introduction by Donald Davie

Douglas Dunn (ed), *Two Decades of Irish Writing: a critical survey*

Maurice Lindsay (ed), *Modern Scottish Poetry: an anthology of the
Scottish Renaissance 1925–1975*

Maurice Lindsay, Alexander Scott, Roderick Watson (eds), *Scottish
Poetry 9*

Paul Mills, *North Carriageway*

Edwin Morgan, *Rites of Passage: selected translations*

Robert Nye (ed), *The English Sermon: 1750–1850: Volume 3*

Robert Nye, *Divisions on a Ground*

Janos Pilinszky, *Selected Poems*, translated by Ted Hughes and Janos
Csokits

Edgell Rickword, *Behind the Eyes: Collected Poems and Translations*

Anthony Rudolf, *The Same River Twice*

Hans Dieter Schaefer, *Strawberries in December and Other Poems*,
translated by Ewald Osers

Michael Schmidt (ed), *Ten English Poets: An Anthology*

Delmore Schwartz, *What is to be Given: Selected Poems*, edited by
Douglas Dunn

Martin Seymour-Smith (ed) *The English Sermon: 1550–1650:
Volume 1*

Jon Silkin, *The Little Timekeeper*

C.H. Sisson, *Anchises: Poems*

C.H. Sisson (ed), *The English Sermon: 1650–1750: Volume 2*

Allen Tate, *Memories and Essays: Old and New, 1926–1974*

Charles Tomlinson, *In Black and White: the graphics of Charles
Tomlinson*, with three prose texts by Charles Tomlinson and an

essay by Octavio Paz

Henry Vaughan, *Selected Poems of Henry Vaughan*, edited by Robert
B. Shaw

Evgeny Vinokurov, *Selected Poems*, translated by Anthony Rudolf
and Daniel Weissbort

David Wright, *To the Gods the Shades: new and collected poems*

1977

The Scottish poet and artist William Sydney Graham (1918–86) was living in Cornwall with his wife, Nessie Dunsmuir, barely making a living from poetry but increasingly in demand as a reader.[1] In this year he read with Harold Pinter, who later wrote: 'W.S. Graham drank and ate poetry every day of his life. [His] letters show an intelligence and sensibility ravished by language and conundrums of language.' Graham wrote to C.H. Sisson in January 1977: 'M'dear (allow that Cornishism) […] I think the advent of your verse is going to help our contemporary English poetry (Whatever that is.) and batter fashion a bit'; and unpredictably added, 'Although you are a very different man from me, so much of your poetry my soul can use.'[2] Faber and Faber published *Implements in their Places* in September 1977, his last single collection, followed by a *Collected Poems* in 1979.

FROM W.S. GRAHAM
Madron
28 March 1977

Dear Michael,

I am writing in great ridiculous ballpoint because Nessie is typing out TO MY WIFE AT MIDNIGHT on the same table. I am encouraging my wife to type and trying not to look at her out of the side of my eye to promote mistakes.

Many thanks for your letter. We had a good day at Plymouth

with Fraser Steel and I think I read my words clear and well.[3]

You are very kind in your remarks about the script. All I need is a tape recorder saying that into my ear day & night. Lovely to hear about you maybe doing the review in *TLS*. If I can help you let me know. For example I hope you will mention [half a dozen 'Chinese' characters drawn here] that I am influenced by Tibetan verse (The Lasha Review). (Joke)

I also, am having (You will see that my calligraphy improves when I am talking about money.) difficulties with finance. Here is the poem. Do you think I could have the £20 on receipt of TO MY WIFE AT MIDNIGHT.

You seem always worried, at the end of your letters. They all close with a phrase about the lack of money. Well my dear, Michael, you must know what you're doing. I don't quite understand the 'drowsy numbness'. Did I write that, or you? I hope you don't let yourself be overwhelmed. Are you a poet first?

'Is not to ring the bell'

'There, at the highway's end'

'Lies hidden where exile
Too easily beckons'

'Done is a battel on the dragon blak'

'Weary of watching round the fire at night.'[4]

I hope among all the fuck-up of finance you are writing your verse.

Viva Mexico
& Manchester,
W.S. Graham

FROM W.S. GRAHAM
Madron
7 April 1977

Dear Michael,

Thanks for your letter and £20 for TO MY WIFE AT MIDNIGHT. I am sending you the complete poem with the lovely title – Johann JOACHIM QUANTZ'S FIVE LESSONS. Two of the 'Lessons' have appeared somewhere before a long time back. My guess is one in the *TLS* and I can't remember where the other came out. The point is, the whole poem coming out in a one'r will make a good thing. I will need the money so can you send it. Nessie and I are being taken to Crete from the 28th April to 15th May by an unmoustached friend who is in wool and his wife, both whom we have a great shoosh towards.[5] Remember we will be away during those dates. I drink an ouzo to you under the tree.

My dear Michael, To get it straight about my book coming out in the Autumn. The book is titled IMPLEMENTS IN THEIR PLACES. Implements in their places is also the title of the long poem in the book. The book has all those poems in it maybe you have seen in Fraser's script. O O O-

[drawing of a boat on the waves, see p.91]

Nessies running for the post. I'll send the QUANTZ. Forgive the cutoff, are you there not too unhappy about your private knut.

Yours sombererian,
Sydney

FROM W.S. GRAHAM
Madron
8 April 1977

Dear Michael,

OK here I write again enclosing this copy of JOHANN JOACHIM QUANTZ'S FIVE LESSONS which is a bit worn. I've taken it from the script. Two 'Lessons' have been printed before, quite a time ago. One in *TLS*, the other I know not where. Or did I tell you in my last letter?

Like you I am broke and the money soon would help me. (a kind of Schmidtzapatan iambic pentameter!)

Our respective wits seem to have crossed each other. Of course I knew it was the nachtigal. Nightly she sings on yon pomegranate tree. Now my Brother Gloucesterring man, I have always been a great Keats supporter and I think the chemist's assistant will go far in spite of his atrocious cockney accent.[6]

I don't understand what you mean when you say 'I have stopped writing verse for the duration.' What duration do you mean?

My wife and I are going down into the big city of Penzance (10,000 inhabitants) to a performance of Faure's Requiem. Good power to you.

Sydney

P.S. Can you let me have proof copies of the poems as usual.
WSG

Michael Schmidt

Carcanet Press Ltd,
330-332 Corn Exchange Buildings,
Manchester M4 3BG

Dear Michael,

Thanks for your letter and £20 for TO MY WIFE AT MIDNIGHT.
I am sending you the complete poem with the lovely title-
Johann JOACHIM QUANTZ'S FIVE LESSONS. Two of the 'Lessons'
have appeared somewhere before a long time back. My guess
is one in TLS and I cant remember where the other came out.
The point is, the whole poem coming out in a one'r will make
a good thing. ~~I and ned the money xxxothell off with your~~ h
~~ead or the tapping wrotter 0 has are you there To start again.~~
I will need the money so can you send it. Nessie and I are
being taken to Crete from the 28th April to 15th May by an
unmoustached friend who is in wool and his wife, both whom
we have a great shoosh towards. Remember we will be away
during these dates. I drink an ouzo to you under the tree.

My dear Michael, To get it straight about my book coming out
in the Autumn. The book is titled IMPLEMENTS IN THEIR PLACES.
Implements In Their Places is also the title of the long poem
in the book. The book has all those poems in it maybe you have
seen in Fraser's script. 0 0 0-

Nessies running for the post. I'll send the QUANTZ.
Forgive the cutoff, are you there not too unhappy about
your private knut.

                Yours sombrerian,

                                        X

FROM W.S. GRAHAM
Madron
16 December 1977

Dear Michael Schmidt,

Forgive me taking so long to write to you after your review. I know you are all out for me. I think you should have stuck your neck out more.[7] I think you should have made use of your space in the *TLS* to show your thinking better. I know how I struggled through my early poetry to gradually get better and clearer. It is not like that. I was disappointed you writing the old cliché about me. My dear Michael, now is your time to say something about how poetry works, from yourself. Why did you make it an extended blurb of a book. You had this area of print given to you (whether it was about me or another poet) to show whether you had any real values about the art of poetry. Why speak like an advert?

Shall I tell you my own measurement of my books? I am getting better I hope. But it is not like a graph saying 'he started out not knowing what he was doing and then went through his Dylan Thomas phase (Which I got a great deal out of) and now he is refining himself (you dont even speak as well as that.) and able to be clear and able to say the great, deeper things which were almost near him anyhow. MALCOLM MOONEY'S LAND is as good a book as IMPLEMENTS IN THEIR PLACES. You see, my dear, you have fallen into the dopiness of your surroundings. Dont let me go on too long or begin to speak about your début in detail. I had thought that because you were the editor of your magazine holding poems and criticism (reviews must be criticism at their best no matter how limited the space) you would have spoken clearer with a fresher attitude. To finish, I thought you would have been greedier to make your mark as an observer of what verse means and how it works. My dear Michael, a dull and uncourageous review. I even had two letters asking why you were not more for me.

I thank you for your 'justice' first paragraph. That is all right and most of the readers will pat you for that.

Dear Michael, Dont let us have a review coming between us. Since I wrote you last I have been reading here from the end of the Celtic Jetty giving readings in Swindon, Oxford and London. I think, my deario, I am getting better at making the good electric at the reading and 'slaying' the people.

What are you doing with your poetry? Have you another book coming up? You better get one out immediately so that I have a chance to know whether you know anything outside.

Come on, Michael, do your best,

Sydney X

P.S. And so I end now with Nessie changing, correcting the stuttering typewriter. And I expect you to write back and say hello and that you send love and a pat on the head. I have been asked to go do a week in and around Loughborough in Leicestershire in the early coming year. OK, WSG

FROM MICHAEL SCHMIDT
Manchester
21 December 1977

Dear Sydney,

Your letter of course burst here like a bombshell. I don't quite understand what you wanted. In fact, I don't understand it at all. Let me say two things. One is that, after proof stage, the review was cut (Fraser has the proofs – or had them, since I gave them to him) of one sentence which said you were now undoubtedly a major poet – 'one of our few best'. That came at the end, and its absence made a hash of the conclusion. The other point is that the piece was a book review for the *TLS*. The brief was to describe the author (it was commissioned as a 'retrospective', as it were) and the book, and its place in the author's development.

Did you want an *ars poetica*? What point would there have been in writing about how poetry works 'from myself', when I was trying to focus on your work, which is rather more important and to the point than any floating notions of my own? And surely the advocacy of the work, and the terms in which I advocated it, the emphases laid upon the last two volumes, show what and indeed how I believe, and why I believe you are one of the three or four best poets writing in English today?

There was no place there for gratuitous theorising. My values should have been clear in my choice to write about you and in the stress I laid on what I took and take to be the best part of your work.

Had I been writing about myself, I should have spoken about how poetry works. But I was trying to write about you. Had I been trying to make my mark, I would not have been doing so in a review of your poetry but in some other context. I was – evidently unsatisfactorily – advocating your work, not mine. And though you had two letters asking why I wasn't more for you, I had several (including one from David Wright, who is my best reader as a poet and prose writer) which thought the review did recommend the book warmly. And they didn't find it dull and uncourageous. Or if they did, they didn't say so.

Your long silence after it had prepared me for your letter, I suppose. I was at first eager and then anxious to know what you thought about it. I'm very sorry it went down badly with you. I would (seriously) like to know what (even sketchily) you see the review as it ought to have been. Could you just do, say, ten headnotes for paragraphs or whatever, showing me what you think I ought to have done?

Meanwhile, though perhaps you're quite off the idea, I'd like to have some more WSG poems in *PNR*. It's probably the wrong time to ask, after I've been unsuccessful with you. But if there's anything, I'd like it.

All the best to yourself and Nessie
– apologies – I try, even if I don't succeed –
Michael

Happy 1978!

*

There is a sweet irony in the image of the poet's wife typing his newly drafted and loveliest poem to her while he, at the same modest table, was writing me a letter. This poem appeared, with 'Johann Joachim Quantz's Five Lessons', in *PN Review* 4 in 1978. By then he had been publishing prominently in *Poetry Nation* and *PN Review* for four years. I very much wanted to add his poems to the Carcanet list. It seemed a possibility. When Nikos Stangos of Penguin approached Faber for rights to publish a selection of the poems in his Penguin Modern Poets series (he was included in *PMP* 17, with David Gascoyne and Kathleen Raine), Faber initially told him (Stangos told me) that the poet was dead (his books were out of print and they had no idea where he was). Stangos and David Wright had encouraged me to correspond with him, and I did. When I told him I was getting married he sent me some delightful drawings for the occasion, and for ten guineas I bought the 'work sheets' for 'The Thermal Stair' from him – at least what purported to be work sheets: in fact it seems to me now that they were worked up in response to my enthusiasm for the poem. Our relations cooled rather after my review of his *Collected Poems*.

We met occasionally, with Fraser Steel, when we were recording poems for *Poetry Now* (he always wanted his cup of tea in studio laced with Teachers). For Graham the first act of literary criticism was to read the poem aloud; you could tell quite soon what the reader understood. We met most memorably at the Cambridge Poetry Festival of 1975 at which he appeared, accompanied by Nessie. He was not very well or very well-behaved and we spoke only briefly. I spent an evening at a loud party trying to hear what Nessie had to say. Eventually she raised the volume of her small voice and I heard her cry out: 'You're not fuckin' listening!' I apologised, naturally, and led her into a quieter space where we tried again.

Roger Hilton used to send him drawings and in return W.S. Graham would send him poems, or sketches. He sent on to C.H. Sisson one or two Hilton drawings because he liked Sisson's poems and Sisson (who valued Graham, much as David Wright did) was generous to him in a private way.

I always associate Graham in my mind with a shamefully neglected poet, Burns Singer, whose work Anne Cluysenaar introduced to me and whose day has yet to dawn. I am persuaded that it will. He is a poet of intense unevenness. He was devoted to Graham and I believe the devotion was reciprocated, though my suggestion was strongly resisted by Nessie. He stayed in the Grahams' garden in Cornwall, they exchanged letters and ideas, until Singer died in 1964 at the age of thirty-six.

Their friendship coincided with the time during which Graham's poetry was undergoing its crucial transition from the whimsical opacity of the Apocalyptic to the compelling luminousness of his mature writing.

NOTES

1. Nessie Dunsmuir (1909–99) married Graham in 1954, after a period of living apart; they had met as students at Newbattle Abbey in 1938. Margaret Snow wrote in her obituary that Graham 'frequently asked for his wife's expenses [for attendance at readings] to be covered too, for, as he put it, "Nessie is necessary"' (*Independent*, 29 July 1999). Anthony Astbury at the Greville Press published her collection *Ten Poems* in 1988.

2. Letter of 24 January 1977, *The Nightfisherman: selected letters of W.S. Graham*, edited by Michael and Margaret Snow (Carcanet, 1999). The comment by Pinter is on the back cover of the book.

3. Fraser Steel (currently Head of the BBC Programme Complaints Unit) was then producer of a series for BBC radio called 'Living Poet', and recorded a session with W.S. Graham. Sending his selection of poems, Graham wrote: 'Don't be frightened of such a shock beginning as "Can you hear me?" My attitude in this program is to set the actual readings of the poems before the public in a less formal, more human way' (8 December 1976, *The Nightfisherman*).

4. 'Is not to ring the bell', from T.S. Eliot's *Little Gidding*, III.182; 'There, at the highway's end', from Schmidt's 'Natalya's Dream' (*My Brother Gloucester*); 'Lies hidden…' from WSG, 'The Dark Dialogues' 4; 'Done is a battel' – opening line of a poem by William Dunbar (1460–1522).

5. Ronnie Duncan, a Yorkshire businessman and art collector interested in poetry, and his wife Henriette took the Grahams to Crete. Duncan co-edited with Jonathan Davidson *The Constructed Space: a celebration of W.S. Graham* (Sunk Island Press, 1994).

6. The nightingale references are to Keats's 'Ode to a Nightingale' ('My heart aches, and a drowsy numbness pains/ My sense…'), and *Romeo and Juliet*: 'It was the nightingale, and not the lark, / That pierced the fearful hollow of thine ear. / Nightly she sings on yon pomegranate tree.' Graham refers to Schmidt's third

collection of poems, *My Brother Gloucester* (Carcanet, 1976).

7. In a letter of 9 December 1999, the poet and critic Dennis O'Driscoll told MNS that he would be reviewing *The Nightfisherman* for the journal *Thumbscrew*, and remarked: 'I could not believe my eyes when I discovered that Graham had chided you over your *TLS* review of *Implements in Their Places* – one of the best-informed and most persuasive things written about his work. I have held on to my copy of your review precisely because it encapsulates the essence of Graham's work. Talk about a poet biting the hand…'.

THE YEAR IN BOOKS

John Ashbery, *Self-Portrait in a Convex Mirror*
Edgar Bowers, *Living Together: new and selected poems*
Charles Boyle, *Affinities*
Glen Cavaliero, *Paradise Stairway*
Donald Davie, *In the Stopping Train and Other Poems*
Michael Drayton, *Selected Poems*, edited by Vivien Thomas
Michael Hamburger, *Real Estate*
Elizabeth Jennings, *Consequently I Rejoice*
Peter Jones, *The Garden End: new and selected poems*
Grevel Lindop, *Fools' Paradise*
Christopher Middleton, *Pataxanadu and Other Prose*
Edwin Morgan, *The New Divan: new poems*
Neil Powell, *At the Edge*
I.A. Richards, *Complementarities: uncollected essays*, edited by J.P. Russo
Burns Singer, *Selected Poems*, edited by Anne Cluysenaar
C.H. Sisson, *Art and Action*
Jonathan Swift, *Selected Poems*, edited by C.H. Sisson
Peter Walton, *Out of Season*
Andrew Waterman, *From the Other Country*
Daniel Weissbort, *Soundings*
Robert Wells, *The Winter's Task*
Clive Wilmer, *The Dwelling-Place*

1978

Myfanwy Thomas (1910–2005) was the youngest child of the poet Edward Thomas and his wife Helen (1877–1967). She made her home with her mother at Eastbury for the last thirteen years of Helen's life. Both women were devoted to the task of keeping E.T.'s memory and work alive and appreciated, and happily saw his reputation rise in their lifetimes. Carcanet published Helen Thomas's *Time and Again*, a collection of memoirs and letters edited by Myfanwy, in 1978. In 1988, the Carcanet publication *Under Storm's Wing* brought together all Helen Thomas's memoirs, extracts from Myfanwy's, and six letters from Robert Frost to Thomas. In her introduction, Myfanwy notes with pride her father's name on the 1985 memorial to the poets of the First World War in Westminster Abbey.

FROM MYFANWY THOMAS
Eastbury, Berkshire
7 September 1978

Dear Mr Schmidt,

Thanks so much for your letter of 22 August. I'm so glad *The Guardian* & *Irish Times* are noticing the book.[1] And a great relief that you are pleased with sales. I do hope the reprint, if any, won't necessitate the price going up – if it is to be only 500, couldn't it be paperback and so keep the prices the same?

And very good news of Edna Longley's book about E.T.'s criticism.[2] I'm so glad it is coming out under your imprint.

Oh, I mistook something you once said or wrote – I thought you preferred TV to radio & thought you were an old hand at it! Alas, I believe the *Sunday Times* colour supplement piece may not appear after all. These capricious newspapers – and all the trouble (and anxiety on my part about precious photographs kept for months) that has been taken. I have my photographs back safely, at Stratford last Sunday – brought by a kind friend who has been keeping an eye on them for me – where there was a programme called 'A Pine in Solitude' with 4 readers, Julian Glover was E.T. and Jane Lapotaire, Helen.[3] There was a bookstall there but unfortunately they'd not managed to get any *T & A* to show.

This winter I'm going to try my hand at my childhood, but I don't really think it will be of enough interest & I don't approve really of 'cashing in'. So I shan't be disappointed if you turn it down. But it will be good exercise & keep the cobwebs away. I shall call it 'Cherries in my Hat' – rather typical of me that I longed to have such a trimming and I can hear the charming chumping sound on the straw – *but* I had to be sure that what I'd been told was true – one by one I squashed them and out came the cotton wool – tears & anguish. I'm afraid my father sized me up very smartly in my poem, ending, 'Wanting a thousand little things that time, without contentment, brings.'[4]

With many good wishes – do many bookshops still have that pernicious 'sale or return' condition? I remember from *Adelphi* days that W.H. Smith used to send back a package of tatty, thumbed copies each quarter.[5]

Yours,
Myfanwy Thomas

Some time please could I have the TS back as I have no copy. Or isn't this usual?

FROM MYFANWY THOMAS
Eastbury, Berkshire
26 September 1978

Dear Michael Schmidt,

Thanks so much for your letter and the copy of the very pleasant *Listener* review. Meantime of course you will have seen the *Guardian* one – Edward would have been amused at the rather belated award of the M.C.![6] How lucky I have been so far in such appreciative notices. And I suppose it is quite a good thing for them to be spread over some months rather than all appear in a heap.

Never mind about the photograph date, I don't suppose it was noticed.[7] Several people have in fact written to say what a pity it was that there was <u>no</u> index to the photographs!

I thought the programme 'No one so much as you' on Sunday radio was good, though I thought it a pity the gloom and despair was no[t] leavened a bit. I did send the young man a very saucy letter of Mother's to Edward 'bending over his Borrow' hoping he would use it, but he didn't.[8]

With good wishes,
Myfanwy Thomas

*

Just before I left Oxford, I began work on a B. Litt. on the poetry of Edward Thomas and Robert Frost. A large bequest of Edward Thomas material had been left to the Bodleian Library and had yet to be shelved. It was piled on a wide window-ledge in the reading room and I was given permission to explore it. My love for Thomas's prose writing and poetry dated from those unsupervised encounters with the whole range of his writings. His reviews and essays were bold and independent-minded (his early response to Pound in particular stood out). Like most busy journalist critics he never found the time to return to enthusiasms once he had taken up lodgings in Grub Street, but his *obiter dicta* were worth many long, considered academic tomes. My research had intended to compare Frost's and Thomas's prosody. I loved Frost and knew many poems by heart but I was coming to love Thomas in a different, a more intimate and personal spirit.

Myfanwy, the poet's younger daughter, and I fell into correspondence. She edited a volume of her mother Helen's writings about Edward. At that time, I was typesetting most of Carcanet's books on an IBM golfball composing machine. Editing as I typeset, I developed a particular kind of closeness with the writing. Some writers were a joy to set because each sentence was a pleasure in itself and typesetting was a particular form of intensive, respectful reading. Others were irksome because of tonal or stylistic qualities which grated. With some I could intervene silently, as it were, and make small adjustments of a crucial kind – to punctuation, diction and occasionally by way of silent, un-signposted omissions which even the authors seldom noted or complained about.

What struck me about *Time and Again* was the fact that Helen had great difficulty in ending a narrative, an account and sometimes a sentence. Things were strung together by 'and' and 'and' or flowed in a single, uninterruptable key. I imagine this was possibly an extension of her speaking style, and that she found it hard to make space for her interlocutor. One of the reasons Edward was so taciturn and often depressed may have been the absence of repose and the impossibility of dialogue at home. When he became friendly with Eleanor Farjeon, one of her attractive qualities was an ability to listen; another was the tact to be silent when silence was required. Typesetting Edward Thomas's own prose was another matter altogether: the lucidity, economy, freshness and transparency of his language were always inspiriting.

I find the end of Helen's essay on Robert Frost deeply sad. Shortly before the war Thomas began to write verses, 'But there was no enthusiastic reviewer to praise his poems. No publisher would take them and only a few of his intimate friends thought well of them. He never saw a poem of his in print under his own name, just two or three under the pseudonym "Edward Eastaway" which he himself had, with a wry smile, included in anthologies he was commissioned to edit.'

NOTES

1. Myfanwy Thomas wrote to MNS on 20 September 1977 with a couple of suggested titles for Helen's memoir: 'All This Thusness (a great expression of hers)' and 'For ever & ever'. Writing again on 27 September, when the title had been agreed, she remarked:

   > I'm glad you like TIME & AGAIN – it was one of Mother's many expressions – she used many of her north country ones. I did think of 'Think me on' which as you probably know is N.C. for 'Remind me'. But it doesn't go so well & these old Southerners would be baulked.

2. *A language not to be betrayed: selected prose of Edward Thomas*, edited by Edna Longley, was published by Carcanet in 1981.

3. 'A Pine In Solitude: A Portrait of Edward Thomas (1878–1917)', devised by Anne Harvey, with Jane Lapotaire, Julian Glover and Benjamin Whitrow, and Anne Harvey, was part of the 1978 Stratford-upon-Avon Poetry Festival. The title is taken from Thomas's poem 'No one so much as you'.

4. Myfanwy tells the story of the disappointing artificial cherries on p.40 of her own memoir *One of These Fine Days*, published by Carcanet in 1982. 'My' poem is 'What shall I give', written by Edward Thomas in 1916, which ends: 'But leave

her Steep and her own world / And her spectacled self with hair uncurled, / Wanting a thousand little things / That time without contentment brings.'

5. The *Adelphi* was a literary journal, founded by John Middleton Murry, published between 1923 and 1955. In 1948-9 it was briefly edited by the novelist Henry Williamson, to whom Myfanwy was secretary.

6. Edward Thomas was killed in the Battle of Arras, shortly after arriving in France as a second lieutenant in the Royal Garrison Artillery. He did not receive the Military Cross.

7. There was a section of photographs at the end of *Time & Again*, and Myfanwy had pointed out that one was wrongly dated. There was a list of photographs at the beginning of the book, which was not noted on the contents page, thus easily missed.

8. Edward Thomas's *George Borrow: the man and his books* was published by Chapman and Hall in 1912.

THE YEAR IN BOOKS

George Chapman, *Selected Poems*, edited by Eirian Wain

Donald Davie, *The Poet in the Imaginary Museum: essays of two decades*, edited by Barry Alpert

Roy Fisher, *The Thing About Joe Sullivan: poems 1971–1975*

Michael Hamburger (ed), *German Poetry 1910–1975*

John Heath-Stubbs, *The Watchman's Flute*

Brian Hepworth (ed), *The Rise of Romanticism: essential texts*

Jeremy Hooker, *Solent Shore*

Helder Macedo and E.M. de Melo e Castro (eds and trs), *Contemporary Portuguese Poetry: an anthology in English*

Christopher Middleton, *Bolshevism in Art and Other Expository Writings*

Paul Mills, *Third Person*

Eugenio Montale, *Selected Letters of Eugenio Montale*, translated by G. Singh

Andrew Motion, *The Pleasure Steamers*
Valentine Penrose, *Poems and Narrations*, translated by R. Edwards
I.A. Richards, *New and Selected Poems*
Edgell Rickword, *Literature in Society: Essays and Opinions II,*
    1938–1978, edited by Alan Young
Robert B. Shaw, *Comforting the Wilderness*
C.H. Sisson, *The Avoidance of Literature: collected essays*, edited by
    Michael Schmidt
Helen Thomas, *Time and Again: memoirs and letters of Helen Thomas,*
    edited by Myfanwy Thomas
Michael Vince, *The Orchard Wall*
Jeffrey Wainwright, *Heart's Desire*
Yvor Winters, *The Collected Poems of Yvor Winters*, introduction by
    Donald Davie

1979

Octavio Paz (1914–98) was a prolific Mexican poet and essayist. He studied at the University of California at Berkeley for two years before entering the Mexican diplomatic service, from which he resigned in protest against his government's massacre of student demonstrators before the Olympic Games in 1968. His postings took him to Paris – where he wrote his influential study of Mexico *The Labyrinth of Solitude* – India, Tokyo and Geneva. He founded the Spanish-language magazine *Vuelta* in 1976, and published in it many of the important international writers of the day. As the letter below makes clear, he was used to moving in highly intellectual circles, but his wife divulged in an interview that he really enjoyed watching *The Simpsons* of an evening. He was awarded the 1990 Nobel Prize for Literature. He and MNS corresponded in Spanish for the most part, and this exchange has been translated by MNS

FROM MICHAEL SCHMIDT
Manchester
16 January 1979

My dear Octavio,

It gave me enormous pleasure to see you and Marie-José in Mexico.[1] And it will give me absolutely enormous pleasure to edit and publish *The Octavio Paz Reader*.[2] I will begin this project during March, and I hope to have both the selection and the translation ready before 1980, to publish it in the spring or autumn of the year following. Thus in March I will need those of the scattered essays that are missing and the books that I don't yet possess. In coming weeks I will send you a list of the books I do have, and perhaps you can send me on those that are missing.

'Quarteto' is a real masterpiece. I am translating it slowly. It's a kind of poem which pleases me more than any other, with an intellectual and formal lucidity which does not darken, one might say, the darknesses! Or the shadows. It has the inevitability of Valéry.[3] More than anything else it reminds me of Sisson's most lucid poetry, and I cannot praise you more highly than that.

I am sending you, first of all, a package which contains *PN Review* 2–8 and my book *A Change of Affairs*. This comes by air mail. After that, next week, I will send you Sisson's work, poetry and essays; Davie's, Popa's and Winters's, and Hamburger's anthology. The book by Lewis is due out the following month and I'll send it to you.[4]

It pleases me greatly that you will allow me to publish various of your things, as I translate them, in *PN Review*. I hope you will like what I have done with the magazine. In the 'Editorial' of number 10 (which will come out in April) I think I will write something about you and about the 'ideological' mind-set that mis-reads you so resolutely.

Gunther says that he *will* provide the design for the cover of *The Octavio Paz Reader*.[5]

I have been reading *Cuadrivio*.[6] The essay on Pessoa in particular pleased me. I was the first to publish in this country collections of Pessoa – four booklets in a little box, one booklet for each heteronym. Your essay makes clear the miracle that Pessoa was.

They have given me six weeks to submit my history of English poetry from Gower to Hopkins – 120,000 words.[7] I have 50,000 to go! That's why I am getting tired. Last night I wrote about Chatterton: 'Grub Street exploited his energy, not his genius.' That's how I feel. As soon as I get home I squeeze out half-fatuous essays, but I need the money!

Abrazos to Marie-José and to Octavio, and a miao for Nevertheless the pussycat.

Michael

FROM OCTAVIO PAZ
Mexico
11 June 1979

Dear Michael,

We were abroad, in Europe and the States, for more than a month. During our absence your letters arrived and that's why it's only now that I reply.

I won't tell you about our trip – that kind of account entertains the teller and bores the hearer. I'll only tell you that, unexpectedly, they told me I had been awarded the Nice International Prize, so on the first of May we had to fly to that city famous for its eccentric Englishmen and its no less eccentric White Russians, not to mention the *cocottes*. We ended up staying in the sumptuous nest of all that *surannée* world – the imposing Hotel Negresco, now pretty battered and its ghosts, as banal as the meringue of its architecture, dissolved in the fumes of the cars which cross the Promenade des Anglais. We were bored for about five days but we distracted ourselves by eating, if not in Lucullus's house, then in a tavern at the port where they gave us a *loup* [*de mer*] browned in Provençal herbs which would have made Brillat-Savarin lick his lips. On the stony beaches we saw the topless bathers, some of them mothers with their children. There's nothing like a state of nature to put paid to desire: civilisation becomes more and more not a system of repression but of inhibition. Later on, we took the Mistral – what a relief for the eyes, the legs and the spirit a train can be! – to Paris. We spent twenty moving and memorable days there. Old and new friends, old and new conversations. In France, at least in certain circles, conversations still occur. A lost art in the remainder of the West. Paris has changed little and this is one of its enchantments; the city, despite many and ugly skyscrapers, has not been irreparably damaged like Mexico and Madrid. What's more, the cuisine is unique. That, and a dozen friends with whom it is still possible to talk about art, literature, and about those nothings which, when we exchange them, provide the feeling that civilisation is almost a form of complicity: it is defined not so much by ideas, manners, monuments or institutions as by signs. Those signs which are more like tokens. I saw Cioran, the most cheerful pessimist I know (Phyrro must have been like him), and Michaux, Bonnefoy, Calvino, Adami, Dominique Aury, Lévi-Strauss, Goytisolo, Tapiès – and among them two Greeks, Castoriadis – whom I had read but never met and who struck me as a man as brilliant as his writing on political philosophy – and Papaiaounou, my old friend – who, unfortunately, I can't read because he hardly writes, but to whom I listen with wonder.[8] I also saw Claude Roy and his wife, subtle and intelligent Parisian Chinese.[9] They have the quality I most admire, since it is the sign of true youth: the capacity for wonder. Speaking with Claude Roy it occurred to me, talking of *Vuelta*, that he could send me each month a *Letter from Paris* – an article discussing the contemporary literary, artistic and political situation. Do you remember the letters Orwell wrote from London for *Partisan Review*? Something of that kind, if not in quality at least in tone and intention. Claude, after hesitating for a moment, accepted… Why am I telling you all of this? Because during the journey to Barcelona, passing through Avignon, I thought that you, too, could send us a letter from London, every two months. Of course, written in English: we will translate it. The extent: ten double-spaced sheets (between 2,500 and 3,000 words). The payment would not be very large yet not negligible either: between 120 and 150 dollars. An attractive supplement. Later the pieces could be gathered into a book. This is what is intended for Roy. What's more, in your case it would be a way of not breaking the links which bind you to the country in which you were born. What do you make of my notion? I hope you'll accept my invitation. It would give me great pleasure.

We stayed in Barcelona for five days for the launch of my book *Poemas (1935–1975)*, a 700-page volume, very nicely turned out, which brings together virtually all my poems without excluding the imaginative prose and which feels more like an English than a Spanish book. We saw various friends, though we were a little weary after the weeks spent in Paris and stunned by the phenomenal, empty noise of the Spanish. Do you know Gimferrer?[9] An excellent poet, perhaps the best younger Spanish poet although locked into the Catalan language. From Barcelona we flew to New York and from New York to Mexico. And in Mexico I was greeted by a hundred letters and parcels, among them the two from you to which I now reply.

[...]

Yes, I had read in the Carcanet catalogue the announcement – with a photograph, too – of the *Octavio Paz Reader*. I was very pleased. Thank you! On re-reading the catalogue I find that I would like to have, among the books that have already been published, the two by Michael Hamburger (*East German Poetry* and *German Poetry 1910-1975*). Among those which you are publishing this year I am interested in Sisson's book: *In the Trojan Ditch*. Can you send them to me? I'll send payment by return. Thank you. Didn't you publish a *Sisson Reader*? I read an essay of his in *Parnassus* which delighted me. It would be worth publishing something of his in *Vuelta*. I hope that, with his permission, you can send us an article by him. Preferably an essay: it's hard to find a good translator of poetry.

[...]

Excellent that there are people who take an interest in the *OP Reader*! In due course you will tell me how I can help you. Why don't you send me a list of the texts you'd like to translate?

What I like best about your splendid translation of *Cuarteto* is the metre you have chosen: the English pentameter is, *roughly*, the equivalent of the Spanish and Italian hendecasyllabic.[10] I also approve of your use of rhyme. As for the quote from Pope: it's from the third Epistle (To Allen Lord Bathurst), line 108. But I changed it slightly. That bit about God not loving the poor Pope puts in the mouth of a person called Blunt and six lines later he says, speaking rather of those 'pobres ricos picaros' ('these poor men of pelf') that 'Each does but hate his neighbour as himself'.[11] The conclusion is devastating: 'Damn'd to the mines, an unequal fate betides / The slave that digs it and the slave that hides.'

That poem – I know only the fragment that appears in Peter Porter's Faber selection – I don't much like. In fact my favourites are the marvellous and entertaining Epistle II (To a Lady) and the *Epistle to Dr Arbuthnot*. For a XXth-century Mexican reader Pope is a very hard poet who requires tremendous effort. But it's worth the effort: not only is the form perfect but each line is a memorable epigram (each time I attend a *Vuelta* editorial meeting, I remember: 'at every word a reputation dies').

I like your translation very much indeed. I think you have caught the tone of the poem – though to me it seems very different from that of Valéry and closer to English than to French poetry. On a separate sheet are some comments and suggestions which, perhaps, could improve your version. You'll tell me if they are worth considering. Don't forget to send me the revised version, when you finish it. Lastly: do you think we might publish this poem not in *PN* but in *The New Yorker*; we could get a few cents for it. If you approve of this idea, you could send the poem – once you have revised it – to the poetry editor of *The New Yorker*. I have worked with them two or three times, and they have asked me to keep doing so. Do you agree?

Un abrazo doble de Maria José y de tu amigo,
Octavio

*

My first literary guru was Octavio Paz. He received me at his home in San Angel, we sat together, he liked the ignorant young man before him, and we remained friends ever after. Not close friends, and it was never quite a discipleship, but there was a strong bond, as of mutual belief and trust. His letters are themselves evidence of this, open and generous. I only wish I could have spent more time with him.

At an event in 2015 at the Mexican Embassy in London I was asked to remember my relations with him. This is how I began:

I met Octavio Paz when I was in my teens, probably in 1965, when I sought him out. Octavio took me seriously and we began to correspond. In 1972 we were planning a book of translations, a Paz Reader that I was going to prepare single-handed. Over time, we exchanged some durable letters. He contributed major work to my magazine *Poetry Nation* (later *PN Review*), and I contributed essays, poems, reviews and a little anthology of British poetry to *Plural* and *Vuelta*. More than any other antecedents, *Plural* and *Vuelta*, in their very different spirits, were models for my magazine *PN Review*, which continues to honour the open, pluralist and critical course Octavio as an editor and writer suggested. I also translated a book of Octavio's essays, *On Poets and Others*, and some of his poems.

In June 1979 Octavio sent me one of those amazing long letters he sometimes wrote after he had been travelling, a letter that was like his best conversation, four close-typed pages in which he recounted adventures in France and Spain, plans for *Vuelta*, an invitation to be a regular contributor, suggestions for *PN Review*, a recommendation of Pere Gimferrer, advice on my love life, a discussion of a book of his I was projecting, of a review I had done of Spanish translations of English poetry for *Plural*, and my translation of his poem 'Cuarteto', of which he approved, though he added two pages of suggestions. I mistook the word *alcahuete* (pimp) for *cacahuate* (peanut), and this provided a good deal of laughter.

Paz refused to put his art to party political use, which does not keep it from being political. He will use his critical skills. He says: 'Criticism is the apprenticeship of the revising imagination – imagination cured of fantasy and resolved to confront the world's reality. Criticism tells us that we ought to learn to dissolve the idols, learn to dissolve them in ourselves. We have to learn to be air, dream set free.' Paz learned his own lesson. 'Criticism reveals the possibility of liberty and this is an invitation to action,' he writes. If an active critical tradition, not deflected by ideology, can develop in time, it may eventually have social consequences. Criticism keeps language to its meanings. 'When a society becomes corrupt,' he writes, 'what first grows gangrenous is language. Thus social criticism begins with grammar and the re-establishment of meanings.'

NOTES

1. Marie-José Tramini (1932–2018), married to Octavio Paz for over thirty years, was born in Corsica, brought up in Morocco and had lived in Paris and India. She was an artist and his muse.

2. 'The Octavio Paz Reader' was never published, although Carcanet published his poetry and prose, beginning with *One Earth, Four or Five Worlds: reflections on contemporary history* in 1985 (translated by Helen Lane). MNS translated a selection of Paz's literary essays, *On Poets and Others* (Carcanet, 1987) and in his Foreword quotes Paz on the writer's tasks: 'The writer should be a sniper, he should endure solitude, he should know himself to be a marginal being. It is both a curse and a blessing that we writers are marginal.'

3. Paul Valéry (1871–1945), of whom Paz was to write in 1986: 'The true French philosopher of our age is not Sartre, but Valéry, as revealed above all in the posthumous publication of his *Notebooks.*'

4. The books referred to were all published by Carcanet in 1978–79; see bibliographies on pp. 104–5 and 116.

5. Gunter Gerzso (1915–2000), major Mexican painter and set designer for theatre and films, much admired by Paz. His son was a close friend of MNS.

6. *Cuadrivio* (1969), essays by Paz on Ruben Dario, Ramon Lopez Velarde, Fernando Pessoa and Luis Cernuda. Pessoa (1888–1935) wrote under about seventy 'heteronyms'; in 1972 Carcanet published four pamphlets translated from the Portuguese by Jonathan Griffith, each pamphlet devoted to one of the major heteronyms. Twenty years later, at a time of extensive activity in the field of Portuguese literature and culture, Carcanet returned to this major author with a handsome edition of *The Book of Disquietude*, translated by

Richard Zenith; this is the 'factless autobiography' of Bernardo Soares, one of Pessoa's most persistent characters. *A Centenary Pessoa* (translated by various hands), published by Carcanet in 1995, has an introduction by Paz that begins: 'Poets don't have biographies. Their work is their biography.'

7. Michael Schmidt's *An Introduction to Fifty British Poets 1300–1900* was published in the Pan Literature Guides series in 1980.

8. A galaxy of intellectuals, writers and artists: Emil Cioran (1911–95), Romanian philosopher and essayist; Henri Michaux (1899–1984), Belgian-born poet, writer and artist; Yves Bonnefoy (1923–2016), French poet and art historian; Italo Calvino, 1923–85), Italian fiction writer, whose *If on a Winter's Night a Traveller* came out in 1979; Valerio Adami (b. 1935), Italian painter who had a major retrospective at the Centre Pompidou in 1980; Dominique Aury, one of the pen names of the French writer and journalist Anne Desclos (1907–98); Claude Lévi-Strauss (1908–2009), French anthropologist whose work was key to the development of structuralism; Juan Goytisolo (1931–2017), Spanish poet, essayist and novelist; Antoni Tàpies (1923–2012), leading Catalan painter, sculptor and art theorist; Cornelius Castoriadis (1922–77), influential Greek-French philosopher, economist and psychoanalyst; Claude Roy (1915–97), French journalist, novelist and poet, had recently published the first volume of his autobiography, *Moi je*.

9. Pere Gimferrer (b.1945), award-winning poet, novelist and critic, writes in Catalan and Castilian. Carcanet published *The Catalan Poems*, translated by Adrian Nathan West, in 2019.

10. 'Quartet' is included in Octavio Paz, *The Collected Poems 1957–1987*, edited by Eliot Weinberger (Carcanet, 1988), in Weinberger's translation.

11. Paz refers to the passage in Alexander Pope's *Moral Essays*, Epistle III:

'God cannot love (says Blunt, with tearless eyes)
The wretch he starves'—and piously denies:
But the good bishop, with a meeker air,
Admits, and leaves them, Providence's care.

12. The sentence about reputation comes from *The Rape of the Lock*, Canto III.

THE YEAR IN BOOKS

David Arkell, *Looking for Laforgue: an Informal biography*
Ian Campbell (ed), *Nineteenth-Century Scottish Fiction: critical essays*,
John Clare, *The Midsummer Cushion*, edited by R.K.R. Thornton and Anne Tibble
Donald Davie, *In the Stopping Train and Other Poems*
Elaine Feinstein (tr), *Three Russian Poets: an anthology*
William Gass, *On Being Blue: a philosophical inquiry*
John Gay, *Selected Poems*, edited by Marcus Walsh
Heinrich Heine, *The Lazarus Poems*, translated by Alistair Elliot
Elizabeth Jennings, *Selected Poems*
Jean de La Fontaine, *Some Tales of La Fontaine*, translated by C.H. Sisson
Simon Lowy, *Melusine and the Nigredo*
Andrew Marvell, *Selected Poems*, edited by Bill Hutchings
John Peck, *The Broken Blockhouse Wall*
Vasco Popa, *Collected Poems* translated by Anne Pennington, introduction by Ted Hughes
Neil Powell, *Carpenters of Light: some contemporary English poets*
Miklos Radnoti, *Forced March: selected poems*, translated by Clive Wilmer and George Gömöri
Michael Schmidt (ed), *Five American Poets*
Paul Wilkins, *Pasts*

1980

Laura (Riding) Jackson (1901–91), born in New York, was briefly associated with the Fugitives, Southern American poets based at Vanderbilt University. At the end of 1925 she travelled to England, and her first book of poems, *The Close Chaplet*, was published by the Hogarth Press in 1925. Her *Collected Poems*, nearly 500 pages, was published in 1938 and, having returned to the USA, she renounced writing poetry. In 1941 she married Schuyler Jackson, also an ex-poet and a scholar of Doughty. In his introduction to *A Selection of the Poems of Laura Riding* (Carcanet, 1993), Robert Nye writes about his excited discovery of her poetry: he admits he might not have understood it; some poems seemed more like 'spells'. But over the years he had come to the conclusion: 'Here is the poetry as an articulation of the most exquisite consciousness, poetry as completely wakeful existence realised in words, with at the end of it news that even poetry will not do.'

FROM MICHAEL SCHMIDT
Manchester
17 January 1980

Dear Mrs Jackson,

Just occasionally, the Gods are unexpectedly kind, allowing one of those wonderful incidences such as yesterday's, when I finished setting your Collected Poems, and rang you, on your very birthday![1] The excitement of the coincidence almost put paid to the flu that was after me; and I am sure that the hot grapefruit juice you prescribed (and I ingested last evening) has at least moderated the intensity of the bout, though I do have flu this morning!

As I mentioned on the phone, our 'new' setting room (for typesetting, that is – we don't keep poultry!) is so cold that even with the electric fan on full, one can bear to work in there for only at most an hour at a time. This is why progress was slower than it might have been. In any case, I sent prelims, etc. yesterday and though corrections may affect pagination, we will be accurate, as accurate as possible.

Your lists have come and I will assiduously attend to them. What I have been sending you are in fact page proofs. We do not go through a galley-proof stage. The bottom margin, however, is consistent on the finished product: the variations on the proofs are due to the fact that they are photocopies differently disposed on the copying machine. The page is much deeper than that on the 1938 collection where there was extra leading, apart from anything else; but there is a good bit of white to the right of each poem and this, our standard format, <u>does</u> look nice when printed, we believe, whatever the impression of the proofs. It is hard if not impossible on my machine to do a centred format unless one has elaborate training which I have not had myself. I hope you will like the finished product. I shall feel very sorry if you don't, but I am confident you <u>will</u>. I will probably ring you at least once more before we go to press (scheduled for 7 February).

Mr Braziller will be using (I instructed him so) our catalogue description in his promotion.[2]

It has occurred to me that we have not yet exchanged an <u>agreement</u> for the book. What special clauses do you want in (especially regarding subsidiary rights)? We pay a straight 10% royalty. I believe Mr Braziller would like us to negotiate a 'sole' contract with you and sub-let the book to him for USA, thus channelling all money etc through Carcanet. Is this acceptable? I would be glad to refer all permission requests to you unless you would trust us to handle them; and if the latter, then we would retain only 10% (the equivalent to agency fee). May I have your reflections? I'll then issue an agreement form.

May the winter prove light, and your endurance great!

With warmest (in every sense!) wishes –

[Michael Schmidt]

FROM LAURA (RIDING) JACKSON
Wabasso, Florida
18 January 1980

Mr Schmidt!

As I told you, your telephone call counted with me as a birthday-present, not just by the accident of its coming to me on my birthday, but by the feeling that moved you to speak with me directly. I was much comforted by the call – the speaking and, concretely, by what you said. – That you receive my lists of my proof-findings, so that I know that all I found has come under your personal attention. And that you judge that the bottom-of-pages margins will be spacious enough to offset the long low-coming of text columns on some pages. I grasped also your point about there being enough airy spaciousness on the right-hand margins of poems-text to balance your style of left-hand title and numbering emphases, with which I found myself uncomfortable. (For myself, where the author puts the title, and the numbering of sections, has for me weight integral with the composition – I at any rate think of my poems with their titles topping them at their textual-mass center, and the numbering, where there are such, likewise. But of course I accept the occurrence of this treatment as an unrevisable finality of circumstance.)

Knowing what has been going on with you – your being arrested in type-setting activity by the extremely cold weather (I had read of this) has eased me in my expectations of what, each day, there might come to me by mail. – I wished, after we spoke, that my suggesting grapefruit to you for help, in keeping down 'flu threat, or actual 'flu-having, had comprised the indication that the warming of it I advised was intended to be understood as warming of <u>juice</u>. This is sworn to by old-timers, here. I have also heard of alternations of grapefruit juice (not necessarily warmed) with intake of water and baking soda (an hour or so between different takings), as useful anti-flu medicine. – (I am sort of an old-timer here, myself, but all this is getting fast lost in the suffusion of this late pioneer area (Florida) with populations seeking 'retirement comfort'.) Earlier comers (among whom I count my husband and myself) came here to <u>work</u>. – Which we did, in fruit growing and shipping, and in the fields of language.

I have already mentioned my having in mind the question of a contract – or contracts to cover specifically relations between Carcanet Press and Persea Books, both. Related to this concern, with me, is the question of publicity – I feel at ease as to this with yourself, but I have nothing to go on as to what Michael Braziller is or will be doing in the U.S.A. I have had no word from him, I know nothing as to whether he has listed, or how he has listed, Collected Poems in his catalogue, whether there is already out a Persea catalogue dealing with C.P. or not. And what, besides catalogue treating of the book, he has planned, if anything. I have already asked of you whether I might have from you a couple of your catalogues, with listing of C.P. included. And mentioned my wondering whether you had used the photograph in later printings. (I gave away the copy of your catalogue sent me quite long ago, with just textual material accompanying the announcement.)

Thank you for speaking of Rational Meaning in your

telephone calling.[3] I have had no word yet from Mr. Walsh. I am waiting for word from the West Coast Press I wrote of, to you – which impressed me by the seriousness of its publishing aspirations, and spirit of interest in my work. That ought to come fairly soon. I shall, then, decide on how to proceed as to Mr. Walsh. And I shall send you what seems to me likely to be of interest to you that presents itself in the latest writing from the West Coast.

I have been working on the introduction to the little Doughty book.[4] I like the way it is going. I plan to give The Day in Britain major space-allowance for the actual presenting of Doughty-poems text – and I mean to exhibit the importance of <u>knowing the meanings of the words</u>, with some reproduction of word-by-word rendering of text into contemporary English. I have got on much more slowly with this than I anticipated, because of work-demands, and some health-experience interferences. But I have been coming to be at better ease about it all, as the introduction takes shape with me, with increasing satisfaction for me in a sense of its possibilities. Just now I have found myself about to touch on Doughty's view of 'right' English in connection with the agitation felt by some in England over the casting out from authorizedness of the Authorized Version. My sympathies are with what you have been doing as to this in *Poetry Nation* and with Mr. Sisson in his writing on the matter printed in a recent issue of *TLS*.[5] I have resisted, however, writing to *Poetry Nation*, and to *TLS*, as to the language of the Authorized Version's (etc.) being 'our language in its first simple and supple splendour'. What I have to say as to this belongs in my writing on Doughty, the only Englishman or man or woman who acquainted himself with where standard of excellence had a steady hold in the language's development – which was a good deal before Renaissance biblical English style – which is perhaps somewhat simpler than regular English literary linguistic usage, but actually quite aged beyond the language's first developed quality of linguistically proficient simplicity – I am planning to send you my introduction at month's end, or a little later, perhaps it will have to be, so that you can judge whether you indeed want the little book from me – whether my treating of Doughty meets the prescriptions for the series.

Before closing I have thought to tell you confidentially – for your interest – that the correspondence that followed Mr. Horniman's (he of A.P. Watt)[6] writing to you, between myself and him, has been extraordinary in what it revealed to me of feeling towards me in the upper, letter-head, figures of the firm in these callow late times; I have been brought to consider what other agent-possibilities there might be for me. (As I have indicated, I tell you this in strict confidentiality.)

I have wondered when you plan to publish Mark Jacobs's review and wondered, of course, when Mr Mathias's article might be appearing. – I must not close without recording my grief that George Fraser did not live to finish his history of English poetry – I take it that he did not finish it. – I cannot forget what he said to Mark Jacobs when he presented to him his wish to write his doctoral dissertation on my work – that it was 'about time' that someone did this.[7] He himself had feelings about it, as he did about much else, expression of which the exigencies of the critic career seemed to call for putting off. But he did have <u>real</u> feelings, rather a rarity in critics-nature, in these times. I had had Christmas word from him and his wife. There came to me also Christmas time word from Edwin Morgan, for whom I have a strong feeling of regard.[8]

May you have warded off the 'flu or, if not, be past the worst of it, when this letter reaches you.

Thanks of glad feeling for your January 16th telephoning!

Laura Jackson

Several long letters dealing with contractual matters and proofs followed this one during March and April, often continued over two or more air letter forms. In her letter of 30 January 1980, which begins 'Michael!', she writes:

> It pleases me that my involuntarily employed 'Michael' in the last moments of our telephone speaking has been followed by your voluntarily signing yourself thus, in your letter of the 17th come to me on the 28th. I am for every first-name using's issuing from a process, not a formal informality custom, in the contemporary manner – being reflective of something that has been happening.

FROM LAURA (RIDING) JACKSON
Wabasso, Florida
12 April 1980

Michael! – I go on from yesterday's writing to you!

To the matter of the blurb, next: recorders of comment. 1) I feel you desire that I be comfortable with what the book itself carries of comment. But if you suppress the planned comment, will the book jacket have nothing whatever of comment? This would, would it not, put a certain bleakness on the presentation to the public of the new edition of these long unavailable poems (become available through your taking interest in the fact of the literary-world's behaviour towards my poetic work)? Thus, I am torn between gladness in your wishing for my happiness in all the features of the new edition and a rather dismal anticipation of a (likely-seeming, now) utterly mute jacket. I assumed that your care for my approval of what your catalogue and possible other publicity statements on the book, earlier, would extend to everything – that any special statements, as for the blurb, would be checked with me well beforehand to their issuance-time. But we all have to live with what there is to be lived with; what is unalterable, between you and myself, as to features of the book, we must keep, to the utmost, from spoiling our sight of what's generally to the good in what results from our working together for the book's coming to be. 2) To say a little on what I found not fitting my sense of my work's experience in the years of its varying availability, before it's being made available <u>now</u> to open acquisition in its 1938 collected form. <u>If</u> it should be desirable that some reference be made to what its experience has been as poetic work that has been a good deal thumbed by poets, this – my view is should be accurately however briefly described. The implication of the blurb's statement is that there was some shortage in the attention given to it by other poets. The quality was that it was very much pawed over in the 'Thirties, in a sort of open secrecy (the secrecy aspect allowing of Hynes', Tolley's, Davies's ignoring it[9] and myself as a, in my work, bandied about, poetic commodity) and has ever since been handled, dug into, combed (very much by Graves,[10] and, for instance, it has been told me, by Tomlinson, Hughes, besides others (some I know of in this country))[11] – but with <u>no one</u> going to it or coming from it with any co-befriending with me of the principles of language's generalities with which my poetic work is animatingly braced, <u>and</u> of those principles as – in so far as poetry has justification as voicing a spiritual trend in human life-interest, – principles of the human raison d'etre. My poetic work, as all the other work of all the years of my working life, has been treated as it has very much because it was not and is not framed within the literary, the categorically literary moulds of value. And thus has absurdly [illegible] that just what the poetic work is not, to use the term applied to it in later years by Robert Graves, in characteristically dishonorable and dishonest shunting me aside with a gesture of pseudo-tribute, the work of 'a poet's poet', is what it is, as in your blurbs telling it's history, where it <u>is</u> referred to with kindness, credited with being. – Do not think that I do not picture to myself how you are burdened with overmany responsibilities, endeavouring – as your nature moves you to, to fulfil all with harmonious nicety. I believe I can trust you not to hold me ungrateful, or ungenerous, or just stupidly puritistic, if I say that I wonder if the solution to your problems may lie not only in more assistance in the editorial ramifications of the Press's programme, but in some reining in of it itself. <u>Please</u>, do not view me as presenting this for <u>answering</u> by you! – I write it, say it, because I feel us to be at a point in communication at which we, one or the other, cannot but naturally move to unhesitant openness.

I cannot try for more writing to you today. But I must note that I had been hoping that the next word from you would bring some report of a possible reply made to Horniman by Cassell, as to the illustrations matter – but perhaps some further word on this matter will be coming from you before long.

I am acting immediately to sign the last contract form, on greenish paper, which duplicates what was written on the roseate to red sheets. – I have already expressed by sense of your having done everything within your reach to make the terms match my ease as to the providing involved as closely as possible. I am not sure that I can find a witness to my signature before I put this into the mails – but there is no indication on the final sheet that you expect such witnessing.

I shall write next on what still remains unwritten by me, of what your last letter held.

I greet you with the devoted feeling that I should have already sent signals of!

Laura

*

According to the preface I wrote for Laura (Riding) Jackson's *The Telling* (Carcanet, 2005):

> In 1978, at the suggestion of Robert Nye, I began a correspondence with Laura (Riding) Jackson which lasted for a decade. During this time she kept a keen, appraising eye on my editorial and critical work. She also allowed me to publish a range of her books, from the 1938 *Collected Poems*, about which I first approached her, to her novels, stories and essays. The book which gave me the most pleasure and astonishment to publish was *First Awakenings: the early poems of Laura Riding*, edited by her official biographer Elizabeth Friedmann, Alan J. Clarke, and by Robert Nye himself. It was published the year after her death, but she had been able to provide a preface and the book had her imprimatur.

She insisted the poems should never be added in to the finished *oeuvre* of the *Collected Poems* but should be kept apart.

She was an exacting correspondent. When I started writing to her I was aware of the many controversies she had courted or been party to, and I asked her for her take on specific people she had known, Edgell Rickword, Hart Crane, Michael Roberts. Her responses were always couched in her extraordinarily periphrastic style, keen to say everything they intended but not to imply more or less. The effort of the writing was replicated in the effort of reading the letters I received, which were numerous and eventually exhausting. She was like Ian Hamilton Finlay in the demands she made of her close correspondents: a complete and unresisting loyalty based, from her point of view, on an understanding of the resolved rightness of her view and the irrefutable nature of her arguments.

I remember meeting with Griselda Ohanessian, the Editorial Director of New Directions in New York, and showing her my forward list which at the time included two

Riding titles. 'I can't offer you those,' I said. 'I wouldn't publish her if she was the last writer in the world.' 'Why?' 'She was a murderer.' 'Come on, surely not.' 'She was my stepmother.' Griselda told the story in her autobiography, *Once: as it was* (2007), a strange footnote to the always vexed biography of Laura Riding.

NOTES

1.   This was a re-publication of the 1938 *Collected Poems* (published by Cassell in London, Random House in New York), with new prefatory material and some supplementary notes. In the little black-and-white Carcanet catalogue for 1979–80, Laura (Riding) Jackson is quoted on her poetry: 'Words were seen to retain their intrinsic properties as words, in her poems, with a distinctness of reality as meaning what they mean as linguistic entities that is hardly found even aimed at in poetical verbal practices generally'. This regard for words as 'linguistic entities' is also evident in her letters.

2.   Michael Braziller and Karen Braziller founded Persea Books in New York in 1975, and still run this independent publishing house.

3.   Laura (Riding) Jackson and her husband worked on what Nye calls 'a monumental book on language', *Rational Meaning: A New Foundation for the Definition of Words*, completed in 1968, but still unpublished at the time of her death. Edited by William Harmon, with an introduction by Charles Bernstein, it was published by the University of Virginia Press in 1997 (640 pages). John Walsh (1944–93), the founder of Black Swan Books (Connecticut) may have been considering it for publication.

4.   Charles Doughty (1843–1926), poet and traveller, whose *Travels in Arabia Deserta* (1888) is his best-known work. Its language is based on the Authorised Version of the Bible, while his epic poem *The Dawn in Britain* (6 vols, 1906),

uses pre-Shakespearian language. His works and language choices are extensively discussed in *Rational Meaning*. The selection referred to here, for Carcanet's Fyfield series, was not published.

5. She refers to *PN Review* 13: *Crisis for Cranmer and King James* (May-June 1980), which the editorial of *PN Review* 70, ten years later, summarised:

    > *PNR* 13 initiated what now appears to have been the last major debate (in and outside the Church of England) about the place of Cranmer's prayer book and the Authorised Version of the Bible in our spiritual and general culture. There were leaders in *The Times*, the *Guardian* and the *Telegraph* and dozens of articles in the press. Some members of Synod condemned the 'Jews and atheists' who arrogated unto themselves the right to comment on the language of worship in a church of which they were not members, even though that Church was the established Church of England.

    > Those protesting in *PNR* 13 against the liturgical changes included John Betjeman, Michael Foot, Herbert Howells, Philip Larkin, Iris Murdoch, A.J.P. Taylor, Mary Warnock. C.H. Sisson, in his essay 'Shared Memory', gave a simple example of a change: 'Would anyone in his right mind sacrifice continuity and familiarity for the sake of changing "as we forgive them that trespass against us" to "those who"? Who ever failed to understand "them that"?'

6. A.P. Watt, founded in 1875, was the oldest literary agency in the world. It is now part of United Agents.

7. James T. Mathias excoriated T.S. Matthew's memoir *Under the Influence* in *PN Review* 14 (July–August 1980), in particular his recollections of Riding and Graves. Mark Jacobs's review of *Selected Poems: in Five Sets* (Faber and Faber) appeared in *PN Review* 15 (September–October 1980). He edited *The Poems of Laura Riding: a newly revised edition of the 1938/1980 collection*

(Persea, 2001). G.S. (George) Fraser (1915–80), Scottish poet, academic and critic, was noted for the quality of his writing about contemporary poetry; Norman MacCaig remarked that it 'has been remarkable, not only for its perceptiveness, but for its civilised good manners and its consistent aim to see and enlarge the best in whatever work he is dealing with.' Carcanet published Fraser's *A Stranger and Afraid: autobiography of an intellectual* in 1983. *Poems of G.S. Fraser* was published in 1981 by Leicester University Press, the university where he taught for twenty years.

8. Edwin Morgan was one of the examiners of Mark Jacobs's doctoral thesis on Laura Riding (supervised by G.S. Fraser), and wrote to MNS on 13 March 1977 that he was 'wondering if Carcanet should perhaps become (pioneeringly) interested in Laura? She is one of the most difficult of modern writers in both verse and prose, but there is undeniably something impressive there, and it ought to be better known.' He goes on to list the books of hers that would be useful to publish:

> If you would like to mull this over in the watches of a few nights and days – (O nights and days, O queen of the night, O graves, O mores!), maybe you could let me know whether I might suggest to Mark Jacobs that he should get in touch with you? The current number of *Chelsea* (New York), by the way, is entirely devoted to LR. It would seem a good moment to do something about her.

In a letter of 1 October 1978, Morgan writes to MNS:

> I hear sometimes from Laura Riding who is clearly very pleased that you are doing her book. I agree that it is hard not to fall into her extraordinary prose style when writing to her: her letters seem almost to demand that the recipient swing (should swing) towards her on the same (at best a similar) kind of (and one uses the word advisedly) trapeze.

9. Laura (Riding) Jackson refers here to: Samuel Hynes, *The*

Auden Generation: literature and politics in England in the 1930s
(where L.R.J. does not appear in the index), 1976; A.T. Tolley,
The Poetry of the Thirties (1975); Donald Davie, *Thomas Hardy
and British Poetry* (1972) – or perhaps some other work by
Davie, but this study has no mention of her poetry.

10. The poetic and personal relationship between Laura Riding
and Robert Graves (1895-1985), which began in 1926 and
ended in 1939, has been much discussed. Writing to his friend
James Reeves about her in 1933, Graves declared, 'She is a
great natural fact like fire or trees or snow and either one
appreciates her or one doesn't' (Miranda Seymour, *Robert
Graves: life on the edge*, 1995, p. 131). They wrote together *A
Survey of Modernist Poetry* (1927) and *A Pamphlet Against
Anthologies* (1928). On his centenary, Carcanet began to re-
issue, in new editions, much of Robert Graves's work, both
poetry and prose.

11. Ted Hughes had written to MNS on 17 June 1979:

> I'm glad you have persuaded Laura Riding to disgorge.
> She wouldn't, for Faber. Everything she says about her
> influence seems to me true. I once tried to say so in a
> review for the *Sunday Times* and 'they' refused to publish
> it – called it outrageous etc, insult to the originality of
> Auden et al. I think you can name every poem that Laura
> R. begat on Auden's muse, and it is quite a bunch – and
> some of the best. That's the point of her claim – she makes
> poets write better – for a brief spell of infatuation – than
> they could without her. They get closer to themselves, and
> a little bolder to go naked. I think she's right.
>
> But her work, in a way, is a severe narrow technique
> for self-discovery – almost a kit.
>
> It's weirdly without substance. It almost is a branch
> of linguistics – an apparatus of specimens and examples,
> appendix to a theoretical approach. But so good! I wonder
> what stopped her – slight shift in the trimming of her
> theories?

THE YEAR IN BOOKS

Cliff Ashby, *Lies and Dreams*

George Buchanan, *Possible Being*

Paul Celan, *Selected Poems*, translated by Michael Hamburger

John Clare, *The Journal, Essays, The Journey from Essex*, edited by
  Anne Tibble

Patrick Creagh, *The Lament of the Borderguard*

Dante Alighieri, *Divine Comedy*, translated by C.H. Sisson

Dante Alighieri, *Literature in the Vernacular*, translated by Sally Purcell

Donald Davie, *Trying to Explain: essays*

H.D. (Hilda Doolittle), *End to Torment: A Memoir of Ezra Pound*,
  with poems from 'Hilda's Book' by Ezra Pound, edited by
  Norman Holmes Pearson and Michael King

Jean Earle, *A Trial of Strength*

Philip French, *Three Honest Men: Edmund Wilson, F.R. Leavis,*
  Lionel Trilling. A Critical Mosaic

Robert Garioch, *Collected Poems*

Robert Herrick, *Selected Poems*, edited by David Jesson-Dibley

Jeremy Hooker, *Englishman's Road*

Peter Jay, *Shifting Frontiers: poems 1962–1977*

Elizabeth Jennings, *Moments of Grace*

Brian Jones, *The Island Normal*

Peter Jones and Michael Schmidt (eds), *British Poetry since 1970: a*
  critical survey

Dennis Keene, *Surviving*

Wyndham Lewis, *Collected Poems and Plays*, edited by Alan Munton
  and C.H. Sisson

Christopher Middleton, *Carminalenia*

Czeslaw Milosz, *Bells in Winter*, translated by Czeslaw Miłosz and
  Lillian Vallee

Edwin Morgan (ed), *Scottish Satirical Verse*

Robert Pinsky, *An Explanation of America*

Jeremy Reed, *Bleecker Street*

Laura Riding, *The Poems of Laura Riding: a new edition of the 1938*
  collection

Michael Roberts, *Selected Poems and Prose*, edited by Frederick
  Grubb
Umberto Saba, *Thirty-one Poems*, translated by Felix Stefanile
Jeffrey Sammons, *Heinrich Heine: a modern biography*
Friedrich Schiller, *On the Naïve and Sentimental in Literature*,
  translated by Helen Watanabe-O'Kelly
C.H. Sisson, *Exactions*
Thomas Traherne, *Selected Writings*, edited by Dick Davis
Andrew Waterman, *Over the Wall*
David Wright, *Metrical Observations*

1981

Bill Manhire (b.1946), New Zealand poet, critic, short-story writer and lyricist, taught in the English Department of Victoria University of Wellington until 2001, when he established the celebrated creative writing school at Victoria, the International Institute of Modern Letters. Manhire was the first NZ Poet Laureate, named in 1997 when the post was created by the Te Mata winery to mark its centenary. He was also a member of New Zealand's inaugural 'Artists to Antarctica' scheme. After he had read some of the resulting poems at base camp, one of the helicopter crew said to him 'he thought this poetry stuff was really interesting. "It's like you're somehow putting words inside the words." It was worth going to Antarctica just for that.'[1]

FROM MICHAEL SCHMIDT
Manchester
14 January 1981

Dear Mr Manhire,

I was surprised to receive your poems. I think they are very good. I would like to accept them all for *PN Review*.

Could you please tell me a little about yourself? This would be useful for our 'notes on contributors' if we print them in future. I will try to include the poems in the next possible issue.

I would welcome a chance to see more of your work.

Yours sincerely,
Michael Schmidt

FROM BILL MANHIRE
London
15 January 1981

Dear Mr Schmidt

Thank you for your note, which arrived this morning, it probably won't surprise you if I say that it gives me a great deal of pleasure.

Of myself – I'm a New Zealander, born there in 1946, the son of a peripatetic publican. I teach at Victoria University, in Wellington NZ – mainly 19th and 20th century poetry, though the field in which I do an almost convincing imitation of minor scholarship is Old Norse Literature. At the moment, indeed for the next twelve months, I'm on sabbatical leave, and will be working on the sagas. My wife and two children are with me.

I've published two small books of poetry, both in New Zealand – *The Elaboration* (1972) and *How to take your clothes off at the picnic* (1978). Both these came from very small presses (a handpress in the case of the latter), and in runs of 200–300. Both are out-of-print.

Which brings me to a reluctant moment of honesty, which in turn may lead you to return the poems after all. With the exception of 'Dettifoss', they've appeared in print in New Zealand. 'Some Epithets' was printed in *How to take your clothes off at the picnic*: the others in small magazines.

I don't think it's simply a 'provincial frame of mind' that makes me wish to see the poems in print beyond New Zealand. I think that verse needs a local habitation; but I think, too, that it needs to cross frontiers. So I saw the act of sending these poems to you as an attempt to push across a border (and New Zealand's borders are exceeding difficult to push beyond, if only because the place is small and distant and quite without the exotic attractions other small cultures seem to offer). I thought of the poems, if you were to accept them, as being <u>translated</u> – as much as Peter Huchel's, really, in the last issue of *PN* Review.[2]

Still, I don't want to offer a tedious apologia. Enough to say that I still believe submitting the poems to you was proper, but I begin to see that you might find reason to disagree. I'd be delighted to see the poems in *PNR* (especially 'The Selenologist', of whom I am inordinately fond),[3] but will understand if you feel differently. In any event, your reaction to the poems has already given me something of what I was looking for – like putting a letter in a bottle and getting a letter from the finder.

Best wishes,
Bill Manhire

FROM MICHAEL SCHMIDT
Manchester
19 January 1981

Dear Mr Manhire,

Thank you for your letter of 15th January. Your confession of previous publication in no way alters my enthusiasm for the work you sent. I only wish I could secure copies of *The Elaboration* and *How to take your clothes off at the picnic*.

I would also like to see more of your work if there is more.

Apart from Baxter (whose work I very much admire), you must be the first native New Zealander whose poetry has actually got through to me![4] Some extraordinarily bad work gets done there! As here of course.

Should we try to meet while you are in the UK? It might be a pleasure, though I appreciate you must be very busy and we certainly are here. The fact is that your residence in

Mecklenburgh Square is directly around the corner from the office (and flat) of our Sales Director, Helen Lefroy, whom I visit from time to time.[5] (This is in connection with Carcanet Press which is also run from the above address.)

I hope to get your poems into the next issue (No. 20). If not, they will appear in No. 21.

I am relieved to know that you are one year older than I am.

Yours sincerely,
Michael Schmidt

FROM BILL MANHIRE
London
22 January 1981

Dear Michael Schmidt,

Thanks for your second letter which cheered me greatly. And I enclose a few more poems, a mixture of the glutinous and the smart – or so they seemed as I typed them out.

Yes, I would enjoy meeting you. I suspect you're a good deal busier than I'm likely to be (Carcanet seems to be a massive enterprise – to judge from the range of titles you produce): so it's probably best if you get in touch and suggest a time that's possible for you. We have the phone: 837 3835. Just ring, if that suits best.

It's odd you mention Baxter. I'm presently trying to write a sort of review essay of his *Collected Poems* for a New Zealand journal. I believe some 4,000 copies, at $35.00 each, were sold within six weeks of publication. Have his late poems been seen over here? The *Jerusalem Sonnets*. Quite remarkable.

I'm glad you are able to use my poems in *PNR* so quickly.

Best wishes,
Bill Manhire

FROM MICHAEL SCHMIDT
Manchester
18 February 1981

Dear Mr Manhire,

Thank you for your letter of 22 January. I am sorry for the delay in writing. Helen Lefroy very much enjoyed meeting you when you delivered your proofs to her. That is obviously an ideal place for us to get together and have a talk.

Before we go any further, might I beg you to lend me your *Collected Poems* of Baxter? I wonder if there would be any chance of our issuing an extended selection in the UK? I know that OUP have published him in the past. He really is a first rate poet – or so I remember. Am I mistaken, or does he not put A.D. Hope to shame?[6]

I have been carting the other poems you sent me around for a long time now. I am not so immediately confident about them as I was about the others, but then of course they did not have 'The Selenologist' as their pilot cross the bar of my taste.

However, I have now read them and like them. I am returning 'The Mutability Cantos' but retaining the other poems for use in *PNR*. I don't know that I shall use them as a group. I may spread them through the magazine over several issues. I hope this is acceptable to you.

I should warn you that there may be one hitch. It is that Donald Davie may dislike the work. If so, I may be compelled to return the other poems I have taken. However, if this should be the case, it will not lessen my commitment to your work now or in future. If I send the poems to him in advance, he will dislike them. Often when he sees things in print, however, he takes a very different and very positive view. I trust this will be the case with your work!

I look forward to meeting you. In the meantime, warm

thanks for your new submissions.

Yours ever,
Michael Schmidt

FROM BILL MANHIRE
London
13 March 1981

Dear Michael Schmidt,

Thanks for your letter of 18 February. I should have replied much sooner.

I'm glad you find the poems I sent you bearable. Still, I won't be distressed if you have, or are obliged to have, second thoughts about these. Your reaction to 'The Selenologist' has given me enough pleasure to be going on with.

And yes, I'm very happy to lend you the Baxter. I'll need to hang on to the book for another six weeks or so, however. I'm going to Germany, to intone and lecture on New Zealand verse (an uneasy journey, since I don't particularly respect the Commonwealth Literature industry yet seem to be taking shameless advantage of it) and will need the *Collected Poems* there. The other reason for delay is that I haven't yet completed a promised review-essay of the volume. I was quite certain of what I would have to say about it before I opened it – and now my mind sticks, and changes, and sticks again.

I'll be interested to know what you make of Baxter. Certainly a Selected Poems would be infinitely stronger than the *Collected*, with its bulk and repetitions. There would have been difficulty six months ago about getting U.K. rights in the poems, but perhaps not now. Oxford are about to become a purely token presence in New Zealand (an 'economy' which won't make a bit of difference to their problems here), and might welcome some form of joint publication where they retained the NZ market and Carcanet held rights elsewhere.[7]

But this rather anticipates your response to Baxter's work – especially the later verse, which you may not like at all. I'll post the book up to you towards the end of April (this will give me time, and a deadline); or, if you're likely to be in London about then, I can give it directly into your hands.

Best wishes,
Bill Manhire

FROM BILL MANHIRE
London
23 March 1981

Dear Michael Schmidt,

I've left my copy of Baxter's *Collected Poems* with Helen Lefroy. Laziness on my part – I don't think the Post Office could particularly add to the damage my thumbings have effected.

Thanks for your tentative thoughts about housing my review in *PNR*. I'm unhappy with the piece I eventually ground out. It's long and lumbering – a thoughtless meandering, affecting to be thoughtful. But it wouldn't in any case suit *PNR*. Too much cultural background is taken for granted; and I've used the review, quite unfairly, as an occasion for tinny thundering about an 'editorial' (leader-writing) habit of mind which I think afflicts New Zealand poetry (along, I suspect, with the rest of the poetries of the 'white Commonwealth').

I could write a separate, short notice for *PNR*. But it would be more interesting, and I'm sure more useful, if someone relatively unfamiliar with Baxter were to look at his work. It should, indeed, be possible to get hold of a review copy. I noticed Oxford advertising the *Collected Poems* in the *TLS* a few weeks ago. I don't imagine they mean to distribute it seriously over here; but presumably hope that a few libraries will buy copies as a matter of course.

Perhaps this means that rights in the poems will be difficult to secure? Baxter's executor is his widow, Mrs J. Baxter. I can't recall her address but a letter addressed to her c/o The New Zealand Room, Wellington Public Library, Wellington, New Zealand should find her easily enough. (She works there.)

In any case, you may find that you dislike Baxter – 600 pages, certainly, are about 400 too many. (You should look, though, at one of Baxter's early set pieces, 'Wild Bees'. It's like, but not like, your own 'Wasps' Nest'.)[8] I enclose, in case it may be of use, a short review of the poems from the *NZ Listener* (a cross between the BBC *Listener* and *Radio Times*). I think it's a useful account of Baxter's range – though Northrop Frye lurks behind it, in ways that don't entirely convince me. Perhaps you can let me have it back when you return the Baxter?[9] There's no hurry about either. We'll be in London until January 1982.

Thanks for the copies of *PNR* 20. 'The Selenologist' looks well, as it were. Or he goes on pleasing me. I'm not sure how many issues make up a single volume of *PNR*. But on the assumption that you've just reached the end of one, I'll write off for a subscription.

Best wishes,
Bill M.

*

What has made correspondence and remote friendship with Bill Manhire such a pleasure over the years is his generosity, his no-nonsense scepticism about certain areas of academic appropriation and pseudo-discipline, and his willingness to talk things through in gently ironic letters. He is not unlike, though quieter than, my dear New Zealand friend Greg O'Brien, who is equally generous, with a Roman Catholic inflection and a greater patience with the elements in Baxter that make Bill Manhire impatient. O'Brien is a compelling visual artist as well as a poet.

On my two visits to New Zealand, spaced apart by decades, I visited Bill Manhire at his handsome apartment which I remember as equally full of light and books. It had the feeling of a boat securely sailing to a destination it was sure to reach in due course. It is the steady lightness of Manhire's poetry that I find irresistible, which is not to say that he is in any sense unserious, only that his command of tone and diction mean he is never solemn and never portentous.

The impression of the room as a boat may derive from 'The Selenologist'. There are moments when you read a poet and you suddenly know the work is wonderful. The Manhire moment for me came with the simple lines:

> There, as it happens, is the outside cat;
> And there are the fox & the flower & the star.
> Among all these his life takes place.

NOTES

1. Bill Manhire, 'A Poet at the Pole', *Doubtful Sounds: essays and interviews* (Victoria University Press, 2000), p. 245.

2. The point about cultural 'translation' crops up in an interview ten years later. Although Manhire says he was 'deeply flattered' that his poem 'Wingatui' (about a NZ racecourse) appeared in *Private Eye*'s Pseud's Corner, surmising that it was read by the British as 'a bit of surrealist waffle', he suggests that they had 'become parochial and provincial without noticing it.' 'Someone suggested to me the other day that if Rupert Brooke had been a New Zealander, instead of "some corner of a foreign field", he would have written "some corner of an overseas paddock"' (*Doubtful Sounds*, p.32); Peter Huchel (1903–81), German poet who lived under surveillance in the GDR from 1962 until he was permitted to leave in 1971.

Carcanet published his *Selected Poems* in 1974, and *The Garden of Theophrastus and other poems* in 1983, both translated by Michael Hamburger.

3. 'The Selenologist' is reprinted in Manhire's first collection from Carcanet, *Zoetropes: poems 1972-82*. Carcanet has published five volumes of Manhire's poetry, including a *Selected Poems* (2014), and one of short fiction, *South Pacific* (1994).

4. James K. Baxter (1926–72) was the most famous poet in New Zealand during his writing life, particularly from the 1960s when he was the counter-culture's guru, a practising Catholic with close connections to Maori culture. His *Collected Poems* ran to about 620 pages of text. Manhire's review was published in *Islands* 31–32 (1981), and partly reprinted in *Doubtful Sounds* (pp.209-12); he remarks of the Jerusalem writings that it is as if they have been 'translated from another language, and might stand free of the niceties of language altogether.'

5. Helen Lefroy was appointed as a director of Carcanet in 1978; as Mark Fisher writes in *Letters to an Editor*, 'an experienced and committed publisher, over the next seven years she made Carcanet a much more professional and responsible operation.' Helen was an Austen scholar and proud of being a cousin four times removed of Jane Austen's youthful flirtation, Tom Lefroy. R.M.: One of my abiding memories of the period I spent working out of her spare room (Carcanet's 'London office') was her very careful management of resources. We parcelled up books to dispatch, often by hand, for review, and I was encouraged to pick up clean cardboard and string when I saw it in Doughty Street and nearby, to re-use as packaging.

6. Nevertheless, Carcanet published the *Selected Poems* of the Australian poet, critic and academic A.D. Hope (1907–2000) in 1986, edited by Ruth Morse. She remarks in her introduction that Hope 'has been stigmatized as an Augustan, a Romantic, a Nietzschean, a Manichee, and latterly an elitist and a misogynist. The list of accusations is perhaps a

compliment to a poet who has always aroused strong feelings'.

7.   Carcanet did eventually issue Baxter's *Selected Poems* in 2010, as the UK publisher of Auckland University Press's edition, edited by Paul Millar.

8.   'Wasps' Nest' is in Michael Schmidt's 1976 collection, *My Brother Gloucester*.

9.   Northrop Frye (1912–91), influential Canadian literary critic and theorist, best known for his *Anatomy of Criticism* (1957).

THE YEAR IN BOOKS

John Ashbery, *As We Know*

Alison Brackenbury, *Dreams of Power and Other Poems*

Donald Davie, *Three for Water Music*

H.D. (Hilda Doolittle), *Hedylus*, edited by Perdita Schaffner

Carlos Drummond de Andrade, *The Minus Sign: selected poems*, translated by Virginia de Araujo

Hans Magnus Enzensberger, *The Sinking of the Titanic*, translated by the author

Thomas Gray, *Selected Poems*, edited by John Heath-Stubbs

Michael Hamburger, *Variations*

Robert Hass, *Praise*

Robert Henryson, *Selected Poems*, edited by W.R.J. Barron

Nicholas Hilliard, *The Arte of Limning*, edited by R.K.R. Thornton and T.G.S. Cain

Randall Jarrell, *Kipling, Auden, & Co.: essays and reviews 1935-1964*

Walter Savage Landor, *Selected Poetry and Prose*, edited by Keith Hanley

David Levy, *Realism: An Essay in Interpretation and Social Reality*

Philip Mairet, *Autobiographical and Other Papers*, edited by C.H. Sisson

Ian McMillan, *The Changing Problem*

Charlotte Mew, *Collected Poems and Prose*, edited by Val Warner

Czeslaw Miłosz, *The Issa Valley*, translated by Louis Iribarne

Czeslaw Miłosz, *Native Realm: A Search for Self-Definition*,
    translated by Catherine S. Leach
Peter Schmidt, *Meyerhold at Work*
Roger Scruton, *Fortnight's Anger*
Roger Scruton, *The Politics of Culture and Other Essays*
C.H. Sisson, *English Poetry 1900–1950: an assessment*
C.H. Sisson, *Selected Poems*
John Skelton, *Selected Poems*, edited by Gerald Hammond
Felix Stefanile (tr), *The Blue Moustache: an anthology of Italian
    Futurist poetry*
Adrian Stokes, *With All the Views: collected poems*, edited by Peter
    Robinson
Edward Thomas, *A Language Not to be Betrayed*, edited by Edna
    Longley
Andrew Waterman, *Out for the Elements*

1982

David Arkell (1913–97), journalist, translator and biographer, spent formative years in France, including four years' imprisonment during the Second World War. When his friend Claire Tomalin asked him what he did then, 'Walked round and round, as prisoners do, was his reply.' He was *PN Review*'s 'literary sleuth', and the Carcanet archives co-ntain a multitude of typed and handwritten notes, often with clippings, sent to the Editor for his delectation and possible inclusion in the 'News and Notes' section.[1] As Tomalin wrote in her Foreword to *Ententes Cordiales: the French in London & other adventures* (Carcanet, 1989), 'it is the discovery of facts that delights him; the charm of anecdote is always backed by serious scholarship.' Carcanet published his biographies *Looking for Laforgue* (1979) and *Alain-Fournier: a brief life* (1986).

FROM DAVID ARKELL
London
30 January 1982

Dear Michael,

My immediate reaction to the ALAIN-FOURNIER idea is a resounding YES, especially as it occurred to you and Claire simultaneously.[2]

I like it for various reasons: I am attracted to A-F without being besotted. I could write about him with a certain irony (which is the mode I like) and the irony would be justified.

He is just about my weight – i.e. has not become the exclusive preserve of academics, who in fact rather cold-shoulder him. For this reason he does not inhibit me, as would Apollinaire, for instance.

The tragic curve of his life dictates a satisfying shape to the book and the risk of insipidity is countered by the great contract between his platonic obsession with the naval man's daughter and his very different affair with the actress.

Though I could not hope to find out anything new about the former, the latter lady is still alive (though 104!!!).[3]

All his papers and impedimenta are kept in impeccable order by a member of the family outside Paris with whom I am persona grata. The project would lend itself to even more profuse illustration than LAF (if you so desired).

These are my spontaneous first thoughts – I would be most grateful for any further thoughts of your own which would fill in the general picture.

All the best,
David

FROM DAVID ARKELL
London
5 February 1982

Dear Michael,

I send the *Morning Dew* just in case (for possible use with the Tom Tit drawing). I tried to get some topical tie-up with Jessie Dwight Orage (the great man's widow) but she never met Beatrice Hastings and the whole affair was long since over when she appeared on the scene, from America.[4]

A few thoughts on your series of writers revisited:

1. In what way are they <u>misprized</u>? I thought Lewis &

Fitzgerald were coming over strong just now; and that Wordsworth and the Brontës were equally secure. Though cold-shouldered by French critics, Alain-Fournier is still a world bestseller...

2. I note that the rules are fairly flexible: in that biography and criticism may be mixed (and this would probably be advisable in my case). I assume, though, that there would be certain constants. Is there any room, for instance, for illustrations? I suppose the title will just be the author's name? I imagine that you and Sisson will decide on the technicalities of how notes, refs etc will be dealt with (and the rest of us will follow style). That is entirely normal – but I am slightly conscious of the fact that in *Looking for Laforgue* I was given free and eccentric rein and that this time I will have to toe the line (with no funny drawings and things to disarm the critics!)

All the best,
David

P.S. I have asked Gallimard: what price an interview with Simone, who's 105 on 3rd April!!!?...

... and if the lady should die, there will be a sad bonus, for she has promised all her letters (most of them unpublished) to the Bibliothèque Nationale and ours could be the first biography to print them.

FROM MICHAEL SCHMIDT
Corn Exchange, Manchester
11 February 1982

Dear David,

I am delighted with your piece on Beatrice Hastings. It is a nice item to have!

'Misprized' in my last letter suggested they had been valued for the wrong reason and in the case of Wordsworth and the Brontës, the misprizing is due to their academic assimilation. As for Fitzgerald, I did not of course mean F. Scott but rather Edward, and I think he is still quite neglected as a letter-writer and as a translator of plays. [Wyndham] Lewis has been systematically excluded from all 'modern masters' lists that exist and therefore cannot be said to have 'made it' in the academy, thank goodness! And your own subject may be a best-seller, but is there much criticism of him? I don't know.

It would be lovely to have an interview with Simone.

There would be no illustrations except, perhaps, an occasional line drawing. That will surely be inevitable in the Lewis. There are to be no footnotes. References should be contained in the text where necessary but should be suppressed where unnecessary. There will be a reading list at the end of the book and perhaps an index. A preface can suggest a latent apparatus.

With every good wish,
Yours ever,
Michael

FROM DAVID ARKELL
London
17 February 1982

Dear Michael,

<u>Alain-Fournier</u>

Many thanks for your letter of 11 Feb.

I think that A-F could rate as a 'misprized' author in the sense that he became famous for the wrong reasons, which now need debunking – i.e. he emerged as a hero of bourgeois (and Catholic) Youth, a sort of Model Adolescent and Super-Scout. This led to his book having enormous sales but being under-rated critically – so that today it is regarded as really a book for children & young girls.

Even the critics who liked it did so for reasons equally misplaced: for them it was the Idyll of Symbolism, in the vein of Maeterlinck's *Pélleas et Mélisande*, a pseudo-mediaeval tale of chivalry & courtly love set in a Never-Never Land (heavy with the kiss of death!).[5]

I would set out to upset these ideas by suggesting that it was firmly based in the sturdy English tradition of adventure stories (*Rob Crusoe* and *Treasure Island*) and Hardy passion (*Tess* and *Jude*).[6]

At the same time I would show that, if A-F suffered from the usual Victorian hang-ups, he was not noticeably more neurotic than his contemporaries – and that (with the help of Simone) he was struggling to get out of the morass when the War cut him down at 27.

This may be a subject where Life and Work should not be separated, but I could certainly separate Biog and Crit if you felt strongly about keeping the unity of the series. (I would like in any case to use my *PNR* piece as intro as it offers a neat way in.)[7]

What is the series to be called? I accept 'no illustrations' and I assume 'no title' other than subject's name. Is 50,000 words a firm figure – and if not – what margin downwards would one have? Am delighted about no notes and no refs – and I agree a reading list and possible index. Please let me know if (in the course of the coming months) there is any change in these specifications. As a journalist I like working to specifications.

Specifically

yours,

David

*

Probably the easiest and most delightful friend Carcanet ever had was David Arkell. His only rival must be Miles Burrows, who shares many characteristics with Arkell but is more immediately hilarious and less a sleuth and scholar. Of all David Arkell's writings, my favourite is *Looking for Laforgue*.

No issue of *PN Review* was complete without one of David's sleuthing contributions, sometimes adjoined to a lively illustration by Philip Norman or Coll Toc, who also illustrated the ambitious but not quite satisfactory large format book *Ententes Cordiales*. He contributed to the magazine forty-six times between 1980 and 1997 (from *PNR* 14 through 113).

I remember visiting David's little flat in Endell Street quite regularly for chats; and when he died his long-time friend Marabel Hadfield invited those who loved him round to his flat for a gentle wake. Each of us was urged to take home a memento. I took the portable Lettera 22 Olivetti which he had used for all his contributions to *PNR* and which had accompanied him through the war. It was this very typewriter about which we corresponded, when he tried to get black ribbons for his heirloom. Long after I disposed of my handsome, vast Adler, the pride of my writing life when I acquired it in 1969 at Pin Farm, I kept David's typewriter, which I still possess and which will become part of his archive at the John Rylands University of Manchester Library.

NOTES

1. There was an exchange about typing between Arkell and MNS in 1993:

> Note to Ed – T.S. Eliot is supposed to have *typed* his
> poems. Not so easy today when old-type ribbons tend to
> hang around the shops long past their sell-by date.
> I bought this one from W.H. Smith's yesterday. Can any of
> your readers (or Pam Heaton?) tell me where I can get a

ribbon that is black and not grey – or must we all use word processors? This is a cry from the heart and nothing to do with NEWS & NOTES. – DA

MNS said in his reply (30 September 1993):

Did you know that the first writer ever to submit a manuscript in typescript was Mark Twain? As for ribbons, we are entirely electronic and use carbon ribbons. [...]

I still believe you should get yourself a little laptop computer. In fact I will try and bring mine down and show it to you next time. You will find it as faithful and responsive a friend as any dog.

2.   MNS had written to Arkell on 26 January that about three weeks previously, he had conceived the idea of a new series for 1983–84 'consisting of literate, non-academic biographical and critical introductions to the work of neglected or misprized authors. I have now got Sisson writing on Fitzgerald, C.J. Fox writing on Lewis and someone writing on the Brontë sisters. I wanted to ask you to contribute a book to this series. [...] Of course the first thought that came to my mind was Fournier (this also occurred to Claire [Harman]).' The series did not eventuate, except for Arkell's book.

3.   Arkell had written to MNS (8 April 1981) that he was 'pondering the ethics of asking a 104-year-old lady what she did to upset her lover (Alain-Fournier) on 20 April 1914'. He was still following up the story in the columns of *PN Review* in 1993, when he reviewed the revelatory *Correspondance 1912–1914* between Henri Alain-Fournier (1886–1914) – author of the European classic *Le Grand Meaulnes* – and his lover, the actress Simone, which ended with Fournier's death in the First World War.

4.   The article on Beatrice Hastings (1879–1943) does not seem to have been published in *PN Review*. She was a poet and literary critic, painted by Modigliani, the mistress of A.R. Orage (editor of *The New Age*), lover of Katherine Mansfield

and Wyndham Lewis.

5. *Pelléas et Mélisande*, a play by Maurice Maeterlinck about the forbidden, doomed love of the protagonists, was published in 1892 and produced in 1893.

6. If Arkell did not mention Defoe's *Robinson Crusoe* in the biography, he did suggest that an admired schoolteacher had recommended Hardy's *Tess of the D'Urbervilles* and *Jude the Obscure* to Fournier. He recorded Mme Simone calling Fournier 'the faithful friend of Stevenson', suggesting that in fact the novel bore more resemblance to *Kidnapped* than to *Treasure Island*.

7. 'The Strange Fête at Gunnersbury' (*PN Review* 21, September–October 1981) begins in typical Arkell fashion: 'Strange as it may seem, one of the prototypes of Alain-Fournier's enchanted château in *Le Grand Meaulnes* may have been a Congregational Church in West London.'

THE YEAR IN BOOKS

Walter Abish, *How German Is It*

John Ash, *The Goodbyes*

John Ashbery, *Shadow Train*

Edmund Blunden, *Selected Poems*, edited by Robyn Marsack

Eavan Boland, *Night Feed*

Charles Boyle, *House of Cards*

Keith Chandler, *Kett's Rebellion and Other Poems*

John Clare, *The Rural Muse*, edited by R.K.R. Thornton

Gillian Clarke, *Letter from a Far Country*

Anne Cluysenaar and Sybil Hewitt, *Double Helix*

Anthony Cronin, *New and Selected Poems*

Michael Cullup, *Reading Geographies*

Ford Madox Ford, *The Rash Act*, introduction by C.H. Sisson

George Gascoigne, *Selected Writings*, edited by Roger Pooley

Michael Hamburger, *The Truth of Poetry: tensions in modern poetry from Baudelaire to the 1960s*

Gerald Hammond, *The Making of the English Bible*
John Heath-Stubbs, *Naming the Beasts*
Thomas Hoccleve, *Selected Poems*, edited by Bernard O'Donoghue
Jeremy Hooker, *The Poetry of Place: essays and reviews 1970-1981*
Jeremy Hooker, *A View from the Source: selected poems*
Elizabeth Jennings, *Celebrations and Elegies*
D.H. Lawrence, *Ten Paintings*
Czeslaw Miłosz, *Visions from San Francisco Bay*, translated by
    Richard Lourie
Edwin Morgan, *Poems of Thirty Years*
Neil Powell, *A Season of Calm Weather*
Laura Riding, *Progress of Stories: a new edition of the 1935 collection*
Michael Roberts, *T.E. Hulme*, introduction by Anthony Quinton
Arthur Schnitzler, *The Round Dance and Other Plays*, translated by
    Charles Osborne
Marcel Schwob, *The King in the Golden Mask*, translated by Iain
    White
Leonardo Sciascia, *Candido or A Dream Dreamed in Sicily*, translated
    by Adrienne Foulke
Seneca, *Thyestes*, translated by Jane Elder
Howard Sergeant and Anthony Thwaite (eds), *The Gregory Awards
    Anthology 1981 & 1982*
Algernon Charles Swinburn, *Selected Poems*, edited by L.M. Findlay
Hans Jurgen Syberberg, *Hitler: A Film Made in Germany*, translated
    by Joachim Neugroschel, preface by Susan Sontag
Myfanwy Thomas, *One of These Fine Days: Memoirs*
Michael Vince, *In the New District*
Virgil, *The Georgics*, translated by Robert Wells
Robert Walser, *Selected Stories*, translated by Christopher Middleton
Sylvia Townsend Warner, *Collected Poems*, edited by Claire Harman
Clive Wilmer, *Devotions*

1983

Frank Kuppner (b.1951), Scottish poet and novelist, described himself as 'semi-unemployed' when he responded to Carcanet's publicity questionnaire in 1983, and apart from stints as a writer in residence at the universities of Glasgow and Strathclyde, he has remained so. Kuppner has, however, published eleven collections of poetry, one non-fiction book and four novels. In the same letter he wrote: 'I read almost anything, provided 1) the local second-hand bookshops have a copy, 2) I can afford it and 3) I think I will like it. In practice, this includes dips into most things, except modern novels and mechanics textbooks.' He described himself then as 'a 19th-century European liberal of the "vanished with the Great War" type'.

FROM FRANK KUPPNER
Glasgow
29 September 1983

Dear Michael,

Thank you for your letters, which both arrived together a week or so ago. I have had great fun antagonising people whom I know by showing them the cover of the anthology and asking them, sweetly, if they write poetry themselves.[1] Rich, if simple, entertainment. Actually, I hadn't realised that the anthology was also coming out in the magazine. Had I done so, I would no doubt not have sent you the two little sequences in such haste, since my main aim in sending them was to obviate what looked to me like unnecessary repetition. But this is by the by.

I have given much thought to your request for suggestions for a cover for the 400.[2] As a result, I have got my friend Alasdair Gray, the writer and illustrator/painter, very enthusiastic about the idea of doing a cover for me himself.[3] He is away at the moment, but I might as well tell you my thoughts in the matter at once, so that if you find them useless you can let us know sooner rather than later. I thought, since the main body of the work deals with Chinese art reflected, refracted or absorbed by an Occidental prism, it might be a neat idea for the cover to show an archetype of Western art in an Oriental guise. To be brief, I have suggested the Mona Lisa, with a Chinese face, in front of Chinese mountains. This is our front-runner. Also in the race is a map of China, variously decorated to avoid imputations of flatness, which includes Glasgow (at least) innocently placed among its towns. I'll not go on, as I probably have you clutching your head with disbelief and sorrow already.

May I say, in a completely level voice, that I do feel obscurely but strongly that the SUNG poems should appear by themselves. It seems to me that they would be happier alone in their strange little world.

With renewed thanks,
Frank

FROM MICHAEL SCHMIDT
Manchester
5 October 1983

Dear Frank,

Thank you for your letter of 29 September. Do you realise that, if things go according to plan, the Prague sequence will come out in *PN Review* 35 with the Swedish sequences coming out in *PN Review* 36, both at the same time. You will thud quite emphatically on to people's doormats!

I like very much the notion of an oriental Mona Lisa for the cover of 'Bad Day'. This is certainly a better notion than the map of China that you propose. Indeed, it is a very compelling notion! So could you work along those lines with Alasdair Gray? We are not in a position to pay very much for covers, no more than £50 unfortunately, but our gratitude is boundless.

I tend to agree with you that the Sung poems should appear by themselves. This raises a great problem regarding the other sequences, as I would not wish not to publish them if you see what I mean. We cannot bring out two of your books at once, but we would have to follow on in 1985 with a second volume incorporating the other sequences or, if the readers of *PN Review* can take it, publish several of them in the magazine. I would like to ask specifically at this time for permission to publish the shorter sequence you sent me last – the untitled – in the magazine. I have been asked to edit a British edition of *Poetry* Chicago and if I do this, it might be possible to print the untitled sequence in that context, getting it quite a good fee. We could then reserve the right to reprint it in *PN Review* ourselves.

Would it be sensible at some stage for us to fund your journey down to Manchester to discuss the strategy for publishing your poems? Of course one thing that would much ease our future planning is if you were less prolific! But let me not urge that. I enjoyed your history of Europe too much to wish you to stop, even to wish you to change your chosen form!

We expect delivery of the anthology and the issue of *PN Review* on 27th October.

With best wishes,
Michael

FROM FRANK KUPPNER
Glasgow
17 October 1983

Dear Michael,

Thank you for your letter of the 5th, to which I only now, after considerable thought, address myself. I have got Alasdair Gray working on the cover for the SUNG poems, and my main contribution in this area is to perpetually curb the man's wilder imaginings, in the hope of finally getting from him a simple witty black and white image. He was all for designing it round the typeface. I would not care to predict how early or late the finished product will emerge. I presume there is no great urgency about it. Or is there?

You have my permission to print the personal sequence. I love the idea of it appearing in America, for something more than sheer cupidity; or rather, I would love it if I didn't feel so keenly that this is usually the sort of work that appears only after the author's death. For years I assumed that no-one would ever read anything I wrote, and this gave me a wonderful freedom of expression. Was it not (of course it was) C.P. Snow who said that the price of total freedom is total neglect? The reverse also seems to apply. It might be better not to keep me in touch with the progress of this sequence, if it does progress, in case I get cold feet; but rather merely present me with a fait accompli (if any should arise). (What a paragraph! It seems the older I get, the more Jamesian I get.)

The sequence had a title, but I suppressed it. Years ago, in a theoretical mood, I tried to devise striking titles for books of poetry (this was more relaxing than actually writing poems) and I eventually came up with an all-time favourite in 'THE SUBTLE OBSERVATION OF NAKED WOMEN'.[4] I still think you could practically sell notebooks with that on the cover. To my discomfort, that line sprang to mind while I was writing the sequence, and I incorporated it in it, without ever feeling entirely happy about it. As the adjective seemed too cheap, I revised it to 'accepted', and changed the title to fit. However, I am still worried that 'accepted' is only the second-best adjective – although I am at a loss to discover the first – and that such a title raises all the wrong expectations anyway. Do you have any thoughts on these matters? I am sorry if this is deeply boring: it bored even me as I was typing it.

It seems to me a good idea that we should meet. The situation is slightly complicated by the fact that I have an uncle who lives in, at or near Lytham, and with whom we are in very precarious contact, so, if I play my cards right, I might be able to arrange some sort of outing within an outing. But I imagine that here too there is no great rush. It seems to me that, merely in carrying out what has already been agreed on, you have done a colossal amount for Kuppner studies, and there is no reason why you should sacrifice your readership to my absurd, and probably pathologically motivated, productivity. The idea of putting out a book with over a thousand poems in it undoubtedly appeals to me, but probably to no-one else. Incidentally, I have finished two more lengthy works. If you have already had enough – and who could blame you – you had better get in touch, appealing to my better nature, within the next couple of weeks. Is it reasonable to suggest that you might wish to keep what you like of them, and I can then try to shove off the dross on other, less deserving souls? You see, I keep thinking: I might wake up tomorrow and no longer want to do this. Or I might forget. These things happen.

With thanks,
Frank

FROM MICHAEL SCHMIDT
Manchester
19 October 1983

Dear Frank,

Thank you for your letter. Your book is published on May 31st and we have to have the jacket artwork complete by February 1st in order to have copies to mail by March 1st. But please don't tell Alasdair Gray this! In fact, give him a much earlier deadline and, if my experience of artists is right, he will deliver on time 2 months late!

We published an interview with Genet in which he reflected that, while in prison, he was free to write whatever [he] wanted because no-one would ever read it.[5] Out of prison, with his books published, people had expectations of him and it made it impossible to write at all. I see you are experiencing the same thing! I do hope the publication will not silence you, though if it slightly reduced the flow of quatrains, it might be a proper ecological measure!

I like 'The Subtle Observation of Naked Women' as a title and ask your permission to use it on the sequence. In fact almost any title is misleading except one which is totally neutral and unattractive. And being misleading is in itself one of the strategies of the poems, surely! Thus let us adopt the title if you have no objection.

If *Poetry* Chicago do not accept the sequence, then we will of course use it in *PN Review* and in your second book.

Concerning your visit, it would be as well if we met some time in December or January so that the text can be finalised. I have a number of small comments, largely to do with specific points in the poems. There is one in which the last lines stretches, amusingly, too far. Unfortunately, the amusement ends about 3 clauses from the end and the line should be shortened and could be without ill-effect. There are other points of this nature which, because of pressure of work, I need a deadline to annotate, and the only deadline that ever seems to work is a visit from the author. This is rather hard on foreign authors!

Could you please send me the two new works? I would be very glad to see them. You must of course broaden your publishing base, but in terms of book publication, I would like to be your exclusive publisher for poetry.[6] I would hate indeed to share you with anyone else! We have in the past occasionally lost poets to OUP, Salamander, Chatto, etc, and this is most distressing for a publisher like me. Thus you must spread the manna on the waters, or whatever the expression is, but when it comes time to gather it in, the basket, I hope, will remain Carcanet!

December and January, particularly the latter, are quite empty so you have free range in my diary. Do let me know soon which day you would like to come here. You would be welcome to stay over at our house in the Peaks (Chapel-en-le-Frith) if you can stand the occasional crying child in the night.

Yours sincerely,
Michael

*

I have a soft spot – unwise in a publisher – for poets who don't seem to care about the reception of their work but who get on with it. It's what they do, they watch their work unfold before them quizzically and are surprised when it takes foreseen forms and unforeseen configurations. You can usually recognise such writers from their publicity photos, acquired perhaps in one of those old photo-booths we went to for our passport mug-shots in pre-iPhone times.

Frank Kuppner began in a very good place for an aspiring

writer, much liked by his contemporaries and his immediate seniors. Alasdair Gray designed a wonderful cover for his first book, a history of whose genesis is recorded above. It was clearly a tightly negotiated collaboration.

Frank visited and stayed with my family, if I remember correctly when we lived in Chapel-en-le-Frith, Derbyshire. He had never experienced a baked potato and addressed it rather as Sir Walter Raleigh must have done in similar circumstances. As a gift for the hostess he brought a panda ashtray from Glasgow Zoo.

It has always been hard to market his books. He is a reluctant public performer. Occasionally a critic will speak up for him. In *The Scotsman* Stuart Kelly wrote, 'That Frank Kuppner is not widely recognised as one of the most ingenious contemporary Scottish writers is a disgrace.' He has fought Kuppner's corner more than once: 'From his surreal short stories (*In The Beginning There Was Physics*) to his haunting memoirs that combine investigations into true crime with meditations on personal loss (*Something Very Like Murder* and *A Very Quiet Street*) to his utterly idiosyncratic poetry – only Kuppner could call his selected poems *What? Again?* – he has consistently tested the limits of literary forms, literary tastes and literary norms.'

He is a writer I cannot imagine being without.

NOTES

1. *Some Contemporary Poets of Britain and Ireland – an anthology*, edited by Michael Schmidt, had a list of eighteen poets on the back cover, including Kuppner, whose 'Svensk Rhapsody' was his first substantial publication. The poets were not all from the Carcanet stable, for example James Fenton, Tony Harrison and Derek Mahon. The book was published in 1983, and also formed *PN Review* 36 (March-April 1984). Kuppner had sent the two sequences 'A Regular Traveller' and 'A Little English Journey'

for consideration for *PN Review*, but MNS found them 'more uneven than the other three. [...] Still my addiction is not cured even by this excess and I look forward to the eventual (final) magnum opusish work you promise in this vein. You cannot keep this up for ever' (2 September 1983).

2. *A Bad Day for the Sung Dynasty* was published in 1984, consisting of 501 quatrains, with a 'Technical Note' on the form in 10 quatrains at the start.

3. Alasdair Gray (b. 1934) has described himself as a 'self-employed verbal and pictorial artist'. His novel *Lanark*, published in 1981, is regarded as a landmark both in its form and its imagining of the city of Glasgow. Gray's murals can be seen in the West End of Glasgow at Hillhead underground and at Oran Mor. He painted the blue and white *Sung Mona Lisa* reproduced as the cover of Kuppner's first book.

4. 'The Subtle Observation of Naked Women' became 'The Intelligent Observation of Naked Women', but Kuppner later had his doubts about that as a title for more than the sequence – 'it sounds like a claim that the author is smugly or arrogantly making for himself' – because repetition as a book title 'in potted biographies etc sounds as if it could easily become a little wearing. What do you think of *Free Translations from the Truth*?' Not much, apparently, as the five sequences appeared under the title *The Intelligent Observation...* in 1987.

5. A transcript of the interview Pierre Vicary conducted with the French novelist, playwright, poet and activist Jean Genet (1910–86) for the Australian Broadcasting Commission in 1982 was published in *PN Review* 32 (July-August 1983).

6. Carcanet has remained Kuppner's exclusive poetry publisher, bringing out his eleventh collection, *The Third Mandarin*, in 2018. It consists of 501 quatrains. Writing to MNS (4 August 1983), Kuppner explained that:

> my poetic technique, poor thing as it is, is a straight lift from the Chinese poetry translators, particularly Witter Bynner.

(Since reading *The Jade Mountain*, I have practically used no other. It is the best poetry I know in English.)[...] Of course I do personal stuff as well, but I find the technique so powerful and captivating that I am reluctant to hang around for months at a time waiting for things worth writing about to happen to me.

1983
Again

The *Times* obituary began 'Robert Gavron's appearance was unmistakable: a sun-bronzed complexion, framed by a woolly mop of white curls, with eyes like shoe-buttons' (9 February 2015). Robert Gavron (1930–2015) became the owner of Carcanet Press shortly after he became owner and Chairman of The Folio Society. His long and distinguished career in printing and publishing was based on his founding and chairing the St Ives printing group. As a Labour peer he was a member of the House of Lords from 1999. He was also Chairman of the Guardian Media Group in the later 1990s, as well as being a director of the Royal Opera House and a trustee of the National Gallery; he was a shrewd, discreet and generous arts philanthropist.

FROM ROBERT GAVRON
London
12 December 1983

Dear Michael,

Although we discussed it on the telephone, I do want to reply to your letter of 5 December.

I believe our aims at Carcanet are to publish good books and then sell them. There is not much point in publishing a good book that won't sell: a book that nobody buys or reads is doing no good to the literary scene. I do, of course, agree with you that a bad book should not be published by Carcanet and the fact that it may sell well should not influence our decision. I do not know about the Powys book on Keats because it is possible that this could be of interest to scholars even if it is, in our opinion, a bad assessment of Keats. For example, if you suddenly discovered a forgotten Shakespeare Sonnet while you were publishing a critical assessment of Shakespeare you would probably want to include it. If you discovered an unknown play by Shakespeare, which was a bad play (as some of his known plays are), you would probably want to publish it.

I think we must publish with an eye to the market because if we are ever to be independent of the Arts Council we must be commercially viable. I believe that our good name is the most important property we have but there is no reason why Mammon and editorial excellence cannot walk hand in hand.

How does that sound as expressed by your newly appointed conscience!

Yours,
Bob

*

When I married and it became clear that Carcanet was likely to remain a perilous liability for a young family, I looked more energetically than ever for 'an investor'. Peter du Sautoy, when Managing Director of Faber and Faber, pointed me towards Robert Gavron. Tom Maschler, at Cape, told me not to bother, he'd never buy such a pup.

I invited Bob to lunch at my club, the Savile. We did not talk at all about poetry publishing but about private matters and gossip. After the lunch he sent me a card to say he thought we might well do business. We met again at the Connaught, at his invitation. He had quail eggs and squirted a yolk up his tie, an amusement and distraction. In the next month or so, instead of his acquiring a half interest in the Press, he bought it outright. It was a generally happy relationship, especially after his first appointee as Chairman, the delightful, exasperating Victor Ross, an Austrian refugee who had been Managing Director of Readers' Digest and for whom small press publishing was a contradiction in terms (for him a run of 10,000 copies was a limited edition, where our longest print runs were 1,500), was removed and replaced at my urgent behest by his new wife Kate Gavron, who had long and relevant experience at Hamish Hamilton and understood the problems and goals of a small operation such as ours.

When he died, I commented in *The Bookseller* (9 February 2015):

> Bob Gavron acquired Carcanet in 1983, under no illusion that he had bought a goldmine. It had been running at a loss for fourteen years, but winning prizes and already quite well-known. After that he supported, under-wrote and encouraged our development. The issue of survival never arose: he was there for the long haul. Kate Gavron has been our chairman for many years now. There has not once been editorial intervention. The occasional raised eyebrow, perhaps, but on the whole lessons in good husbandry, good design, and cheerful support. Bob understood publishing in all its aspects, from the mass market to the most specialized, and he knew that there was a place for each. I think he liked our books – poetry and prose – as books, each one delivering a different surprise.

THE YEAR IN BOOKS

Elizabeth Barrett Browning, *Selected Poems*, edited by Malcolm Hicks

T. Carmi, *At the Stones of Losses*, translated by Grace Schulman

Charles Cotton, *Selected Poems*, edited by Ken Robinson

Donald Davie, *Collected Poems 1971–1983*

Stevie Davies, *Emily Brontë: The Artist as a Free Woman*

George Dekker, *Donald Davie and the Responsibilities of Literature*

Padraic Fallon, *Poems and Versions*, edited by Brian Fallon

Ford Madox Ford, *The English Novel*

George Sutherland Fraser, *A Stranger and Afraid: autobiography of an intellectual*

John Gower, *Selected Poetry*, edited by Carole Weinberg

Ivor Gurney, *War Letters*, edited by R.K.R. Thornton

Michael Hamburger, *A Proliferation of Prophets: essays on German writers from Nietzsche to Brecht*

J.F. Hendry, *The Sacred Threshold: a life of Rilke*

Peter Huchel, *The Garden of Theophrastus and other poems*, translated by Michael Hamburger

Juvenal, *Sixteen Satires Upon the Ancient Harlot*, translated by Steven Robinson

Jean de La Ceppède, *Theorems: LXX Sonnets*, translated by Keith Bosley

Giacomo Leopardi, *Moral Tales*, translated by Patrick Creagh

Wyndham Lewis, *Self-Condemned*, afterword by Rowland Smith

Katherine Mansfield, *The Aloe* with *Prelude*, edited by Vincent O'Sullivan

Ian McMillan, *Now It Can Be Told*

Christoph Meckel, *The Figure on the Boundary Line*, translated by Brian Harris, Margaret Woodruff and Christopher Middleton

George Meredith, *Selected Poems*, edited by Keith Hanley

Christopher Middleton, *111 Poems*

Christopher Middleton, *The Pursuit of the Kingfisher and Other Essays*

Adolf Muschg, *The Blue Man and Other Stories*, translated by Marlis Zeller Cambon and Michael Hamburger

Idris Parry, *Hand to Mouth and Other Essays*
Pier Paolo Pasolini, *Lutheran Letters*, translated by Stuart Hood
Michael Schmidt (ed), *Some Contemporary Poets of Britain and Ireland*
Roger Scruton, *The Aesthetic Understanding*
C.H. Sisson, *Anglican Essays*
C.H. Sisson (tr), *The Song of Roland*
George Holbert Tucker, *A Goodly Heritage: a history of Jane Austen's family*
Daniel Weissbort, *Modern Poetry in Translation: an annual survey*

1984

Elizabeth Jennings (1926–2001) first appeared on Carcanet's list in 1975 with *Growing Points: new poems*, having been published previously by André Deutsch and Macmillan. Her first collection, *Poems* (Fantasy Press, 1953) brought her to Robert Conquest's attention, and he included her as the only woman in his 1956 anthology which launched 'The Movement'. She gained a very wide readership over the years. A resident of Oxford almost all of her life, a practising and troubled Catholic, she devoted herself to her writing, living frugally in rented rooms. Her mental and physical frailty was a concern to her small but constant circle of friends. Her obituarist in *The Guardian* remarked on her rarely missing a new production of Shakespeare at Stratford; 'a connoisseur of ice-cream, she was a regular at the Häagen-Daz's ice-cream parlour. So avid was her filmgoing that her local cinema, in Walton Street, was rumoured to have given her a free pass for life.'[1]

FROM ELIZABETH JENNINGS
Oxford
11 January 1984, 1.20 a.m.!

Dear Mike,

This is just a follow-up from my last. It is to raise a literary, critical question. I notice how often you use words like 'civic', 'responsibility' and so on when you are evaluating poetry or individual poems. I take it that you are judging in a moral sense; the poem is written by an 'act of will', a poet is not to be thought of as the poet but a human being who makes certain choices when he writes. I know this is a gross over-simplification because all sorts of other forces are engaged, primarily the imagination. Well, I wouldn't question any of this unless I thought something rather large seems to be being left out. No one, I take it, believes any longer in art for art's sake or art for beauty's sake. If these didn't die forever in the 1890s, then the worst Georgians and the publication of *The Waste Land* very neatly buried them. But, poetry elevates and pleases. Surely you would not quarrel with the sheer zest of, say, Keats's *Nightingale* or Hopkins's *Spring* or the great heights of *Tintern Abbey* or Rilke's *Duino Elegies*. Pleasure is the bait, the rest comes when it has been swallowed. I really would be most grateful if you, when and only when you have time, would clear my mind a little about all this.

You have seen the hour, my small hours! I went for tests to the consultant today and had a rather unsuccessful time when they tried to get a specimen of my blood. My veins are tiny and I always come away with bruised arms! I have to have a Cardiogram and Cephalogram and an ex-ray of my head. I am literally having my brain and heart examined. I have a book to review for the *D[aily] Telegraph* and *The Tablet* want to print my poems more often, I had a very pleasant letter from the Editor. I do hope you are all well and safely back after a lovely time.

Love, Elizabeth

FROM MICHAEL SCHMIDT
Manchester
19 January 1984

Dear Elizabeth,

Thank you for your letter. I reply in tremendous haste since the pressure here is unrelenting.

You may remember that some time ago in *PN Review* we published a translation of Valéry by G.S. Fraser. It was his poem called 'The Young Fate'.[2] He had given up writing poetry and, when the First World War came, he was asked to write a poem to help the French cause, as it were. He wrote a poem in which there was no allusion to contemporary events, to the French nation, to French ambitions or realities. However, it was a poem which used every resource of the French language. It proved that the French language was the supreme literary tool that it is simply by example. It strikes me that this is the highest possible form of civic poetry. It celebrates language which is our only common possession, it extends, cleans and strengthens it. There are other forms of civicism which I also like in poetry (as should be evident from our list).

You may say that I am defining the term so widely that it has no meaning at all. But I think it does have meaning. Especially if it is taken in reference to the way in which the language is employed – as a <u>common</u> language – it is the only word I can think of to define the responsible writer. Poetry is, as David Jones said, our one intransitive act, the one act we perform (I suppose other forms of art fall into this category) in which we do not expect to have a result in action – it is not a cause of an effect or a means to an end.[3] It is an end in itself. But it exists in the language and for it, and the more you reflect on language as our common possession (not a fluid or democratic element, as the French critics and new philologists would have us believe), the more I think you will see what I mean when I use the word. It would be silly for any poet to write deliberately 'civic' poetry in a cruder sense. In fact, civicism is not an end but one of the many contributing means in a writer.

I am very sorry indeed to learn you have been unwell again and hope that 1984 will be the year in which your health levels off! It would be nice to have you working to the full and not having these blackouts any more.

I am not keen to read manuscript poems en masse again if I can help it. That is why I very much hope it will be possible for you to continue to have poems typed. If it is impossible, however, I will accept manuscript poems, but you must appreciate how much longer it takes me to read them! I do feel that it is best for me to see as much of your work as possible since there is so much of it and I am always afraid that you will unvalue your better poems and over-value your most recently written ones! I always feel that we should publish a book by you every month so as not to miss the poems which get overlooked as you move on at such speed!

The question of a Collected Poems to coincide with 1986 I will bear in mind.[4] It will depend to some extent on the sales of the *Selected* and to an even greater extent, on the success or otherwise of our large rash of Collected Poems coming out this year. If the H.D., Sisson and Hamburger (not to mention the Mina Loy) come unstuck, we will be so much the poorer that I do not think we will risk [a] Collected again for some time! I know you are a different category altogether, but these books will give us some indication.

With love from us all,
Michael

P.S. Charles was delighted with your message!

FROM ELIZABETH JENNINGS
Oxford
24 January 1984
Why red? The pen nearest to me.

Dear Mike,

Thank you for your lovely, long letter. It was so good of you to reply to my critical points at once. How I wish we could <u>talk</u> about them. I think I do know what you mean, about language, and in view of the dire *clichés* etc. that are spoken in it now, I feel how very much each language in each country needs to be purified by every living line of poetry. Steiner has much to say of this in *After Babel*.[5]

Yes, poetry is an end in itself. I think that, perhaps very rarely, it can move to action but, as a rule, it does not but doesn't it civilise also? I think that's important.

I will give you a very lofty analogy for poetry; it is like the Eucharist, words are spoken, a simple element is offered and the words <u>transform</u> that element. I think D. Jones would go along with this.[6]

And, yes, the poet is a highly responsible person. He, by his own talent, is responsible both to his language and to the poetry of the past for cleansing <u>and</u> making new our common tongue (I speak of English). Your Valéry was a perfect example of 'civic' verse.

Please, Mike, do not over-work. It is important for you, your family and all of us to keep <u>well</u>. It is good of you to ask after my confounded health. I've been having neurological tests at the old Radcliffe, but I've also been having more blackouts. But I am working furiously…

(Continued later)

I have the results of tests – brain X-ray, electroencephalogram and electrocardiograph on St Valentine's day. I rather dread this.

I shall have a few typed poems soon and more to come.

A great piece of news came a couple of days ago. Puffin want to do a *Quintet of Poets* which means children's poems from Ted Hughes, Causley, John Fuller, John Walsh (?) and me.[7] Isn't it exciting? It also means I can earn a bit of much-needed money.

Try this childhood joke on Charles. Ask him to say to his sister – 'Is a bell necessary on a bicycle?'!

And much love to all of you,
Elizabeth

*

A poet finding her way into poetry as an undergraduate in the 1980s wrote, 'Jennings was always the "one" female poet conjured by the "canon" to have even existed in Britain in the 1950s (aside from Plath)'. I was at Oxford in the late 1960s and this was not the case then. At Oxford the first poet of any sex I met was Anne Ridler. There was Elizabeth, certainly, whom I met in my early weeks (my partner gave me a book of her poems and I went to cadge her autograph, the beginning of a long friendship). But there was also the scholarly, hedonistic, eccentric Sally Purcell; and E.J. Scovell, and on Boar's Hill Elizabeth Daryush. Many others came to read for the Poetry Society, some at my invitation – Stevie Smith, Rosemary Tonks, Kathleen Raine and Anne Stevenson; there was Ruth Pitter, too, and Patricia Beer, and Elaine Feinstein who – like Muriel Spark – had been a significant editor. And Denise Levertov who abandoned the English. Plath was a prevailing absence, and other substantial Americans – Adrienne Rich in particular, even then – cast shadows. These are poets we still remember, more than many of their male contemporaries. Ruth Fainlight survives with her readership, and Fleur Adcock. Sylvia Townsend Warner and Frances Bellerby were of an earlier generation. In the darker past loomed Charlotte Mew, a favourite of Elizabeth's, and Edith Sitwell for whom she had a soft spot.

In my four years at Oxford I used to visit Elizabeth almost every week, sit with her for an hour taking tea and listening to her problems and her poems. She read her poems down the phone to Dame Veronica Wedgwood, one of her most devoted friends, and gave them one or two or occasionally three stars in response to her listener's response. She wrote copiously in lined foolscap notebooks. She wrote in them from back to front and, after *Growing Points*, when she felt a new book was due she would give me twenty or thirty of these books to sort through, select from and type up the poems. This I did, and sometimes I made free with her never entirely consistent punctuation, tampered with the diction and even cut stanzas where they seemed to be weak. As the years passed, the gleanings of good work from the notebooks became more and more sparse.

In an obituary, I wrote:

She compared making poems to the practice of prayer, which reconciles an individual with the world outside. Self is subsumed in a larger stability. 'Each brings an island in his heart to square / With what he finds, and all is something strange / And most expected.' Prayer and poetry also risk the terrifying world of shadows. In a poem on Rembrandt's late self-portraits she implicates herself: 'To paint's to breathe / And all the darknesses are dared.' It was intensely exciting for me when a fine poem managed to burst free of the undergrowth of difficult handwriting and repetitive tropes (seasons, sleeplessness, remote love) to dazzle eye and ear.

At the end of the obituary I recalled her investiture:

It was her habit in later years to wear plimsolls, socks, a woollen skirt, a knitted sweater and, in the street, a knitted hat. Before she went to the Palace to receive her CBE in 1992, friends urged her to dress appropriately. She reassured us: she had bought new socks, a new skirt, a new jumper. Also, new plimsolls. A week or so after the investiture she joined me for lunch at Rules (her choice, she had always wanted to go there). She came in carrying six plastic bags and wearing the outfit she had worn to the Palace. The maître d' had to be reassured: this was a great poet. A headline in *The Times* described her as 'the bag-lady of the sonnets'. The effect was cruel, because to herself she never seemed eccentric, difficult, unusual. Out of confusion, anguish and pain she had drawn a humane, consoling body of poetry that will remain popular for generations. What could be more normal?

NOTES

1. Grevel Lindop, *The Guardian*, 31 October 2001.
2. Paul Valéry's 'La Jeune Parque', translated by G.S. Fraser, appeared in *PN Review* 33 (September–October 1983).
3. David Jones (1895–1974), Welsh poet and painter, whose work was informed by his Catholic faith and Welsh traditions. He said something slightly different than MNS remembers here, after quoting the (unascribed) dictum 'Art is the sole intransitive activity of man': 'It is the intransitivity and gratuitousness in man's art that is a sign of man's uniqueness, not merely that he makes things, nor yet that those things have beauty.' ('Art and Sacrament', in Harman Grisewood (ed.), *Epoch and Artist: selected writings*, Faber and Faber, 1959, p.149)
4. Carcanet did bring out the *Collected Poems 1953–1985* in 1986, to celebrate Jennings's 60th birthday. It comprised poems selected from seventeen volumes, including her translations of Michelangelo's sonnets. Jennings wrote in her short Preface that 'once a poem is published it ceases to have much to do with oneself. Art is not self-expression while, for me,

"confessional poetry" is almost a contradiction in terms.' The volume gained the prestigious W.H. Smith Literary Award the following year. She published seven more collections with Carcanet, including the *New Collected Poems* in 2001.

5. George Steiner's *After Babel* (OUP, 1975) is a comprehensive study of linguistics and translation. Steiner (b. 1929), literary critic, philosopher, essayist and academic, directed a number of important writers to Carcanet, of which he remains a 'critical friend', contributing a dozen essays to *PN Review*. Jennings may also have been prompted to her reflection by a recollection of T.S. Eliot's 'To purify the dialect of the tribe' (*Little Gidding*), adapting Mallarmé.

6. In the essay 'Art and Sacrament', David Jones did write about his discovery that 'an analogy between what we called "the Arts" and the things that Christians called the Eucharistic signs became (if still but vaguely) apparent. It became increasingly evident that this analogy applied to the whole gamut of "making"' (p. 171).

7. *Poets in Hand: a Puffin quintet of poets*, edited by Charles Causley and Anne Hardy, was published by Penguin Books in 1990. The poets besides Jennings were Causley, John Fuller, Vernon Scannell, and John Walsh.

THE YEAR IN BOOKS

John Ash, *The Branching Stairs*

John Ashbery, *A Wave*

Jean-Louis Baghio'o, *The Blue Flame-Tree*, translated by Stephen Romer, afterword by Maryse Condé

Joachim du Bellay, *The Regrets*, translated by C.H. Sisson

Alison Brackenbury, *Breaking Ground and Other Poems*

Christine Brooke-Rose, *Amalgamemnon*

Dino Buzzati, *Restless Nights: selected stories*, translated by Lawrence Venuti

William Cowper, *Selected Poems*, edited by Nick Rhodes

H.D. (Hilda Doolittle), *Collected Poems 1912-1944*, edited by Louis Martz

Paul Durcan, *Jumping the Train Tracks with Angela*

Ford Madox Ford, *A Call*, afterword by C.H. Sisson

Natalia Ginzburg, *Family Sayings*, translated by D.M. Low

Desmond Graham, *The Truth of War: Owen, Blunden, and Rosenberg*

John Gray, *Park: A Fantastic Story*, afterword by Philip Healy

Michael Hamburger, *Collected Poems, 1941-1983*

Christopher Hewitt, *The Living Curve: Letters to W.J. Strachan 1929-1979*, foreword by William Anderson

Peter Hoyle, *The Man in the Iron Mask*

R. C. Hutchinson, *The Quixotes and Other Stories*, edited by Robert Green

Ben Jonson, *Epigrams and The Forest*, edited by Richard Dutton

Dennis Keene, *Universe and Other Poems*

Karl Kraus, *In These Great Times*, translated by Harry Zohn

Frank Kuppner, *A Bad Day for the Sung Dynasty*

John Masefield, *Letters to Margaret Bridges 1915–1919*, edited by Donald Stanford

John Masefield, *Selected Poems*, edited by Donald Stanford

Sir Walter Ralegh, *Selected Writings*, edited by Gerald Hammond

Gareth Reeves, *Real Stories*

Laura Riding, *A Trojan Ending*, afterword by Laura (Riding) Jackson

Christina Rossetti, *Selected Poems*, edited by C.H. Sisson

Leonardo Sciascia, *The Day of the Owl and Equal Danger*, translated by Archibald Colquhoun and Arthur Oliver; Adrienne Foulke

C.H. Sisson, *Collected Poems*

Iain Crichton Smith, *The Exiles*

Botho Strauss, *Tumult*, translated by Michael Hulse

Georg Trakl, *Selected Poems and Letters*, edited by Frank Graziano, translated by Michael Hamburger et al

Malachi Whitaker, *The Crystal Fountain and Other Stories*, edited by Joan Hart

1985

Marina Warner begins her tribute to John Ashbery (1927–2017) by saying 'Through thick and thin, Michael Schmidt kept publishing John in the UK (and it was mostly thin when it came to an American poet like Ashbery)', although no one was quite like Ashbery. Recognised as one of the greatest American poets of the twentieth century, he was modest and charming in conversation, and generously encouraging to younger poets. Warner suggested that he combined a 'rapt quality of attention with inconsequentiality, a kind of mood I associate with Paris' of the fin-de siècle. He lived in Paris for ten years, otherwise in New York and upstate. Carcanet published him first in 1977 and kept up with his output until the end, thirty-five books in all, including volumes of translation and one of art criticism. Warner recalls Ashbery's championship of Mary Butts at a London dinner party: 'I was the only female in the company' she writes, 'and utterly outclassed as to drink and, as it turned out, expertise, not only in Mary Butts, but also in the complete wit and wisdom of Dame Edna Everage.'[1]

FROM JOHN ASHBERY
New York
21 March 1985

Dear Michael:

My agent, George[s] Borchardt, just sent me a xerox of a letter from Richard Scott Simon's office concerning the *Selected Earlier Poems* that John Ash proposed while he was over here.[2] Since then, however, I've decided at long last to go ahead and publish a *Selected Poems* with Viking, which will include poems from all my books to date, so I suppose you would prefer to bring this out in the U.K. I haven't yet signed the contract with Viking and will let you know details later on. Borchardt will be in touch with you, but I thought I'd best get this off straight away.

Did I mention Mary Butts to you when I was in England?[3] I'm surprised that even such super sleuths as Messieurs Ash and Lenton haven't heard of her. I suppose she might be England's equivalent of Djuna Barnes if Djuna Barnes were really as good as everyone says she is.[4] Mary Butts is rather uneven, but her novels *Armed with Madness* and *Ashe of Rings* might intrigue you. Even better are her short stories in the collections *Speed the Plough*, *Several Occasions*, and *Last Stories*. Her dates, I believe, are approximately 1895 to 1937. Her brother Tony, a painter, was the lover of William Plomer.

Well, that's all for now,
John

FROM MICHAEL SCHMIDT
Manchester
28 March 1985

Dear John,

Thank you very much for your note of 21st March. I would love to do the 'Selected Poems' with Viking. I will let Richard Scott Simon know and if you keep Borchardt apprised of my interest, all should be well. John will be disappointed I expect but he will get over it.

You did not mention Mary Butts but, oddly enough, I am at present considering her stories for publication![5] Your recommendation will spur me on.

I look forward to seeing you at Cambridge where I will be recording the Festival for the BBC and intend to fill the programme with Ashbery.[6]

Yours ever,
Michael

FROM MICHAEL SCHMIDT
Manchester
21 June 1985

Dear John,

It was a real pleasure to see you over here. I wish I could have made the farewell party. I hope you enjoyed yourself as much as most of us did.

I would like to see *A Nest of Ninnies*.[7] I would also, if they really are free, like to have some of the poems you read last at the Cambridge Poetry Festival for *PNR*. I have now signed a contract for the *Selected Poems* which looks like a real barn-dance!

The new printing of *Self-Portrait in a Convex Mirror* is selling like warm cakes.[8]

With every good wish,
Michael

FROM JOHN ASHBERY
New York
28 June 1985

Dear Michael,

It was a great joy to see you again, in London and Cambridge, being so friskily efficient. I loved the lunch with all the young blond grey eminences. I wish I could remember all their names. Tom Sutcliffe's is the only one I can remember. (I wonder why?) Maybe you could remind me of the name of the nice man who edits the *TLS* as I want to send him some poems at some point.[9] I want to send you some too. However, sending them out is a chore and I only contemplate it a couple of times a year. I would rather wait till some time later in the summer when I will presumably have accumulated some more. I have feelings about which I would like to publish in England and which in America, and presumably will have them also about the ones I haven't written yet. For instance, 'Daffy Duck in Hollywood' would be right for England (it was published in the *TLS*) because the English seem so much more knowledgeable about American pop culture than we are. At any rate, let me thanks you again for the lunch – as I told you, such an event is inconceivable in New York, at least as far as Viking Press is concerned.

I'm sending you a copy of *A Nest of Ninnies* in a plain brown wrapper. As you know, I would love it if you publish it, but that of course is not for me to decide. I do think the English reader would be pleased to have a book with my name attached to it that he or she could understand and perhaps even enjoy.[10]

To quote the opening lines of Malcolm Elwin's biography of Landor, one of the books I bought at Rota's, 'The English have always preferred mediocrity and the commonplace to magnanimity and genius. Comfort is the condition most to be desired – perhaps because, as Hazlitt said, "the English are certainly the most uncomfortable of all people in themselves" – and they glance askant at the disturber of their peace.'

I just went to Viking today to look at the type and jacket design of my *Selected Poems* (I also signed the Carcanet contracts today and sent them back to Borchardt).[11] I think the jacket will be very pretty – they're using a handmade paper I bought in France, in dull shades of black, white, rose, apple green, and toast. The label on the front will be toast with rose lettering shaded by green. You'd be welcome to use this design and there's of course no artist's fee to pay. My editor, Elizabeth Sifton, is alerted that you might be in touch with her about this.

Please give my best to Robyn and keep up the good work – publishing all those inspiring tracts, I mean.

Love,
John

P.S. As an afterthought, I'm sending you a copy of my three plays, along with *A Nest of Ninnies*.

*

When Carcanet published *Self-Portrait in a Convex Mirror* in 1977, two years after its American publication, there was a sense of our having dragged our feet. What catalysed publication was my meeting the poet at the Cambridge Poetry Festival where I heard him read in his wry, throw-away manner, as if he himself was surprised and a puzzled by what was on the page before him. (He told me of a reading he gave at West Point. Looking down from the podium he spotted a particularly dashing pupil in the front row. Leaning over, he said, 'Do you want me to sign your *book*?') Hearing the poet read: my decisions on several poets have been taken after, tempted by the manuscript, I hear the way their voices bring the poems alive. This happened with Jeffrey Wainwright, Iain Crichton Smith, Sorley MacLean and others. I could also list those poets whose readings have doused my enthusiasm for their work. Readings disclose the poet's attitude to the poem, unless the poet is focused on the audience and the exercise is less in interpretation than in marketing.

Writing in 1994 in an editorial in *PN Review* 99, with a substantial supplement about Ashbery's work, I reflected on how his readership had changed in Britain. I also tried to identify some of the qualities which I, as editor, most enjoyed, and to consider his impact on other writers:

> I regret the opaque patristics which now attach to his work. He answers – inadvertently, I believe – to certain current theoretical prescriptions. Critics conjure Ashbery to legitimise arguments, attributing to him deliberate strategies, where the pilot of his poem is not a scheming post-Modern opportunist. He is a writer with a remarkably finely-tuned sense of syntax and prosody, an informed, a *refined* freedom from conventionality in approach, and actual occasions, real feelings. If he is programmatic it is in his instinctive avoidance of predictable sequence, his unwillingness to take things and themes on accepted terms. [...]
>
> He deploys varieties of voice – spoken voices, written voices, period tones. These he orchestrates: verbal material from the world we live in, and echoes of worlds of language, art and social discourse which came before, with a hint of those that may come after. Such language negotiates a vivid way through commonplace, cliché, familiar trope, getting to another side (not the other side: things are never dialectical in Ashbery). His approaches, rooted

in his particular culture, his wide and often eccentric reading, are strictly inimitable.

This means of course that he has dozens of imitators, and a few poets who have learned their own, rather than his, lessons from him. He offers two kinds of freedom: a freedom from conventional constraints which is enabling, and another freedom which issues in the 'ludic' inconsequentialities of his lesser disciples and is to be found in the less successful of his own poems.

Writers considering his work in *PN Review* 99 included F.T. Prince, Miles Champion, Christopher Middleton, Mark Ford, Sujata Bhatt, Eavan Boland. A big adjustment in *PN Review*'s editorial stance is reflected here. Ashbery remains a central strand in Carcanet's DNA, and also in the magazine's.

NOTES

1. Marina Warner in 'Remembering John Ashbery', *PN Review* 239 (January–February 2018). Mark Ford, in the same issue, comments that 'Although famous as a poetic innovator and as a champion of the avant-garde, John derived pleasure from a very wide spectrum of sources', obviously including the Australian comedian and satirist Barry Humphries's alter ego Dame Edna, star of stage and television. In a conversation with John Ash, published in *PN Review* 46 (November–December 1985), Ashbery remarks:

   I think there are now people who know my name but don't know what I do. I'm famous for being famous – I'm a superstar, almost like Edna Everage! I find this very strange. I'm certainly still terribly controversial as a poet. The jury is still out on the question of whether I'm a poet at all, yet I get my picture taken for *Women's Wear Daily*.

2. Richard Scott Simon, well-known literary agent in London; Georges Borchardt and his wife Anne established their distinguished literary agency in New York in 1967.

3. Djuna Barnes (1892–1982), American novelist and poet, mainly remembered for her novel *Nightwood* (1936). It was praised by T.S. Eliot for its 'great achievement of a style, the beauty of phrasing, the brilliance of wit and characterization, and a quality of horror and doom very nearly related to that of Elizabethan tragedy'. Carcanet published her poems in 2003 and *Ladies Almanack* in 2006.

4. Antony Butts (1900–41) was fictionalised by William Plomer (1903–73), novelist, poet and literary editor, in his novel *Museum Pieces* (1952).

5. Mary Butts (1890–1937) wrote fiction, essays and poems. Her work was championed by Pound and Ford, but had fallen into neglect. In 1988 Carcanet re-issued her 'partial autobiography', *The Crystal Cabinet*. It described her childhood at Salterns, the family house in which there were forty-two pictures by William Blake, collected by her great-grandfather who was Blake's patron and friend. *With and Without Buttons & other stories*, a collection of fourteen stories edited by Nathalie Blondel, was published by Carcanet in 1991.

6. This was the final iteration of the biennial Cambridge Poetry Festival, founded by Richard Berengarten (Burns) in 1975. Poets who took part in the festival were featured in *PN Review* 46 (November–December 1985), which was in effect a programme for it, guest-edited by Clive Wilmer. It included two poems by Ashbery, 'Railroad Bridge' and 'Forgotten Song'.

7. Carcanet published *A Nest of Ninnies*, the novel by John Asbery and James Schuyler, in 1987. It had been published in the USA in 1969, when W.H. Auden reviewed it approvingly: 'My! What a pleasant surprise to read a novel in which there is not a single bedroom scene… there are to be sure some scenes of violence, but the violence is meteorological'. He concluded, 'I am convinced that their book is destined to become a minor classic.'

8. *Self-Portrait* was first published by Carcanet in 1977, reissued
    in 1981, and in a larger paperback format with a severe black,
    green-lettered cover in 1985. It was the first of Ashbery's
    collections to be published by Carcanet, two years after its
    publication by Viking in the USA.

9. Tom Sutcliffe, journalist and arts editor, was then editor of
    BBC Radio 4's arts programme *Kaleidoscope*, and the next
    year went on to become the first arts editor of the *Independent*
    newspaper. In 1981 the Editor of the *Times Literary
    Supplement* was Jeremy Treglown; the lunch guest might have
    been Alan Jenkins, then the poetry and fiction editor of the
    TLS.

10. Writing to Mark Ford (18 March 1992), Ashbery commented
    philosophically on his reviewing history::

    > These things tend to be cyclical; after a few bleak years
    > review-wise in the US I came out rather well with *Flow
    > Chart*. Undoubtedly this stimulated a counter-reaction in
    > the UK, even if no one there was aware of the American
    > reviews, the two countries being rather like the woman
    > with the watering can and the mackintosh-clad man in
    > my Swiss barometer; when the former emerges from their
    > chalet you can expect the heavens to unzip. (*PN Review*
    > 239, p.46)

11. Carcanet published Ashbery's *Selected Poems* (with the Viking
    jacket described here) in 1986. Alan Jenkins, reviewing for
    The Sunday Times (27 April 1986), suggested that this would
    be the volume that could help 'English readers who haven't
    already made up their minds' as to whether Ashbery was 'too
    odd a poet to be really good'. He concluded: 'Ashbery *is* a really
    good poet, a legitimate though rebellious heir of Eliot, Pound,
    Stevens and Auden, seriously and often amusingly trying to
    make it new; he is also one of those rare and attractive species, a
    late-flowering dandy'. Ashbery's *3 Plays* was published in 1995.

THE YEAR IN BOOKS

Guillaume Apollinaire, *The Poet Assassinated and Other Stories*, translated by Ron Padgett

Cliff Ashby, *Plain Song: collected poems 1960-1985*

Machado de Assis, *The Devil's Church and Other Stories*, translated by Jack Schmitt and Lorie Ishimatsu

Alistair Brotchie and Malcom Green (eds), *An Atlas Anthology III*

Dino Buzzati, *The Tartar Steppe*, translated by Stuart Hood

Gillian Clarke, *Selected Poems*

Arthur Cohen, *An Admirable Woman*

C.B. Cox, *The Two-Headed Monster*

Guy Davenport, *Thasos and Ohio: poems and translations*

Donald Davie, *Selected Poems*

Keith Douglas, *A Prose Miscellany*, edited by Desmond Graham

H.D. (Hilda Doolittle), *Helen in Egypt*

H.D. (Hilda Doolittle), *Tribute to Freud*, foreword by Norman Holmes Pearson

Mark Frutkin, *The Alchemy of Clouds*

Natalia Ginzburg, *All our Yesterdays*, translated by Angus Davidson

Natalia Ginzburg, *The Little Virtues*, translated by Dick Davis

Emma Hardy, *Diaries*, edited by Richard Taylor

Michael Hartnett, *Collected Poems: volume 1*

John Heath-Stubbs, *The Immolation of Aleph*

Zbigniew Herbert, *The Barbarian in the Garden*, translated by Michael Marsh and Jarosław Anders

Zbigniew Herbert, *Selected Poems*, translated by Czeslaw Miłosz and Peter Dale Scott, introduction by A. Alvarez

Gert Hoffman, *The Spectacle at the Tower*, translated by Christopher Middleton

Stuart Hood, *Carlino*

Stuart Hood, *A Storm from Paradise*

Elizabeth Jennings, *Extending the Territory*

Brian Jones, *The Children of Separation*

Clarice Lispector, *Family Ties*, translated by Giovanni Pontiero

Mina Loy, *The Last Lunar Baedeker*, edited by Roger L. Conover, note from Jonathan Williams

Bill Manhire, *Zoetropes: poems 1972–1982*

Harry Mathews, *The Sinking of the Odradek Stadium*

Czelaw Miłosz, *The Land of Ulro*, translated by Louis Iribarne

Bruno Monsaingeon, *Mademoiselle: conversations with Nadia Boulanger*, translated by Robyn Marsack, introduction by Elliott Carter

Edwin Morgan, *Selected Poems*

Samuel Palmer, *The Parting Light: selected writings*, edited by Mark Abley

Pier Paolo Pasolini, *A Violent Life*, translated by William Weaver

Octavio Paz, *One Earth, Four or Five Worlds: reflections on contemporary history*, translated by Helen R. Lane

John Cowper Powys, *Three Fantasies*, afterword by Glen Cavaliero

Leonardo Sciascia, *The Wine Dark Sea*, translated by Avril Bardoni

Vikram Seth, *The Humble Administrator's Garden*

Iain Crichton Smith, *Selected Poems*

Henry Howard, Earl of Surrey, *Selected Poems*, edited by Dennis Keene

Jeffrey Wainwright, *Selected Poems*

Sylvia Townsend Warner, *Selected Poems*, edited by Claire Harman

1986

John Ash (b. 1948) was first published by Carcanet in 1982 (*The Goodbyes*). He left his native city of Manchester for New York in 1985 and formed strong friendships with poets of the New York School. He continued to contribute reviews and essays to *PN Review*, and to publish poetry collections with the press. The reviewer of *The Burnt Pages* in the *Washington Post* wrote: 'many of [Ash's] best poems are prose poems, with a kind of Frank O'Hara-like grace: "Until I came to the island of Manhattan I always wanted to live in some other place where I could be loved or ignored as I wished, where it would seem that the great currents of the world converged..." ("Fifth Spring, Sixth Autumn"). Art and music, especially music, are central subjects – because they make us for a moment happy –' (19 January 1992). After teaching in Iowa and California, Ash left NY in 1996 to settle in Istanbul, writing and teaching there, a transition described in his 2007 collection *The Parthian Stations*. He moved back to Manchester in 2017.

FROM JOHN ASH
New York
[n.d., 1986]

Dear Michael,

Today the Ash energy is at a low ebb after a particularly exhausting salon which ranged over Sapphics and pantoums and ended with Harry (the Great) reading a chapter from his new novel which made my hair stand on end.[1] But first, thanks to you and Pam for doing what you could to get Quartet Books moving.[2] Needless to say I haven't heard a thing from them. A stiff letter is in order.

Next a message for Mike (Freeman).[3] It was nice of him to ask me to review Calvino's *Mr. Palomar*. I'd love a chance to write on Calvino, but there are problems. All my books are in England, – but I guess I could borrow here. Also I've looked at *Mr. Palomar* and found it rather disappointing. It seemed oddly dated, – rather like the stuff that Robbe-Grillet and other *Nouvelle Vague-istes* were doing all those years ago – and I wouldn't want to write a piece of half-hearted praise.[4]

But, of course, I haven't read the whole thing. I suppose my answer is yes, providing the review doesn't have to be in soon. Regarding my review of the reprehensible Mr. Reynolds, – I finished this some time ago and you're welcome to take a look at it, but I wonder whether *PNR* should pay him any attention at all.[5] His work is so utterly worthless perhaps we should just stand aside and wait for his little career to die a natural death. What do you think? I mean. The real criminal is not Reynolds, but Raine. And talking of criminals – have you seen Ms Fenton's abominable 'review' of John's *Selected Poems*?[6] The man should be shunned by all right-thinking people. John took it very hard. I have a suggestion. Why don't I do a long essay-review on John, – I've never done this for a 'major' publication and would relish the opportunity. It wouldn't take me long, either, since I could use material from my Brooklyn College talk. Let me know what you think about this. Please say yes. We'd both appreciate it very much.

Resumed somewhat later. That is to say 3.30 in the morning, after a tour of the gay bars on the Westside, preceded by dinner at Doug Crase's.[7] […]

I've just received payment for something that appeared in *PNR* 47, for which much thanks, – but what exactly am I being paid for? Have I seen a copy of *PNR* 47? The last two things I saw in proof were my review of James Merrill and the long essay on music.[8] Which, if either, appeared in *PNR* 47? Talking of music, John Lenton has just sent me some Robin Holloway tapes (or to be exact, they just arrived) including one of his Second Idyll – a marvellous piece which has gone straight to the top of my playlist. I took it to Doug's dinner party and the guests were ravished!

I've got some part-time work, sorting out Kenneth Koch's unpublished manuscripts, – a kind of literary Augean stables.[9] I'm still wading through the early sixties. I sort everything into 3 piles – 1 Of Small Interest, 2 Of Some Interest, 3 Of great Interest. Kenneth is a notoriously awkward character, but he seems to be delighted by the things I've unearthed, so at the moment I can do no wrong, - especially as I'm also reviewing his new book for the *New York Times*!

Anyway all of this is helping to plug the gaping hole in my finances, so I can begin to think about paying off my debtors. [...]

But are you going to be in Nueva York in February? You mentioned something about this in your last letter. Whatever you do, don't come between Feb 3rd and 8th, because I'll be in Texas visiting the wonderful Mr Middleton.[10] I'm looking forward to this immensely. It would also be terrific to see you and read more of your long poem. Did I tell you that I have taken to writing Moral Essays in verse. Can you believe this? The longest is *On Friendship* (22 pages of <u>very</u> long lines) and you make an appearance as 'M.S., my favourite lunch companion.' I have to warn you that I will soon have enough poetry for a new collection. Could you suggest an appropriate publishing date? There's no hurry, but it would be nice to have some idea.

Well, what else? Hmmm, I feel settled here and much of the time I can lead a quiet life without feeling that I'm missing something. I now stay in at least 3 evenings a week and work. I have a solid circle of loyal friends, - John, Maggie (Paley), Harry (when he's here), Stephanie, Paul (my landlord and neighbour), John Wells (artist), Doug (when I can prise him out of his shell), Darragh (a wonderful painter), Martin (Earl), Eugene (John's assistant) and his wife Rosanne, Ted Castle, and so on...[11] But every now and then I go out and play the field, - for example, at a P.E.N. party last week, which was like every New York intellectual/High Society party you have ever seen in films, - an illusion enhanced by the presence of Warren Beatty. Also present was Nawmin Mailer, Arthur Miller, Czeslaw Miłosz (who is a conceited little man and nothing like such a good poet as his distant cousin – O.V. de L. Miłosz) and William Gass (who was very agreeable, – as was his wife) and Elizabeth Hardwick, Barbara Epstein, etc...[12]

I'm glad to hear that you're entertaining the idea of publishing Jimmy Schuyler's poetry.[13] It will mean so much to him, since he has this sentimental attachment to an England he has never visited. But hold out for a *Selected Poems*, – the new book – *A Few Days* –, is wildly uneven though containing much that is charming, witty and touching. Did you get anywhere with Doug's *The Revisionist*, by the way? He's good you know.

Next week I go for an interview at Brooklyn College. They are considering me for the post that John has vacated. Pray for me. It seems such a neat substitution, I think it might happen. I miss you very much, so write soon. How are Claire and the young Schmidts?

Love,
John

Manchester
26 February 1986

Dear John,

Thank you for your recent and characteristically undated letter. I do not know how out of date I am in replying to you now. And this reply will necessarily be short. To speak of the woe that is in publishing! At least I hope to see you in April if you are still there and I am able to fulfil my travelling plans.

Your letter was delightful. It sounds to me as though you have found your environment and it would be churlish of me to wish you back here, though for selfish and gustatory reasons I might, from time to time, pine for lunch. Your letters are a treat.

I missed the Fenton review of Ashbery and would like to see it, if only to be able to respond to it in the editorial pages of *PN Review*. The *Selected Poems* is a wonderful book, and I would have thought Fenton would have the sense to like it. He is, after all, someone nurtured on Stevens.[14]

I would certainly welcome a long review of the *Selected Poems* by you. Indeed, it could be an essay for *PNR*. But do please rein yourself in a bit and do not exceed 4,000 words. If you could encourage James Tate to send us a story or two I would be grateful and also if you could suggest to Harry Mathews that he send us 'Armenian papers', we would be delighted to run them.[15]

Please remember me to Doug Crase. I hope to see him when I am over. You are being paid in *PN Review* 47 for your Ginzburg poem, I believe. Or something else. I cannot remember.

Delighted that you will be reviewing for the *New York Times*, that you are giving readings for such huge fees and that there is the possibility of employment. If you would like to pay me for your air ticket in fragments, please do so. I'll leave it to you! And I hope that Texas proves a delightful experience.

When I come to New York, I hope I will coincide with one of your literary evenings. I could do with a bit of literature after all the number work I have been doing.

A proper and human letter will follow eventually. In the meantime, affectionate regards from everyone at Carcanet.

Yours ever,
Michael

*

I cannot remember where I first encountered John Ash's poems and person. It might even have been a submission of poems, though it is not like John to submit work: he waits to be asked. Perhaps we met at an event in Manchester and I asked him. It is not impossible that he had been in correspondence with John Ashbery and that John recommended him to me, or me to him. I believe the poem that clinched my enthusiasm and led to my long-term commitment to his writing was 'An Idyll for Ellie and Ruth', published in *PN Review* in 1984, which he mischievously omitted from his 1996 *Selected Poems*. The first poem by him that I published was 'The Stranger in the Corridor' with its 'bonkers' epigraph from Coleridge, 'O sole, true Something – This!...'

The four years that I knew him when he lived in Manchester, we lunched most weeks and he was a wonderful, if expensive, education in contemporary literature, music and much else. When he went to New York he opened a window on a world in which some of my favourite poets moved, and when I visited New York he pulled back the curtain just a little so I could see in.

His sudden, to say the least reluctant, return to Manchester from Istanbul in 2017 was a trauma from which he has been making a gradual but decisive recovery, and he has started writing poems again, the first of which, 'After Long Absence', re-inhabits his experience of near-death 'in the country of my sickness'. One has a sense that other climates have marked his card.

NOTES

1. Harry (the Great) refers to Harry Mathews (1930–2017), experimental prose and poetry writer, and translator, who divided his time between Paris, New York and Key West. His new novel was *Cigarettes*. Carcanet re-published *The Sinking of the Odradek Stadium* in 1985, and three more of his novels in paperback in 1988: *Cigarettes*, *The Conversions* and *Tlooth*. *A Mid-Season Sky: poems 1954–1991* was published in 1992, with John Ashbery quoted in the catalogue: 'His poetry is both bizarre and deeply moving.'

2. Pam Heaton was MNS's secretary and Carcanet's general administrator from 1981 until the early 2000s. She was invaluable.

3. Michael Freeman began working for Carcanet in 1983 on a voluntary basis and then became the fiction reader and editor until 1993. Ash did not review anything by Calvino in *PN Review*, although he mentions the Italian author in his long essay 'Reading New York', *PN Review* 54 (March–April 1987).

4. Alain Robbe-Grillet (1922–2008), French writer and film-maker, associated with the *nouveau roman* (new novel) writers of the 1960s, rather than the *nouvelle vague* (new wave) of film-makers of the same period.

5. Oliver Reynolds (b. 1957), poet and critic, whose first collection, *Skevington's Daughter*, was published in 1985 by Faber & Faber, where Craig Raine was the poetry editor. Reynolds has published four further collections.

6. James Fenton (b. 1949), poet, journalist and literary critic

(Oxford Professor of Poetry 1994-99), reviewed Ashbery's *Selected Poems* for the *New York Times* on 29 December 1985 under the heading 'Getting Rid of the Burden of Sense'. He wrote:

> On the one hand we have the poet as he presents himself to the interviewer and at times in the poems – easy-going, anti-didactic, aware of the haphazard nature of life and consciousness, undemanding of our attention. On the other hand, in sharp contrast, we have the exorbitantly demanding poet, asking of the reader impossible feats of attention, taxing our patience, yielding only a minimum of reward, parsimonious with clarity, hedged about with obscurity and nevertheless always hinting at a profundity of philosophical insight which is designed to make a non-philosopher uneasy. The entirely permissive poet and the overbearing ego at one and the same time. It is a highly complex performance.

He concluded the review by saying that 'I still respect the talent, but not the resort to the sad shadows.' Marjorie Perloff quoted from this review as an example of 'What we don't talk about when we talk about poetry' in her article of that name published in *PN Review* (May-June 1997).

7. Doug Crase (b. 1944), American poet and critic, is best known for his volume of poetry *The Revisionist* (Little, Brown & Co.,1981). He and his husband are the title couple in James Schuyler's poem 'Dining Out with Doug and Frank'. Carcanet published *The Revisionist and The Astropastorals* in 2019.

8. Ash's article 'The Poet's Grandmother and other dilemmas', on Christopher Middleton's essay collection *The Pursuit of the Kingfisher* , was published in *PN Review* 47 (January-February 1986). James Merrill (1926–95) was one of the leading American poets of his generation. 'On Being Bronze', Ash's enthusiastic review of Merrill's collection *Late Settings*, was published in *PN Review* 49 (May–June 1986). Robin

Holloway (b.1943), English composer, academic and writer, was featured in Ash's long essay 'Music and Literature', published in *PN Review* 51 (September-October 1986).

9. Kenneth Koch (1925–2002), poet, playwright and academic, prominent member of the New York School of poets. Carcanet published his *Selected Poems* in 1991, and his last collection, *One Train*, in 1997 (originally published by Knopf in 1994).

10. Christopher Middleton, poet, translator and academic – see below, pp.341 ff.

11. Maggie Paley (b.1939), American novelist and literary journalist; Darragh Park (1939–2009), an American artist best known for his book-cover illustrations, was also the literary executor of James Schuyler. Eugene Richie and Rosanne Wasserman started publishing chapbooks for poets reading at the Intuflo series in NY in the late 1980s, and went on to edit Ashbery's translations from French: *Collected French Translations: poetry* and *Collected French Translations: prose* (Farrar, Straus & Giroux, 2014), published in paperback by Carcanet in the same year. (See their interview at https://www.wordswithoutborders.org/dispatches/article/eugene-richie-rosanne-wasserman-on-john-ashbery-part-one, accessed 2 March 2019). (Frederick) Ted Castle (1938–2006) was an experimental novelist and New York art critic. In 1969 he co-founded the Vanishing Rotating Triangle Press, which lasted about ten years and published work by John Ashbery, Guy Debord and the first two novels of Kathy Acker.

12. Czeslaw Miłosz (1911–2004) and William Gass (1924–2017) were both Carcanet authors; Gass with just one book, *On Being Blue: a philosophical inquiry*, published in 1979. Carcanet published six of Miłosz's books, beginning with the poetry collection *Bells in Winter* in 1980, the year he was awarded the Nobel Prize for Literature, and ending with *Facing the River: new poems* in 1995. Elizabeth Hardwick (1916–2007), American novelist and critic, second wife of Robert Lowell;

Barbara Epstein (1928–2006), literary editor and co-founder of the *New York Review of Books*.

13. James Schuyler (1923–1991), a central figure in the New York School of poets; Carcanet indeed held out for a *Selected Poems*, first published by Farrar Straus Giroux in 1988, and in the UK in 1990.

14. In the letter from James Fenton printed in *Letters to an Editor* (pp.257–8), written in 1989, he complains that the *TLS* publishes 'fatuous attacks' on what he is 'supposed to represent' and then hopes to lure him into replying. 'But – Ashbery apart – I haven't the foggiest notion of what they're on about. And I resent the unexamined assumption that it was wrong of me when asked to say what I thought about Ashbery.' He remembers from their Oxford days a feeling that everyone who wrote poetry tended to form into camps and to accuse the other camps of missing the point. People had, for instance, rival sets of American heroes – but perhaps they shared a feeling that American poetry was superior to anything in England. Fenton goes on to suggest what counts as 'seriousness' in poetry in the late 1980s; one aspect is 'anything that can be attributed to the Wallace Stevens tradition? Poor Stevens! Once we were allowed to <u>enjoy</u> him. (Or: some of us were.)'

15. Ash does not appear to have reviewed Ashbery's *Selected Poems* for *PN Review*. James Tate (1943–2015), author of over twenty poetry collections, was teaching creative writing at the University of Massachusetts at Amherst at this period. Carcanet was his first British publisher, issuing his Pulitzer Prize-winning *Selected Poems* in 1997. Neither his stories, nor Harry Mathews's 'Armenian Papers' appeared in *PN Review*.

THE YEAR IN BOOKS

Henri Alain-Fournier, *Towards the Lost Domain: Letters from London 1905*, translated by W.J. Strachan

David Arkell, *Alain-Fournier: A Brief Life*

John Ashbery, *Selected Poems*

Christopher Barker, *Portraits of Poets*, edited by Sebastian Barker

Emmanuel Bove, *My Friends*, translated by Janet Louth

Christine Brooke-Rose, *Omnibus: Out, Such, Between & Thru*

Christine Brooke-Rose, *Xorandor*

Christopher Caudwell, *Collected Poems: 1924-1936*, edited by Alan Young

Paul Celan, *Collected Prose*, translated by Rosmarie Waldrop

John Cornford, *Collected Writings*, edited by Jonathan Galassi

George Crabbe, *Selected Poems*, edited by Jem Poster

Ford Madox Ford, *The Ford Madox Ford Reader*, edited by Sondra Stang

Natalia Ginzburg, *The City and the House*, translated by Dick Davis

Jon Glover, *Our Photographs*

Michael Hamburger, *After the Second Flood: essays on post-war German literature*

A.D. Hope, *Selected Poems*, edited by Ruth Morse

Peter Hoyle, *Brantwood: The Story of an Obsession*

Elizabeth Jennings, *Collected Poems*

Gabriel Josipovici, *Contre-Jour: a triptych after Pierre Bonnard*

Karl Kraus, *Half-Truths and One-and-a-Half Truths: selected aphorisms*, translated by Harry Zohn

Clarice Lispector, *The Foreign Legion*, translated by Giovanni Pontiero

Clarice Lispector, *The Hour of the Star*, translated by Giovanni Pontiero

Christopher Middleton, *Two Horse Wagon Going By*

Les Murray, *Selected Poems*

Pier Paolo Pasolini, *The Ragazzi*, translated by Emile Capouya

Charles Péguy, *The Mystery of the Charity of Joan of Arc*, translated by Jeffrey Wainwright

Leonardo Sciascia, *Sicilian Uncles*, translated by N.S. Thompson

Abdelhak Serhane, *Messaouda*, translated by Mark Thompson

Iain Crichton Smith, *A Life*
Virgil, *The Aeneid*, translated by C.H. Sisson
Val Warner, *Before Lunch*
Andrew Waterman, *Selected Poems*
Daniel Weissbort, *Leaseholder: new and selected poems*
Dieter Wellershoff, *Winner Takes All*, translated by Paul Knight
Robert Wells, *Selected Poems*

1987

In the 1980s Carcanet branched out into fiction, both in English and in translation, with a particular emphasis on Italian fiction. Stuart Hood (1915–2011), a Scottish novelist and translator, also an influential television executive and producer, an academic and a radical activist, published his novel *A Storm from Paradise* with Carcanet in 1986. He translated Pasolini's essays and Dino Buzzati's novel *The Tartar Steppe* (reprinted by Carcanet in 1985). The story of his wartime experiences as a POW and then as a resistance leader in Italy had first been published as *Pebbles in My Skull* in 1963, and was reissued as *Carlino* by Carcanet in 1985.[1]

FROM STUART HOOD
Brighton
28 January 1987

Dear Michael,

You will be pleased to know that on Monday I handed the MS of Busi into the London office of Carcanet.[2] I hope you like it.

This was one of the most difficult translations I have ever tackled. Reasons: Busi's love of oxymorons; his way of slipping in and out of realism; the occasionally baroque nature of his style. The problem was how to translate rather than paraphrase or interpret.

There are (as you will see) a couple of points where I cannot 'read' him and have asked him for elucidations. He is not averse to a certain mystification of the reader!

To translate a book is to submit it to a severe test in that one lives with it, dissects it, finds oneself drawn into a critical examination of the author's thought processes. I found that *Seminar on Youth* stood up to the test so that it was with regret that I finished the work.

I seem to remember Mike saying that there had been an interesting notice of the book in the *TLS* (?).

I wonder whether he has a photocopy of the article. It would interest me.

When shall we talk about *The Upper Hand*?[3]

All best wishes for 1987,

Yours,

Stuart

FROM MICHAEL SCHMIDT

Manchester

2 February 1987

Dear Stuart,

I started reading the translation of the Busi on the train back from London on Monday with considerable puzzlement and fascination. It is a very difficult text and I feel a prefatory note by you explaining some of the difficulties of style might deflect certain forms of mis-reading. I have not yet finished it. I can see how impossible the task must have been, not least because of the sentence structure. I have queried one or two places where the oxymorons seem to me unfunctional – or at least where there may be excessive use of negatives, for example six which makes three affirmatives unless I am mistaken!

I think you have done a very heroic job and I expect, by the time I have completed the reading, that I will like the book as much as you do at the end of the task of translation.

I will ask Mike to send you a copy of the *TLS* review.

Let us get together and talk about 'The Upper Hand' as soon as we can. February is more or less a write-off now but March would be a good time. Indeed we may have to talk about it in February, come to think of it, given the publication schedule. Perhaps we could be in touch some time during the next week?

With every good wish,

Michael

FROM STUART HOOD

Brighton

1 May 1987

Dear Michael,

Appropriate greetings for May Day!

You may remember that Gini Alhadeff in New York got on to me through Carcanet and expressed interest in some excerpts from Busi.[4] I sent her the passages in which she was interested and thought you might be cheered – as I was – to have her reactions. She writes: I am still reeling from the beauty of your translations of Busi. I know how difficult it must have been but you really do find his voice in English and it is <u>him</u>. It felt precisely as though I were re-reading it in Italian.

Since we spoke last Busi has answered some of my outstanding queries.[5] When we meet to look at the MS I can insert the answers.

All best wishes,

Stuart

PS The Scottish Arts Council event went off painlessly in John Smith's in Glasgow.[6] The sticker you had managed to get on to the copies on display impressed everyone!

PPS Am deep in various Italian authors. Brancati is interesting and funny! At least he makes me laugh. Will be reporting soon.

FROM MICHAEL SCHMIDT
Manchester
16 July 1987

Dear Stuart,

I will shortly be sending you a photocopy of Octavio's speech and some other material from the Congress.[7] I was very grateful for your telephone call. The thing that interested me with Vargas Llosa was the nature of his speech to the Congress. He was one of the few writers who took the occasion to make, as it were, an aesthetic statement which was not entirely bound up with ethics and politics. Not that his speech was without its political dimension. Part of that political dimension was in the relative absence of ideological content. In fact, it was a beautifully structured talk and very trite in content. In the television debate which I mentioned, the intellectuals generally played up to Paz[,] and Semprún and Vargas Llosa were the main contributors.[8] Vargas Llosa was hauled over the coals by Octavio because of his rather sentimental meliorism and one had the feeling that while Paz had lived his politics, with some rather devastating consequences in his own life, Vargas Llosa, despite the turbulence of Peru, had somehow become too westernised and had forgotten the lessons [of] his own history and the history of his continent.[9] It was rather like seeing Madero in conversation with Porfirio Diaz![10] You know which is the greater of the two!

I will do my best to see Busi and make him feel less unloved,
though not more loved I hope!

Yours ever,
Michael

*

Stuart Hood wrote one of the most powerful Italian books
we published, the memoir of his time in Italy after being
released from POW camp in 1943, his time in the hills
among the peasants and the Partisans. It was a world familiar
to me from Carlo Levi's *Christ Stopped at Eboli* and Natalia
Ginzburg's *All Our Yesterdays,* as well as from Hood's own
translation of Dino Buzzati's *The Tartar Steppe* – probably the
best novel Carcanet published – and the fact that *Carlino* can
be mentioned unapologetically in the company of those books
says something about the quality of Hood as a memoirist.
He was also one of that great, unostentatious and dedicated
generation of translators that made English readers aware of
the modern world. His politics were an aspect of his culture.

His translation of Busi was not without its comic side: the
author came to visit the translator and was arrested for what he
described as an Oscar Wilde crime in the public conveniences
at Oxford Circus. It appears he had propositioned a policeman.
He insisted on returning to London for the hearing of his
case and asked me to appear as a character witness. I only met
him when I got to court, and the proceedings were comically
English. A representative of the gay press was there (Busi had
given a gay newspaper quite a candid interview, including
statistics of how many sexual encounters he had had), hoping
for an exemplary scandal. But the magistrate was disobliging.
He proved sympathetic to the accused and said in a tone
which Aldo might have chosen to misread as flirtatious, 'Well,
Mr Busi, I'd like to give you an unconditional discharge...'

Stuart Hood and I drifted apart, as I remember, when I turned down a novel he had written.

NOTES

1. Dino Buzzati (1906–72), Italian novelist and journalist, is best known for *Il deserto dei Tartari* (1940), originally published in English in 1952, and widely acclaimed on its Carcanet reissue.

2. *Seminario sulla gioventù* was the first novel by Aldo Busi (b. 1948); the *New York Times* reviewer of the American edition (published by Farrar, Straus in 1989) suggested that he had 'come to represent the successful misfit, the all-too-articulate, exhibitionistic incarnation of marginality and iconoclasm in a country where flamboyance has long been a sure ticket to fame and fortune.' Hood translated two more of Busi's books, which were published by Faber and Faber: *Sodomies in Elevenpoint* and *Uses and Abuses: journeys, sleepwalkings and fool's errands.*

3. Hood had written to MNS in 1984 that he was turning over 'the thought of another book on the Blunt generation (to which I belong). I have always been interested in the mole – not in the thriller sense – but in the sense of the man or woman who leads the schizoid existence required for the penetration of an organisation, whether it be a governmental one or a left-wing one.' *The Upper Hand* was published in 1987.

4. The writer and translator Gini Alhadeff founded and edited *Normal: a quarterly of art and ideas,* published by Rizzoli; the first issues came out in 1986, so she may have been considering an excerpt for the magazine.

5. Busi had written to MNS the previous year to ask him to make the translator aware 'that I am totally at his disposal'; as a translator himself, he would 'understand any, but really any, demand of explanation (slang, two-level-meaning of sentences etc.).' He was then working on *Sodomie in Corpo 11,* 'a demented essay on literary critics and literary sex' (26 May 1986).

6. Hood was awarded the Royal Bank of Scotland/Saltire
   Society Scottish Book of the Year for *A Storm from Paradise*.
   The *Glasgow Herald* headlined an article by one of the judges,
   Alan Taylor: 'Marxist view wins premier book award' and
   the subhead began: 'A major Scottish book award has been
   given, after much animated debate, to a seventy-one-year-old,
   little known author born in Edzell, Tayside' (22 November
   1986). This event would have been a reading at John Smith's
   bookshop, once a Glasgow landmark in St Vincent Street
   (closed down in 2000).

7. The International Congress of Intellectuals and Writers was
   held in Valencia in June 1987, the fiftieth anniversary of the
   Second International Congress of Writers held in Valencia,
   Madrid and Barcelona during the Spanish Civil War, with
   a later session in Paris. The writers Stephen Spender, André
   Malraux, Langston Hughes and Pablo Neruda were among
   the participating delegates of the 1937 Congress, as was Sylvia
   Townsend Warner. MNS reported on the 1987 event for the
   BBC in a programme broadcast on 3 July, and printed in *PN
   Review* 59 (January–February 1988).

8. MNS described the television debate in his report:
   > Paz was Voltaire, enlightened, devil's advocate, corrective,
   > rejecting the pieties of progress and the seductions of
   > fashionable politics. Vargas Llosa emerged as a very young
   > man, charming but intellectually out of his depth. Semprún,
   > who fought in the French resistance and spent years in a
   > German concentration camp, was emancipated from the
   > Communist Party but still played by its rules. This was a
   > brilliant confrontation of rhetorical styles. It also brought the
   > Congress into focus – a focus it never achieved in its own
   > debates.

9. The Peruvian novelist Vargas Llosa (b. 1936) was already
   famous in 1983 when he was asked by the Peruvian President
   to sit on the Investigatory Commission into the killing of

eight journalists in the village of Uchuraccay, and was widely criticised after its findings were released.

10. Francisco Madero challenged the Mexican President Porfirio Diaz (running for his sixth re-election) in the elections of 1910, as a candidate seeking social justice and reform. Madero was elected President but assassinated in 1913, aged 39.

THE YEAR IN BOOKS

John Ash, *Disbelief*

John Ashbery and James Schuyler, *A Nest of Ninnies*

Sebastian Barry, *The Engine of Owl-Light*

Eavan Boland, *The Journey and Other Poems*

Nicolas Bouvier, *The Scorpion Fish*, translated by Robyn Marsack

Emmanuel Bove, *Armand*, translated by Janet Louth

Charles Boyle, *Sleeping Rough*

Aldo Busi, *Seminar on Youth*, translated by Stuart Hood

Dino Buzzati, *A Love Affair*, translated by Joseph Green

Arthur Hugh Clough, *Selected Poems*, edited by Shirley Chew

Andrew Crozier and Tim Longville (eds), *A Various Art*

Anne Finch, Countess of Winchilsea, *Selected Poems*, edited by Denys Thompson

Natalia Ginzburg, *Valentino & Sagittarius*, translated by Avril Bardoni

Natalia Ginzburg, *The Manzoni Family*, translated by Marie Evans

Guido Gozzano, *The Colloquies and Selected Letters*, translated by J. G. Nichols

Ivor Gurney, *Severn and Somme & War's Embers*, edited by R.K.R. Thornton

Michael Hartnett, *Collected Poems: Volume II*

Denis Hirson, *The House Next Door to Africa*

Gert Hoffman, *Our Conquest*, translated by Christopher Middleton

Molly Holden, *Selected Poems*, edited by Simon Curtis

Stuart Hood, *The Upper Hand*

Robinson Jeffers, *Selected Poems*, edited by Colin Falck

Gabriel Josipovici, *In the Fertile Land*

Frank Kuppner, *The Intelligent Observation of Naked Women*

Djanet Lachmet, *Lallia (Le Cowboy)*, translated by Janet Still

Jorge Lewinski, *Portrait of the Artist: twenty-five years of British art*

Grevel Lindop, *Tourists*

Richard Lovelace, *Selected Poems*, edited by Gerald Hammond

Cecily Mackworth, *Ends of the World*

Brian Maidment, *The Poorhouse Fugitives: self-taught poets and poetry in Victorian Britain*

Ian McMillan, *Selected Poems*

Alistair Niven (ed), *Under Another Sky: The Commonwealth Poetry Prize Anthology*

Octavio Paz, *On Poets and Others*, translated by Michael Schmidt

Umberto Saba, *Ernesto*, translated by Mark Thompson

Delmore Schwartz, *The Ego is Always at the Wheel: bagatelles*, edited by Robert Phillips

Leonardo Sciascia, *The Moro Affair & The Mystery of Majorana*, translated by Sasha Rabinovitch

Leonardo Sciascia, *One Way or Another*, translated by Sasha Rabinovitch

Sir Philip Sidney, *Selected Writings of Sir Philip Sidney*, edited by Richard Dutton

C.H. Sisson, *God Bless Karl Marx!*

Jon Stallworthy (ed), *First Lines: Poems Written in Youth from Herbert to Heaney*

Klaus Wagenbach, *Franz Kafka: pictures of a life*

Michael Westlake, *Imaginary Women*

Malachi Whitaker, *And So Did I*

William Carlos Williams, *Collected Poems volume I 1909–1939*, edited by A.Walton Litz and Christopher MacGowan

1988

Correspondence between MNS and Charles Hobday, Edgell Rickword's biographer, is more revealing of the Press than letters from Rickword himself, although three very genial ones from the 1970s are printed in *Letters to an Editor*. Rickword (1898–1982), who served in the First World War (losing one eye), was a poet, critic and journalist, and editor of the most influential literary journal of the 1920s, *The Calendar of Modern Letters*. He joined the Communist Party in 1934, and left it quietly after the events of 1956. He was bemused to see that his famous poem of the 1930s, 'To the Wife of a Non-Interventionist Statesman', was published in a Polish anthology in 1964 under the name Edgell Rickwordova, along with poems by E. Sitwellova and E. Jenningsova. He was interviewed by MNS and Alan Young for the first issue of *Poetry Nation*.

FROM CHARLES HOBDAY
London
21 November 1988

Dear Mr Schmidt,

I enclose Chapter XV, which has been delayed by one correspondent's delay in sending me some information I needed. I'm still finding scraps of Edgell's writing – there's a nice couplet on p.476, despite the grammatical slip.[1]

Chapter XVI (the last) is well on its way. I would be grateful for any information you can let me have on your own relations with Edgell – how you first came across his work, personal impressions etc.

Yours sincerely,
Charles Hobday

FROM MICHAEL SCHMIDT
Manchester
29 November 1988

Dear Mr Hobday,

Thank you for your letter of 23rd November. I am delighted that we are so near the happy conclusion of the book. I will then look forward to going through it with you in some detail.

The information I can give you about my meetings with Edgell is not copious. I first heard of him from Frank Kermode and Ian Hamilton when Eric Walter White was considering the possibility of launching a new literary journal under Arts Council patronage.[2] Eric invited Edgell as one of the most distinguished living editors that he could think of and Kermode as one-time editor of *Encounter* to dine with me and Hamilton who at that time was still editing *The Review*.

I believe that Eric White's idea was to have an editorial board consisting of Edgell, Frank and Ian. This would have given credibility of an unusual quality to a new journal. In the event, of course, the money was given to Hamilton and the magazine that resulted was *The New Review* with its controversial, chequered and finally fatal history.

Some time after this meeting – which I find hard to date though it must have occurred in 1970 or 1969 – I moved to Manchester where I undertook my academic post. I met Alan Young who became a close friend. He and I spent some time discussing Edgell's work and when Brian Cox and I had launched our new magazine, *Poetry Nation* as it then was, we – Alan Young and I – decided that it would be sensible to interview Edgell because at that time the orientation of the magazine was Marxising if not Marxist. Edgell was very helpful. The interview you have read. It was severely edited from a rather rough tape made at Beatrix's house in London.[3]

Thereafter I exchanged a number of letters with Edgell, assembling a more or less complete collection of his books (and translations) and developed so keen an enthusiasm for his early prose – the work collected in the first volume of criticism – and for his poems that I must have regarded myself as something of a disciple, even though my own politics were moving in the opposite direction from Edgell's. He was enormously generous to me and I think appreciated the quality of my commitment to his work – always as it were mediated through Alan Young who was my only contact with Edgell. I did visit him in Colchester on one occasion and we went to the sea together. I visited him in London several times and he managed to come to most of our Carcanet parties and festivities in London. There are one or two nice photographs of him in 1973 and later on as well.

I wrote a long poem about him which is in all likelihood un-useful to you. I am sure that Alan Young, with whom you have no doubt been in touch, would be able to tell you much more than I am able to do. The problem with being a disciple is that an unrealistic glow attaches to the chosen mentor and to the period of one's life which one found oneself rooting one's certainties in the life and work of an older, wiser man.

With best wishes,
Michael

FROM CHARLES HOBDAY
London
2 December 1988

Dear Mr Schmidt,

Thank you for your very interesting letter of November 29. I think you have misdated your first meeting with Edgell. By a coincidence I received your letter the day after a number of photocopies of his letters to Jack Beeching arrived, one of which contains this passage: 'Frank Kermode informed us (I met him at Eric White's) that the Arts Council is preparing to back a Lit. Mag. And that there will be a Trust to run it.'[4] That was evidently the occasion when you met him, and the letter is dated October 16, 1972.

I don't know if you're aware that between 1971 and 1974 Edgell, Arnold Rattenbury, Roy Fuller and later William Empson were involved in a plan to launch a magazine to be called 'The New Calendar', with Edgell as one of the editors.[5]

The Arts Council's plan inevitably complicated matters, and 'The New Calendar' seems finally to have failed to appear because of its inability to find a financial backer and the inflation of 1973–4.

Edgell doesn't mention you in connection with that particular occasion, but you'll be pleased to hear that his references to you and Carcanet in later letters are rather flattering.[6]

I was interested in your remark that *Poetry Nation* was 'Marxising' in its early days. Edgell described you and your associates at Carcanet in 1974 as 'good lads, but only mildly pro-Marxist at present'. That ties in with what has struck me about Carcanet, that you have almost a corner in Marxist poets (Edgell, Sylvia Townsend Warner, Cornford, Caudwell), while publishing others who are more or less at the opposite extreme politically, such as Wyndham Lewis and Sisson.[7] (No aspersion on Sisson is intended; I greatly admire his poetry, if not his politics.)

Talking of Marxist poets, have you ever read Randall Swingler's work?[8] I think he has been shamefully neglected, especially his war poems in *The Years of Anger*. A selection might be worth considering. I believe his daughter has a mass of unpublished poems which may repay examination.

I've just noticed one of Edgell's references to Carcanet which may amuse you: 'I think Carcanet must be supported. It would be fine to have a cultural revival based on Manchester instead of Oxbridge. But my god, the city is a ghastly dump.'

Yours sincerely,
Charles Hobday

FROM MICHAEL SCHMIDT
Manchester
12 December 1988

Dear Mr Hobday,

Thank you very much indeed for your letter of 2nd December. It is useful to have that date confirmed. My view was that it was Eric White's initiative and I did not realise that ranked against the Ian Hamilton brigade was so massive and impressive a potential magazine which did not come to fruition. Probably one of the larger misfortunes of recent literary life in this country.

The reason Carcanet and *PN Review* started off as it were on the Left has much to do with my own politics at the time. I was, I suppose, as an activist in 1968 (and a member of the SDS at Harvard!) quite left-wing.[9] At Oxford I remained to a degree active, to the degree that I did not enjoy myself very much in the traditional areas or indeed in the radical areas

I entered. In my last year I began to be inoculated against the Left by having Terry Eagleton as a tutor at Wadham.[10] I moved to Manchester and set up *PN Review* (initially *Poetry Nation*) with Brian Cox, who has never been as far on the Right as has been assumed and was assumed at the time. I was still very interested in Marxist criticism which is why I described the magazine as 'Marxising' rather than 'Marxist'. I don't suppose I was ever a thoroughgoing Marxist. My move to the Right was in response to various acts including the introduction of the closed shop,[11] my growing familiarity with the work of Sisson and Davie and a general sense that the English Left was losing its direction after the 1960s, not least in the sphere of cultural politics.

I was also intolerant of the intolerance of the Left to major writers of the Right whose work is essential, it seems to me, to the tradition. Thus when Carcanet – at least in the form of its Managing Director – moved 'to the Right' this did not affect my literary judgements that much. I am fascinated by the work of Cornford and was intrigued by Caudwell. The work of Edwin Morgan, Christopher Middleton and others intrigued and enriched me too much not to publish it. I think I have never published a book for political reasons nor not published a book for political reasons – this is the 'freedom' my 'politics' gives me. It is interesting that among the people who most firmly advocated that we should publish the work of Edgell Rickword was C.H. Sisson, who himself had written on Rickword in his book on modern poetry. And Sisson, too, has urged me to publish a number of other volumes which could not by any stretch of the imagination be considered on the Right: Botho Strauss, Jean Louis Baghio'o, Abdelhak Serhane, Emmanuel Bove and of course Ford Madox Ford.[12] His enthusiasm for Lewis is rather less pronounced now than it was but he did help me to put those programmes together too, of course.

I was urged to publish Randall Swingler's poetry by Edgell but never read it. He was always on the verge of sending me copies. Certainly it is not something I would turn down sight unseen. And if you had a 'selected', or a collection you think I might possibly read – *The Years of Anger* perhaps? – I would be very happy to do so.

True, Edgell did not like Manchester very much. Like Beatrix, he had a decadent taste for the picturesque! You Southerners are all the same!

Warm regards,
Michael

NOTES

1. Carcanet had published Rickword's *Essays and Opinions 1921–1931*, edited by Alan Young (1974), *Behind the Eyes: collected poems and translations* (1976), and *Literature in Society: essays and opinions II, 1931-1978* (1978). *Edgell Rickword: a poet at war* was published in 1989. Its author, the journalist Charles Hobday (1917-2005), was also a poet, and had served on the editorial board of the communist literary journal *Our Time*, edited by Rickword. He may have been referring to the couplet 'I have slept in all the beds in all the world / And seen dawn from the beggar's gutter', which he quotes in the penultimate chapter of the biography.

2. Frank Kermode (1919–2010), influential literary critic and editor of the Fontana Modern masters series of introductions to new thinkers, author of over fifty books and dozens of essays. He was on the editorial board of *Encounter*, co-editor from 1965, but resigned less than two years later when the CIA's funding the magazine was revealed. Ian Hamilton, see p.51. Eric Walter White (1905–86) was the first Literature Director of the Arts Council of Great Britain; Charles Osborne's affectionate obituary for him was published in *PN Review* 49 (May–June 1986).

3. Beatrix Hammarling (née Moore) was Rickword's partner from 1965 until his death; they lived in her house in London but spent the weekends at his in Halstead, near Colchester. She was Beatrix Potter's god-daughter.

4. Jack Beeching (1922–2001), poet, historian, novelist and journalist, was also a board member and contributor to *Our Time*. He spent much of his working life in France and Spain. A selection of his poems was included in *Penguin Modern Poets* 16. Carcanet very nearly published a collection by him.

5. Arnold Rattenbury (1921–2007), poet and exhibition designer. The *Guardian* obituarist comments that Rattenbury's work for *Our Time* 'brought him into contact with such luminaries as Montagu Slater, Randall Swingler, Sylvia Townsend Warner [...] and, most significantly, the novelist Patrick Hamilton, to whose rooms in The Albany, Piccadilly, he was regularly dispatched for funds when money at *Our Time* ran out' (John Lucas, *The Guardian*, 30 July 2007).
   Roy Fuller (1912–1991), poet, novelist and solicitor, Professor of Poetry at Oxford. Carcanet published his *Crime Omnibus* in 1993; his *Selected Poems* in 2012, edited by his son John Fuller, poet, publisher, and Fellow in English at Magdalen College, Oxford.
   William Empson (1906–84), poet and critic, author of the seminal *Seven Types of Ambiguity: a study of its effects on English verse* (1930). G.S. Fraser wrote that his books and essays had become 'part of the furniture of any good English or American critic's mind' (in *Great Writers of the English Language: Poets*).

6. In his biography, Hobday quotes from a letter from Rickword to David Holbrook about MNS: 'He is both intelligent and humorous, an ideal combination, and works like a nuclear reaction' (p.288).

7. John Cornford (1915–1936), poet, who joined the Communist Party as an undergraduate at Cambridge, worked for the Communist Party of GB from 1933. He served with the

International Brigades in the defence of Madrid in 1936 and was killed near Cordoba at the end of that year. Carcanet issued *Understand the Weapon, Understand the Wound: selected writings of John Cornford, with some letters of Frances Cornford*, edited by Jonathan Galassi, in 1976, and in a revised edition in 2016.

Christopher Caudwell was the pseudonym of Christopher St John Sprigg (1907–37). He left school at fifteen and became a reporter on the *Yorkshire Observer*. A Marxist writer and poet, also a member of the Communist Party of GB, he was killed in action in the Spanish Civil War at the battle of the Jarama river. Much of his writing was published posthumously. Alan Young edited his *Collected Poems* for Carcanet (1986).

8. Randall Swingler (1909–67), poet, librettist and literary journalist, was a member of the Communist Party of GB 1934–56. He was the Literary Editor of the *Daily Worker* and involved in setting up various journals, including *Our Time*. His *Selected Poems* were published in 2000 by Trent Editions (Nottingham Trent University), edited by Andy Croft, who also wrote his biography.

9. Students for a Democratic Society (SDS) was founded at Ann Arbor, Michigan, in 1960 and grew rapidly across American university campuses in the mid-1960s, its activism fuelled by opposition to the Vietnam War. It wound down in the early 1970s.

10. Terry Eagleton (b. 1943), literary theorist and critic, whose widely read *Literary Theory: an introduction* (1983) is rooted in Marxist tradition. He taught at Wadham College, Oxford, 1969–89, and in 2001 became John Edward Taylor Professor of Cultural Theory at the University of Manchester.

11. A 'closed shop' is a union agreement by which an employer agrees to hire union members only and employees must maintain continuous membership of their union to remain employed. This was made illegal in the UK after the

introduction of the Employment Act 1990.

12. Botho Strauss (b. 1944), German playwright and novelist;
his novel *Tumult*, translated by Michael Hulse, was published
by Carcanet in 1984. The catalogue entry refers to 'his
controversial play *Great and Small*, starring Glenda Jackson',
which was staged in London in 1983; it was probably
optimistic to think that Strauss' name had 'become familiar in
Britain' as a result.

Jean Louis Baghio'o was the pseudonym of Victor Jean-Louis
(1910–94), born in Martinique, and member of the French
Resistance. He was a sound engineer for radio and cinema.
His strongly anti-colonialist novel set in Guadeloupe, *Le
Flamboyant à fleurs bleues*, won the Prix des Caraïbes in 1975,
and was translated for Carcanet by Stephen Romer (*The Blue
Flame-tree*, 1985).

Abdelhak Serhane (b. 1950) grew up in the Middle Atlas
region of Morocco, and his autobiographical novel *Messaouda*
gives his view of the decline of peasant culture and the
brutality of French colonial domination in the 1950s. It was
translated from the French for Carcanet by Mark Thompson
and published in 1986.

Emmanuel Bove (1898–1945), French journalist and novelist
of no particular political complexion, was admired by Rilke
and Beckett. Carcanet published *My Friends* (*Mes Amis*, 1924)
– described by Bove as a 'novel of impoverished solitude' – in
1986 and *Armand* (1927) in 1987, both translated by Janet
Louth.

Ford Madox Ford (1873-1939) wrote over eighty books,
and Carcanet began to republish a number of them at
Sisson's urging, beginning with *The Rash Act* in 1982, with an
introduction by Sisson. *The Ford Madox Ford Reader*, edited by
Sondra Stang, came out in 1985, introducing and representing
'the no longer neglected work of a most civilised, brilliant and
stimulating author', as the catalogue described it. Carcanet has

twenty of Ford's books on its list, including the four volumes of his masterpiece *Parade's End* and a new *Selected Poems*, edited by Max Saunders (2003).

THE YEAR IN BOOKS

John Ashbery, *April Galleons*

John Ashbery, *Three Plays*

Patricia Beer, *Collected Poems*

Patricia Beer, *Moon's Ottery*

Sujata Bhatt, *Brunizem*

Alison Brackenbury, *Christmas Roses and Other Poems*

John Burnside, *The Hoop*

Mary Butts, *The Crystal Cabinet: my childhood at Salterns*, foreword by Camilla Bagg and afterword by Barbara Wagstaff

Gabriele D'Annunzio, *Halcyon*, translated by J.G. Nichols

Donald Davie, *To Scorch or Freeze*

Yury Dombrovsky, *The Keeper of Antiquities*, translated by Michael Glenny

Caradoc Evans, *Nothing to Pay*, afterword by John Harris

Ford Madox Ford, *Ladies Whose Bright Eyes*, afterword by C.H. Sisson

Roy Fuller, *Crime Omnibus*

Natalia Ginzburg, *Family*, translated by Beryl Stockman

Oliver Goldsmith, *Selected Poems*, edited by John Lucas

Michael Hamburger, *Selected Poems*

John Heath-Stubbs, *Collected Poems 1943–1987*

P.J. Kavanagh, *People and Places: a selection 1975–1987*

Edward Lear, *Edward Lear's Tennyson*, edited by Ruth Pitman

Harry Mathews, *Cigarettes*

Harry Mathews, *The Conversions*

Harry Mathews, *Tlooth*

Michelangelo, *Sonnets*, translated by Elizabeth Jennings, introduction by Michael Ayrton

Elsa Morante, *Arturo's Island*, translated by Isabel Quigly

Edwin Morgan, *Themes on a Variation*
Les Murray, *The Daylight Moon*
Octavio Paz, *Collected Poems 1957–1987*, edited by Eliot
    Weinberger
Rodney Pybus, *Cicadas in their Summers*
Fabrizia Ramondino, *Althénopis*, translated by Michael Sullivan
Laura Riding, *Lives of Wives*, afterword by Laura (Riding) Jackson
Peter Robinson, *The Other Life*
Leonardo Sciascia, *The Council of Egypt*, translated by Adrienne
    Foulke
E.J. Scovell, *Collected Poems*
Michael Teague, *In the Wake of the Portuguese Navigators*
Theocritus, *The Idylls*, translated by Robert Wells
Helen Thomas with Myfanwy Thomas, *Under Storm's Wing*
William Carlos Williams, *Collected Poems Volume II 1939–1962*,
    edited by Christopher MacGowan
David Wright, *Selected Poems*

1989

Sujata Bhatt was born in Ahmedabad, India, and received her MFA from the Writers' Workshop at the University of Iowa. She has published nine collections with Carcanet to date; her first, *Brunizem* (1988), won the Commonwealth Poetry Prize (Asia) and an Alice Hunt Bartlett Award. Her *Collected Poems* (2013) was a Poetry Book Society Special Commendation. She lives in Bremen (Germany) with her husband, the poet and broadcaster Michael Augustin. In interviews in *PN Review*, Bhatt has said 'I have never been monolingual, so I don't know what that feels like. I think sometimes I experience my languages like a concrete medium: like different colours of paint, for example'; and reflecting again on this experience with Gujurati, English and German as her chief languages, 'Multilingualism is such an innate part of me, and the silences between different languages – a sort of musical silence, heard in my mind – are something that accompanies that multilingualism.'[1]

FROM SUJATA BHATT
Bremen
20 November 1989

Dear Michael,

This is just a quick note to say 'hello'. It was nice to talk with you again this morning – however briefly. I'm sorry if I sounded so reserved. You're so good at identifying my voice on the telephone – while I'm never quite sure whether it's you or Mike F. or Nick who answers.[2]

Well, life goes on in Bremen... It's a bit exciting these days, crowded with visitors from the GDR.[3] Michael already dashed off to East Berlin last week to have a discussion with some writers over there. We're relieved that there hasn't been any violence so far. Otherwise I don't think anyone knows what will happen next!

My parents will arrive the day after tomorrow. They'll be staying with us for three weeks. I'm very much looking forward to their visit and to the hours they'll want to spend with their granddaughter who they'll meet for the first time!

I am writing a bit more these days and I promise to send you the next batch of poems for *PN Review*. By the way, I really did take your major suggestions for revisions regarding the poem 'Mozartstrasse 18'.[4] It's shorter now that I've deleted the names of the great dead as well as the statements at the beginning of the poem. The dream, however, (in its shortened form) had to stay.[5] At the risk of sounding defensive, I didn't invent the dream. I hope you don't think that vain or hubris-filled. But in the end I realised how much the names of those famous people (who would each deserve a poem of their own, at least) interfered with the rest of the poem. Thank you again for your patient and honest commentary. I've sent it off to another magazine – out of curiosity – but I also thought you might be getting tired of that poem and would prefer something else!

Speaking of dreams, last year I dreamt that a secret door out of Carcanet's Manchester office led to another earth: a sort of paradise free of economic, political or environmental problems! It was such a vivid and believable dream that I was sorry to wake up and realise it wasn't true. However, I don't think I'll ever forget it: walking through the Corn Exchange, then through piles of Carcanet books and then through the hidden door into an unspoilt earth – maybe someone could write a gripping science-fiction novel about it!

Meanwhile, if you're looking for a good book to read, I highly recommend Sara Suleri's *Meatless Days*, Univ. of Chicago Press, 1989. I think she's an incredibly brilliant writer. She is Pakistani but her mother was Welsh. Strangely enough, *Meatless Days* leads me to pick up *The Love of Strangers* again![6] There is a connection! It has to do with your stance towards history and autobiography. To my mind the two of you are kindred souls – of course, no one might agree with me. I was impressed and moved by the tone of your narrative – it's your narrator's voice that pulls one in, that seduces. My one complaint is the cover – or do you like it?

Believe it or not, this 'note' was intended to be brief!

More soon –

In haste with warm wishes to all the Carcanetti

Sujata

P.S. I hope your wife and children are well and happy. Our baby remains our constant source of entertainment.

FROM MICHAEL SCHMIDT
Manchester
3 December 1989

Dear Sujata

Many thanks for your letter. As you may have heard, Nick has gone to pastures lucrative and new, much to my sorrow. With Mike Abbott's departure and Mike Freeman now freelancing, Carcanet is very unpeopled.[7] This is sad since we are doing rather well and doing well implies huge clerical efforts to keep customers happy. So we are overworked. I write from home on my old steam typewriter.

Germany must be fun just now. I tend to feel that Carcanet is like East Germany, with everyone getting out while the borders are open. I intend to close them again as soon as possible. You are lucky to be living so near the centre of events.

I am glad you redid the Mozartstrasse 18 poem. I look forward to a new batch when they are ready to be pushed out of the nest. How is the baby?

Your dream is terrifying, like something out of C.S. Lewis![8] The only world free of environmental problems would be a world without people!

I'm writing to Chicago about the Suleri book. It sounds fascinating. The cover of my book of poems is one of the things I like least about it. It is hideous. I had hoped for a full demy page and rather larger type-size and better leading, to make the poem <u>easier</u> to read. [handwritten addition: Is it <u>poem </u> or <u>poems</u>?] In fact the format makes it opaque and difficult, whereas the poems are simplicity itself. I am so glad you have read them. I wish I could write more.

With affectionate regards to you, Michael and the baby!

Michael (Schmidt)

*

In 1977 while Sujata Bhatt was away (I imagine in New Haven visiting with her father), Michael Augustin sent me a batch of her poems for the magazine and almost by return I asked to see as much material as he had in order to consider book publication. Her free verse had a beguiling movement and in terms of theme and landscapes it was full of surprises, not least those of a variety of cultural antecedents with which I felt a natural affinity. We seem to have been able to communicate quite directly, without resorting to irony.

Throughout her work, the question of cultural difference is sharply raised. There is always a problem of translation or accommodation, between English (which is now pretty much her first language) and Gujarati, or English and German which – given how long she has lived in Bremen – vies with English. And within English there are the gulfs between American (in which she was educated) and British dialects. In her early poem 'Udaylee' she evokes the room into which women withdraw during their periods. This custom of monthly exile from the routine of women's lives (itself an escape from and a part of that routine) has a positive aspect, the consolidation of a 'sisterhood' apart, turning a condition to advantage. But this is a release from, not a release into. Her poems explore partial and whole releases, including the release into the erotic. She is often witty, seldom ironic, and always candid in her poetry, and in her letters. Her dream of a rabbit-hole out of Carcanet into another, problemless world often presents itself to me in the small hours as a delicious impossibility.

'Search for my Tongue' is her most anthologised poem, partly bilingual, with Gujarati script, transliteration and translation. Each language reflects reality quite differently, translation is at best partial and sometimes entirely inadequate.

Brunizem, her first book, was long, and I have always urged her to write expansively, at length. She is not entirely at home with lyric, it won't do everything she wants to do in verse; and she likes to range well beyond the English tonalities that go with the conventional lyric. For all its questing and experimentation, her work does not feel 'literary' or worked up, and the erotic is a natural, un-coy part of her imagination and thus of the world of the poem which the reader shares and is refreshed in.

NOTES

1. Interview with Vicki Bertram, *PN Review* 138 (March– April 2001); interview with Helen Tookey, *PN Review* 213 (September–October 2013).

2. Nick Rhodes was Carcanet's Marketing Manager 1987–89, and also managed Canto Publications, which included recordings of a number of Carcanet poets. 'Donald Davie's fine reading for the new Canto series of poetry cassettes has just been selected for *Gramophone*'s prestigious annual *Critics' Choice* list. This is something of a breakthrough for spoken poetry and some vindication of the belief that tapes can help to introduce poetry to a wider audience. Mary Postgate, the magazine's spoken-word critic, says: "I found Davie a surprising and disarming poet and his cassette a delight."' News & Notes, *PN Review* 54 (March–April 1987).

3. The Berlin Wall was opened on 9 November 1989, leading to the reunification of Germany in October 1990.

4. MNS had written about 'Mozartstrasse 18' on 15 June 1988:

    > It seems to me one of your most ambitious and in some respects one of the best poems, but I am very troubled by the reductiveness of your list of Jews. [...] The names stand for the people but as counters – the process is one of de-personalisation because what links them together is their Jewishness and their very different anxieties which are somehow made equal by the 'a long procession' phrase and by the list itself. [...] I am also troubled here by an excess of language in pursuit of your meanings. [...]
    > I wonder if there is not a certain hubris in the fact that 'they greet me'? Also in your 'I remember all their different eyes'. It is the difference that matters and it is the difference which your catalogue denies. The tone of reverie, almost hypnotic, ought I think to be effected more by the dynamics of your rhythms which work well here rather than by the accretion of too many words.

    'Mozartstrasse 18' was included in Bhatt's second collection, *Monkey Shadows* (1991).

5. In her interview with Vicki Bertram, Bhatt said:

    > Dreams are important to me – and sometimes they can be

powerful. A dream, however, is not a poem. One has to be very careful when using dream material in a poem. There's always the danger that the dream fails to come to life within the poem or that the dream doesn't allow the poem to acquire the freedom it needs in order to become a poem in its own right. Myths pose similar problems. Sometimes a dream will clarify a poem that I'm in the process of writing. Sometimes lines will occur to me in a dream.

6. *The Love of Strangers* (Hutchison, 1989) was MNS's sixth collection of poetry, described in the blurb as an 'extended poem sequence which cumulatively amounts to a dazzling essay in autobiography, rich in language and also in experience'.

7. Mike Abbott was Carcanet's Sales Manager 1986–89.

8. C.S. Lewis (1898–1963), critic, novelist and author of Christian apologetics, best known for the fantasy *Narnia Chronicles*.

THE YEAR IN BOOKS

David Arkell, *Ententes Cordiales*, illustrations by Philip Norman, foreword by Claire Tomalin

John Ashbery, *Reported Sightings: Art Chronicles 1957–1987*, edited by David Bergmann

Anthony Bailey, *Major André*

Eric Bentley, *The Brecht Memoir*

Thomas Bewick, *Selected Works*, edited by Robyn Marsack

Eavan Boland, *Selected Poems*

Emmanuel Bove, *A Man Who Knows*, translated by Janet Louth

Bo Carpelan, *Axel*, translated by David McDuff

Gillian Clarke, *Letting in the Rumour*

Samuel Taylor Coleridge, *Selected Poetry*, edited by William Empson and David B. Pirie

Leroy Judson Daniels, *Tales of an Old Horse Trader*

Luis de Camoes, *Epic & Lyric*, edited by Helder Macedo, translated by Keith Bosley

Donald Davie, *Under Briggflatt: A History of Poetry in Great Britain 1960–1988*

H.D. (Hilda Doolittle), *Selected Poems*, edited by Louis L. Martz

Alistair Elliot, *My Country: collected poems*

Mark Fisher (ed), *Letters to an Editor*, booklist compiled by Teresa Doering

Ford Madox Ford, *A History of Our Own Times*, edited by Solon Beinfeld and Sondra Stang, foreword by Gordon A. Craig

John Gallas, *Practical Anarchy*

Roger Garfitt, *Given Ground*

Natalia Ginzburg, *The Road into the City & The Dry Heart*, translated by Frances Frenaye

Michael Hamburger, *Testimonies: selected shorter prose 1950–1987*

Jean Hartley, *Philip Larkin, The Marvell Press and Me*

Charles Hobday, *Edgell Rickword: A Poet at War*

Stuart Hood, *The Brutal Heart*

Elizabeth Jennings, *Tributes*

Elias Khoury, *Little Mountain*, translated by Maia Tabet, foreword by Edward Said

Paddy Kitchen, *Gerard Manley Hopkins: a life*

Eric Korn, *Remainders*

Frank Kuppner, *Ridiculous! Absurd! Disgusting!*

Marghanita Laski (ed), *Common Ground: an anthology*,

Sorley MacLean, *From Wood to Ridge: Collected Poems in Gaelic and English*

Christopher Middleton, *Selected Writings*

Les Murray, *The Boys Who Stole The Funeral*

Idris Parry, *Speak Silence*

Rainer Maria Rilke, *The Duino Elegies*, translated by Stephen Cohn

Leonardo Sciascia, *To Each His Own*, translated by Adrienne Foulke

Leonardo Sciascia, *1912 + 1*, translated by Sasha Rabinovich

L.M.E. Shaw, *Trade, Inquisition and the English Nation in Portugal*

C.H. Sisson, *On the Look-out: a partial autobiography*

William Turner, *A New Herball*, edited by George Chapman
Sebastiano Vassalli, *The Night of the Comet*, translated by John Gatt
Michael Westlake, *The Utopians*

1990

F.T. Prince (1912–2003), was born in South Africa, lived in England for most of his life, and taught for two decades at the University of Southampton. His first collection caught T.S. Eliot's attention and was published by Faber and Faber, but his subsequent books came from a variety of publishers, including Carcanet towards the end of his life: *Collected Poems 1935–1992* (1993). His 1974 letter in *Letters to an Editor* is a vigorous defence of his changing verse-forms: 'all "forms" are *equally* rigorous, and only seem less so if they are badly used'. He was an admirer of John Ashbery's poetry, and the admiration was mutual. Introducing him to an audience at a New York reading in 1983, Ashbery said: 'Prince is one of the best twentieth-century poets. Like Landor, he stands somewhat apart from mainstream modern poetry; like him, he is a poet to whom poets turn when they feel they cannot write, that is, he is a source of poetry.'[1]

FROM F.T. PRINCE
Southampton
2 July 1990

Dear Michael,

Would you be interested in this group of poems? I have been amusing myself this year with these and others on the same lines. These are the best so far, but I was hoping, and still am, to run to about twenty-five.

The note on the reference-book would be needed, I think, because without it people might not realise that the starting point is heraldic family-mottoes.[2]

I have been amused by the writing, but most of the mottoes are very boring.

With best wishes,
Yours sincerely,
Frank Prince

FROM MICHAEL SCHMIDT
Manchester
5 July 1990

Dear Frank,

Thank you very much indeed for your letter of 2 July and for the fascinating mottoes. I love them. There is [a] split infinitive at the end of number six which makes me uneasy but apart from that they are extremely 'spoken' and compelling.

Thank you for them!

With every good wish,
Yours ever,
Michael

FROM F.T. PRINCE
Southampton
27 July 1990

Dear Michael,

I hope you will be patient with me if I ask you to return the 'Notes on Mottoes' I sent you not long ago. As you know, they are part of a larger scheme, and I have been uneasy about it, and them, for some time. Some 'guardian' has now pronounced definitely against them.

With my apologies for being a nuisance (but one must be allowed that sometimes?).

Yours sincerely,
Frank Prince

FROM MICHAEL SCHMIDT
Manchester
31 July 1990

Dear Frank,

Further to your letter of 27 July and our phone conversation this morning, I return with the greatest reluctance your 'Notes on Mottoes'. Of course you must be true to your Taskmistress Muse. On the other hand, these pieces are so thrifty and precise, and work together so well, that I cannot see how they might be improved except by extension.

It would be wonderful if your second thoughts could be brisk and friendly to these poems so that I might still feature them in *PN Review* 76. But if they come later, they can expect to grace 77 or 78 – or 87 or 88 should we live so long.

Is it foolish of me to ask whether you are building towards another collection, and if so, whether Peter Jay will be publishing it?[3] I remember once making a serious error at Carcanet about your work. It is not an error which – given the opportunity of a second chance – I would repeat.

With kind regards,
Michael

FROM MICHAEL SCHMIDT
Manchester
7 August 1990

Dear Frank,

I am delighted to have Notes on Mottoes back again, with the extra pair which make the sequence even better. In (ii), is <u>Quid prod sodali</u> correct, or should it be <u>pro</u>?[4] Or is this my error?

Professor Hackett writes to warn me that 1991 is the Rimbaud centenary. He suggests – a suggestion I welcome – that you might be willing to write an essay on Rimbaud for *PN Review*.[5] Would you do this for us? We would certainly welcome it – anything up to 5,000 words would suit our needs. We would need the piece by about March of 1991. I may ask one or two other poets whose work I respect to contribute too, though I do not envisage a formal 'supplement' or special issue. I have a strong resistance to much of Rimbaud, though he meant a great deal to me when I was an undergraduate and I was stunned by him again about seven years ago.

Warm greetings as always,
Yours ever,
Michael

FROM F.T. PRINCE
Southampton
8 August 1990

Dear Michael,

Yes, I would like to write on Rimbaud for *PN Review*. It would be an informal piece on my reading him and what I tried to get from it between the ages of 17 and, say, 22. I have not cultivated him for many years.

As for <u>prod</u>, my Latin dictionary gives it as an alternative form of <u>pro</u>. I wish I were enough of a Latinist to be able to place some of the mottoes as tags from classical authors. Many are obvious, but I suspect there are more than one realises. I would like also to have time to look into the whole background – the dates of the various honours, the system by which the heralds chose or found the mottoes, etc. But my 'little knowledge' may be preferable to my losing myself in too much.[6]

With best wishes,
Yours ever,
Frank Prince

*

My copy of Carcanet's edition of Frank Prince's *Collected Poems 1935–1992* falls open naturally at 'The Yuan Chen Variations'. I remember when reading the proofs remarking how the poems moved from long decisive lines in the early work to shorter and shorter lines, purer perhaps, but no less complex in their syntax and the demands they made of the reader, to speak them aloud in order to draw out their sense. This poem still fascinates me and frustrates my tongue. My first encounter with Prince was through his exemplary writing on Milton. I admired in particular *The Italian Element in Milton's Verse*, which told me so much about the great Italians and gave Milton a European context. His work is certainly enabling, from the unforgettable first poem in the *Collected*, 'An Epistle to a Patron', to the last, entitled 'Last Poem', out of Hardy and his world of eloquent gravestones, where he awaits 'My own silence'.

NOTES

1.   John Ashbery, 'F.T. Prince', *PN Review* 147 (September–
     October 2002); this issue contained several tributes to Prince
     on his 90th birthday.

2.   The mottoes referred to can be found in *Fairbairn's Crests of
     the Families of Great Britain and Ireland*. Prince uses them as a
     starting point for his reflections, for example:

> *Dulces ante omnia Musae*
> 'Sweet above all else the Muses':
> Comes like a true sigh
> After wounds and bruises
> In body and mind,
> From one who looks
> About at last, to find
> Like balm, his books.

3.   Peter Jay (b.1945), poet and translator, set up Anvil Press
     in 1968, also expanding from the base of a magazine, *New
     Measures*. When he decided to close the press in 2015 to
     concentrate on his own writing, it was merged with Carcanet,
     the founders of both being old friends and Anvil 'like family',
     as MNS remarked. Anvil published Prince's *Later On* (1983)
     and *Walks in Rome* (1987).

4.   Twelve 'Notes on Mottoes' were published in *PN Review* 76
     (November–December 1990); '*Quidni prod sodali*' ('Why not,
     / For a comrade?') is the first line of number ii. Nine more
     appeared in *PN Review* 80 (July-August 1991).

5.   F.T. Prince's 'Rimbaud after Sixty Years' (*PN Review* 78,
     March–April 1991) was the only article about the poet in that
     issue, which had a set of tributes to Laura (Riding) Jackson at
     90. Prince observed:

> Age and experience, years of professional middle-class
> life, may be of no advantage in dealing with so adolescent
> a genius. Yet I find that one 20th-century experience has
> a certain relevance: that of living through the turmoil of

the emerging 'youth culture' of the 1960s in America and Western Europe. Hundreds of thousands – it seemed millions – of young people then acted out such attitudes as the seventeen-year-old Rimbaud brought from Charleville to Paris in 1871. But of course they were without his genius.

6. Alexander Pope, 'An Essay on Criticism':

A little learning is a dangerous thing ;
Drink deep, or taste not the Pierian spring:
There shallow draughts intoxicate the brain,
And drinking largely sobers us again

THE YEAR IN BOOKS

Christine Brooke-Rose, *Verbivore*

Maurice Collis, *The Grand Peregrination: Being the Life of Fernão Mendes Pinto*

Donald Davie, *Collected Poems*

Donald Davie, *Slavic Excursions: essays on Russian and Polish literature*

D.J. Enright, *Memoirs of a Mendicant Professor*

Padraic Fallon, *Collected Poems*, introduction by Seamus Heaney and edited by Brian Fallon

Richard Francis, *The Land Where Lost Things Go*

Natalia Ginzburg, *Voices in the Evening*, translated by D.M. Low

Fulke Greville, *Selected Poems*, edited by Neil Powell

Ivor Gurney, *Selected Poems*, edited by P.J. Kavanagh

John Heath-Stubbs, *Selected Poems*

Richard Hooker, *Ecclesiastical Polity: selections*, edited by Arthur Pollard

Leigh Hunt, *Selected Writings*, edited by David Jesson-Dibley

Brian Jones, *Freeborn John*

Gabriel Josipovici, *Steps: Selected Fiction and Drama*

William Law, *Selected Writing*, edited by Janet Louth

Clarice Lispector, *Near To the Wild Heart*, translated by Giovanni Pontiero

Rose Macaulay, *They Went to Portugal, Too*, edited by L.C. Taylor
Henry Miller, *Letters to Emil*, edited by George Wickes
Nicholas Moore, *Longings of the Acrobats: selected poems*, edited by
    Peter Riley, introduction by John Ashbery
Edwin Morgan, *Crossing the Border: essays on Scottish literature*
Edwin Morgan, *Collected Poems*
Cristopher Nash, *The Dinosaur's Ball*
Orhan Pamuk, *The White Castle*, translated by Victoria Holbrook
R.E. Pritchard (ed), *Poetry by English Women*
Peter Sansom, *Everything You've Heard Is True*
James Schuyler, *Selected Poems*
Leonardo Sciascia, *Death of an Inquisitor and other stories*, translated
    by Ian Thomson
Roger Scruton, *The Philosopher on Dover Beach*
C.H. Sisson, *In Two Minds: literary essays*
Iain Crichton Smith, *Selected Stories*
Julian Symons, *The Thirties and the Nineties*
Jeremy Taylor, *Selected Writings*, edited by C.H. Sisson
Federigo Tozzi, *Eyes Shut*, translated by Kenneth Cox
Kurt Tucholsky, *Germany? Germany!*, translated by Harry Zohn

1991

Robert Wells (b. 1947) first approached Carcanet ('Dear Sir, I enclose a book of poems to be considered for publication...') in 1976, and his collection *The Winter's Task* was published in 1977. He worked as an editor for Carcanet for a couple of years, as a forester on Exmoor and a teacher in Iran and Italy; he has lived in France for some years. Carcanet published his translations of Virgil's *Georgics* (1982) and the *Idylls* of Theocritus (1988). Wells reported to MNS (16 September 1980), 'Yesterday morning I finished the first draft of the Georgics, after a record day of 38 lines, and sat down on the floor at 1.30 a.m. with a bowl of tomato soup, to celebrate. [...] How do you make water-nymphs speak believably?' Carcanet issued his *Collected Poems and Translations* in 2009. He wrote to MNS in 1984 that 'the two activities [writing poetry and translating] belong together and are finally the same [...] A gesture against the predominant "look at me" view of poetry.'

FROM ROBERT WELLS
Blois
18 November 1991

Dear Michael,

I'll keep my account of Cheltenham until we next meet, or at least my account of Hulse[1] [...]. After his three-hundred liner about the Gulf War, a lady in the audience lent across to me and intoned 'It may be very well between the covers of a book, but it won't do in Cheltenham.' I didn't think it would do anywhere.

I enjoyed meeting Bo Carpelan – very direct and funny and engaging.[2] He told a nice story about a critic who had accused him of writing 'summer-cottage poetry'. 'So I called him to ask why he say this horrible thing – but he was in his summer cottage.' Among the famous young I briefly met Michael Hofmann, charming and highly intelligent.[3] It would only be necessary to exchange a couple of words with him to discover that.

But despite these encounters, and the courtesy of Lawrence Sail,[4] who is also obviously a very effective organiser, a sort of fog wrapped me the moment I set foot on the station platform at Chelters (so Stephen Romer calls it)[5] and didn't lift until I left. England seemed a place of lost connections. Is that me or England or both? I talked and was talked at a lot. But not the conversations one hopes for. Too little sleep that week, too much drink, too much moving around.

But good, nevertheless, to find myself in Charles Sisson's sitting-room once again after it must be six or seven years, with an equally fine view of the bookcase and the Dorset hills.[6] The same slightly baffled friendship still prevailing – and the soup 'from the garden' still as good. I wanted to talk poetry and he wanted to talk friends and family, but somewhere between the two we met. Nora entertained me just as if I were a wandering Telemachus – including morning tea in bed, something not countenanced in France.

News from Blois: Benoit nearly six months old now, sitting up in his pram like the infant Hercules looking for serpents to strangle. Eating enormously, but a charming and easy baby, much smiling and laughter, especially for his mother and sister. He goes to the crèche now (which means I can get back to work) where he spends much of the day locked in the embrace of various French girls. Constance is nearly four. My notions that one day she might come hill-walking with me on the Pyrenees are never to be fulfilled I think. She keeps all her energies for the city, and would jump along the entire length of the Boulevard St Germain, if given the chance.

I have begun a new set of poems, in free verse this time. Though rhyme will creep in the interstices.

I thought Michael Longley's new book wonderful.[7] Years since I've liked something so much, or felt such sympathy with the tact and taste and principle which lies behind the writing. There are some great things too in the new Bunting: 'Such syllables flicker out of grass' and 'Now we've no hope of going back' above all, also the close of 'Against the tricks of time'.

What do you know about Bunting's editor Richard Caddel? His poems are the only ones I take to at all in the recent PBS anthology. The only ones, that is, where the form has imposed some sense of selection.

In PNR the best thing remains the Tredell interviews.[8] Scruton, as usual, comes over as not believing anything he says and not disbelieving it either.[9] An attitude, a mental disposition or predicament is there and sadly real, but the actual views are just there to fill the space appropriately. I enjoyed Davie on Niedecker.[10] Why is it necessary to pay some shark of a bookdealer about £50 before one can get hold of her poems? Is there any possibility of Carcanet producing an edition?

I have another publishing selection. One of the most difficult of all Collected Poems to get hold of is John Marston's (as against the plays), and they're much sought after too.[11] A fine edition long out of print, the only one, was produced by the Liverpool U.P. (as no. 7 in their Liverpool English Texts and Studies) edited by Arnold Davenport. Could you buy the rights and reissue the book, waiving in this case Carcanet's interdiction on scholarship – since a satirist above all needs notes? Marston is an extraordinary poet. Don't write back and tell me to do a Fyfield.

Re the Tredell interviews. I think he should do one with Martin Bernal, chiefly about his work *Black Athena*, of which the second volume has just been published.[12] Have you heard of it? It's a rewriting of the origins of Greek civilisation, as well as an account of 'the fabrication of ancient Greece' over the last three centuries. But the true subject is what the word Europe means, and the book reaches out beyond its scholarship in essential ways. Please pass the idea on to Tredell.

Good to have David Wright's versions of Caeiro (my favourite of Pessoa's characters).[13] Can we have some more?

What news of you? Of the Friend? Of Children? Of Poetry? Of England? Be indiscreet. And what of this Canadian trip you dangled briefly before me? Is anything to come of that?

Lots of love,

Rob

P.S. I would like to order Padraic Fallon, *Collected Poems*, Laura Riding, *Collected Poems*. I owe Carcanet for Davie's Pound book, but can't find the invoice. Will you send another, please. P.P.S. You are the only fixer I know. Don't you think the ground should be laid for Yves Bonnefoy to get the Nobel Prize?[14]

*

When Robert Wells sent his first collection I was still in thrall to Edward Thomas, and Wells's poems seemed built on similar ground, in both senses: a poetry rooted in landscape and profoundly alive to the pastoral tradition and to that tradition's wider context. In Wells's case the context was broadened out by his classical education, and his eventual translations of Virgil's *Georgics* and Theocritus's *Idylls*, first mooted soon after we met, are core elements in his small but resonant *oeuvre*. I hope Anglophone readers will not lose the ability to hear these strains for what they are. Wells and Sisson are at the very heart of Carcanet's first decade and without them my editorial approach would have been quite different.

Robert was never shy about saying what he liked in *PN Review* and among the books we published. His approbation was something I waited for in vain much of the time: he was not a diplomat but a reader, editor and friend.

He was part of a trio of poets comprising Clive Wilmer and Dick Davis also, the three in the end all turning up on the Carcanet list, which also accommodated poets who meant a great deal to them in their formative years, Yvor Winters and Edgar Bowers in particular. They were also in debt to Thom Gunn who perhaps pointed them in Winters's direction. These three Cambridge contemporaries styled themselves *Il Movimento Inglese*, the Italian title affirming a confident European and a renaissance affiliation.

My first introductory anthology, *Ten English Poets*, featured all three members of the *Movimento*. I had hoped to draw older poets – Davie and Sisson in particular – behind the grouping, which was not entirely pastoral or entirely formal, but it was not to be. I commissioned Donald Davie to review the book, and was not prepared (I ought to have been) for what he produced for *PNR 3*. I titled it – unless he did – 'On the Wrong Track'. He takes Wells in particular to task, and traces the source of his main complaint to Winters's door, Winters whose chair at Stanford he himself occupied and whose work he has written about with great insight. Winters seemed to absolve Wells and some of his contemporaries whose work I admired from registering and responding to the counter-challenge of Ford and of Pound, whose prose and poetry so deeply inflect the poems of Sisson.

For Davie, the primary issues are diction and anachronism, and he insists that certain changes or adjustments are total and inexorable. 'The initial miscalculation about diction infects other dimensions of verse-writing,' he says. His response to this anthology, and to Wells's poems in particular, remained an open disagreement between us down the years. Re-reading Wells's first book today, I realise that Davie reacted against the timelessness of the poems' manner, their resistance to what to Wells would have been mere contingencies, and their place in a living, working landscape. I can see what all the objections might be, 'marmoreal' and the rest of it, but I am moved now as I was then by poems such as 'Deus Loci' on whom the poet waits and who is 'withheld / Only by so slight a thing as his absence.'

Odd how the old battles persist, and the old trenches have not quite vanished from memory's map…

NOTES

1. Michael Hulse (b. 1955), prolific translator from German, critic and poet, currently teaches poetry and comparative literature at the University of Warwick. He was a regular contributor of reports and reviews to *PN Review* through the 1980s–1990s.

2. Bo Carpelan (1926–2011), Finnish poet and novelist. Carcanet published *Axel* (translated by David McDuff, 1989) a fictional account of the friendship between Carpelan's great-uncle and the composer Jean Sibelius, and in 1993 three collections of his poetry under the title *Homecoming*, translated from the Finland-Swedish by David McDuff.

3. Michael Hofmann (b. 1957) had published two collections of poetry with Faber and several translations from German at this point; he contributed poems, reviews and articles to *PN Review* in the 1980s and 1990s. Carcanet published two of his father Gert Hofmann's novels, *The Spectacle at the Tower* (1985) and *Our Conquest* (1987), both translated from the German by Christopher Middleton.

4. Lawrence Sail (b. 1942), poet, critic and anthologist, was

programme director, 1991, and co-director, 1999, of the Cheltenham Festival of Literature. He has been a regular contributor of reviews and reports to *PN Review* for forty years.

5. Stephen Romer (b. 1957), poet and translator from French, has lived in France since 1981, and was Maître de Conférences at University of Tours. Carcanet published his *Set Thy Love in Order: new and selected poems* in 2017.

6. MNS took Wells to meet C.H. Sisson in 1976, and in thanking him for this opportunity, Wells wrote:

> What will remain with me is a picture of him, walking across Somerton Moor, with his slightly stumbling gait, and the talkative attempt to be good company. [...] He is a moving presence. A pre-Bagehot England alive in him. To meet him is to be put in touch with this. I came away with an awareness of having a lot to learn – and some sense of where to learn it. (17 August 1976)

When Wells read with Sisson in Cambridge in 1982, he reported back to MNS:

> The new poems he read sound as if they have some fine stuff in them. Geoffrey Hill was at the reading. I heard him say to Charles at the pub afterwards: 'You are a gloomy old bugger.' [...] Hill glowered through my reading. I noticed at the edge of my vision that he brightened when I got to Virgil. (28 October 1982)

Telemachus searched for his father, Odysseus, in his wanderings.

7. Michael Longley's collection *Gorse Fires* was published by Cape in 1991 and won the Whitbread Poetry Prize. Basil Bunting's posthumous *Uncollected Poems* was published by OUP in 1991, edited by Richard Caddel, a poet and at that time Director of the Basil Bunting Poetry Centre at Durham University.

8. Nicolas Tredell (b. 1950), a prolific writer on literature, culture

and film who taught at the University of Sussex, contributed a series of twenty-one interviews to *PN Review*, some of which were collected in *Conversations with Critics* (1995). He edited a special issue in 1986, *PN Review* 49, challenging the 'new orthodoxy' of post-structuralism, and in 1993 Carcanet published his study of the 1980s' revolution in critical studies, *The Critical Decade: culture in crisis*.

9. Roger Scruton (b. 1944), philosopher especially of aesthetics and political thought, contributed articles to *PN Review* in the 1980s; Carcanet published his novel *Fortnight's Anger* in 1981, and four books on aesthetics. This interview was published in *PN Review* 81 (September–October 1991). Some Carcanet authors regretted the presence of such a conservative public figure on the list and in the pages of *PN Review*. Wells comments, 'I'm sorry to find myself taking this callow swipe at Roger Scruton. You don't have to be of one mind with Scruton on everything to feel, as I do now, respect and admiration for him.'

10. Donald Davie, 'Postmodernism and Lorine Niedeker', *PN Review* 82 (November-December 1991). The *Collected Works* of Lorine Niedeker (1903–70) was eventually published by the University of California Press, edited by Jenny Penberthy, in 2002.

11. John Marston (1576–1634), playwright, poet and satirist; the University of Leeds currently hosts an online project of editing his complete works. Carcanet did not take up Wells's suggestion.

12. Nor did Tredell interview Martin Bernal (1937–2013), whose *Black Athena: the Afroasiatic roots of classical civilization* was published in three volumes in 1987, 1991, 2006.

13. David Wright (1920–94) was born in Johannesburg and lived in England from the time he was 14, attending the Northampton School for the Deaf before studying at Oxford. He lived in Cumbria and spent time in Portugal. He was

editor with Patrick Swift of *X* magazine, 'discovering' C.H. Sisson, who introduced him to MNS Carcanet first published his poetry in 1976, when he wrote to MNS, 'To be in Carcanet now confers the same kind of cachet that Fabers had in the 30s and 40s' (*Letters to an Editor*, no. 106). 'Four Poems of Alberto Caeiro' were published in *PNR* 81. His *Poems and Versions* (1992) includes translations of Pessoa.

14. Yves Bonnefoy (1923–2016): named to the Collège de France in 1981 to fill the chair left vacant by the death of Roland Barthes, Bonnefoy was the first poet honoured in this way since Paul Valéry, but he did not win the Nobel Prize. Carcanet published his *New and Selected Poems*, translated by John Naughton and Anthony Rudolf in 1996, and *Poems* (2017), of which Romer was co-editor and one of the translators.

THE YEAR IN BOOKS

Sujata Bhatt, *Monkey Shadows*

C.R. Boxer, *The Portuguese Seaborne Empire 1415-1825*

Alison Brackenbury, *Selected Poems*

Christine Brooke-Rose, *Textermination*

Mary Butts, *With and Without Buttons*, edited by Nathalie Blondel

David Craig, *King Cameron*

John Crowe-Ransom, *Selected Poems*

Donald Davie, *Studies in Ezra Pound: chronicle and polemic*

Paavo Haavikko, *Selected Poems*, translated by Anselm Hollo

Donald Hall, *The One Day and Poems 1947–1990*

Gabriel Josipovici, *The Big Glass*

P.J. Kavanagh, *Enchantment*

Mimi Khalvati, *In White Ink*

Kenneth Koch, *Selected Poems*

C.A. Lejeune, *The C.A. Lejeune Film Reader*, edited by Anthony Lejeune

Grevel Lindop, *A Prismatic Toy*

Bill Manhire, *Milky Way Bar*

Jack Morpurgo, *Master of None: an autobiography*
Les Murray, *Collected Poems*
Les Murray, *Dog Fox Field*
Hugh Nissenson, *Tree of Life*
Frank O'Hara, *Selected Poems*, edited by Donald Allen
John Peck, *The Poems and Translations of Hi Lo*
Fernando Pessoa, *The Book of Disquietude*, translated by Richard
    Zenith
Dilys Powell, *The Dilys Powell Film Reader*, edited by Christopher
    Cook
Neil Powell, *True Colours*
James Reed (ed), *Border Ballads: A Selection*
Edgell Rickword, *Collected Poems*, edited by Charles Hobday
Dante Gabriel Rossetti, *Selected Poems and Translations*, edited by
    Clive Wilmer
C.H. Sisson, *Antidotes*
Meic Stephens (ed), *The Bright Field: An Anthology of Contemporary
    Poetry from Wales*
Raymond Tallis and Howard Robinson (eds), *The Pursuit of Mind*
Javier Tomeo, *The Coded Letter*, translated by Anthony Edkins
Andrew Waterman, *In the Planetarium*

1992

Les Murray (1938–2019) grew up on a dairy farm in Bunyah, New South Wales, where he also spent much of his adult life. 'If I sometimes boast that I was Subject Matter at my university before I graduated, that is partly a rueful admission of the inordinate time I took in graduating.'[1] From 1971 he made literature his full-time occupation; Carcanet has been his publisher since 1986. *Subhuman Redneck Poems* (1996) won the T.S. Eliot Prize, and Murray was awarded the Queen's Gold Medal for Poetry in 1999. *New Selected Poems*, Murray's choice of his own work, was published in 2012, and his last book, *On Bunyah* (2017), tells the story of his community in verse and photographs. In his *Guardian* obituary for Murray, MNS observed that Murray 'preferred the pastoral gossip of creatures (rural human beings among them), "bush balladry" with roots in actual ballads and hymns.'[2]

FROM LES MURRAY
Bunyah
2.9.92 (This year's palindromic date, you notice)

Dear Michael,

How to describe *Translations from the Natural World* in a catalogue note?[3] I leave that essentially to you, but Janet tells me you'd like some background to work from.[4] Hmm. It's essentially the *Presence* sequence, of course, with poems from the human realm fore and aft, for variety and padding. What to say of those? Varied. Travels in NW Australia and on the poet's native North Coast of NSW: 'North Country Suite' essentially replies to and continues a poem Kenneth Slessor published 50-odd years ago about this coast, under the title 'North Country'.[5] Back then, it was a world of small farms, butter factories & dead ringbarked forests: now it's halfway to extinction, & socially far more varied: lots of disguised long-term poverty then as now. Back then, that was indigenous, now it's often ex-urban too: long-term dole people & the semi-employed. The rest of the human poems should present no problem of reference. In *Presence*, I tried to go outside of the human & human time & find verbal renderings for the non-verbal *life* (not languages: they don't have them) of the creatures out there. Each poem's a different experimental way of coming at the job, every technique from Aboriginal legendry (Cattle Ancestor: <u>not</u> a trad. legend, but one I constructed on the trad. model) to the depressed slum language of imprisoned species (pigs) to lots of mimesis of sound (elephants, lyrebird etc.) & so on. One piece, 'Honey Cycle', respectfully parodies a famous Irish Gaelic poem ('Gile na Gile'), another alludes to Iain Crichton Smith's 'Deer on the High Hills' but is utterly different.[6] And lots of 'em are dead SENSUOUS! Best of luck.

Here's a pic. which you or Janet also wanted.

Best wishes –

Les

*

Writing about Les Murray at the time of his death, I stressed the aspect of his own approach to poetry which I find most challenging and at the same time enabling as an editor working through what were once the mountains, and now are the cyber-clouds, of submissions which find their way to Carcanet. A Murrayesque poet must prepare to be a medium for voices of experience. A 'Cockspur Bush' speaks through Murray:

I am lived. I am died.
I was two-leafed three times, and grazed,
but then I was stemmed and multiplied,
sharp-thorned and caned, nested and raised,
earth-salt by sun-sugar. I was innerly sung
by thrushes who need fear no eyed skin thing.
Finched, ant-run, flowered, I am given the years
in now fewer berries, now more of sling
out over directions of luscious dung [...]

What is wonderful is the plant's enactive syntax. This is inscape in Hopkins's sense, what elsewhere Murray calls 'wholespeak'. He insists that every form of expression can be poetry: some make it with language, others with dance, skating, chopping wood. Poetry, a universal making, a universal kind of engagement, is not confined to language, though (fortunately) his own is. Neglect of writers not from the 'central cultures', neglect of the eccentric, the misfit, he will not tolerate. He is a sharp critic and warm advocate of Australian writing neglected by Britain and America. He said, 'Of course, that I suppose has been the main drama of my life – coming from the left-out people into the accepted people and being worried about the relegated who are still relegated.'

NOTES

1. 'On being Subject Matter', *The Paperbark Trees: selected prose* (Carcanet, 1992). Murray concludes the essay with a wry reflection on the importance of the writer's profession, since it is 'subject to public scrutiny of a sort granted to no other'; imagine reviews of surgeons or barristers, he suggests:

> 'With his move to the cardiac field, Mr Broadribb-Cleaver
> appears to have left behind the timid bourgeois formalism of
> his earlier appendectomies and acquired an almost daredevil
> attack in his incisions. […] With the appearance of this
> superb stylist, Australian heart-surgery has come of age.'

2. The *Guardian*, 1 May 2019.

3. Translations *from the Natural World* was published in 1993;
   the central *Presence* sequence is a virtuoso rendering of the
   experience of the natural world in its 'own' voices.

4. Janet Allan, former Librarian of Manchester's Portico Library,
   was Carcanet's Production Manager for several years from 1992.

5. Kenneth Slessor (1901–71), leading Australian poet, whose
   work is included in the anthology *Fivefathers: five Australian
   poets of the pre-academic era* (Carcanet, 1994), edited by Murray.

6. Murray had a particular regard for Scottish poets, based
   on a feeling of ancestral kinship; see his essay 'The Bonnie
   Disproportion' in *The Paperbark Tree*. Iain Crichton Smith
   (1928–98) was first published by Carcanet in 1985, with a
   representative *Selected Poems*; his *New Collected Poems*, edited
   by Matt Maguire, was published in 2011. Murray refers to
   Crichton Smith's 1962 sequence 'Deer on the High Hills',
   which begins: 'A deer looks through you to the other side /
   and what it is and sees is an inhuman pride.'

THE YEAR IN BOOKS

John Ashbery, *Hotel Lautréamont*

Iain Bamforth, *Sons and Pioneers*

Donald Davie, *Older Masters: essays and reflections on English and
American literature*

Donald Davie, *Purity of Diction & Articulate Energy*

Alain Dugrand, *Trotsky In Mexico 1937–1940*

Roger Finch, *According to Lilies*

Franco Fortini, *Summer is Not All: selected poems*, translated by Paul
Lawton

Gerald Hammond, *Racing: a book of words*

Thomas Hood, *Selected Poems*, edited by Joy Flint

Elizabeth Jennings, *Times and Seasons*

Gabriel Josipovici, *Text and Voice: essays*

P.J. Kavanagh, *Collected Poems*

Clarice Lispector, *Discovering the World*, translated by Giovanni Pontiero

Hugh MacDiarmid, *Selected Poetry*, edited by Alan Riach and Michael Grieve

Hugh MacDiarmid, *Selected Prose*, edited by Alan Riach

Cecily Mackworth, *Lucy's Nose*

Harry Mathews, *A Mid-Season Sky: poems*

Carlo Mazzantini, *In Search of a Glorious Death*, translated by Simonetta Wenkert

Chris McCully, *Fly Fishing: a book of words*

Christopher Middleton, *The Balcony Tree*

Edna St Vincent Millay, *Selected Poems*, edited by Colin Falck

Adelaida Garcia Morales, *The South & Bene*, translated by Sarah Marsh

William Morris, *Selected Poems*, edited by Peter Faulkner

Les Murray, *The Paperbark Tree: selected prose*

Octavio Paz, *The Other Voice: poetry at the fin-de-siècle*, translated by Helen Lane

Morris Philipson, *The Wallpaper Fox*

Janos Pilinszky, *Conversations with Sheryl Sutton*, translated by Peter Jay and Eva Major

Fernando Mendes Pinto, *The Peregrination*, translated by Michael Lowery

Eça de Queiros, *Cousin Bazílio*, translated by Roy Campbell

Eça de Queiros, *The Illustrious House of Ramires*, translated by Ann Stevens

Laura Riding, *First Awakenings*, edited by Elizabeth Friedmann, Alan J. Clark and Robert Nye

Rainer Maria Rilke, *Neue Gedichte/New Poems*, translated by Stephen Cohn

Peter Robinson, *Entertaining Fates*

A.J.R. Russell-Wood, *A World on the Move: the Portuguese in Africa, Asia and America 1415–1808*

Carmelo Samona, *Brothers*, translated by Linda Lappin

Leonardo Sciascia, *To Each His Own*, translated by Adrienne Foulke

Walter Scott, *Selected Poems*, edited by James Reed

Mary Sidney, *The Sidney Psalms*, edited by R.E. Pritchard

C.H. Sisson, *English Perspectives: essays on liberty and government*

Iain Crichton Smith, *Collected Poems*

Oscar Wilde, *Selected Poems*, edited by Malcolm Hicks

William Carlos Williams, *Paterson*, edited by Christopher MacGowan

Clive Wilmer, *Of Earthly Paradise*

Gregory Woods, *We Have the Melon*

David Wright, *Poems and Versions*

Judith Wright, *A Human Pattern*

1993

Ted Hughes introduced MNS to the poems of Seán Rafferty (1909–93), who grew up in Dumfriesshire but had lived in Devon since the 1940s, working as a publican. He had gardened for years: 'I like vegetables, you can eat them and they don't talk to you.'[1] Sorley MacLean remembered him from '1929–30 when he was amazing us at Edinburgh University with his brilliance' in poetry.[2] Rafferty went to London in 1932, 'to get lost' in a city. There he wrote songs and sketches for revues. He said to Nicholas Johnson, 'I've never written an easy poem. Some of them have taken three years.' When he surfaced in *PN Review* it was the first time he'd been visible since *16 Poems* published by Grosseteste in 1973. He began writing again in the 1990s: 'this last batch has pleased me a lot, because I didn't know they were still there.' His *Collected Poems* were published posthumously.

BEGINNINGS 1981–82

On 11 November 1981, Ted Hughes sent MNS an order for a couple of books. He added a postscript:

> I'm enclosing a manuscript by Sean Rafferty. He's about 70. Used to write plays for the Players Theatre. Kept a pub in Devon for 25 years. Now he's a gardener. Remarkable chap. I don't think he's ever published a poem (I'm not quite sure).

In his letter of 24 November, MNS replied:

I will be reading the Rafferty manuscript in the next few days. Though it is quite certain we could not offer publication in book form, I might consider these for the magazine?

FROM MICHAEL SCHMIDT
Manchester
1 December 1981

Dear Ted,

I have now got round to reading the Sean Rafferty poems. I must be very careful here. I find the poems so direct and so clearly in the rhetoric that I must respond to[,] that I cannot 'judge' their merits. Because of my predisposition – partly Sissonian, partly Yeatsian – I feel I would respond to these poems even if they were bad! They have the force, for me, and the transparency of the best of recent Barker.[3] (I am very keen on recent Barker!)

I propose that we run the whole poem – I estimate that it will come to about 10 pages – in *PN Review*. This would in a sense be better than book publication because there would be an immediate 'circulation' of about 2,000 copies. It would draw the poetry into much more public attention than a book would do. I don't know whether to suggest that we put a headnote identifying the poet or let the poem stand quite naked and eloquent. What do you think? Perhaps a note would be sensible to 'place' the poet, though if so perhaps it could come at the end rather than at the beginning of the poem. Could you possibly draft a short paragraph?

I am sure this work will not please Donald Davie! I cannot see how it could help but please C.H. Sisson, David Wright, and the other poets on my side of the divide!

Amazed if cautious thanks for this offering!

Yours ever,
Michael

North Tawton, Devon
27 December 1981

Dear Michael,

Sorry for this delay. I was in Ireland – the coldest freeze and the highest winds this century, according to Irish telly, combined to make the visit exhilarating. I actually saw fish blown out of a lake – which could only happen in Ireland. Very small fish to be sure.

Your letter gave me great joy and I think it gave Sean Rafferty great joy too, though he'd never show it. After his years of isolation. He's an exceedingly retiring figure and I imagine you and I are the only people who've seen the sequence.

The thought of an introductory paragraph about him gave him a worried hour or two, but eventually he agreed to:

Born in 1910, in Ayrshire. [*sic*] For many years he kept The Duke of York in Iddisleigh, in Devon.

That's all. It's quite likely some of the Magazine's readers will know of him – his pub was quite famous in its way. His wife Peggy is an unusual character (so is he) and she ran a restaurant that became eventually as I say quite famous.[4] She refused ever to charge more than £1-50 a meal. When they retired about five years ago they had about £200. She was a great friend of Allen (Alan?) Lane's. Sean is now a gardener for Alan Lane's daughter who runs a Farm for City Children near Iddisleigh – a place where schoolchildren from inner Birmingham, inner London etc come and work on the farm for a week – thirty at a time, with their teachers.[5]

Sean used to write drama – worked for the Players Theatre in the thirties and forties.[6] But better keep information about him to just those two sentences above.

He's the unlikeliest fellow to keep a pub – not exactly

dour but silent enough, except among a very small circle. Completely unspoiled, very true to himself.

[letter continues on other matters]

FROM TED HUGHES
North Tawton, Devon
8 March 1982

Dear Michael,

Sean Rafferty is dazed with joy, seeing his poems in the Magazine.[7] They look pretty good.

Could you let me have 12 copies – bill me for postage and everything.

Who did the interview with Herbert?[8] I assume he was a Pole and in Poland – or about to return to Poland.

A complete Herbert would be a great book. Are all his early poems really as good as the ones that keep on appearing? Very fine essay, the Piero d[ella] Fran[cesca]. Very good to publish that, & to find it.

Keep well
yours
Ted

CORRESPONDENCE WITH THE AUTHOR, 1993

FROM MICHAEL SCHMIDT
Manchester
13 July 1993

Dear Mr Rafferty,

Nicholas Johnson kindly brought me some of your more

recent work which has strengthened my commitment to your writing expressed earlier in the inclusion of your sequence of poems in *PN Review*.[9] We would very much like to do a collection of your writing in book form. Ideally we could work through Nicholas Johnson who seems to know you and your work very well.

I would like to schedule publication, if it is congenial to you, for early in 1995. I would like Nicholas to work on an article/interview with you which need not be formal in nature but which ought ideally to have your approval in detail.

I would also welcome the opportunity to publish some of your new poems in the magazine during 1994, leading up to publication.

Do let me know either directly or through Nicholas that these proposals are acceptable. If they are, I will issue you a contract for publication and hope to see a finished manuscript by 1st July 1994.

With kind regards,
Yours ever,
Michael Schmidt

FROM SEAN RAFFERTY
Iddesleigh, Devon
[n.d.]

Dear Michael Schmidt

I am pleased all the poems will be published and that Carcanet will publish them. It is best you deal with Nick Johnson because I am old and slow. I will find it easier to talk to him than I would a stranger: not that I have much to say. Publish any poems you find suitable: if I write any more, which is doubtful, I will send them to you.

The opening sentence is a massive understatement. I am

absolutely delighted that Carcanet will publish the poems.

Yours
Sean Rafferty

FROM MICHAEL SCHMIDT
Manchester
21 July 1993

Dear Mr Rafferty

Thank you so much for your letter. I have heard, too, from Nick Johnson. I am really delighted. I have suggested to him what I hope an interview might yield, primarily an evocation of your early years, early landscapes, antecedents, formative reading, musical and artistic enthusiasms, and the narrative detail of a long life which may help put the poems into a chronology. I'm also interested to know which writers have 'stayed the course' with you. I always imagine you must read Herbert as often, and as attentively, as you do Yeats.

It was a special pleasure to meet Nick here – he seems a person of unusually pure and admirable motive, quite refreshing when most of the writers and journalists one meets are jockeying for position in a world of little fames and reputations which is vertiginously ephemeral.

When Nick returns from France we will exchange contracts for the book and start the long march towards publication.

I am absolutely delighted we will be publishing your poems.

Yours ever
Michael Schmidt

FROM SEAN RAFFERTY
Iddesleigh, Devon
[n.d.]

Dear Michael Schmidt

I will try to give an honest account of my life and opinions. Looked at objectively, the only thing extraordinary about my life is its length.

It has occurred to me that I should tell you that before I knew you were going to publish the poems Kevin Perryman (Babel) suggested he should publish half a dozen of the later poems in a booklet and I agreed.[10] I don't know when they will be published because he works very slowly.

I was touched by what you said about Nick. It was perceptive and true. He has an unselfish, untutored passion for poetry. I'm devoted to him.

Yours
Sean Rafferty

FROM MICHAEL SCHMIDT
Manchester
9 August 1993

Dear Mr Rafferty

Thank you for your letter. There is no objection on my part to Kevin Perryman of Babel doing a booklet of six of your poems. On the contrary, it sounds an attractive proposal and does not affect our book. Material from the pamphlet might not then be available for *PN Review*? Before the book I'd like to make a song and dance in the magazine.

On Friday I go to Cornwall with my little tribe (three children) for a week. I expect the rain will be warmer down there, the beer waterier. The big clay boats that come into Fowey harbour (we stay in Polruan, opposite) are one of life's pleasures, tugged in quietly humming and all ablaze with lights at 3 a.m. past the bedroom window. And by day hundreds of sails and (even nowadays) a million butterflies on the buddlia (sp?). Perhaps on a later visit to one of my authors I might come shake your hand at Winkleigh? I go once or twice a year to see Charles and Nora Sisson.

With kind regards
Michael Schmidt

FROM SEAN RAFFERTY
Iddesleigh, Devon
[n.d.]

Dear Michael Schmidt

Thank you for your letter. I will write to Perryman: there are no other complications of that sort. I understand about the magazine and hope there will be material for that.

West Country weather seems to be improving. With any luck Cornwall will be sunny. I hope for your sake and the children's it will be and the harbour full of boats.

If you are ever near this part of Devon, please do come to see [me]. I would like to thank you personally and for me Manchester is as far off as the moon.

Yours
Sean Rafferty

NOTES
1. The *Collected Poems*, edited by Nicholas Johnson, was published in 1995. It included a 'conversation' between editor and poet, from which Rafferty's words here are taken.
2. Sorley MacLean is quoted on the back cover of the *Collected Poems*. MacLean (1911–96), born on Raasay, studied at the University

of Edinburgh (1929–33), graduating with a first-class degree in English Literature. He was the leader of the Gaelic poetry renaissance in Scotland. Carcanet published a bilingual collected poems in 1989, with a revised and corrected edition in 1999.

3. George Barker (1913–91); his posthumous collection *Street Ballads* was reviewed by David Wright in *PN Review* 89 (January–February 1993), who remarked, 'all the poems in this collection were written by a man in his late seventies. Such is their vitality, drive and exuberance, it's hard to believe'. Barker's poems were published in *PN Review* in the 1980s.

4. His first wife, Betty Caldecourt, died in 1945 'almost the day peace was declared'. They had one daughter. He married Peggy Laing in 1946 and moved to the village of Iddesleigh the following year.

5. Clare (daughter of Allen Lane, founder of Penguin Books) and Michael Morpurgo (author of *War Horse* and many other works for children) set up Farms for City Children in 1976 at Nethercott House, on the outskirts of Iddesleigh.

6. The Players' Theatre was founded in London in 1936, attracting gifted musicians and performers as well as designers, and drawing on the traditions of the Victorian music-hall.

7. The poems were published in *PN Review* 26 (July-August 1982), but the handwritten date on Hughes's letter is clear; perhaps Rafferty saw a proof? Yet the following remarks suggest that Hughes had seen the whole issue. In his reply to Hughes, MNS notes 'The Rafferty poems have attracted a good deal of positive (and some negative, as I predicted) response' (11 March 1982).

8. 'A Poet of Exact Meaning', an interview with Zbigniew Herbert by Marek Oramus, a Polish student (*PN Review* 26, July–August 1982). Carcanet did not publish the poems of Herbert (1924–98), but did publish a volume of his essays, *Barbarian in the Garden* (1985), translated from the Polish by Michael March and Jarosław Anders, which included the essay on Piero della Francesca.

9. Nicholas Johnson, who was born in Devon, is a poet and publisher. He edited a revised and enlarged *Poems* (<u>etruscan books</u>, 1999), and Rafferty's *Poems, Revue Sketches, and Fragments* (<u>etruscan books</u>, 2004).

10. Kevin Perryman's *Babel* magazine, founded in 1983, features new poetry in English and German chiefly, but also other languages, with poems presented bilingually; *Babel* VII (1993) included six poems by Rafferty. *Salathiel's Song/ Salathiels Lied* (from the Babel fine press) consists of ten late poems, published in 1994 on what would have been Rafferty's eighty-fifth birthday.

THE YEAR IN BOOKS

Patricia Beer, *Friend of Heraclitus*

Aphra Behn, *Selected Poems*, edited by Malcolm Hicks

Eavan Boland, *In a Time of Violence*

C.R. Boxer, *The Christian Century in Japan 1549–1650*

Charles Boyle, *The Very Man*

Bo Carpelan, *Homecoming*, translated by David McDuff

John Clare, *Cottage Tales*, edited by Eric Robinson, David Powell and Paul Dawson

Gillian Clarke, *The King of Britain's Daughter*

C.B. Cox, *Collected Poems*

Robert Duncan, *Selected Poems*, edited by Robert J. Bertholf

Mircea Eliade, *Bengal Nights*, translated by Catherine Spencer

Alistair Elliot, *Turning the Stones*

Caradoc Evans, *Selected Stories*, edited by John Harris

William Feaver, *Pitman Painters: the Ashington Group 1934-1984*

John Gallas, *Flying Carpets Over Filbert Street*

Graham Greene, *Mornings in the Dark: The Graham Greene Film Reader*, edited by David Parkinson

Ivor Gurney, *Collected Letters*, edited by R.K.R. Thornton

Martin Harrison, *Theatre: a book of words*

John Heath-Stubbs, *Sweet-Apple Earth*

Humphrey Jennings, *The Humphrey Jennings Film Reader*, edited by Kevin Jackson

Gabriel Josipovici, *In a Hotel Garden*

Michael Krüger, *Diderot's Cat*, translated by Richard Dove

Charles Lamb, *Charles Lamb and Elia*, edited by J.E. Morpurgo

Hugh MacDiarmid, *Complete Poems Volume I,* edited by Michael Grieve and W.R. Aitken

Hugh MacDiarmid, *Selected Prose*, edited by Alan Riach

Hugh MacDiarmid, *Scottish Eccentrics*, edited by Alan Riach, note by Norman MacCaig

Chris McCully, *Time Signatures*

Paul Mills, *Half Moon Bay*

Czeslaw Miłosz, *Provinces: poems 1987-1991*, translated by the author and Robert Hass

Les Murray, *Translations from the Natural World*

John Peck, *Argura*

Sandro Penna, *Remember Me, God of Love: selected poems and prose*, translated by Blake Robinson

F.T. Prince, *Collected Poems 1935–1992*

Eça de Queiros, *The Maias*, translated by Patricia McGowan and Ann Stevens

Eça de Queiros, *The Yellow Sofa and Three Portraits*, translated by John Vetch

Vicki Raymond, *Selected Poems*

Gareth Reeves, *Listening In*

Edmond Rostand, *Cyrano de Bergerac*, translated by Edwin Morgan

Gāmini Salgādo, *The True Paradise*, edited by Fenella Copplestone

Norm Sibum, *In Laban's Field: selected poems*

C.H. Sisson, *Is there a Church of England?*

Gavin Smith, *Whisky: a book of words*

Kevin Stratford, *Songs of the Adept*

Michael Teague, *In the Wake of the Portuguese Navigators*

Nicolas Tredell, *The Critical Decade: culture in crisis*

Cesar Vallejo, *Trilce*, translated by Rebecca Seiferle

Daniel Weissbort, *Nietzsche's Attaché Case*

1994

Denise Riley (b.1948) is a poet, philosopher and literary critic, currently Professor of the History of Ideas and of Poetry at the University of East Anglia. Her third collection, *Mop Mop Georgette* (Reality Street Editions) came out in 1993, a *Selected Poems* from the same publisher in 2000; and in 2016 *Say Something Back* (Picador), a new collection, included 'A Part Song', which had won the Forward Prize for Best Single Poem in 2012. *PN Review* carried an interview with her in 1995, in which she said 'I suppose I've got an obstinate attachment to musicality (and "musicality" is a vague word, as is "cadence"). If I entitle things "Lyric" it's because the main property that I've aimed at in those poems is some musical brightness.' And: 'I hope I would not be the heroine of my own work – although it's always a fragile balance, to use the stuff of your life while refusing to shine as the guiding light of it.'[1]

FROM DENIS RILEY
London
23 April 1994

Dear Michael Schmidt,

It was very kind of you to write.[2] But I should say that I did my very best, although in vain, to persuade my interviewer *not* to send her piece off to *PNR*, but to stick to an Anglo-American periodical with established interests in those 'issues'.

I am enclosing some issue-free offprints. But emphatically not *for* anything – except possible interest.

Perhaps one difficulty concerns currently-pursued ways of reading, really – my impression is that one of the routes that critics now use to approach contemporary poetry (especially, for contingent historical reasons, if it happens to be the work of a woman author) is to approach it with a conceptual or thematic template, and to then read the poetry for its 'fit'. To try to render the writing legible in terms of its faithfulness or its capacities to illustrate a set of 'theoretical' terms; but without taking apart the historical formations or metaphoricity of those theories themselves.

(This ensures that critics expect an illustrative poetry. Those few people who enquire about my work never believe me if I explain that I work 'blind' in poetry, and that I don't *know* 'what I'm doing' other than practically and in retrospect, and very imperfectly at that. And that if I need to write thematically, I do so through the channel of journalism, or of intellectual history.)

The other main critical approach-road now is, I suppose, worse: the demarcating and shepherding of factions and schools; a direction in which the sociology of allegiance veers to gossip.

If you like Michael Haslam's work (I have run his fan club for a quarter of a century) you might just like the American poet Fanny Howe's.[3] Both of them have what seems (to an agnostic reader!) the advantage of spiritual conviction on top of extraordinary technical gifts. Like Elena Shvarts; whose new collection I expect you're having reviewed.[4]

Yours sincerely,
Denise Riley

FROM MICHAEL SCHMIDT
Manchester
6 May 1994

Dear Denise Riley,

Thank you so much for your letter of 23 April and for the poems which I have just seen. The interviewer whose piece I returned has written again to ask whether an interview more *ad rem* would be of interest and in a speculative way I shall reply and say perhaps. I would certainly welcome a conversation or interview which opened your work towards our readers.

What you say about 'working blind' in poetry seems to me to make perfect sense not only in relation to your own poems but to most of the poetry that I most enjoy. Prosodically, the surprises that such poetry can yield and the clarifications that come are often the durable ones.

In an oblique and rather awkward way I think I am beginning to learn quite a bit from your *PNR* piece but also from snatches of correspondence with you and with Michael Haslam. His objection to a proper 'Collected' or 'selected' poems in chronological order I have found particularly illuminating, in a way that one of Andrew Crozier's early essays on the formation of readership startled me into a different approach.[5]

Michael Haslam said that three of the most important people in his firmament were called Riley and also indicated to me how very real your support for his work has been.[6]

I had a letter from Fanny Howe offering to send me her work, an offer which I declined because our list at the moment can hardly accommodate the tenants lodged on it and queuing up down the street. Editorially speaking, I seem to go through periods of excessive enthusiasm followed by periods of excessive restraint. A period of enthusiasm may be coming to an end at present, and much adjustment of ear will have to follow my discovery of Michael Haslam's work and, also, my response to those poems you sent for *PN Review* which I retained. A young Irish poet called Sinéad Morrissey has also done interesting things to my reading in the last few weeks.[7] Apparently Eliot used to claim that editors ceased to develop and ceased to hear after the age of 40. He may have been wrong – or perhaps I now suffer from new kinds of deafness! I hope not: it is strange to be so drawn by something I find so opaque.

With kind regards,
Yours ever,
Michael Schmidt

FROM DENISE RILEY
London
9 July 1994

Dear Michael Schmidt,

Many thanks indeed for inviting me to contribute to the 100th issue [of *PN Review*], which is a great privilege – and one I don't feel I merit, especially as I'm so new a contributor as to ~~not yet~~ only just! have been published.

I am very glad nevertheless to offer you 217 lines of poems, including their titles (there are more than five poems, but within the 220-line count you're allowing) and my short comments, in about 480 words. I have set them all out, poems and comment, in the running order I'd like, if possible, and I've indicated the publisher at the top of the notes. Copyright is mine for everything here.

But if there's matter here that you really don't like, do please cut it! There are lots of other, maybe more tolerable, poems to fish out of.

Can I suggest you look at an excellent new book by R.F. Langley called *Twelve Poems*, published by Infernal Methods [address]; a review copy will probably be around your office. My *guess* is that you'd greatly enjoy it.[8]

Warmest congratulations on the 100th anniversary. I have an inkling of the effort and struggle it will all have entailed.

With best wishes,
Denise Riley

FROM DENISE RILEY
London
22 November 1994

Dear Michael,

Thank you for your letter. The *Calander* [*PNR* 100] is a fine production, and I hope you've had many serious compliments on it. – I've fought an intermittent corner for so long against the profoundly misleading categorising drives which afflict contemporary poetry that it's a great relief to see this fight being enacted as an editorial policy. I'm taking out a subscription at once to *PN Review*.

Best wishes
as ever,
Denise

FROM MICHAEL SCHMIDT
Manchester
2 December 1994

Dear Denise,

Thank you for your note of 22 November. I was certainly grateful for your response as I was for our brief conversation at the party. Just as I hate the narrowing English nationalism that besets us, so, too, I hate categorisations which limit, exclude and in the end warp readership. It is such a joy to be able to respond, with surprise and clarification, to poems like yours, to Michael Haslam's, to Langley's, and to some of the American poets that I am now 'taking on board'. The pleasure is that these poets actually submit work – which is almost the only way I come to read these days – and feel that *PN Review* belongs to them as it does to Davie, Sisson, Boland, Middleton and Ashbery. I think there are certain lengths that I will be unable to go – including the challenge of Tom Raworth, a favourite with some of my students.[9] But teaching combined with the magazine managed to keep me less stale than I would otherwise be and the freedom one has with support from the Arts Council carries with it a responsibility to be, perhaps, more open and catholic than one would were one governed by a tyrannical accountant.

I hope we will have occasion to meet again soon.

With warm regards,
Yours ever,
Michael

*

Until Robyn Marsack reminded me of my correspondence with Denise Riley, I had forgotten that it was she who pointed me in the direction of R.F. Langley who, as a poet and diarist, is one of my favourite writers. Revisiting her generous and open letters, I experience once again that vexatious sense I have had as an editor of being torn between: Sisson and Davie for starters. Writers including Christopher Middleton and Andrew Crozier wrote prose which made me uneasy with the relatively narrow (as it seemed to me then) wake that Carcanet drew. But from a very early date we had been instrumental in bringing W.S. Graham back into circulation, and this had been noted; and Haslam; and in a different spirit Seán

Rafferty. We had a very strong translation list. And was not Ashbery on board as well? Even so, I felt the intellectual pull of writers like Denise Riley (and her poetry, more than in the case of Crozier). A full reorientation was not possible because, while I could be convinced by an argument, what had to persuade me was poems themselves, and as an academic I had a settled distrust for poetry written from the academy, though inevitably many of my favourite poets worked in education.

It is refreshing in retrospect to see that the wider dialogue which opened up when I spent two and a half years at Cambridge in 2015–18 was already begun, tentatively, at this time. I do now wish we had published the work of Fanny Howe; also of Denise Riley, had the opportunity arisen.

NOTES

1. Romana Huk, 'in Conversation with Denise Riley', *PN Review* 103 (May–June 1995).

2. In his letter of 20 April about the interview he had been offered, MNS reflected: 'Unfortunately a publisher and full-time academic seems to have very little leisure to "think" and therefore the editorial hunger is never quite defined sufficiently to look for the sustenance it desires in a logical and continuous fashion. Not, of course, that logic and continuity would be likely to locate the thing desired.'

3. Michael Haslam (b. 1947) knew Riley and other poets through their Cambridge connections. He was published by scattered independent presses, then Carcanet published a gathered and revised collection of his work as *A Whole Bauble* in 1995. Haslam moved on to Arc and later to Shearsman; there is a narrative bibliography on his website.
   Fanny Howe (b.1940), an American poet and novelist, whose work has been recognised by the award of the Ruth Lilly Prize (2009) among other distinctions. She is published by Graywolf in the USA; her latest collection is *Love and I* (2019).

4. John Pilling, a regular contributor, reviewed Elena Shvarts' *Paradise: selected poems* (Bloodaxe, 1993), in *PN Review* 98 (July-August 1994).

5. Andrew Crozier (1943–2008) is described on the Carcanet website as 'a poet and energiser of poetry': 'A champion of work excluded from the familiar canon, he brought to the English literary landscape of the 1960s and 70s an engagement with the energies of American poetry.' Carcanet published *A Various Art* (1987), edited by Crozier and Tim Longville, an anthology of poems written by a generation of poets who began writing in the 1960s and were published by small presses (Veronica Forrest-Thomson is the only woman represented); also *An Andrew Crozier Reader* (2012), edited by Ian Brinton.

6. The three Rileys would be the poets Denise, John and Peter (not related). John Riley (1937–78) met Tim Longville at Pembroke College, Cambridge; they founded the Grosseteste Press in 1966, and the Grosseteste Review in 1968. Grosseteste published *John Riley: The Collected Works* in 1980, after Riley died in an attack by muggers in his hometown of Leeds. Carcanet published his *Selected Poems* (1995), edited by Michael Grant. Peter Riley (b. 1940) is also an alumnus of Pembroke; *The Glacial Stairway* (2011), a collection of poems and prose, is his most recent work from Carcanet.

7. Sinéad Morrissey (b. 1972) grew up in a Communist household in Belfast; her first collection was published by Carcanet in 1996. *Parallax* (2013) won the T.S. Eliot Prize and *On Balance* (2017) won the Forward Prize for Best Collection.

8. MNS wrote to Riley: 'Incidentally, I am most grateful to you for suggesting that I get hold of the work of Roger Langley which I have been astonished by and enjoyed tremendously' (15 September), and she replied: 'And I'm glad you liked the Roger Langley work; it's a collection I'm astonished by. It has something of a late-WS Graham-feel to it, yet not quite' (11 October).

9. Carcanet did later publish Tom Raworth, see pp. 393–8.

THE YEAR IN BOOKS

Mark Akenside, James MacPherson and Edward Young, *Selected Poetry*, edited by S.H. Clark

Matthew Arnold, *Selected Poems*, edited by Keith Silver

John Ashbery, *And the Stars Were Shining*

Eavan Boland, *In a Time of Violence*

C.R. Boxer, *The Golden Age of Brazil 1695–1760*

John Burnside, *The Hoop*

Roberto Calasso, *The Ruin of Kasch*, translated by William Weaver and Stephen Sartarelli

Paul Carter, *Baroque Memories*

Vincenzo Consolo, *The Smile of the Unknown Mariner*, translated by Joseph Farrell

William Cookson (ed), *Agenda: An Anthology: the first four decades 1959–1993*

Abraham Cowley, *Selected Poems*, edited by David Hopkins and Tom Mason

Elaine Feinstein, *Selected Poems*

Boris Ford (ed), *Benjamin Britten's Poets: an anthology of the poems he set to music*

Jon Glover, *To the Niagara Frontier; poems new and selected*

Elizabeth Jennings, *Familiar Spirits*

Adam Johnson, *The Playground Bell*

Gabriel Josipovici, *Moo Pak*

Michael Kennedy, *Music Enriches All: The Royal Northern College of Music, the first twenty-one years*

Thomas Kinsella, *From Centre City*

Frank Kuppner, *Everything is Strange*

Giacomo Leopardi, *The Canti: with a selection of his prose*, translated by J.G. Nichols

Lya Luft, *The Red House*, translated by Giovanni Pontiero

Hugh MacDiarmid, *Complete Poems Volume II*, edited by Michael Grieve and W.R. Aiken

Hugh MacDiarmid, *Lucky Poet*, edited by Alan Riach

Bill Manhire, *South Pacific*

C.B. McCully (ed), *The Poet's Voice and Craft*

Ian McMillan, *Dad, The Donkey's on Fire*

Sasha Moorsom and Michael Young, *Your Head in Mine*

Edwin Morgan, *Sweeping Out the Dark*

Les Murray (ed), *Five Fathers: Five Australian Poets of the Pre-Academic Era*

Gregory O'Brien, *Days Beside Water*

Neil Powell, *The Stones of Thorpness Beach*

Rodney Pybus, *Flying Blues*

Eça de Queiros, *The City and the Mountains*, translated by Roy Campbell

Eça de Queiros, *The Sin of Father Amaro*, translated by Nan Flanagan

Laura Riding, *Selected Poems*, edited by Robert Nye

Laura Riding, *The Word 'Woman'*, edited by Elizabeth Friedmann and Alan J. Clark

Anne Ridler, *Collected Poems*

José Saramago, *The Manual of Painting and Calligraphy*, translated by Giovanni Pontiero

Peter Sansom, *January*

Michael Schmidt (ed), *New Poetries I*

Roger Scruton, *The Classical Vernacular*

C.H. Sisson, *What and Who*

Iain Crichton Smith, *Endings and Beginnings*

Nicolas Tredell, *Conversations with Critics*

Jeffrey Wainwright, *The Red-Headed Pupil*

James McNeill Whistler, *Whistler on Art*, edited by Nigel Thorpe

Clive Wilmer (ed), *Poets Talking: 'Poet of the Month' interviews from BBC Radio 3*

Judith Wright, *Collected Poems*

1995

MNS had been keen that Jorie Graham should join the Carcanet list since 1993, and in 1994–95 she proceeded to do so. Graham (b. 1950) won the 1996 Pulitzer Prize for Poetry with *The Dream of the Unified Field: Selected Poems 1974–1994*, and was the first American woman to win the Forward Prize for Best Collection, with *PLACE* in 2012. She is currently the Boylston Professor of Rhetoric and Oratory at Harvard University, the first woman to hold the position. Interviewed for *Prac Crit* on the publication of her most recent collection, *Fast* (2017), Graham said in answer to Sarah Howe's question 'What can poetry do?': 'It is one of any civilization's most ancient and mysterious means for shaping the very tension between rupture and continuity, so that one has to take the measure, in every line, of one's nearness to the "edge" while also conjuring and experiencing the fall, or perhaps leap, to what may lie beyond that edge. In that sense every succession of verses invents or models both death and resurrection. They are both rehearsals and survivals.'[1]

FROM MICHAEL SCHMIDT
Manchester
29 September 1994

Dear Jorie Graham,

I have been speaking with Dan Halpern at Ecco about your
work because I would like to be your British publisher. It was
Eavan Boland who alerted me to your poems quite a while ago.

Given the existing body of work, it's hard to know how best
to 'present' it to British readers. My long-term objective would
be to publish a volume that gave British readers a sufficient
sense of what has come before, and then to follow on with
each of your new books, publishing here at roughly the time
of US publication. When I first discussed this with Dan, I had
in mind a *Selected*. An alternative would be a compendious
volume which we would not have the effrontery to call a
Collected but which could in effect, in a preliminary way, be just
that. The new work represents new departures; British readers
should know what you are departing from.

I'd like to ask whether, in the first place, you would like to be a
Carcanet author? We have a strong, diverse American element,
beginning with Williams, H.D., Riding, Ransom, Jeffers,
Winters, Millay (among others) and then concentrating on
Ashbery, Schuyler, Koch, O'Hara, Guest and in my generation
John Peck and (I hope again – we published him long ago)
Pinsky. We once published Bob Hass. Mark Strand and James
Merrill will appear.[2] Our British and Commonwealth list is
equally catholic (not, I trust, eclectic).

I would wish to introduce your work in 1996, ideally in the
spring, or in the late autumn of 1995.

You will be appearing at the Poetry International: it will
be a pleasure to meet you.[3] We will be celebrating its 25th
birthday. Eavan, Murray and Ashbery will be among the guests

of honour. It would be good if you could meet my colleagues and me at that time.

If you find this proposal attractive, can we begin to put the pieces in place? I look forward to hearing from you.

Yours sincerely,
Michael Schmidt

FAX FROM JORIE GRAHAM
11 January 1995, 6.07 p.m.

Michael –
I have sent, Federal Express, a rough draft of a *Selected Poems* to you today. Dan Halpern tells me you will contact Princeton University Press directly for permission to print from the first 2 books; the subsequent 3 are with Ecco. He also asked me to tell you to inform him if Princeton is at all difficult, as he knows people there and will take care of any problems... My draft ended up being 18 pages over your limit – but perhaps a change in type-face (point size) will take care of that. Let me know when you get it.

All best to you (and wishes for the New Year) –
Jorie (Graham)

FAX FROM JORIE GRAHAM
2 March 1995, 11.58

Michael –
Do you want work for *PN* that's post *Selected*? Or do you wish me to pick key poems from the book, and add a few new ones? My new work – from an as yet unpublished book called *Secrecy* – might not be representative of what readers will find in the *Selected*.[4] As you can tell, no doubt, each new book tends to differ somewhat from previous ones, and this new one is no exception.

Tell me – preferably by fax – what you prefer. Also, we need to discuss the interior design of the *Selected*: I'm very concerned about page-breaks, poem lay-out, stanza integrity and so on – with poems in as many different styles as these, it's hard to find one design that can accommodate different stanzaic structures, for example, I'm used to re-writing, re-punctuating and altering sequence in order to preserve the flow and music of the poems. So I need to see galleys at a stage where I can still make those kinds of minor alterations (to preserve Left to Right flow of poems, for example).

Can you let me know what our schedule is? Do you need any jacket material? Should I provide a photo? I ask all this now as I will be in Italy between March 12th and August 30th and, if that period should turn out to be important to your time-frame, we need to recall the state of the Italian mails – Let me know –

All Best

Jorie (Graham)

*

No Carcanet poet has had a clearer proleptic vision of her books than Jorie Graham: the importance of the unbroken long line naturally affects format and extent, the cover image, the quality of its colours, the accuracy of the printing register for text and cover, all of these affect reading itself, how the poems mean. Her vision of each book is quite stable and the publisher's job is to approximate it. One can almost get there, but never *quite*.

She is a generous poet: her public readings are real occasions because of the way in which she inhabits and propels her poems. The complexities of the long lines and sometimes of the extended syntactical periods all become functional when she speaks the poem. She is always larger than life, and, away from the lectern, always a companion so alert to the world and so candid (and sometimes mischievous) that one comes away from each encounter with a dozen new projects.

NOTES

1. https://www.joriegraham.com/node/312 (accessed 30 July 2019)

2. Many of these authors have been footnoted elsewhere. Carcanet was the UK publisher of two handsome volumes of the *Collected Poems* of William Carlos Williams (1883–1963) plus *Paterson*. The major Modernist H.D. (Hilda Doolittle, 1886–1961) was championed early in Carcanet's history, her *Tribute to Freud* being published in 1971, with an introduction by Peter Jones (reissued in 1997, edited by Norman Holmes Pearson); Pearson also edited her *Trilogy* (1974) of WWII poems and, with Michael King, *End to Torment: a memoir of Ezra Pound* (1980). Besides her prose books, Carcanet published Louis L. Martz's editions of HD's *Collected Poems 1912–1944* (1996) and *Selected Poems* (1997). Filling in gaps for British readers in the 1990s, Carcanet published John Crowe Ransom (1888-1974), *Selected Poems* (1995); Edna St Vincent Millay (1892–1950), *Selected Poems* (1996); Frank O'Hara (1926–66), *Selected Poems* (1991); Barbara Guest (1920–2006), *Selected Poems* (1996); Robert Pinsky (b. 1940), *The Figured Wheel: new and collected poems* (1996) – his *An Explanation of America* had been published in 1980; Mark Strand (1934–2014), *Selected Poems* (1995).
   John Peck (b. 1941), poet and Jungian analyst, who studied with Donald Davie at Vanderbuilt University, has published five volumes of poetry with Carcanet, including his *Collected Shorter Poems* (1999). He was one of the *Five American Poets* MNS introduced in 1979, along with Hass and Pinsky; the collection was revisited in a new edition in 2010.

3. Poetry International was initiated in London by Ted Hughes

as a response to the polarisation of the Cold War; the first festival took place in July 1967, lapsed ten years later, and was re-launched effectively as a biennial event in 1988. See Chris McCabe's account at www.southbankcentre.co.uk (accessed 30 July 2019).

4. Graham's next volume was called *The Errancy* (Ecco, 1997; Carcanet, 1998). Replying about arrangements for the *Selected*, MNS assured her that in Bryan Williamson, Carcanet had 'the best poetry typesetter in England'. Bryan worked with Carcanet for fifteen years, from the Old Fire Station in Todmorden and then from Frome, an 'anarcho syndicalist libertarian, five-a-side footballer, poetry buff and typesetter extraordinaire' as his family described him at his death in 2009 (www.hebdenbridge.co.uk, accessed 30 July 2019). MNS also mentioned that 'we have a fine lettering artist as our designer': this was Stephen Raw, who established the distinctive look of Carcanet's covers, jackets and catalogues in the 1980s, and remained a mainstay of the Press for thirty or so years.

THE YEAR IN BOOKS

Lancelot Andrewes, *Selected Writings*, edited by P.E. Hewison
John Ash, *Burnt Pages*
John Ashbery, *Flow Chart*
Sujata Bhatt, *The Stinking Rose*
Eavan Boland, *Collected Poems*
Eavan Boland, *Object Lessons: the life of the woman and the poet in our time*
Alison Brackenbury, *1829*
Sir Thomas Browne, *Selected Writings*, edited by Claire Preston
Lewis Carroll, *Selected Poems*, edited by Keith Silver
Robert Carver (ed), *Ariel at Bay: reflections on broadcasting and the arts*,
Paul Celan, *Poems of Paul Celan*, translated by Michael Hamburger
John Clare, *Northborough Sonnets*, edited by Eric Robinson and
     David Powell
Donald Davie, *Church, Chapel and the Unitarian Conspiracy*

Donald Davie, *These the Companions: recollections*

Geoff Dench, Tony Fowler and Kate Gavron (eds), *Young at Eighty:
the prolific public life of Michael Young*

Peter Gizzi (ed), *Exact Change Yearbook 1995*

Luis de Gongora Y Argote, *Selected Shorter Poems*, translated by
Michael Smith

Robert Graves, *Collected Writings on Poetry*, edited by Paul O'Prey

Robert Graves, *Complete Poems 1*, edited by Beryl Graves and
Dunstan Ward

Robert Graves, *Complete Short Stories*, edited by Patrick Quinn

Robert Graves, *The Centenary Selected Poems*, edited by Patrick
Quinn

Ivor Gurney, *Best Poems* and *The Book of Five Makings*, edited by
R.K.R. Thornton and George Walter

Sophie Hannah, *The Hero and the Girl Next Door*

Michael Haslam, *A Whole Bauble: Collected Poems 1977-1994*

Hildi Hawkins (ed), *On the Border: New Writing from Finland*

Molly Holden, *New and Selected Poems*

Stuart Hood, *The Book of Judith*

P.J. Kavanagh, *The Perfect Stranger*

Mimi Khalvati, *Mirrorwork*

Thomas Kinsella, *The Dual Tradition: an essay on poetry and politics
in Ireland*

Leena Krohn, *Doña Quixote and Other Citizens*, translated by Hildi
Hawkins

Clarice Lispector, *The Besieged City*, translated by Giovanni Pontiero

Roger Little, *The Shaping of Modern French Poetry: reflections on
unrhymed poetic form1840–1990*

Hugh MacDiarmid, *Contemporary Scottish Studies*, edited by Alan
Riach

José Rodriguez Migueis, *Happy Easter*, translated by John Byrne

Czeslaw Miłosz, *Facing the River*, translated by Czeslaw Miłosz
and Robert Hass

Les Murray, *Selected Poems*

Alan Myers, *Myers' Literary Guide to the North East of England*
John Peck, *Selva Morale*
Fernando Pessoa, *A Centenary Pessoa*, edited by Eugenio Lisboa
    with L.C. Taylor, translations by various hands
Edgar Allan Poe, *Poems and Essays on Poetry*, edited by C.H. Sisson
Neil Powell, *Roy Fuller: Writer and Society*
John Cowper Powys, *Petrushka and the Dancer: the diaries of John*
    Cowper Powys 1929-1939, edited by Morine Krissdóttir
Eça de Queiros, *To the Capital*, translated by John Vetch
Justin Quinn, *O'o'a'a' Bird*
Seán Rafferty, *Collected Poems*
Robert Rehder, *Compromises Will be Different*
Antonio Pinto Ribeiro (ed), *The State of the World*
John Riley, *Selected Poems*, edited by Michael Grant
Ralph Russell, *Hidden in the Lute: an anthology of two centuries of*
    Urdu literature
John Russell-Wood, *World on the Move*
Adam Schwartzman, *The Good Life The Dirty Life*
Leonardo Sciascia, *One Way or The Other*, translated by Sasha
    Rabinovitch
C.H. Sisson, *An Asiatic Romance*
Iain Crichton Smith, *Collected Poems*
Jon Stallworthy, *The Guest from the Future*
Mark Strand, *Selected Poems*
Susanna Tamaro, *For Solo Voice*, translated by Sharon Wood
Miguel Torga, *Tales and New Tales from the Mountain*, translated by
    Ivana Carlsen
Andrew Waterman, *End of the Pier Show*
Clive Wilmer, *Selected Poems*
Richard Zenith, *113 Galician Portuguese Troubador Poems*

1996

Christine Brooke-Rose (1923–2012) came to Carcanet on the advice of George Steiner, sending MNS her new novel *Amalgamemnon* at the end of 1983. At that time she was still living in Paris, where she taught at the University of Paris VII for twenty years. During the war she had worked in intelligence at Bletchley Park, and that decoding experience informed her approach to language and structure. Although she knew Hélène Cixous very well, 'the very idea of a "feminine writing" irritated her: she found it too essentialist'. Jean-Michel Rabaté remarks in his affectionate 'Farewell' article that 'her structuralism was tempered by humour', and that the writing constraints she imposed on herself 'were the very devices that allowed her to advance. She said that she could never have written an autobiography, as she did with the spectacular *Remake* (1996), had she not found it interesting to write about her life without using the first person.'[1] Carcanet published nine of her books, including a *Brooke-Rose Omnibus* (1986) collecting her earlier work.

FROM CHRISTINE BROOKE-ROSE
Cabrières d'Avignon
7 February 1996

Dear Michael,

Many thanks for your very nice letter. I'm glad we've reached a stage in our friendship when I can occasionally criticise minor things (I know I've also done worse). Believe me, I'm very happy at Carcanet, the contact is much easier & more personal than in a huge firm; the production is beautiful etc. etc. I just get slightly distressed at not selling for you, and therefore more so when occasions of selling a few copies are missed. But think how much worse it would be if a big firm did everything with huge ads (it wouldn't of course, since I don't sell! vicious circle), and I still didn't sell.

Of course I wouldn't resist V and X (or rather X & V) together.[2] I even suggested it. And of course the idea of redividing the Omnibus was barmy.

I hope your heart won't sink, but I'm actually working on a new novel. So *Remake* did, finally, unblock me, which is why I undertook it (blocked since *Txt*). It's going very slowly and I have no idea whether it's any good or not, but it's lovely to be writing again. Heather Reyes, who is doing a PhD on me, read the first 25 pages when she was here & liked it, and brought me some documentation.[3] It's about people who sleep in the street so I needed to know the GB admin situation, even if I don't stick to it literally or in detail. It's a huge effort of imagination but I needed to invent again after five years of various versions of putting things down merely because they happened, then worrying about what to cut, etc. etc.

So it's very slow, some 65 typed (still on computer) pages so far. Called *Next*. This is absolutely *entre nous*, please don't talk about it as I may never finish it.

To get back to your plans. I'm glad *Verbivore* as first was a mistake for *Textermination*, not only because it's more accessible but because you liked it so much. And it seems to be out of print, though probably not in U.S. (I get no info about that, perhaps because I hate reading royalty statements with any attention).

I was very sorry to read, late, in *LRB*, of Donald Davie's death last autumn. I used to know him years ago when he was at Essex, and he was always very nice to me (we had Pound and poetic diction in common), for all his apparent later grumpiness. I think he was a disappointed writer.[4] Did brilliantly as professor but perhaps didn't pierce through as he'd hoped qua poet. Well, we have that in common too, but I try to take it in my stride. That was a very nice article.[5]

(No reply expected)

Love,

Christine

FROM MICHAEL SCHMIDT
Manchester
20 February 1996

Dear Christine,

So far the response to *Remake* from the people who have solicited review copies has been very warm and I hope that other reviews will follow apace.[6] The book is published in two weeks' time.

Thank you very much for your letter of 7th February. I had a very pleasant lunch the other day with Raymond Tallis who told me about your rather ghastly conference at Warwick.[7]

Concerning *Remake*, my only criticism of the production is that there should have been a blank page at the end. It is horrible to pass from the final page to the inside board of the paperback binding. Gillian, too, was particularly agitated by this inadequacy.[8]

We had a memorial service for Donald Davie last week in Cambridge. Unfortunately Frank [Kermode] was away in Houston and could not come and George [Steiner], though I invited him, did not reply. It was a rather beautiful service with a choir in St Catherine's Chapel and readings by Tomlinson,

Wilmer and Heaney as well as an address by your publisher.[9]
You are right I think in your diagnosis of Donald as a
disappointed writer – not that he could have written better (he
could hardly have written better than the poems in *To Scorch
or Freeze*, which are magnificent) but that he felt he deserved a
better readership. Somehow we cannot provide – 'we' meaning
lecturers and teachers – the kind of readership that responds at
any depth or with any intensity to the work of the Modernists
or of those who have learned from them without succumbing
to post-Modernism.

With love as always,
Michael

PRESS RELEASE   PRESS RELEASE   PRESS RELEASE   PRESS RELEASE

CARCANET'S OFFICES DEVASTATED IN BOMB BLAST

The bomb that struck central Manchester on Saturday, 14 June, severely damaged
the offices of Carcanet Press. It is uncertain when, or whether, they will open again
for business.

The Corn Exchange, where Carcanet has had office for 25 years, is still within the
police 'no-go' cordon and is said to have sustained severe structural damage. A police
spokesman described it as 'a wreck. It will be a long time before access is permitted.'

Viewed from Salford, at present the closest access that can be obtained, it is clear
that windows, window frames and part of the roof are destroyed. Fortunately on the
Saturday of the blast none of Carcanet's staff was at the office.

Carcanet, one of Britain's permiere poetry ad literary publishing companies, will
establish temporary offices by Friday 21 June, address to be notified.

'The September launch of the new paperback fiction list, the relaunch of *PN Review*,
and the ambitious autumn poetry programme, will not be delayed,' said Managing
Director Michael Schmidt. 'We have had crises before. This certainly is a change from
cash-flow problems. On balance, I prefer the more conventional kinds of crises.' […]

PRESS RELEASE   PRESS RELEASE   PRESS RELEASE   PRESS RELEASE

FROM CHRISTINE BROOKE-ROSE
Cabrières d'Avignon
25 June 1996

Dear Michael,

I rang several times after the bombing and could get no reply, then after several days I got Carol, at home, who told me no one had been hurt but that all the files etc. etc. would have to be built up again slowly. What a disaster for you. I hope you'll get compensation. She told me anything sent to the old address would reach you at the provisional premises, so I'm sending the novel, registered, and will of course be patient in the circumstances (but try not to take 5 months again). I thought it would be better to send it before the summer vacation as arranged.

Frank Kermode read it while he stayed with me last week and liked it, says all my work has a 'signature'. But he was slowed down by the very things I intend as slowing down (all my novels have something to try and force the reader to read attentively!), as no doubt you will be too. Namely: the different layers of Cockney, though the spelling is very consistent and one should in theory get used to it; and, more needful of concentration, the abolition of conventional announcements or even spaces for switches of viewpoint (i.e. there are no 'chapters' or even spaces between sections). This is voulu, partly for concentration but also to express our feelings that these people are indistinguishable from the outside, like 'niggers' in the old days... If the reader has concentrated it should be absolutely clear we are in someone else's mind or in a different dialogue, from what is thought or said, and apart from the absence of marking I give plenty of other clues, immediately or very soon. These are the 'visibles'. Another visible, but which should cause no problem is that I scatter the text whenever a character is alone, and, if it's a homeless character, he loses his 'I', recovering it only when he's with others. This last does not apply to the other poor characters who do have homes (Jacinto, Blake, Adelina).

Secondly, the alphabet theme is important, and recurs with explanation at the end, i.e. all the characters have names beginning with one of the 26 letters, but the ten homeless ones have names beginning with the top row of keys on a typewriter. Also, I don't use the verb 'to have' (for obvious reasons, these are have-nots). I did a search but will remove any that have crept in in proof and in a last close reading before I send the disk. So don't bother to look for them, or about literals. These are the 'invisibles' I like to play with. The 'visibles' will be pounced on. Be patient therefore. I just warn you of both so that you don't make them the subject of criticism, as I don't intend to change them. Any other criticism welcome.

My printer conked out just before the last two pages, so I typed them out, the print is a bit larger so the scattering may be a bit different, but it will be OK on disk. I've had to type this letter too.

All the best, and 'courage mon ami', and love,
Christine

FROM CHRISTINE BROOKE-ROSE
Cabrières d'Avignon
25 June 1996

Dear Michael,

Here are the last two pages which my printer, after complex manip[ulation]s, unexpectedly delivered. So please (when you get my TS & letter) replace my two typed ones, they look better.

I received your sad circular this morning. Of course I'll cooperate. But all my reviews except those for *Remake* are in my archive at Austin Texas (Harry Ransom Humanities Center) so if you really need all the back ones you'll have to write to them. As for the photo I prefer to have a new one when (& if) you next publish me. And I'll send a Xerox of my <u>last</u> contract, unless you specifically tell me you want them all (they're all the same, I think). With copies of the few *Remake* reviews.

Did you send this circular to Jerzy?[10] I assume the Norwid is bombed, & hope he kept a copy of it all. That wasn't a real Q. you need answer, just a reminder in case he wasn't on the list.

You should be getting the novel next week, I posted it yesterday, registered, with a framed request to forward to post-bomb premises.

Good luck, and courage.

Maybe the damage is less than you surmise.

Love,
Christine

Replying to Brooke-Rose on 1 July, MNS wrote that 'it appears we may not have access to our offices for some time yet. The damage was very extensive.' He had asked all the authors to send in materials in order to reconstitute their files: contracts, photographs, reviews. In a letter of 10 October to Brooke-Rose he states 'I cannot refer to past correspondence since the correspondence is all at the disaster warehouse being hoovered.' In order to reconstruct the Carcanet mailing list, MNS sent out a circular on 11 July requesting names of 'up to five individuals who you feel might like to receive information about Carcanet… we are naturally especially anxious that our readers miss none of the major books we are publishing this autumn. The new list is our most ambitious ever. We are re-launching fiction in paperback. The range and depth of the poetry, Fyfield and Lives and Letters programme are impressive. The Graves and MacDiarmid programmes make significant advances too.'

Carcanet did manage to publish 36 books in 1996.

FROM MICHAEL SCHMIDT
Manchester
21 August 1996

Dear Christine,

Many thanks for your letter of 9 August. I <u>believe</u> we have worked out a strategy to have copies of *Remake* and other titles at your conference in Switzerland (they have already been despatched), which looks like being quite an impressive intellectual spread. I am agonising still over reissuing the *Omnibus*. The book is so long that when we reprint we will have to charge £14.95 on a 500 run or £12.95 on a 1000 run. There is no way we can pull it back to £9.95, which is where it could attract students. Its absence is a real problem. I hope to have a decision on it by mid-September. We are putting *Textermination* into paperback next year as you know.

I have made a very slow start on *Next*. So far I have the sense of a novel which goes 'back' to develop some areas of your work which many of your readers most like, in terms of structuring and reification of language. I find it very hard to read continuously.[11] It may be that I am tired and old, but I suspect that this is a novel to which I will find myself unequal. I will persist, after Japan, and hope to like it. I will not burden you with one of my enormous letters unless I feel it's necessary.

My unease with the novel does not mean that – if I don't warm to it in the end – we will not publish it. You are a Carcanet author. I feel that you wrote *Remake* for me, so I would be churlish not to let you write *Next* for yourself and those readers who can warm to it.[12] My difficulty will be in 'presenting' it. I hope that after thirty more pages I'll be taken over by it, as I was by *Xorandor* and *Textermination*, though not by *Amalgamemnon* or *Verbivore*. I am your middle-brow and sub-intellectual publisher.

Would you be content to have *Next* published in February or March of 1998? We have *Textermination* in 1997, and the costly reprint of the *Omnibus* in whatever form we finally decide. If you have a problem with 1998 we can discuss alternatives, though we are extremely constricted in scheduling. Delaying the book into 1998 would not mean delaying considerations till then: I want to give you a less incomplete response soon.

Love as always,
Michael

FROM CHRISTINE BROOKE-ROSE
Cabrières d'Avignon
4 October 1996

Dear Michael,

I forgot to tell you in my last letter, just posted, that I followed your brilliant suggestion of omitting possessive pronouns, and to thank you for it.[13] It was more difficult than I thought: not only did I have to search for the dialect forms as well (me, mah etc.), but I couldn't, as you thought, simply replace with 'the' (the most alienating word in current English). Sometimes a demonstrative would do (this, that) or the indefinite article, but sometimes I had to rephrase ('what are you called' for 'what's your name', etc.), and once or twice, to omit altogether. And I had to give up Ivy's 'mah raobics' for 'my aerobics' (replaced with the less funny 'nahraobics', as if from Nairobi). But it was interesting and, you were right, it should add (by my own theory) to the unconscious feeling of non-possession.

I only did it for the ten homeless. And even when they're talked *to* or *about* (i.e. no 'your', yours' or 'his/her'). All the other characters (the Goan family, the woman at the job centre and her husband, the wife, the interviewer etc.) keep their possessives. So it will be invisible, like my other constraints.

But you can add it to the blurb if you like.

Love,
Christine

MNS wrote to Doreen Davie on 5 November 1996 to thank her for sending flowers to the new office (4th Floor Conavon Court, 12–16 Blackfriars Street), which he described as 'a kind of Edwardian lantern on top of a Victorian building':

> We receive back from the storage centre in Worsley today the debris from the Corn Exchange and it will be possible at last to assess the extent of actual loss and damage. It will be interesting to greet this material, last seen on 14 June when the offices were put to bed for the night, never to wake up again. We have reason to believe that the archive material, which was boxed pending removal to the Rylands, may have survived intact.

Postscript: On 22 May 2017, as people were leaving a concert by Ariana Grande at the Manchester Arena, a radical Islamist detonated a home-made bomb, which killed 23 people (including the bomber) and injured 139, more than half of them children. MNS emailed Alison Brackenbury on 30 May:

> I had occasion to Facebook your lovely poem about the previous bomb. Then I got some nasty comments from people saying we were exploiting the present tragedy by remembering the earlier one. That certainly saddened me. It has been a hard place to live this last week, Manchester. Probably England itself, of which we are a metonym...

Brackenbury emailed back on 31 May:

> I am very sorry about the Facebook comments. The Internet can be a magnet for crazy and destructive people. There's usually one of these on any busy bus. But most of the other people on the bus are fine, shaking their heads over their shopping. Manchester is the place, I've found, where people are kindest on the buses. I am sure your city will, in the end, keep its good heart.

My friend and colleague Michael Freeman was and remained enthusiastic about Christine Brooke-Rose's novels, and he had a wonderful way of dealing with her: patient, calm, intelligently acquiescent. Others were less emollient. When we published her quartet of early experimental novels *Out*, *Such*, *Between* and *Thru* in *The Brooke-Rose Omnibus*, a colleague mused aloud, 'Will the next novel be called *Bitch*?' Creative, if a little harsh. Christine was a formidable writer who once stood, beside her then-friend Muriel Spark, on the threshold of a great popular success. In *The Novel: a biography*, I wrote:

> At first Brooke-Rose and Spark were taken together, as if growing from a common trunk. In 1965 Spark was awarded the James Tait Black Memorial Prize for *The Mandelbaum Gate*. The following year, for her second experimental novel, *Such*, Brooke-Rose received the same award. In their early careers Spark and Brooke-Rose were friends, but Spark managed her life and her career efficiently, did not bother with husbands after the first one, and after limping along the poor, hard lanes found the main highway. Christine Brooke-Rose became a more obviously experimental and theoretical writer. She was five years Spark's junior. None of her books made a breakthrough, those who praised her – Angela Carter, Frank Kermode, Lorna Sage – come to her with critical and interpretative tools sharper and subtler than general readers are expected to possess.

There was a good deal of affection underpinning our carping, which went in both directions. Her concern for Carcanet after the bomb soon gave way to a concern for her own work. I have often been a slow editor and her five-month wait was not unusual, especially for fiction writers on the list. It must be infuriating (I know it is, from an author's point of view), and not uncommon in publishing at that time.

The main disappointment Christine experienced with Carcanet, apart from my tardiness in response and, in some cases, my failures as a reader, was Carcanet's inability radically to improve – that is, to increase – her readership. In terms of reviews, essays and academic attention she always had a strong pull, though it did depend on the progressive fascination of her writing which became more and more difficult for her as she progressed, refusing to repeat herself and always avoiding the boredom of conventionality.

It has been a disappointment that we did not gain a wider readership for our fiction list. Christine stayed with us, and we with her, despite slow sales. Gabriel Josipovici, another novelist/critic deeply engaged with European modernism and with an innovatory style, has been with us for four decades and his work has found a slowly expanding and committed readership. Our translation list was ahead of its time – now Clarice Lispector, Leonardo Sciascia, Natalia Ginzburg and others are being re-rediscovered. The same is bound to happen to these remarkable British novelists.

NOTES

1. Jean-Michel Rabaté, 'Farewell to Christine Brooke-Rose', *Textual Practice* 32:2 (2018).

2. Her novels *Xorandor* and *Verbivore* were published by Carcanet in 1986 and 1990, and *Textermination* in 1991.

3. Heather Reyes's PhD thesis 'Delectable metarealism/ethical experiments: re-reading Christine Brooke-Rose' was presented at the University of London in 1998.

4. Brooke-Rose wrote a *ZBC of Ezra Pound* (Faber and Faber, 1971) and *A Structural Analysis of Pound's Usura Canto: Jakobson's method extended and applied to free verse* (Mouton, 1976).

5. Michael Wood, 'In Love', *London Review of Books* Vol. 18 no. 2 (26 January 1996).

6. Lorna Sage, reviewing *Remake* for the *LRB* (4 April 1996)

concluded:

> It's a disconcerting performance – sometimes dry,
> sometimes moving, sometimes eccentric and evasive. But
> this is another way of saying that she leaves you wondering
> whether this is a book about someone experimenting
> in writing, simply *telling* it differently, or someone who
> experimented in living; and that uncertainty is exciting,
> like the unreasonable feeling of being on the verge (only
> on the verge, but never mind) of something new.

7. Raymond Tallis (b. 1946), a retired physician and clinical neuroscientist, is a philosopher, novelist and cultural critic. He was a frequent contributor to *PN Review*, and for Carcanet co-edited a book on *The Pursuit of Mind* (1991).

8. Gillian Tomlinson, Carcanet's Marketing Manager at this period.

9. Charles Tomlinson, Clive Wilmer, and Seamus Heaney. In talking with Dennis O'Driscoll about the Movement poets, Heaney remarked 'Donald Davie, for example, would be considered your typical Movement bard, but the book of Davie's that meant most to me was *Essex Poems*, a Poundian swerve away from all that straight down the line *New Lines*-y ratiocination' (*Stepping Stones*, Faber and Faber, 2008, p.127).

10. Jerzy Peterkiewicz (1916–2007), novelist and academic, left Poland in 1939 and made his way to Britain. He obtained a doctorate in English Literature in 1947, and married Brooke-Rose soon afterwards, but the marriage did not last. In 2000 Carcanet published his selection of the work of the exiled Polish writer Cyprian Norwid (1821–83), *Poems, Letters Drawings*, translated by himself, Brooke-Rose and Burns Singer.

11. *Next* was issued as a paperback in March 1998. It is presented in the catalogue as 'a murder mystery' and also 'a harrowing chronicle [...] of the world of dispossession'. The *Omnibus* is listed in the September 1997–August 1998 catalogue at

£14.95, but in an earlier catalogue at £9.95.

12. In a lecture, Brooke-Rose admitted to having been totally
    blocked for several years after writing the ominously titled
    Textermination, and had reacted negatively to MNS's
    suggestion that she might write an autobiography, but then
    thought it might serve as an 'exercise' to unblock her. The
    difficulty was that while in novels she liked not to know where
    she was going, here all the material was ready-made. Then
    she 'decided to scrap all personal pronouns and all possessive
    adjectives. [...] Suddenly, I got interested again. I had found
    the constraint I needed.' It allowed her to 'have fun with
    language again'.

13. In the preceding day's letter, Brooke-Rose wrote:
    > I'm sorry you were sorry [the novel] ended as it did.
    > Can't change that, but you must have missed the sudden
    > metafictional author-intrusion towards the end. I don't
    > understand your 'essayistic': I'm inside Tek's mind (as with
    > all the characters, no narrator-voice except for above), and
    > he's gone mad. In fact I've added a lot in that vein, as I did
    > to the Tek/Ulysses conversations. But I'm doing no more
    > changes, out or in.

THE YEAR IN BOOKS

John Ashbery, *Can You Hear, Bird*

Cliff Ashcroft, *Faithful*

Jane Austen, *Collected Poems and Verse of the Austen Family*, edited by
David Selwyn

Iain Bamforth, *Open Workings*

Nina Berberova, *Aleksandr Blok: a life*, translated by Robyn Marsack

Bernard Bergonzi, *Heroes' Twilight: a study of the literature of the
Great War*

Yves Bonnefoy, *New and Selected Poems*, edited and translated by
Anthony Rudolf, John Naughton, and Stephen Romer

Christine Brooke-Rose, *Remake*

Bo Carpelan, *Urwind*, translated by David McDuff

Miles Champion, *Compositional Bonbons Placate*

John Clare, *By Himself*, edited by Eric Robinson and David Powell

Donald Davie, *Poems and Melodramas*

Ford Madox Ford, *The Good Soldier*, edited by Bill Hutchings

Louise Glück, *The Wild Iris*

Jorie Graham, *The Dream of the Unified Field: selected poems*

Barbara Guest, *Selected Poems*

Sophie Hannah, *Hotels Like Houses*

John Heath-Stubbs, *Galileo's Salad*

Elizabeth Jennings, *Every Changing Shape: mystical experience and the making of poems*

Elizabeth Jennings, *In the Meantime*

Elizabeth Jennings (ed), *A Poet's Choice*

James Keery, *That Stranger the Blues*

Danilo Kiš, *Homo Poeticus: essays and interviews*, edited by Susan Sontag

Chris McCully. *Not Only I*

Ernst Meister, *Not Orpheus: Selected Poems*, translated by Richard Dove

James Merrill, *Selected Poems*

Christopher Middleton, *Intimate Chronicles*

Edwin Morgan, *Collected Translations*

Sinéad Morrissey, *There Was Fire In Vancouver*

Les Murray, *Subhuman Redneck Poems*

Robert Pinsky, *The Figured Wheel*

John Rodker, *Poems and Adolphe 1920*, edited by Andrew Crozier

C.H. Sisson, *Collected Translations*

Iain Crichton Smith, *The Human Face*

Miguel Torga, *The Creation of the World*, translated by Ivana Carlsen

Sir Thomas Wyatt, *Selected Poems*, edited by Hardiman Scott

1997

Poets on Poets

Carcanet's major project for this year involved correspondence (not emails) with over fifty poets, of which a sample appears below. The editors' pleasure was the matching of present poets to past poets; the copyeditor's pain the late arrivals, second thoughts, hurried proof-reading. The response to the invitation seems to be almost invariably one of pleasure at the task. Seamus Heaney politely declined the invitation to select Yeats – Thomas Kinsella did that; and late in the day, having selected poems for the Australian mini-anthology, Les Murray backed away from Shakespeare. Edwin Morgan stepped up to the plate ('Fortunately I know my sonnets and turtles fairly well, and shall plunge into the pages tomorrow. I refuse to make any pun about saving your Bacon,' he wrote on 9 June 1997); he had already delivered his choice of poems by Gerard Manley Hopkins. While Andrew Motion on Keats, Thom Gunn on Ben Jonson, and Don Paterson on Burns were orthodox partnerships, Wendy Cope on A.E. Housman, Simon Armitage on Lord Byron, Alice Oswald on John Skelton and Roger McGough on Kipling were some of the less expected combinations. It was in Waterstone's for National Poetry Day in October.

FROM MICHAEL SCHMIDT MANCHESTER
[late 1996 – early 1997]

Dear [poet]

Nick Rennison of Waterstone's, who compiled the *Guide to Poetry Books* and I are assembling an anthology of English poetry.[1]

Ours is an anthology with a difference. It includes writers who began their careers before the turn of the twentieth century, and we're inviting poets we admire to make primary selections from fifty of the major poets, starting with Gower and running up to Yeats. We will not limit ourselves to British and Irish writers but include work in English from around the world.

Waterstone's designers will give the book a visual distinction. It will run to 400+ pages in a handsome columnar format. Published by Carcanet in paperback at £9.95, for the first year [it] will be sold exclusively by Waterstone's. We intend to publish in October 1997.

Our aim is to emphasise vital continuities: this is demonstrated in the range of poets we are inviting to make selections quite as much as in the unusual geographical scope of the volume.

We invite you to select from the work of [poet's name] a maximum of 240 lines [varied according to the poet] and spaces (allowing 3 lines for each title) and to write a headnote of no more than 300 words to describe the choice. We need selection and headnote by 5 March 1997. Each contributor will receive a copy of the book and a modest honorarium of £50. The book, given [its] scope, will not make a profit: we aim to encourage a wider readership of classic English poetry and to signal the generative connection between new poetry and the best of the past.

We have decided to exclude dramatic verse, but translation and extracts from long poems are admissible. The selection can be as radical and distinctive as you wish.

Please let us know if you can join us in this project. We would welcome your reply by 20 January if possible.

Yours sincerely,
Michael Schmidt & Nick Rennison

FROM CHRISTOPHER LOGUE
London
29 December 1996

Dear Michael & Nick:

An honour accepted. One snag: I am completing a memoir. Quite taxious. Having given a promise to others to finish by Jan. 31st, I must do my best to keep it. I will let you know how things stand before Jan 20th.

Sincerely,
Christopher L.[2]

FROM MICHAEL SCHMIDT
Manchester
7 January 1997

Dear Christopher,

Thank you so much for your card of 29th December. I am delighted that you can do Dryden for us. It is one of the crucial selections of the book!

I appreciate there may be a little bit of a glitch in terms of scheduling but we are so keen to have you in that if you over-run our proposed deadline by a week or two it would not matter. It must be extremely taxing to write a memoir – I look forward to reading it!

With warm regards,
Yours ever
Michael

FROM CHRISTOPHER LOGUE
2 February 1997

Michael:
I am getting on with the DRYDEN – I shall need more space.

Best.
Christopher

PS Am away for 10 days.
PPS Shakespeare will have to give up some of his space.

FROM CHRISTOPHER LOGUE
London
25 April 1997

Dear Michael Schmidt:

My Dryden mini-antho herewith. A little under 600 lines. I wanted to make his work interesting in fact as well as art – hence contextual notes. Apologies for the delay.

My best,
Christopher L.

FROM MICHAEL SCHMIDT
Manchester
1 May 1997

Dear Christopher Logue,

That selection of Dryden is absolutely first-rate. I am delighted with it even though you broke my rubric about including dramatic verse! Also the rubric about linking narrative – but all is forgiven in the light of the quality of what you have produced. I am most grateful.

With kind regards and best wishes,
Yours ever,
Michael Schmidt

FROM CHRISTOPHER LOGUE
London
5 May 1997

Dear Michael Schmidt,

I am glad you liked the Dryden select. Agreed, your letter of 12.12.96 did exclude dramatic verse which I took to mean 'from the play texts' – Hammond ('96) Kinsley ('58) & Gilfillan (1855) include under 'Poems' (in their editions of such) the Songs, Prologues & Epilogues. As for the commentary/ narrative, JD is so close to his own day an inexperienced reader really needs a hand up – and you have to admit Gwynne playing St Cecilia is a remarkable contrast...[3]

Best
CL

MNS TO RLM, I AUGUST 1997

It looks as though we should have complete proofs by the end of the week of August 16th and we will have two weeks to turn them around and get CRC to Mike Nicholls if we are to get delivery before the end of the third week of September and get the books out to the Waterstone's branches in time for National Poetry Day.[4] In fact we should aim for completion of the whole operation no later than 16th September (Mexican Independence Day). That is the date by which I feel we should have books ready to go into the warehouse. I know this is a horrendously tall order. Can we square our holiday plans? I shall be away from August 16th through 23rd.

MNS TO RLM, II AUGUST 1997

Here is a section of a fax we have had from John Ashbery:

I want to make another teeny change to my note on Beddoes on page 10 (ten) of the anthology. In my last communication I made the change 'Edmund Gosse, whose pioneering edition of Beddoes's work appeared in 1890...' I now want to change 'pioneering edition' to 'landmark edition'. (My problem is that Gosse's edition actually wasn't the first edition as I originally wrote therefore it can't really be called pioneering either. 'Landmark' seems a suitable face-saving alternative.)[5]

MNS TO RLM, 27 AUGUST 1997

Here are Elaine Feinstein's Wyatt proofs, and Penny has sent a batch of others that came here by mistake.[6]

[...] We ought to have delayed it but National Poultry Day is The Occasion, and if we miss that we will lose the

Waterstone's order and have one hell of a lot of books to dispose of. Sorry, sorry, sorry.

I enclose Kenneth Koch's Herrick.[7] In the battle between *we're* and *w'are*, I think we side with the former despite the cogency of the latter prosodically.

Neil Powell sounds almost human again after the Waterstone Ravages. I am sorry, again, to have given you both, not to mention Pam and Penny, such a nightmare. Next year let's publish one book, preferably a straight reprint, and nothing more.

NOTES

1. Nick Rennison is a writer, editor and bookseller. His books include *Sherlock Holmes: An Unauthorised Biography*, the Bloomsbury Good Reading Guides and *100 Must-Read Historical Novels*.

2. Christopher Logue (1926–2011) is best known for his bold, brilliant, blank-verse adaptations of the *Iliad*; his other poetry was often political. He also wrote screen-plays, limericks, and pornography under a pseudonym. His memoir, *Prince Charming*, was published by Faber and Faber in 1999.

3. Actually it was St Catherine of Alexandria, in Dryden's play *Tyrannic Love* (1669), although the contrast between her fate and that of Charles II's mistress Nell Gwynne is still marked. In his headnote Logue calls Dryden 'the master poet of his age': 'quick, witty, sane, fertile, conversational, better able to argue in verse than any other English poet'.

4. Mike Nicholls was the genial, brisk but patient Sales Director of Short Run Press, based in Exeter, which still prints Carcanet's books.

5. While Logue's headnote was a crisp 16 lines, Ashbery's to
    Thomas Beddoes (1803–49) ran to 114 lines. He savoured the
    poet: 'Pound evokes the "odour of eucalyptus or sea wrack" in
    Beddoes; one could add those of rose, sulphur and sandalwood
    to that unlikely but addictive bouquet.'

6. Feinstein remarks of Thomas Wyatt (1503–42) that he was
    'the earliest English exponent of that tug between speech
    and melody on which a whole tradition of English language
    depends'. Elaine Feinstein (1930–2019), poet, novelist,
    biographer and translator, first came to Carcanet with her
    translations of *Three Russian Poets* (1979), and then with
    her own *Selected Poems* in 1994. Her most recent Carcanet
    publication is *The Clinic Memory: New and Selected Poems*
    (2017). Penny Jones began her career in press and marketing
    at Carcanet, and is now one of the founding directors of Kirby
    Jones Management.

7. Koch's brief headnote begins: 'In the poems of Robert Herrick
    (1591–1674) there is a music that seems to belong exclusively,
    and naturally, to the English language but which has appeared
    nowhere before or since.'

THE YEAR IN BOOKS

John Ashbery, *The Mooring of Starting Out*
Charles Baudelaire, *Complete Poems*, translated by Walter Martin
Silvio Bedini, *The Pope's Elephant*
Patricia Beer, *Autumn*
Sujata Bhatt, *Point No Point*
Elizabeth Bishop, *Exchanging Hats*, edited by William Benton
Michael Brander, *The Language of the Field*
Sophia de Mello Breyner, *Log Book*, translated by Richard Zenith
Gillian Clarke, *Collected Poems*
Anne Cluysenaar, *Timeslips*
Allen Curnow, *Early Days Yet: new and collected poems*
John Eddowes, *The Language of Cricket*

Hazel Edwards, *Follow the Banner: an illustrated catalogue of the Northumberland miners' banners*

Alistair Elliot, *Facing Things*

Salvador Espriu, *Selected Poems*, translated by Louis J. Rodrigues

Elaine Feinstein, *Daylight*

Ford Madox Ford, *Parade's End*, edited by Gerald Hammond

Ford Madox Ford, *Selected Poems*, edited by Max Saunders

John Gallas, *Grrrrr*

Natalia Ginzburg, *The Things We Used to Say*, translated by Judith Woolf

Louise Glück, *The First Five Books of Poems*

Robert Graves, *The Complete Poems Volume 2*, edited by Beryl Graves and Dunstan Ward

Robert Graves, *The White Goddess: a historical grammar of poetic myth*, edited by Grevel Lindop

Ivor Gurney, *Eighty Poems Or So*, edited by George Walter

Lincoln Psalter: Versions of the Psalms, translated by Gordon Jackson

Mimi Khalvati, *Entries on Light*

Thomas Kinsella, *The Pen Shop*

Kenneth Koch, *One Train*

Frank Kuppner, *Second Best Moments in Chinese History*

Eugenio Lisboa, *The Anarchist Banker and Other Stories*

Eugenio Lisboa, *Professor Pfiglzz and His Strange Companion and Other Stories*

John Lyly, *Selected Plays and Other Writings*, edited by Leah Scragg

Hugh MacDiarmid, *Albyn: Shorter Books and Monographs*, edited by Alan Riach

Hugh MacDiarmid, *The Raucle Tongue Volume One: Hitherto Uncollected Prose*, edited by Angus Calder, Glen Murray and Alan Riach

Edwin Morgan, *Virtual and Other Realities*

Alistair Niven and Michael Schmidt (eds), *Enigmas and Arrivals: an anthology of Commonwealth fiction*

Neil Powell, *The Language of Jazz*

Frederic Raphael, *The Necessity of Anti-Semitism*
Nick Rennison and Michael Schmidt (eds), *Poets on Poets*
Rainer Maria Rilke, *Neue Gedichte/New Poems*, translated by
    Stephen Cohn (revised edition)
Peter Robinson, *Lost and Found*
Sylvia Rodgers, *Red Saint, Pink Daughter*
José Hermano Saraiva, *Portugal: a companion history* edited by Ian
    Robertson, translated by Ursula Fonss
Harvey Shapiro, *Selected Poems*
Adam Schwartzman, *Merrie Afrika!*
Stephen Tapscott, *From the Book of Changes*
James Tate, *Selected Poems*
Thomas Traherne, *Select Meditations*, edited by Julia Smith
Izaac Walton, *Selected Writings*, edited by Jessica Martin

1998

Anne Stevenson (b. 1933) has been an occasional contributor to *PN Review* for over thirty years, mostly of poems but some articles as well. Raised in New England, she has lived in Britain since the mid-1950s, moving to Sunderland in 1982 and thence to Durham. Her poetry was published by OUP, and then by Bloodaxe, which issued her *Poems 1955–2005* in 2005; she is also the author of a biography of Sylvia Plath and two studies of Elizabeth Bishop. Asked by Cynthia Haven about teaching creative writing, Stevenson said: 'The Muse, I suppose, really isn't all that nice! She hates rules, hates conformity, favours her special pets, gleefully drives worshippers to drink or drugs, happily drives other worshippers to suicide, is politically completely unreliable, and, being an unmitigated snob, she takes flight as soon as she hears the word "creativity". Goodness, how she detests the word and makes fun of it over drinks with her cronies!'[1]

FROM MICHAEL SCHMIDT
Manchester
14 July 1998

Dear Anne,

Thank you for your letter and the poem ['Arioso Dolente']. I do not like the first line at all: the conceit (and the rhythm) are awkward to my ear; but the poem itself rises like the Yeats ring and the last two stanzas, especially the penultimate, are wonderful – as wonderful as anything of yours I have read. I'm delighted to have the poem for the magazine. It's got *Saturday Evening Post*, Rockwelly colours with a sense of aftermath which is as much history as time.[2] I don't generally let poems move me in the way I let this one do. It may have been that you plunked me on my grandmother's porch in Calhoun, Georgia! That screen door and twang. If Chekhov had been a Southerner, just think how much <u>better</u> *The Cherry Orchard* might have been!

In Durham you may know Gareth Reeves, who set up Carcanet with me and Peter Jones at Oxford. We have fallen unaccountably out of touch. I did not know Michael O'Neill was chairman of the English Department there.[3] My own impatience with academia had led to my resignation. In the life of a slow man, as Donald [Davie] would have said, 27 years is long. I have somewhere to go, I trust, and should not be out of commission for long.

All the best,
Michael

FROM ANNE STEVENSON
Llanbedr, Gwynedd
17 July 1998

Dear Michael,

Very happy to have your letter of July 14th. I have taken to heart your criticism of the first line (Arioso Dolente) so am sending you a revised version – thanks to you, better.[4] Or I hope so, rhythmically surely so. The image of the jug and cup seems right to me; it was that image that set the poem going in the first place; it does accurately describe my mother's addiction to lecturing to her assembled family over supper every evening. She was an extraordinarily intelligent woman who should have been a history or English teacher; high-principled, well-read, a dedicated Democrat and ardent member of the League of Women Voters in Ann Arbor. The present stanza gives her more of her opinionated character (she predicted disaster for the U.S. if Ronald Reagan should ever become President. Clinton she would have thought a vulgar light-weight).[5] My father, who was a lecturer in philosophy and a fine amateur pianist, always relied on mother to tell him how to vote. They were both first-generation intellectuals who met in their Cincinnati high school, married after college and came to England, where my father studied under I.A. Richards, G.E. Moore and Wittgenstein in '30s Cambridge.[6]

All their lives they were determined to share with their three daughters all they themselves valued in the arts. I drank it all in greedily until I married; after which I rebelled against them and their Bourgeois Culture and all they stood for. Of course, now I share most of their attitudes and beliefs and much lament the amount of time I spent wasting my substance in riotous living.

I didn't know that you'd had a grandmother in Georgia. As a passionate Chekhovian, I'm not sure that *The Cherry Orchard* could be better than it is. In some ways it <u>has</u> been re-written in the South by the likes of Carson McCullers and Faulkner.[7] It's true, I think, that when literature is really top-notch, it ceases to depend on a period or nation and becomes 'universal'.

NB. In the last stanza of Arioso I originally tried to avoid the word 'universe'. I've restored it because it seems more accurate, though a cliché. What do you think? Also made other changes to clarify meaning; and I've regularized the stanzas so that the broken four lines in each 'line up' with each other. I hope that the ode-like form reflects the breaking up of an entire way of life. I've made pretty free with the stresses throughout, though there's sort of an iambic back-beat.

Do I gather from your letter that you are resigning from Carcanet after 27 years? And from *PN Review*? Today's academia is mostly antithetical to literature; I'm so glad I have squeezed through without having to join up, as it were. Gareth Reeves is an old friend and a good guy. I learned yesterday that my little guide to the poetry of Elizabeth Bishop is ready to send out for review.[8] I'm sure Bellew will send you a copy, but if he doesn't, do let me know. The Michigan book of essays is also on the way, after two and more years! Much of it may be out of date now. Anyway, these books now exist.

I can't tell you how grateful I am for your support; *PN Review* has been, for many years, much the best literary journal in England; for poetry it has been almost the only one to take seriously. So whatever you think now, you can look back on a life nobly spent!

With all best wishes,
Anne

FROM MICHAEL SCHMIDT
Manchester
[July 1998]

Dear Anne,

Thank you very much for your letter of 17th July with the revised poem. I approve of all your revisions and return the earlier version to you.

Like you I am passionate about Chekhov and was only jesting when I suggested that he might have been better had he lived in Georgia.

I must have given you entirely the wrong impression. I am certainly not resigning from Carcanet or *PN Review* – they are what I live for and by. I am probably resigning from the University of Manchester and, I hope, moving on to a different academic job which is less taxing in terms of teaching hours.[9]

I could never leave Carcanet or *PN Review* – they would have to collapse under me.

All the best,
Michael

*

The stanza that so much moved me in Anne Stevenson's poem reads, in the magazine:

> Consciousness walks on tiptoe through what happens.
> So much is felt, so little of it said.
> But ours is the breath on which the past depends;
> 'What happened' is what the living teach the dead –
>   – who, smilingly lost to their lost concerns,
>   in gray on gray
> are all of them deaf, blind, unburdened
>   by today.

Two years after the Manchester bomb, it is curious to see how vehemently I express my continuing commitment to the press and magazine: 'they are what I live for'. And, reflecting on this from a distance of twenty-one years, I think I meant it.

NOTES

1. In *The Courtland Review* no.14 (November 2000) Accessed on 27 May 2019, http://www.cortlandreview.com/issue/14/stevenson14.htm
2. Norman Rockwell (1894–1978), popular American painter and illustrator, best known for his cover illustrations of everyday life for the *Saturday Evening Post*.
3. Michael O'Neill (1953–2018), who had taught at the University of Durham since 1979, was also a poet, his later collections being published by Arc, including the posthumous

Crash and Burn (2019).

4. Stevenson discusses the process of revising 'Arioso Dolente' in her essay 'Purifying the Cistern', published in *PN Review* 131 (January-February 2000), beginning:

> Dissatisfaction is a painful spur, but it can be an inspiration. I don't know how many times I redrafted 'Arioso Dolente', a poem that first appeared in *PNR* in January 1999. [...] After I received his letter I set to work drafting and redrafting the opening, sending Michael so many versions that I wonder he didn't throw the lot in the wastepaper basket. As it happens, 'Arioso Dolente' [...] had gone through umpteen drafts and stages (all kept in a manila folder) before it even reached Schmidt, but it was months before I realized why the opening phrases in both first and second stanzas sounded rhythmically limp.

   She mentions that W.B. Yeats's poem 'Among School Children' was '(rather remotely) a model'.

5. The political sex scandal involving President Bill Clinton and a White House intern, Monica Lewinsky, came to light in 1998, and the court case was to begin in August.

6. I.A. Richards (1893–1979) graduated in philosophy and used his knowledge of this and other fields to inform his influential books on literary criticism; he published a revised edition of *Practical Criticism* in 1930 and *The Philosophy of Rhetoric* in 1936. Carcanet published a *Selected Poems* by Richards and a book of his essays. G.E. Moore (1873–1958) was Professor of Philosophy at Cambridge; with Ludwig Wittgenstein (1889–1951) and others he founded a school of analytic philosophy.

7. Carson McCullers (1917–1967) was born in Georgia, and the South is the setting for much of her fiction; William Faulkner (1897–1962) grew up in Oxford, Mississippi, and wrote most of his novels from that base, tracking the decline of the South.

8. *Five Looks at Elizabeth Bishop* (Bellew, 1998), reprinted by Bloodaxe in 2006; *Between the Iceberg and the Ship: Selected*

Essays (University of Michigan Press, 1998).
9. MNS was the founding Director of the Writing School
    at Manchester Metropolitan University 1998–2005, and
    Professor of English there from 2000 to 2005.

THE YEAR IN BOOKS

John Ash, *Selected Poems*
John Ashbery, *Wakefulness*
Frank Bidart, *Desire: collected poems*
Peter Bland, *Selected Poems*
Eavan Boland, *The Lost Land*
Christine Brooke-Rose, *Next*
Gillian Clarke, *Five Fields*
Donald Davie, *With the Grain: essays on Thomas Hardy and British
    poetry*, edited by Clive Wilmer
Louise Glück, *Meadowlands*
Jorie Graham, *The Errancy*
Robert Graves, *I, Claudius* and *Claudius the God*, introduction by
    Richard Francis
John Heath-Stubbs, *The Literary Essays*, edited by Trevor Tolley
Friedrich Hölderlin and Osip Mandel'shtam, *What I Own: Versions
    of Hölderlin & Mandel'shtam*, translated by John Riley and Tim
    Longville
T.E. Hulme, *Selected Writings*, edited by Patrick McGuinness
Kevin Jackson, *The Language of Cinema*
Elizabeth Jennings, *Praises*
Gabriel Josipovici, *Now*
Hugh MacDiarmid, *The Raucle Tongue: Volume Three*, edited by
    Angus Calder, Glen Murray and Alan Riach
E.A. Markham, *A Papua New Guinea Sojourn*
Ian McMillan, *I Found This Shirt*
Christopher Middleton, *Jackdaw Jiving*
Les Murray, *Fredy Neptune*
Neil Powell, *Selected Poems*

Stephen Raw, *The Art of Remembering*
Norm Sibum, *The November Propertius*
Iain Crichton Smith, *The Leaf and the Marble*
Jon Stallworthy, *Rounding the Horn: collected poems*
Shuntaro Tanikawa, *Selected Poems*, translated by William I. Elliott
  and Kazuo Kawamura
Ninette de Valois, *Selected Poems*
Val Warner, *Tooting Idlyll*
Gregory Woods, *May I say Northing*
Andrew Young, *Selected Poems*, edited by Edward Lowbury and
  Alison Young

1999

Alison Brackenbury (b. 1953) published her first collection, *Dreams of Power and other poems,* with Carcanet in 1981; it was a Poetry Book Society Recommendation. Ten more collections have followed, most recently *Gallop: selected poems* (2019). She is descended from generations of skilled farm workers. After taking a degree in English at Oxford, she married and moved to Gloucestershire, where she combined writing with horse-keeping, parenthood, grassroots politics and working for her husband's small metal-finishing firm in various capacities. In her interview with Vicki Bertram, Brackenbury remarked: 'Poems get written. They ought to be written in pencil on lined paper but they have been written in green felt-tip on the back of shopping lists. They are written under their own pressure, either soon after something has happened (or been thought of), or a little later. They will not wait for ever and they will not survive interruption, so a crowded life can both find them and destroy them.'[1]

FROM MICHAEL SCHMIDT
Manchester
26 July 1999

Dear Alison,

Where are we up to with Vicki Bertram? Am I losing my mind? I am certainly late again in replying to you. Forgive me (again).

There have been various things eating up my time, though I appear this week to have begun to return to the normal earth. The change of job was a move from the Victoria University of Manchester to the Met, the old polytechnic, where I am setting up a writing school. I have on my teaching staff Jeff Wainwright, Carol Ann Duffy, Sophie Hannah etc – not a poor turnout, and with extremely numerous and time-consuming responses.[2]

We took over the OUP list, and now seem to be suffering a welter of malicious untruths about the arrangement and other matters. I had not anticipated so much agro!

Minhinnick himself is writing very well.[3] I like his *Poetry Wales* just now also. He came to read in Manchester and is every bit as alarming and electric as I expected. Rather more so, in fact, with a toothache.

I am sorry that engineering has the brakes on. The economy is most peculiar just now. I believe we are in the middle of a recession and that somehow the spin doctors have made people believe we are having a mini boom. Spin doctors don't walk through the shopping streets and see the dreadfully deeply discounted sales.

I am very much taken with the new book. I hope with the kinds of things Gaynor does, and with a *PNR* interview etc, we will be able to increase the Brackenbury Velocity somewhat! I also like the dedication of the book.[4]

With love,
Michael

Peter Scupham, an OUP poet, had written to MNS on 18
November 1998:

> Well, I had a go at ringing you this Wednesday early to tell you the
> news which is now old hat – about Oxford's incredible hatchet-job
> on their list. These things all seem to fit the same pattern. Silence,
> rumours, then Jacky [Simms] called in to tell her the list is finito,
> napoo, kaput. (And it would be nice not to make a fuss, but for
> everyone to go quietly, in an orderly queue, saying thank you and
> touching their forelocks.) […] no doubt from Jura to Java, from Wick
> to Weimar the air will be full of banshee wailings and the disconsolate
> cries of the ghosts of bards and bardlets looking for somewhere to go
> haunting. It is clearly an absolute disgrace for a House like OUP to
> take this decision and I hope that all hell breaks out round the ears
> of their Delegates, Dogsbodies, Syndics, Satraps, Number-Crunchers
> and Nobodies.

In the meeting of the OUP delegates which voted to support the
finance committee's decision to chop the contemporary poetry list
– it had been going for 30 years – one delegate was reported as
saying: 'The meagre sums of money you will save by cutting the
poetry list will hardly compensate for the flood of opprobrium
that will ensue.' Alan Howarth, the Arts Minister, spoke against
the decision at a poetry reading on 3 February 1999, which he
attended because he shared the community's 'dismay and distress'.
On 7 March 1999 OUP issued a press release announcing that
it had agreed with Carcanet Press for the Oxford Poets list to be
published jointly by the two firms: 'all living poets on the OUP
list have been invited to join this new venture'. In July 1999, the
Independent noted that two of the poets who had been dropped
were shortlisted for the Forward Prize for Best Collection: Jo
Shapcott (who had gone to Faber and Faber), who won it that
year; and Jane Draycott, published by Carcanet.

FROM ALISON BRACKENBURY
Cheltenham
28 July 1999

Dear Michael,

I was delighted to hear from you. I am sorry I never see you. It would be good for me if Manchester were nearer to Cheltenham, but it would not be good for Manchester. There are removal vans in every hot street. Half the population seems to be selling their houses. This has always been a foolish town. Cobbett hated it.[5]

Vicki Bertram! In brief: the interview is scheduled to take place by post, 'two weeks into August'.

In detail – Vicki and I have been carrying on an amicable correspondence, which I have just looked up. [details of dates and arrangements follow]

I will be quick [in replying to VB's questions], but I'm going to be a bit careful about this interview. First, I don't want to bore the reader. I tend to skip interviews myself. On the other hand, I don't wish to dash off any ill-considered one-liners which become hostages to fortune. I have seen very well-known poets have careless remarks eagerly seized upon. If you start these rows, you have to finish them. My views are frequently fierce. If I reviewed I wouldn't live long.[6] I have never had much spare mental energy for literary politics. The little I have is devoted to marginal activity in wider conflicts.

I am very sorry about all the sniping over OUP. The reports I have read have been so confused that I am sure most readers have given up, befogged.

Your new job sounds very exciting. Will there be a Manchester School? No, I'm sure there won't be. The tutors start varied & the students will end so too. I do remember thinking, in my earlier twenties, that I would welcome technical advice, and then having to scrabble for it from a range of sources. I once saw the brief for teachers on the Arvon courses which said you should <u>not</u> give technical advice. I would have thought that was all that you could give! I look forward to your venture with great interest.

Summer is odd, it seems endless, then it is gone. There are gardens to water, and the pony to gallop in the warm wind; but the dews are getting heavier, and I am still writing. The poems are sharp ballads with nothing of summer in them. I will send them off to editors who seem to be getting younger!

I am glad you like the book. Chris (Gribble) has been very helpful already.[7] I have been diligently placing work, so perhaps we can raise some interest. I will try to find you some good poems, at a suitable time.

I admired *Meadowlands*, a remarkably varied book, with the little Latin animula alive again, and some wickedly funny poems.[8] I very much liked the last *PNR* with Christopher Middleton's glances at the red bird, and John Ash's Turkish poem.[9] Perhaps summer should banish ghosts. But I think we need to talk to them from time to time.

The moon is [as] hazy as my brain! I wish you clearer thoughts.

Love & best wishes,
Alison

FROM MICHAEL SCHMIDT
Manchester
11 August 1999

Dear Alison,

I dragged all my colleagues off to watch the eclipse (we got 85%) from my balcony. We drank wine, and I cannot be certain that what I write to you here is consecutive or cogent.

It was a very real pleasure to get your long letter of 28 July. You are one of the people I would like to see regularly. I have very few people to talk to about poetry (almost no one) or life or liberty or the pursuit of 'appiness.

Vicki is a modern sort of academic. She did not like Eavan Boland because Eavan was not keen to be interviewed, gave in the end an excellent interview, proceeded to revise it entirely in transcript, etc. Now, Eavan is a powerful thinker and kept drawing Vicki up short. Mimi was altogether more her cup of tea. [...][10] I am glad you are writing your responses to her questions, not least because you can give the questions a more interesting inflection if you ruminate a little upon them.

A long time ago I decided that new poets should 'do a Boland', which is to help create a prose context in which their poems might thrive. Eavan always gives her readers (and critics) a thorough context: a major essay and often a major printed interview at roughly the same time. It is not marketing as such: it's making sure the initial record is controlled.

My whole endeavour in creative writing courses is to respect the difference of students who would not have been admitted if there were not something rather exceptional about them (apart from the fact that they can afford the fees without recourse to grants!). So if there were to be a Manchester School I would have failed in my task. It is largely a matter of discussing technical questions and providing immovable deadlines.

Love to you and Zoe and all!

Yours ever,

Michael

*

Ever since Carcanet started publishing Alison Brackenbury – I could not resist and I still like the vocal range of *Dreams of Power*, both the book and the title sequence – she has been acutely aware of readership. She never sees it as market, and as a writer she maintains as many close connections with it as she can. Readers' responses mean as much to her as reviews, and she engages her readers in the composition of her books. When we were discussing the pricing of her selected poems, *Gallop*, she argued the case for keeping the book – a relatively long one – under £10. In persuading me she took evidence from her readers, and persisted forensically until she had worn me down. She is a skilful but not a calculating user of social media, always sharing and never selling herself or her readers short. Many of her readers become followers, and it is always, with Alison, a two-way traffic.

She also avoided revision for revision's sake of her earlier poems. Though there is a deep continuity in her work, the tonalities and the themes have evolved and tampering from a later perspective might have introduced falsifications. The few changed notes were governed by her experience of reading the poems aloud in public, and finding what went right and what went wrong in public presentation. She retained the whole 'Dreams of Power' sequence in *Gallop*, which was a great relief to me. Its omission would have removed a keystone from the arch that her work represents.

The mention of Robert Minhinnick's visit brings to mind the presence of Welsh writers on Carcanet's list, with strong continuities, notably in the work of Gillian Clarke. Published by Carcanet since 1985 as a poet and prose writer, she is one of our most popular and generous authors, a Welsh laureate, sought after on the reading circuit and a favourite with younger readers.

NOTES

1. Vicki Bertram, who taught at Manchester Metropolitan University, contributed six interviews to *PN Review*, as well as reviewing occasionally for the journal. Her interview with Alison Brackenbury appeared in *PN Review* 132 (March–April 2000).

2. Jeffrey Wainwright (b. 1944), poet, translator and playwright, taught at Manchester Metropolitan University until 2008. His first collection with Carcanet was *Heart's Desire* (1978), and his most recent is *What Must Happen* (2016).

   Sophie Hannah is another Carcanet poet, though best known for her psychological crime fiction. Her first collection was *The Hero and the Girl Next Door* (1996); *Marrying the Ugly Millionaire: new and collected poems* was published in 2015.

   Carol Ann Duffy (b. 1955) published *The World's Wife*, one of her best-known collections, in 1999 (Anvil Press). She served as the UK Poet Laureate 2009–2019, and is Professor of Contemporary Poetry at MMU.

3. Robert Minhinnick (b. 1952), Welsh poet, novelist, translator and essayist, was editor of *Poetry Wales* 1997–2008. In 1999 he published (and frequently performed) his poem 'Twenty-Five Laments for Iraq', which won that year's Forward Prize for Best Single Poem. Carcanet began publishing his poetry with a *Selected Poems* in 1999; his most recent collection is *Diary of the Last Man* (2017).

4. *After Beethoven* (2000) was dedicated to the poet's daughter.

5. William Cobbett wrote of Cheltenham in 1826: 'What a figure this place will cut in another year or two! I should not wonder to see it nearly wholly deserted. It is situated in a nasty, flat, stupid spot, without anything pleasant near it' (*Rural Rides*, 1830).

6. Brackenbury in fact reviewed often for *PN Review* after 2005, particularly chapbooks and pamphlets. She and MNS had an exchange about reviewing in 2017, prompted by his concern over an online article commenting on the lack of ethnic (also

gender) diversity in reviewers and books reviewed, pointing the finger at *PN Review* among others. Brackenbury replied (31 May 2017):

> Reviewing, unless you skimp, takes a lot of time. It also needs the terrified respect for deadlines that we had for decades in a small industrial business. A very good (and I'd say, efficient) young poet – a woman – admitted to me recently that she'd just missed two reviewing deadlines because of the pressure of everything else she was trying to do. Poetry reviewing needs some knowledge of poetry, at least as a reader, if not also as a writer. If you simply appealed for would-be reviewers, I suspect you would attract many unsuitable candidates.
>
> One interesting thing I have learnt about reviewing is that some writers I know – often women – who are well-qualified to review, don't, because no editor has invited them to do so. I have suggested that they approach the magazine for which they'd most like to review. This has often worked out well. So, without issuing riskily general invitations, I think it is worth encouraging any writers you know, who you think would make good reviewers. I'm sure you already do this. Writers who seem very strong characters can be surprisingly passive!

7. Chris Gribble worked for Carcanet 1998–2001, first as Sales and Production Manager, and then as Publicity and Marketing Manager. He is now Chief Executive of the National Centre for Writing in Norwich.

8. Louise Glück's *Meadowlands* was published by Carcanet in 1998. Glück (b. 1943) was awarded the Pulitzer Prize in 1993 for *The Wild Iris*, which Carcanet published in 1996, becoming her UK publisher. She was the US Poet Laureate 2003–04.

9. *PN Review* 128 (July–August 1999) published Christopher Middleton's poem 'The Redbird Hexagon' and John Ash's 'The Anatolikon'.

10. Bertram interviewed Eavan Boland for *PN Review* 124
(November-December 1998) – her collection *The Lost Land*
had been published in September; and Mimi Khalvati for *PN
Review* 130 (November-December 1999) – her *Selected Poems*
came out in March 2000.

THE YEAR IN BOOKS

John Ashbery, *Girls on the Run*

Thomas Lovell Beddoes, *Selected Poetry*, edited by Judith Higgens
and Michael Bradshaw (new edition)

Christine Brooke-Rose, *Subscript*

Jane Draycott, *Prince Rupert's Drop*

William Dunbar, *Selected Poems*, edited by Harriet Harvey Wood

Ford Madox Ford, *Return to Yesterday*, edited by Bill Hutchings

Ford Madox Ford, *War Prose*, edited by Max Saunders

John Gallas, *Resistance is Futile*

Louise Glück, *Proofs and Theories*

W.S. Graham, *The Nightfisherman: Selected Letters of W.S. Graham*,
edited by Michael Snow and Margaret Snow

Robert Graves, *The Complete Poems Volume 3*, edited by Beryl Graves
and Dunstan Ward

Robert Graves, *The Sergeant Lamb Novels*, introduced by Caroline
Zilboorg

Sophie Hannah, *Leaving and Leaving You*

John Heath-Stubbs, *The Sound of Light*

Thomas Kinsella, *Godhead*

Hugh MacDiarmid, *Annals of the Five Senses*, edited by Roderick
Watson and Alan Riach

Gabriella Maleti, *Bitter Asylum*, translated by Sharon Wood

Robert Minhinnick, *Selected Poems*

Eugenio Montale, *Collected Poems 1920–1954*, translated by
Jonathan Galassi

David Mourao-Ferreira, *Lucky in Love*, translated by Christine
Robinson

Les Murray, *Conscious and Verbal*

John Needham, *The Departure Lounge: travel and literature in the post-modern world*

Michael Palmer, *The Lion Bridge: selected poems 1972–1995*

John Peck, *Collected Shorter Poems 1966–96*

Aleksandr Pushkin, *After Pushkin*, edited by Elaine Feinstein

Justin Quinn, *Privacy*

Jose Regio, *Flame Coloured Dress*, translated by Margaret Jull Costa

Michael Schmidt (ed), *New Poetries II*

Adam Schwartzman (ed), *Ten South African Poets*

Jorge de Sena, *Signs of Fire: Selected Poems*, translated by John Byrne

Manuel Teixeira-Gomes, *Erotic Stories*, translated by Alison Aiken

Marina Tsvetaeva, *Selected Poems*, translated by Elaine Feinstein

Jeffrey Wainwright, *Out of the Air*

Robert Wells, *Lusus*

Isaac Watts, *Selected Poems*, edited by Gordon Jackson

Paul Wilkins, *Truths of the Unremembered Things*

Clive Wilmer, *Selected Poems*

Nikolai Zabolotsky, *Selected Poems*, translated by Daniel Weissbort

2000

Neil Powell (b. 1948), poet, critic and biographer, has been associated with Carcanet Press and *PN Review* for many years as writer, editor and proofreader. He taught at Kimbolton School and St Christopher School, Letchworth, where he became Head of English; he was the founder-owner of The Baldock Bookshop in Hertfordshire; and since 1990 he has been a full-time author and editor. Among his publications are biographies of Roy Fuller, George Crabbe, Amis father and son, and Benjamin Britten; he has edited Fulke Greville's *Selected Poems* (1990) Donald Davie's *Collected Poems* (2002) and Adam Johnson's *Collected Poems* (2003) for Carcanet; his latest book is his own collected poems, *Was and Is* (Carcanet, 2017). In 'Forgetting How to Read', Powell wrote at the end of the twentieth century: 'there are times when a perception of cultural decay might actually be accurate, and perhaps this is one of them. […] [T]his collapse is different in kind and scale from previous shifts in our culture, because it involves a devastating and potentially irreversible disconnection from the past.'[1]

FROM NEIL POWELL
Bungay, Suffolk
3 October 2000

Dear Michael,

I've been looking again at the mass of material from which I hope to produce a book (or two) of essays; and it occurs to me that there *is* a coherent collection there, absolutely at the heart of it – one which seems somehow completed by the Winters piece I've just done for *PNR*.[2] It's still called *Virtues and Necessities*, a title which sums up the twin purposes of my essaying and reviewing, and it could be subtitled 'Essays on Twentieth-Century Poets'. (That would leave me with the option of assembling a more wide-ranging companion book – after *V&N* has proved an astonishing and resounding success – to be called *Airs and Variations*.)

The pieces, which I propose to arrange in thematic clusters rather than in order of writing or publication, fall into four substantial groups: (1) Graves, Sassoon, Edward Thomas, pieces on First World War poets in general; (2) writers of the mid and later century, including Winters, R.S. Thomas, W.S. Graham, Roy Fuller, Heath-Stubbs, Davie, Larkin, Gunn; (3) shorter essays, mostly deriving from *TLS* reviews – on a range of late twentieth-century poets (Fanthorpe, Scupham, Dobyns, Doty, Kantaris, Wells and others), ending with my *PNR* piece about Adam;[3] (4) general pieces and polemics – a couple of reviews of major anthologies (the 1993 *New Poetry* piece and 'The Bonfire of the Anthologies')[4] and articles from 'The Poet, the Public and the Pub' (*PNR*, 1978) to 'Forgetting How to Read' (*PNR*, 1999). Looks like a terrific book to me! 320pp at a guess. What do you think? I feel lost without a Carcanet project in the pipeline.

I am also thinking, but slowly, about the memoirish thing: it has to be right, and it's the sort of book which needs to be approached very sanely (or else in a spirit of reckless lunacy). I hope there will also be, eventually, a new book of poems.

Crabbe, meanwhile, may have found a good home, about which I'll say nothing more until it's settled (or not).[5]

Best wishes,
Neil

FROM MICHAEL SCHMIDT
Manchester
5 October 2000

Dear Neil,

Thank you for your letter of 3rd October about 'Virtues and Necessities'. It is an attractive title.

There is a serious absence in the work you outline of essays on what one might call the Rickword, Empson, Auden line as well as the Modernists. 'Essays on Twentieth-century Poets' has a kind of comprehensive air.

You are clearly not making exclusions on national grounds in view of the fact that you include Welsh, Scottish and American writers (I see no Irish there!).

If the book is to be anything more than a miscellany of good reviews, we must make it cohere a bit more intensively.

Let us discuss this matter soon. I certainly would like to do another book of you, prose or verse. My feeling is that a prose book based on, for example, your anthology reviews, could be made a lot of fun whereas the larger collections you envisage are for the most part too miscellaneous to make sense. I wonder indeed whether a book on the modern anthology, cannibalising your reviews in various ways, might not be in itself quite original and quite wonderful? It could, for example, reproduce and collate contents lists or take 'sections' and see what poets are anthologised in which ways and how many anthologists cannibalise each other's work rather than going to the fountainhead. I have often contemplated writing such a book myself but have not had sufficient incentive. It could start briefly with Tottel[6] and the Elizabethan books which made the fortunes of their publishers and proceed, possibly with brief character sketches of the publishers where they were important and of the editors where they were self-important, to the present day.

Much of the work seems to me to have been done already in your excellent reviews!

You may think this is a non-starting idea from your point of view but I love it! I would almost go to contract immediately!

With warm regards,

Yours ever,

Michael

P.S. I had a long letter from Anthony Thwaite this morning.[7] What a shock.

*

Neil Powell was a very close and central figure in Carcanet and *PN Review* for decades. He writes with clarity and confidence, as a poet is a fine formalist, a kind of cousin of the poets in *Il movimento inglese* (Wells, Davis and Wilmer) without the Wintersite colouring. For me, a foreigner in love with England, he is the epitome of certain values I relished. He was also a schoolmaster rather than a university lecturer, which was very much in his favour in my book: he was in touch with people coming to, and coming to terms with, poems, not yet strung out on the racks of theory. But as Carcanet changed, finding new poets, different kinds of poetry and new directions, and as the times changed, Neil was an unwobbling pivot.

He has not taken up the gauntlet of the short book on anthologies which I threw down, after his excellent and perceptive essays. It could still prove the kernel of a larger project.

NOTES

1. 'Forgetting How to Read', *PN Review* 125 (January–February 1999).

2. 'Winters' Talents', *PN Review* 136 (November–December 2000).

3. Powell wrote a tribute to his friend and fellow poet Adam Johnson (1965–93) in *PN Review* 93 (September–October 1993); Johnson had delivered the typescript of *The Playground Bell* – published in 1994 – to Carcanet three weeks before his death of an AIDS-related illness.

4. 'Sparklers and Bangers', *PN Review* 133 (May–June 2000): 'Domes and wheels and other such questionable edifices apart, the thrilling fact that all four of the year's digits happened to change at the end of 1999 provided an excuse for various literary fireworks; I wrote about a couple of fat rockets – Peter Forbes's *Scanning the Century* and Michael Schmidt's *Harvill Book of Twentieth-Century Poetry in English* – in *PNR* 130. Here are some of the lesser explosives, sparklers and bangers as it were, and much the most sparkling of the bunch is Simon Rae's *News that Stays News*.'

5. Powell's *George Crabbe: An English Life 1754–1832* was published by Pimlico in 2004.

6. The London publisher Richard Tottel published *Songes and Sonnettes*, the first printed anthology of poetry in English, in 1557.

7. Anthony Thwaite (b. 1930), poet and critic, editor notably of Philip Larkin's poems and letters. He published poems

in *PN Review* in 1987 and 1993. In Powell's interview with Peter Scupham, the latter said: 'Some remarks do have an impact on one: I remember Anthony Thwaite leaning across and regarding me balefully once and saying, "Lay off the churchyards for a bit." And he was dead right' (*PN Review* 37, March–April 1984). Thwaite recalled this in his affectionate tribute to Scupham at 85 in *PN Review* 240 (March–April 2018): 'in 2016, Peter and I found ourselves more fully represented than any other poets in Kevin Gardner's anthology *Building Jerusalem: Elegies on Parish Churches*.'

THE YEAR IN BOOKS

John Ashbery, *Your Name Here*

Sujata Bhatt, *Augatora*

Aleksandr Blok, *Selected Poems*, translated by Jon Stallworthy and Peter France

Alison Brackenbury, *After Beethoven*

John Clare, *A Champion for the Poor: political verse and prose*, edited by P.M.S. Dawson, Eric Robinson and John Powell

David Constantine, Hermione Lee and Bernard O'Donoghue (eds), *Oxford Poets 2000: an anthology*

William Cowper, *The Centenary Letters*, edited by Simon Malpas

Donald Davie, *Two Ways Out of Whitman: American essays*, edited by Doreen Davie

John F. Deane, *Toccata and Fugue: new and selected poems*

Keith Douglas, *The Letters*, edited by Desmond Graham

Elaine Feinstein, *Gold*

Jonathan Galassi, *North Street*

Roger Garfitt, *Selected Poems*

Lorna Goodison, *Guinea Woman: new and selected poems*

Jorie Graham, *Swarm*

Robert Graves, *The Complete Poems in One Volume*, edited by Beryl Graves and Dunstan Ward

Robert Graves, *Some Speculations on Literature, History and Religion*, edited by Patrick Quinn

Ivor Gurney, *Rewards of Wonder: poems of Cotswold, France, London*, edited by George Walter

Mimi Khalvati, *Selected Poems*

Thomas Kinsella, *Citizen of the World*

Thomas Kinsella, *Littlebody*

Frank Kuppner, *What? Again? selected poems*

Jean de la Fontaine, *The Complete Tales in Verse*, translated by Guido Waldman

Maggie Lane and David Selwyn (eds), *Jane Austen, A Celebration*

R.F. Langley, *Collected Poems*

Hugh Latimer, *The Sermons*, edited by Arthur Pollard

Grevel Lindop, *Selected Poems*

Richard Mayne, *The Language of Sailing*

Ian McMillan, *Perfect Catch: poems, collaborations & scripts*

Andrew McNeillie, *Nevermore*

Paula Meehan, *Dharmakaya*

Christopher Middleton, *Faint Harps and Silver Voices: selected translations*

Edwin Morgan, *AD: a trilogy of plays on the life of Jesus*

Edwin Morgan, *New Selected Poems*

Cyprian Norwid, *Poems, Letters, Drawings*, edited by Jerzy Peterkiewicz

Petrarch, *Canzoniere*, translated by J.G. Nichols

Karen Press, *Home*

Eça de Queiros, *Eça's English Letters*, translated by Alison Aiken and Anne Stevens

Jean Racine, *Phaedra*, translated by Edwin Morgan

Peter Riley, *Passing Measures: selected poems*

Rainer Maria Rilke, *Sonnets To Orpheus & Letters To a Young Poet*, translated by Stephen Cohn

Peter Sansom, *Point of Sale*

Michael Schmidt (ed), *Commonplace Book*

Alan Shapiro, *Selected Poems 1974–1997*

Iain Crichton Smith, *Country for Old Men & My Canadian Uncle*
Edward Thomas, *Letters to Helen*, edited by R. George Thomas
Andrew Waterman, *Collected Poems 1959–1998*

2001

Mimi Khalvati (b. 1944) was born in Tehran and has lived most of her life in London. She has worked as an actor and director in both the UK and Iran, and is the founder of The Poetry School, which provides poetry tuition by established poets. Her first collection with Carcanet, *In White Ink*, came out in 1991; *Child: new and selected poems* was published in 2011; *Afterwardness* appeared in 2019. '[T]he lyric "I" is my front door – the place I go out from to meet the world. When I write in the first person I don't feel as though I'm going to write about myself, I feel that's the way language comes initially into my mouth,' Khalvati explained in an interview with Maitreyabandhu; 'if my work is "at home" anywhere, it would be within the English lyric tradition, starting with my first love of Wordsworth. But, like many writers living away from their home country, I am constantly remaking my home in the language.'[1]

FROM MIMI KHALVATI

London

24 March 2001

Dear Michael,

I send you the typescript of *The Chine*. I do hope it's OK because I've had to put it together under the most peculiar circumstances.

I find it impossible to write something formal about it for

the author questionnaire form, so please forgive me if I just note here my thinking about it.

It falls into three sections: roughly, my childhood, my children, and love stuff. I had a quintessentially English childhood in Shanklin on the Isle of Wight. Shanklin is famous for its chine and Shanklin Chine ran through the school grounds.[2] My early years in Iran are a total blank, and people have often misread poems as being based on Persian childhood memories. I have none. Losing my first language meant losing memories encoded in that language I believe, and living thereafter with an appalling memory for facts, histories, narratives, including my own. I have been trying to reclaim some of this lost territory.

This is my most autobiographical book, I think. Much of it written while my family fell apart – divorce, my daughter diagnosed with a congenital disease [...], my son, as you know, still ill. I don't know if and how this information should be conveyed or if it's necessary to the reading of some of the poems.

The book is also very formal. Everything with either rhyme, or metre, or both. Lots of blank verse, fixed forms – and some longer poems: the corona, one in ottava rima (with two rhymes) and the elephant sequence. There's also quite a lot of dream material.

Michael, I hope some of this is helpful. I really am sorry to be so tacky in presenting things like this – but I must get this off to you before the week starts and March ends. Please do let me know, as of course you will, of any changes you'd like, poems to omit (I have omitted several I had doubts about) and anything else.

I have still not cleaned up odd lines here and there, particularly in the sonnet sequence, so please don't consider this the final manuscript. I hope to incorporate your suggestions and give you the final thing as soon as I can after hearing from you.

Thank you so much, Michael, I hope you think the book will do.

Much love,
Mimi

*

Much as I dislike poetry competitions, they can have two positive effects. They pay the judges quite generously, and just occasionally one turns up an outstanding poet either *in posse* or *in esse*. Mimi Khalvati was a relatively late starter and she broke rules. 'For me, there is a surfeit of [...] particularity, too much concrete detail in poetry: a huge emphasis on the concrete and the particular that I wanted to redress. I have taken the risk of using abstracts and generalities and more conceptual things: calling a tree a tree, rather than an ash or an oak. It doesn't go down well here,' she declared in an interview with Vicki Bertram. This is an aspect of her poetic openness to the reader. She does not pursue 'voice' in the current sense but deliberately rejects eccentric speech. The poems, whether they are in conventional formal shapes or in free verse, with a wonderful unfolding syntax, are mimetic, spoken and eminently speakable, but they are written towards us, as it were, rather than towards herself. Any reader's voice can, without distortion, without impersonation, ride on her cadences.

English is her second or 'foster' language. She has lost the first almost entirely, it is an empty space in memory. 'In losing your first language [...] you retain the memories that are body memories, sensations, like smell and taste. You can't remember what town it was, how old you were, who was with you, where you lived: any of that stuff, but you can remember a sensation of a battle in your mind between bewilderment and trust.'

NOTES

1. Maitreyabandhu, 'In Conversation with Mimi Khalvati', *PN Review* 221 (January–February 2015).
2. *The Chine* was published in 2002. 'Chine' is a word used on the Isle of Wight and in Dorset to refer to deep, narrow ravines in which water flows down to the sea. In a letter to Fanny Brawne, Keats wrote: 'The wondrous Chine here is a very great Lion: I wish I had as many guineas as there have been spyglasses in it' (July 1819).

THE YEAR IN BOOKS

Homero Aridjis, *Eyes to See Otherwise: selected poems 1960–2000*, edited by Betty Ferber and George McWhirter

Thomas Blackburn, *Selected Poems*, edited by Julia Blackburn

Eavan Boland, *Code*

Joseph Brodsky, *Collected Poems in English*, edited by Ann Kjellberg, translated by various hands

Paul Celan, *Fathomsuns & Benighted*, translated by Ian Fairley

Linda Chase, *The Wedding Spy*

David Constantine, Hermione Lee and Bernard O'Donoghue (eds), *Oxford Poets 2001: an anthology*

Brian Cox, *Emeritus*

Allen Curnow, *The Bells of St Babel's: poems 1997–2001*

Greg Delanty, *The Blind Stitch*

Rebecca Elson, *A Responsibility to Awe*, edited by Anne Berkeley, Angelo Di Cintio and Bernard O'Donoghue

Louise Glück, *The Seven Ages*

James Grant, *Selected Poems*

Robert Gray, *Grass Script: selected earlier poems*

Robert Graves, *The Greek Myths*, edited by Michel W. Pharand

Robert Graves, *Homer's Daughter & the Anger of Achilles*, edited by Neil Powell

Victor Hugo, *Selected Poetry*, translated by Stephen Monte

Elizabeth Jennings, *Timely Issues*

David Kinloch, *Un Tour d'Ecosse*

Thomas Kinsella, *Collected Poems*

Hugh MacDiarmid, *New Selected Letters*, edited by Dorian Grieve,
O.D. Edwards and Alan Riach

Bill Manhire, *Collected Poems*

Patrick Mackie, *Excerpts from the Memoirs of a Fool*

Christopher Middleton, *The Word Pavilion: new and selected poems*

Dom Moraes, *In Cinnamon Shade*

Les Murray, *Learning Human: New Selected Poems*

Jeremy Over, *A Little Bit of Bread and No Cheese*

Frederic Raphael, *Personal Terms: notebooks 1951–1969*

John Redmond, *Thumb's Width*

Laura Riding and Robert Graves, *Essays From Epilogue 1935–1937*,
edited by Mark Jacobs

Peter Robinson, *About Time Too*

Burns Singer, *Collected Poems*, edited by James Keery

Pedro Tamen, *Honey and Poison: selected poems*, translated by Richard
Zimler

Charles Tomlinson, *American Essays*

2002

Christopher Middleton's long association with Carcanet began in 1975 with *The Lonely Suppers of W.V. Balloon*, and continued with a variety of poetry collections, translations and essays; he was also a regular contributor to *PN Review*. Born in Truro, Middleton (1926–2015) served in the Royal Air Force before going to Oxford, graduating in 1948. He was for many years Professor of German at the University of Texas in Austin. During a steamy Austin August, when he was busy translating a novel by Gert Hofmann, he wrote to MNS: 'Elation is rare. Rare, too, the old moments when one hears the distant sea, feels the sun, smells the universe, and tastes a Gauloise – when imagination feels good and right. These are my moments, bless them. They really take your life away.'

FROM CHRISTOPHER MIDDLETON
[Austin]
7 May 2002

Dear Michael,

I hope this won't be a literary letter, but I have a thing in mind that I want to release, and, rooting round for responsive recipients, I thought of yourself. You'll know how I worry, that the books of mine, which you publish, sell so seldom; and that I'm improperly sensitive to adverse reviews, when they're mean-spirited and ignorant. Well, these past few days have cleared my mind as to a number of matters along those lines.

To a considerable extent, one writes from a 'blind spot' – and in obedience to impulses that come seemingly from nowhere. But I'm beginning to 'see'. It probably started, this seeing, in Berlin: I had to give a reading at the American Academy, so wrote a brief preamble, indicating that I was a polite poet – that my language was polite, at least. I might have realized there and then, but did not, that politeness could be precisely what offends reviewers in England who, wittingly or not, mistake me for a 'poshocrat'. Probably I should take a few steps back now.

The Thirties spawned those gallant pinko poets who, as tail-enders of a British bourgeoisie, wanted to disavow their class and join the proletariat. This entailed some ill-considered, but at the time commendable, vituperation against 'individualism': the Marxist jargon crammed the cortex of young poets who had no political experience, but could theorize freely about revolution, and all that. My generation had the task of extracting something fresh from the bourgeois rhetoric – or its lingo, its total linguistic horizon.

We saw the revolutions fizzle out, Stalinism prevail, dissidence a difficult option, or the only option. Our poets were not proles, but the victims, like Mandelstam, or else, for me, foreign poets such as Seferis or St John Perse, who'd never been subjected to the pinko fiddle-faddle of the English stripe: I was exogamic.[1]

At the same time, the class structure was changing. 'Larkin' (I put the name in quotation marks because I mean a mood not the man) was on top: craftsman, depressive, catcher of the wry mood, a real downer, I suppose? And once the changes got going, my sort of English (developed entirely apart from Eng. Lit. and what my good contemporaries knew) became increasingly distinct from the utilitarian grey idiom of suburban intellectuals crouched over their pints.

For me, Côtes du Rhône, pastis, & whiskey. For them the demotic, for me, I fear, the mandarin. – And isn't English still divided along such lines? (Marius is Mandarin, anyhow; and Tomlinson, for better or worse, likewise.)[2] The political dimension, meanwhile, had become for yours truly anything but uninterestingly English: I got intrigued by Germany; my political education came through, say, Kunert, earlier through people at Bush House (Erich Fried, Christiane Hansen).[3] And the gist was that transformations in society are apt to throw onto thrones the vilest Philistines, not philosopher kings; so the Hope was dashed, and one's friends, if not on the run, were under interrogation everywhere.

I'm telescoping decades here. For I come to a certain truth now. Curse Bourgeois and Philistine as one may, the poet-qua-artist (as a special and occasionally inspired human type) walked as a resistant individual through the century of revelation and massacre. The 'vulgar Marxist' demotion of the individual had its heat, historic necessity, no doubt, but it was proved wrong, a metaphysical error and, even, a misprision of the legend of history. What was in question was not the individual as Tom, Dick and Harry, or as artist, but the false sublimations that individualism had driven into social discourse. And, hereabouts, the sexual came into the picture, notably in England. If individualism, inspired by renaissance ideals and Christianity, was intent on sublimating sperm into spirit, the English hadn't done a successful job of it, at least as regards some social implications. But the mess could not be cleared away by a team of homosexual bourgeois-individualist poets charging into the proletariat in search of lovers. That was rather a freakish phase (the Thirties) in a series of transformations still ongoing, and complicated enormously by the influx of Commonwealth citizens after 1950, whose *mores* didn't rhyme with either working-class (now middle-class?) or upper-crust modes of repression. What a difficult story…

But to cut it short: individualism underwent a deep mutation, and one symptom of that was the division internal to the grand or small outreaches of the English language. At least I now think that I was saddled with the language of high individualism, and that I've really tried to extract some honey out of it. (I'm aware that the mixed metaphor indicates what a paradox the task entailed.) Of course, everyone went his or her own way, all the ways being critically assessed, more often than not, on grounds not of an idiom as such, but of subject-matter, orientation, content. Davie strikes me as a peculiar case here: how come he so seldom saw that poetry might be intelligent without being intellectual (or intellectualist)? Hughes hyperbolized and ferocified the language. Larkin cut it down to size; very parochial it became, as English folks prefer. Tomlinson is another intellectualist. Well, those were some of idiomata that were being extracted from an individualist discourse still untouched, really, by the 'demotic' now current, or only bouncing off it.

So the language track, snarled as it is from passage through the last fifty years, can be seen to be divided. Whatever else the other track entails, the one I'm on is 'polite', which doesn't mean at all that it's not bumpy. Certainly my immersion in other languages, other cultures, and my years in a foreign domain, have relieved me of pressure from shifting patterns in the British class-conflict; but my polite English is not the idiom of my detractors, which is precisely why they so viciously or vapidly deplore my endeavours (Reading in the *TLS*, Lovelock in *Oasis*).[4]

Perhaps I should keep this sort of meditation to myself? But no, this time I won't. Because you just might, after all, appreciate a letter that has nothing to do with business.

I haven't dressed these thoughts up in the magisterial complications, let alone the dialectical subtleties, of a regular essayist. Possibly, too, everything I've said is and already was as plain as a pikestaff, and I might have simply been slow on the uptake? It's easy to forget about British history here. – I was only reminded of it, these past few days, by Frank Kermode's lectures in *History and Value*: what a fine, patient and generous mind he has. Inexhaustible attention, and no fuss. What a gentleman! I hope he is still going strong. I'd like to send him my *Twenty Tropes*, but have no address.[5]

I'm wondering if I have omitted, from the above, a whole slew of burning issues? Was I only poking around in the ashes?

Love as ever,
Yours,
Christopher

FROM MICHAEL SCHMIDT
Manchester
25 July 2002

Dear Christopher,

I am terribly sorry for the long delay in replying to your excellent letter of 7th May outlining what you take to be the reasons for the response – or lack of response – to your work. We have had the Literatures of the Commonwealth Festival to deal with and it is now over with a hideous aftermath.[6]

I have been having thoughts not unlike yours though not quite so located in the reception of my own work. The reception of your work and that of a number of other writers inspired by continental and American modernism is extremely vexing. It is as though my generation has been succeeded by a generation without historical roots. My generation gave up God and this generation has given up history. There is very little to keep us on this planet now.

My concern at the moment is a simple one: will the usual pendulum swing occur or, as appears more likely by the day, will the swing towards populism and anti-intellectualism continue? As image-culture and TV continue to alter the nature of imagination in this country and, I suspect, throughout Europe and America, is there any chance for attentive readership to re-develop in any but the most marginal way? The loss of the Classics and in this country the loss of second languages are indications of a shift away from the philological in which the culture that you value and that I value is rooted.

There are no strategies for dealing with this I think. The only way in which one could increase readership would be to appeal to the mean and that, I think, would be a form of cop-out quite intolerable to any real writer or artist.

I owe you another letter and I will write it soon.

With love,
Michael

*

In 1991 Christopher Middleton described most of the poems in an anthology he was reviewing as 'dilated anecdotes': 'Whatever can have happened,' he asked, 'to the understanding that poetry – and not only at outer limits – universalises words, or works and plays words up to a condition of clearest starlight?' Most of what he wrote in prose underlines the difference between his 'polite' sense and the prevailing demotic as outlined in his pained and candid letter here.

He was a prolific writer, and Carcanet published many more of his books than we could sell. At the launch of his *Collected Poems*, I presented him with an early copy of the 720-page tome. He took it with one hand and with the other handed me the manuscript of his *next* collection. *Collected Poems* was not a monument, a final payment as it were. In 2014 Carcanet repeated the monumental gesture with a *Collected Later Poems* (440 pages). Again, there was more to come. Sheep Meadow

Press published *Nobody's Ezekiel* (2015), 48 further pages.

When I first published him in *Poetry Nation* in 1975, I wanted to see whether I liked the work. The best way to do that was to edit and print it and see how it stood up. When he submitted work for book publication in 1974, I asked other poets for advice. They urged against it. He was eccentric, Germanic, experimental. I kept re-reading *The Lonely Suppers of W.V. Balloon* and could not bring myself to reject it.

NOTES

1. Osip Mandelstam (1891–1938), poet and translator, one of the four great poets of the Russian Silver Age. Carcanet published *What I Own: versions of Hölderlin & Mandelshtam*, translated by John Riley & Tim Longville, in 1998. The *Complete Poems* of George Seferis (1900–71), translated from the Greek by Edmund Keeley and Philip Sherrard, was published as a Carcanet Classic in 2018 (originally an Anvil title). Saint-John Perse (pseudonym of Alexis Leger), French diplomat and poet, won the Nobel Prize for Literature in 1960. Henry King described Middleton as 'the most comprehensively European poet to have been born in England in the 20th century'. See https://www.eborakon.com/bog/in-memoriam-christopher-middleton (accessed 31 May 2019).

2. Marius Kociejowski (b.1949), poet, essayist and travel writer; Carcanet has published his essays *God's Zoo: artists – exiles – Londoners* (2014) and his *Collected Poems* (2019).

3. Gunter Kunert (b. 1929), born in Berlin, was 'encouraged' to leave for West Germany in 1979. In the prefatory note to his translations of Kunert's poems in *PN Review* 110 (July–August 1996), Middleton writes: 'Straight-on and steely grey as much of his writing is, a rich comic vein runs through it.' Examples of his poems can be found in Middleton's *Faint Harps and Silver Voices: selected translations* (2000). Michael Hamburger also translated his poetry. Erich Fried (1921–1988), poet and

translator, fled to England after the murder of his father in Vienna in 1938. He worked as a political commentator for the BBC's German service 1952–68, based at Bush House in London. *100 Poems without a Country* (John Calder, 1978) and *Love Poems* (Calder, 1991) were translated into English by Stuart Hood.

4. Peter Reading (1946–2011), poet in a very different style from Middleton's; Yann Lovelock (b.1939), writer and translator, perhaps reviewing *The Word Pavilion* (2001), a new collection plus 110 poems selected from Middleton's previous books.

5. Frank Kermode's *History and Value: the Clarendon lectures & the Northcliffe lectures 1987* (Clarendon Press, 1989) looked back at the books of his youth in the 1930s. *Twenty Tropes for Doctor Dark* (Enitharmon, 2000).

6. Manchester was the host for the Commonwealth Games and Carcanet ran a literature festival for the week 17–23 June 2002, with all the organisational and financial burden that entailed.

THE YEAR IN BOOKS

John Ash, *The Anatolikon & To the City*

John Ashbery, *Chinese Whispers*

Patricia Beer, *As I Was Saying Yesterday: essays*, edited by Sarah Rigby

Sujata Bhatt, *A Colour for Solitude*

Caroline Bird, *Looking Through Letterboxes*

Anthony Burgess, *Revolutionary Sonnets and Other Poems*, edited by Kevin Jackson

David Constantine, Hermione Lee and Bernard O'Donoghue (eds), *Oxford Poets 2002: an anthology*

John Donne, *Selected Letters*, edited by P.M. Oliver

Antony Dunn, *Flying Fish*

Elaine Feinstein, *Collected Poems and Translations*

Ford Madox Ford, *Critical Essays*, edited by Max Saunders and Richard Stang

John Gallas (ed), *The Song Atlas: a book of world poetry*

Jorie Graham, *Never*

John Heath-Stubbs, *The Return of the Cranes*

Malcolm Jack, *Sintra: a glorious Eden*

Dawson Jackson, *Selected Poems*, edited by Nicola Simpson

Elizabeth Jennings, *New Collected Poems*

Gabriel Josipovici, *Goldberg: Variations*

Sidney Keyes, *Collected Poems*, edited with a memoir by Michael
   Meyer

Mimi Khalvati, *The Chine*

Edward Lucie-Smith, *Changing Shape: new and selected poems*

Chris McCully, *The Country of Perhaps*

Andrew McNeillie, *Now, Then*

Robert Minhinnick, *After the Hurricane*

Edwin Morgan, *Cathures*

Edwin Morgan (trs), *Beowulf*

David Morley, *Scientific Papers*

Sinead Morrissey, *Between Here and There*

Les Murray, *Poems the Size of Photographs*

John Henry Newman, *Selected Writings to 1845*, edited by Albert
   Radcliffe

Mary O'Malley, *The Boning Hall: new and selected poems*

Laura Riding and Robert Graves, *A Survey of Modernist Poetry* & *A
   Pamphlet Against Anthologies*, edited by Patrick McGuiness and
   Charles Mundye

Michael Schmidt (ed), *New Poetries III*

Peter Scupham, *Collected Poems*

Joe Sheerin, *Elves in the Wainscotting*

Jon Silkin, *Making a Republic*

Gregory Woods, *The District Commissioner's Dreams*

William Wordsworth, *The Earliest Poems 1785–1790*, edited by
   Duncan Wu

2003

Peter Scupham (b. 1933) went to Cambridge after his period of National Service. His teaching career culminated in the position of Head of English at St Christopher School, Letchworth. With John Mole he founded The Mandeville Press, which uses the traditional letterpress method of printing. He now writes, and runs Mermaid Books, a second-hand/antiquarian book business, out of the Elizabethan manor house he restored with his wife, Margaret Steward, in Norfolk. In his interview with himself, he quoted Richard Wilbur: 'The strength of the genie comes of his being confined in a bottle,' advice he found pertinent: 'Make good bottles; hope for genies. And I suppose I've always preferred the church to the cathedral, the hedgerow to the forest, the song to the symphony. Start small, go big.'[1] His decorated envelopes are always opened with pleasure at Carcanet, which published his *Collected Poems* in 2002.

FROM MICHAEL SCHMIDT
Manchester
21 October 2003

Dear Peter,

It was a pleasure to talk to you today and find that my library is to be enhanced with so many nice volumes.

I am quite serious about Golding.[2] William Cookson was supposed to be doing it and never made any progress with it at all, I fear.[3] He would have done it, as it were, out of Pound. I imagine you will do it, as it were, out of a different mare.

What I would have in mind would be a selection from the Ovid with any other material you thought was pertinent and exciting, the whole book running to no more than 180 pages. The passages that would be especially valuable – indeed indispensable – would be those that are clearly echoed in Shakespeare. But that should not be the only determinant on the selection of material.

The introduction would be biographical and critical of course with, I would hope, some indication of the modernisations required of the text. In particular I imagine the punctuation will require quite a lot of judicious Scuphamian attention.

I would have [hoped] that we could sell this book to the Americans but I am not entirely confident on this score. In any case, it would make an excellent Fyfield book for us here.

The usual fee for producing a Fyfield is a £300 advance against a 5% royalty. We would be able to work with a photocopied text if required. I hate the idea of your cutting up one of the big editions. (I prohibit you to cut up the £350 edition!)

If you are interested seriously, I will draw up an agreement forthwith or even fifth-with!

With warm regards, dear Peter,

Yours ever,
Michael

FROM PETER SCUPHAM
Norwich
Wednesday 8 October 2003
NO! Wednesday 22 October 2003

Dear Michael,

Well, I think the Golding/Ovid proposal is a smashing ideah, so here goes.

I take the points made about the Shakespeare Connection!!

Yes, can do the 'modernisation of the text bit'. Would need to think and raise queries – talking to Neil [Powell] might be good at some later date.

The idea of a £300 advance against a 5% royalty is fine. I could probably afford to buy the Mermaid copy in crushed mulberry signed by Ovid for Rouse in biro for that, and might well do so.[4]

In English, this means I accept your proposal and look forward to the agreement.

Thanks
Peter

FROM PETER SCUPHAM
Norwich
faxed 24 November 2003

DEAR MICHAEL STOP HAVE STARTED READING
GOLDING STOP
IS THIS WRONG STOP HAVE WRITTEN OFF CAR BY
BEING STRUCK
SAVAGELY (IF NOT DUMB) BY IDIOT STOP
NON-DRIVERS MAY
LARF HO HO STOP AM I TO RECOUP ENSUING FI-
NANCIAL CAR-

TASTROPHE (NEXT CAR WILL COST ME A COOL
    THOU MORE
THAN INSURANCE WILL GIVE ME CHIZZ CHIZZ) BY
    SOME
<u>METAMORPHOSES</u> STOP YOU WILL RARELY HAVE
    MET A MOR
PHOSESIOUS LETTER THAN THIS STOP (SEE B.
    ALDISS
'BRIGHTFOUNT DIARIES') IF I DON'T GET THIS
    CHANCE TO EDIT
GOLDING MAY THE GODS TURN YOU INTO A DELIA
    SMITH
COOKERY BOOK IN A TORN DW AND GIVE YOU TO
    OXFAM STOP[5]

*

Carcanet has been known to be slow to pay advances, hence Peter Scupham's telegraphic letter of 24 November soliciting his contractual advance.

Many readers are addicted to Peter Scupham's catalogues, which arrive in eccentrically illustrated envelopes and in which the descriptions of books he is selling are so witty that he could – in effect he does – sell snow to the esquimaux. More than once I have been on the brink of buying the same book from him twice, but like a Heraclitus he remembers and deflects me. He generally sends books out before he takes payment. Thus debt collection becomes a creative task, as in the following exchange over a purchase I made in 2013. He wrote 'Nursery Rhymes for Christmas':

> Christmas is coming, tycoons are getting fat —
> Please to put a penny in the Merman's hat.
> If you haven't got a penny, then thirty-three pounds 60p will do,
> If you haven't got thirty-three pounds 60p, then God help you.

Hark, hark, the dogs do bark,
The beggars are coming to town,
The poets in rags, the publishers in jags,
and it's thirty-three pounds 60p for a small velvet gown nowadays.

There was a crooked poet and he ran a crooked mile,
And found a crooked sixpence beneath a crooked stile.
He prayed to St. Michael, and as quick as eye could see,
It turned into a cheque for thirty-three pound sixty 60p

Ayez pitie, seigneur, ayez pitie

One is compelled to reply in verse; sometimes limericks are
called for, but generally one tries to respond in register. In this
instance, for lack of a cheque book I paid cash. My ostensible
motive for taking long credit was to elicit a poem from the
bookseller. Here is 'Bou-lingerie; Or don't get your twists in
35 knickers':

It's a silly excuse at Christmas
To say I haven't a cheque
But it's true: the bank haven't sent one
Though I've tried and I've tried. Oh heck.

I am sending an envelope, Peter,
With thirty five smackers for fudge.
When you get it, don't treat it like junk mail.
'It is Pound's,' shrieks the late Olga Rudge.

The reason I stretch out my credit
The way any editor would
Is because the Musa Cunctatrix
Makes the Merman swim out of the wood

With a poem on his fluorescent Speedos
And a grin on his sweet puckish face.
Adam Smith, Chuck Darwin, Eliza:
Bear my greetings to Old Hall apace:

Tell Margaret and Peter Good Cheer
At the end of this torybull year.
Maybe two fourteen will be better.
All the best! from the lonely baguetter.

NOTES

1. Interview in *PN Review* 240 (March–April 2018); some of his envelopes are also reproduced in this issue.
2. Arthur Golding (c. 1636–1606) translated over thirty works of Latin into English, but is best-known for one, his translation of Ovid's *Metamorphoses*, because it was used by Shakespeare. Peter Scupham did edit this for Carcanet: *Ovid's Metamorphoses* was published in 2005.
3. William Cookson (1939–2003) was a poet and literary editor, who founded the magazine *Agenda* in 1959, after meeting Pound. Carcanet published *Agenda: an anthology 1959–1993* in 1994.
4. W.H.D. Rouse was the editor of *Shakespeare's Ovid – Being Arthur Golding's Translation of the Metamorphoses* (Southern Illinois University Press, 1961).
5. It seems excessive to annotate this playful fax, but for the sake of readers who might enjoy it more for having the references: 'chizz chizz' (a swindle) comes from the 1950s novels about the incorrigible schoolboy Nigel Molesworth by Geoffrey Wilans, illustrated by Ronald Searle; 'Grand Master of Science Fiction' Brian Aldiss collected a series of columns based on his bookselling experience in *The Brightfount Diaries* (1955); Delia Smith, doyenne of English cookery writers; 'DW' dust wrapper (book jacket), familiar abbreviation in booksellers'

catalogues; Oxfam, the anti-poverty British charity, has about 150 bookshops selling secondhand books.

THE YEAR IN BOOKS

John Adlard (ed), *Restoration Bawdy*

Djuna Barnes, *The Book of Repulsive Women & Other Poems*, edited by Daniela Caselli

Thomas Lovell Beddoes, *Death's Jest-Book*, edited by Michael Bradshaw

Eavan Boland (ed), *Three Irish Poets*

Donald Davie, *A Travelling Man: eighteenth-century bearings*, edited by Doreen Davie

John F. Deane, *Manhandling the Deity*

Greg Delanty, *The Ship of Birth*

Sasha Dugdale, *Notebook*

Padraic Fallon, *'A Look in the Mirror' and Other Poems*, edited by Brian Fallon

Ford Madox Ford, *England and the English*, edited by Sara Haslam

Nigel Forde, *A Map of the Territory*

Robert Graves, *Antigua, Penny, Puce & They Hanged my Saintly Billy*, edited by Ian McCormick

Robert Graves, *The Story of Marie Powell, Wife to Mr Milton & The Islands of the Unwisdom*, edited by Simon Brittan

Sophie Hannah, *First of the Last Chances*

Adam Johnson, *Collected Poems*, edited by Neil Powell

P.J. Kavanagh, *A Kind of Journal*

Charles Lamb, *Selected Writings*, edited by Jack Morpurgo

Hugh MacDiarmid, *The Revolutionary Art of the Future: rediscovered poems*, edited by John Manson, Dorian Grieve and Alan Riach

Stéphane Mallarmé, *For Anatole's Tomb*, translated by Patrick McGuinness

Robert Minhinnick (ed), *The Adulterer's Tongue: Six Welsh Poets – a facing-text anthology*

Les Murray, *New Collected Poems*

Frank O'Hara, *Why I'm Not a Painter and Other Poems*, edited by
  Mark Ford
George Oppen, *New Collected Poems*, edited by Michael Davidson
Ovid, *Amores*, translated by Tom Bishop
Frederic Raphael, *The Benefits of Doubt; essays*
Tom Raworth, *Collected Poems*
Peter Riley, *Alstonefield: A Poem*
Peter Robinson, *Selected Poems*
Robert Saxton, *Manganese*
Adam Schwartzman, *Book of Stones*
Ossian Shine, *The Language of Tennis*
Charlotte Smith, *Selected Poems*, edited by Judith Willson
James Sutherland Smith, *In the Country of Birds*
Charles Tomlinson, *Metamorphoses: poetry and translation*
Charles Tomlinson, *Skywriting*
William Tyndale, *Selected Writings*, edited by David Daniell
Giuseppe Ungaretti, *Selected Poems*, translated by Andrew Frisardi
Matthew Welton, *The Book of Matthew*
Duncan Wu (ed), *Wordsworth's Poets*

2004

R.F. Langley (1938–2011) was a teacher for nearly forty years, and Head of English at Bishop Vesey's grammar school in Sutton Coldfield from 1980 until his retirement. He read English at Cambridge, where he met and became close friends with J.H. Prynne, but his chief interests were in painting and drawing. Peter Riley wrote in his obituary: 'Roger sought occasions when he was "alone and perfectly still" and allowed words to freely elaborate from that point.'[1] *PN Review* published over fifty entries from his journals in the years after he had retired to Suffolk, and more entries posthumously. When Carcanet published Langley's *Collected Poems* in 2000, it was shortlisted for the Whitbread Prize; the book contained seventeen uncollected poems.

FROM R.F. LANGLEY
Halesworth, Suffolk
8 August 2004

Dear Michael,

Just done the proofs for the extracts from my journal for the next *PN Review*… number 159.

Two slight queries. You seem to be printing two extracts this time, giving me twice as much space as usual. Which is very generous and pleasing, of course. It will, however, run you out of the extracts you have in store… so I wondered if this double blast was sort of a closing trumpet call. If so… fine. You have given me a terrific run for my money, and thanks a lot.

If you want any more, let me know. I enclose two more, in case, which could be presented together or apart. I wouldn't like to have the responsibility for falling out of the system that has been running so long and so much to my advantage!

But please let me know what the intentions are.

Meanwhile, the poetry comes as slowly as ever. I have another, but am somewhat uncertain of its value and want to sit on it and think. The total number of poems is now at twenty-nine![2] What an output! Here's to rarity value! Hope you are well, and, preferably, somewhere excellent on a summer holiday.

Thanks again,
Roger Langley

FROM MICHAEL SCHMIDT
Manchester
9th September 2004

Dear Roger,

I do not want the blast in *PN Review* 159 – an error in fact – to be a final trumpet call. On the contrary, I want your journal extracts to continue for ever. I am most grateful for the new pair. Can you please continue supplying?

I certainly look forward to the new poem as well. I think you have produced as many poems as a poet should and most other poets simply lack your proper mechanisms of self-control.

I wonder if your son told you of the strange synergy that occurred at Leeds?[3] It was as though I had stepped on a very nice snake.

With warm regards,
Yours ever,
Michael

FROM ROGER LANGLEY
Halesworth
19 September 2004

Dear Michael,

Thanks for the letter and for the request for more journal. I comply with pleasure. I include here the poem I mentioned, 'Touchstone', which, as do most of my things, has given me some uneasiness. It is a very old-fashioned poem. Long ago Bernstein said it would be better not to consider the poet himself as the prime source of the poem, but to credit the culture, the language, history etc as prime movers.[4] No telephone from writer to reader. Instead the live wires… You know all that of course. And, I must admit, avoiding just speaking as myself in a biographical setting, offering my views on what it looks like to me, has always been in my mind, as part of the Cambridge inheritance, where most writers take it much more seriously than I do so that they disappear conclusively. But my poems have always been struggles, in this scenario, since they are basically autobiographical in origin, whatever happens to them in transit, as it were. I seem to find it hard to do what seems to me one of the best things being done, ever since Pound, never mind Bernstein. The Pound tradition, I love it. But this last poem gives up on all this and just speaks from my back garden and offers naked ideas in that setting. Rather grim ideas, maybe. Anyway, see what you think.

One of the journal extracts I am sending, the one for August 23 2003, is the source of the poem. I did this once before, you recall, with the poem about the Funeral, the one that started this whole series of journal extracts. The trouble with doing it is that the journal extracts, possibly interesting because linked to the poem, are not necessarily the best journal extracts in themselves. So, here again, I throw it over to you to decide if the extract is worth having in at all. So the poem and the extract are both, so to speak, in question. There if you can use them, together or not.

The other extract is one I sent ages ago, but it has not, I think, been used. The only one of that first batch not used. Maybe there was a reason for that, but, if not, here it is again. I will now set about choosing more. You have the two bits from my previous letter, and now these two more, the one to fit the poem if you think so. Whew.

I was astounded to see myself as 'Highly Commended' in the Forward anthology.[5] To some extent it felt like being back at school, doing tests! The poem was charged with quotation from Iris Murdoch and Rilke, but I suppose it was well concealed.[6] I think competition poems probably should not be charged with Rilke and Murdoch! But it shows that my work has some effect, so I am grateful. Thanks for including me in the process.

We are just back from St Ives, where I gave a reading at the Salthouse Gallery to a small but enthusiastic audience which included Tony Frazer of Shearsman.[7] On the way there and back we called at Dartington College to see my friend Andrew Brewerton who had just taken over as Principal of the Art School. Merce Cunningham and Cage and Rauschenberg were at the college back when my uncle was involved with the place.[8] I have most fond memories and hope to do a reading there in the spring. John Hall is there, for one thing.[9] And, yes, Eric told us about the little snake you trod on. Most odd, but, indeed, neat and nice.

Thanks again for everything.
Roger Langley

*

I am puzzled in this correspondence by the reference to 'a very nice snake', surely not intended to describe Eric Langley, the poet's son. The connection between the two Langleys, and Eric's request that his first book appear in the traditional Carcanet livery, out of a proper *pietas*, were a particular pleasure.

R.F. Langley's *Complete Poems* and Miles Burrows's *Waiting for the Nightingale* are the two books always on my bedside table – not supporting the lamp but enlarging the small hours.

NOTES

1. Peter Riley, R.F. Langley obituary, *The Guardian*, 7 March 2011.

2. Carcanet published a second collection in 2007, *The Face of It*, with twenty-one poems; his *Complete Poems* was published in 2015, edited by Jeremy Noel-Tod, including his late uncollected poems.

3. Eric Langley is a Shakespeare scholar who lectures at University College London. His first collection, *Raking Light*, was published by Carcanet in 2017 and shortlisted for the Forward Prize for Best First Collection. He is quoted on the Forward website as saying: 'When the real poet of the family died, I found that writing poetry was a way of continuing conversations which we'd had.' http://www.forwardartsfoundation.org/poet/eric-langley/ (accessed 31 May 2019)

4. Charles Bernstein (b.1950), American literary critic and poet, was co-editor 1978–81 of L=A=N=G=U=A=G=E magazine, and co-founder of PENNsound, the archive of recorded poetry based at the University of Pennsylvania. A key collection of his essays is *A Poetics* (Harvard University Press, 1992).

5. Langley won, posthumously, the Forward Prize for Best Single Poem in 2011, with 'To a Nightingale'.

6. Iris Murdoch (1919–99), English philosopher and novelist.

Carcanet has published three collections of poems by Rainer Maria Rilke (1875–1926) translated by Stephen Cohn, and since acquiring the Anvil list, a collection translated by Michael Hamburger. It also published J.F. Hendry's *The Sacred Threshold: a Life of Rilke* in 1983. (RM: It was the first book I edited for Carcanet. Coming straight from university, I found it insufficiently rigorous, and asked MNS why he had accepted it: 'Because I liked the first sentence,' he replied.)

7. The Salthouse Gallery for contemporary art was established in St Ives in 1979. Tony Frazer (b. 1951) is the founding publisher of the long-running *Shearsman* magazine: 'there is a clear inclination towards the more exploratory end of the current spectrum', Frazer states on the website. He also edits the Shearsman book imprint (founded 1982), which published R.F. Langley's *Journals* in 2006.

8. Dartington College of Arts is now incorporated in Falmouth University, but was for many decades an independent organisation offering innovative education in music and the arts, based at Dartington Hall in Totnes, Devon. Langley's maternal uncle, Eric Langford, was a teacher closely associated with the College over a long period. John Cage, his partner Merce Cunningham and Robert Rauschenberg (composer, choreographer/dancer and painter respectively) presented their interdisciplinary collaboration *Story* at Dartington in 1964, when Rauschenberg remarked that people there had 'that Black Mountain beatnik kind of look'. See http://theatredanceperformancetraining.org/2018/10/visual-performance-a-way-of-being/ (accessed 31 May 2019).

9. John Hall (b. 1945), poet, essayist and teacher, spent most of his working life at Dartington College. His most recent collection, *As a Said Place*, was published by Shearsman in 2017.

THE YEAR IN BOOKS

John Ashbery, *Selected Prose,* edited by Eugene Ritchie

Patricia Beer, *Mrs Beer's House*

Alison Brackenbury, *Bricks and Ballads*

Carmen Bugan, *Crossing the Carpathians*

Robert Burton, *The Anatomy of Melancholy: a selection*, edited by
    Kevin Jackson

Gillian Clarke, *Making the Beds for the Dead*

Ken Cockburn and Robyn Marsack (eds), *Intimate Expanses: XXV
    Scottish Poems 1978–2002*

David Constantine, Hermione Lee and Bernard O'Donoghue
    (eds), *Oxford Poets 2004: an anthology*

Donald Davie, *Modernist Essays: Yeats, Pound and Eliot*

Jane Draycott, *The Night Tree*

Mark Ford (ed), *The New York Poets: an anthology*

John Gallas, *Star City*

Douglas Gifford and Alan Riach (eds), *Scotland: Poets and the
    Nation*

Robert Graves, *Count Belisarius & Lawrence of the Arabs*, edited by
    Scott Ashley

Robert Graves, *The Golden Fleece & Seven Days in New Crete*, edited
    by Patrick Quinn

Ivor Gurney, *Collected Poems*, edited by P.J. Kavanagh

P.J. Kavanagh, *Something About*

Rudyard Kipling, *The Long Trail: selected poems*, edited by Harry
    Ricketts

Frank Kuppner, *A God's Breakfast*

Carola Luther, *Walking the Animals*

Kevin Jackson, *Letters of Introduction*

Peter McDonald, *Pastorals*

Patrick McGuinness, *The Canals of Mars*

Cyprian Norwid, *Selected Poems,* translated by Adam Czerniawski

Cesare Pavese, *Disaffections: Complete Poems 1930-1950*, translated
    by Geoffrey Brock

2004

Neil Powell, *Halfway House*
Frederic Raphael, *Rough Copy: Personal Terms II*
Sarah Raphael, *Drawings*
Lou Andreas Salomé, *You Alone Are Real To Me: Remembering Rainer Maria Rilke*, translation by Angela von der Lippe
Evelyn Schlag, *Selected Poems*
Muriel Spark, *All the Poems*
Jon Stallworthy, *Body Language*

2005

The anonymous writer of the obituary for Patrick Creagh (1930–2012) in the *Daily Telegraph* provides an irresistibly quotable account of his life, from his schooldays at Wellington, where he was disciplined for answering an exam question 'on Cromwell's foreign policy not in the form of an essay, but with a limerick', to his brief stint in the RAF, 'managing to get himself discharged on the grounds of mental instability after wearing red socks on the parade ground', and beyond.[1] With his second wife, he lived in a farmhouse with a vineyard in Radda-in-Chianti, north of Siena. 'Creagh demonstrated an enthusiasm for the production and consumption of red wine. His only subsequent collection of poems would be *The Lament of the Border Guard*, published by Carcanet in 1980. As his own creative output diminished, however, he emerged as one of the great Italian translators of his generation. He approached translation much as he had poetry, with assiduous attention to every syllable'. The Leopardi project discussed in the letters never came to fruition, but Creagh won awards for his translations of Italian fiction.

FROM PATRICK CREAGH
Panzano, Tuscany
16 January 2005

Dear Michael,

I see it's a year now since I sent you some stuff, so it's pretty clear that you didn't think much of my Leopardi versions, or else of my snooty attitude towards my rival's work.[2] Almost certainly both. In any case, I have thoroughly offended you and am heartily sorry. That is the first reason for this letter.

The second is that I have begun, tentatively, writing poems again. Very little so far, but spurred on by having come across some old things left behind me in another house. Now I have a few poems in hand, and some scraps and fragments that might yield some return. But I can't remember what you printed in *PNR* all those years ago. I haven't even the printed 'Epistularium' (I have your translations, but only as sent to me in typescript, with a query about 'ayas', which should have been 'hayas', so I hope I answered it).[3] But you printed other poems, which are simply lost to me. Would it be possible to find and photocopy them? A tall order, I'm afraid, but if I could see what I've got it would be a great encouragement to go on and write more. Meanwhile, in a day or two, I'll send you two or three things I'm sure you haven't seen.

And the third and last reason for this letter is to summon up the courage to ask you, should you hear of anyone in the business actually looking for a translator from Italian, to remember me. Nearly three years of health trouble and the collapse of Harvill as a source of work have left me high, dry and very worried.[4]

I beg you to forgive me, within reason, for imposing on you, as for everything else, and I hope to hear from you in due course.

With best wishes,
Patrick

FROM MICHAEL SCHMIDT
Manchester
10 January 2005

Dear Patrick,

Your bated breath must now have abated. I am desperately sorry for the long delay in replying to your letter of 22 February [2004] with your versions of the Canti. I have read and re-read these versions (hoping you have continued with the project). My only misgivings are to do with diction, certain locutions which are horrendously arch and Victorian and which I feel ought to be re-considered. The first, but not the only one, is 'Blithesome' in 'The Lone Blue Rock Thrush'.

Having said that, it does feel to me as though the prosodies you have adopted are miraculous; the very famous poems, which one knows by heart, with a great fidelity. So, too, the huge abstractions suddenly have a kind of specific gravity about them.

I am not sure where we go from here. I hope that my long silence will not put you off altogether. Perhaps you could send me as an attachment on email a complete file of the versions you have done so far? I would love to see them and see what emendations you have made in those you sent in February. We can then look into which ones will shine in *PN Review* and whether we might consider proceeding to a book.

With warm regards and best wishes for the New Year,

Yours ever,
Michael

FROM PATRICK CREAGH
Panzano, Tuscany
5 February 2005

Dear Michael,

Indeed our letters did cross, and with a vengeance: I got yours less than two minutes after posting mine. I'm sorry not to have answered at once, but my old typewriter collapsed on me, so I've had to start again on a hand-me-down laptop, which delayed me a bit as it had no instruction manual and I've never touched a computer before in my life.

I have not abandoned the Canti project, and indeed am working on it now, but it was interrupted by a) a novel to translate for *actual cash*, and b) even more by a spot of surgery that took me six months to recover from.[5] I am re-revising everything as I transfer them onto computer, which serves two purposes at once: taking a fresh look and practising on this new machine (this is my first letter, so it may go into gobbledegook at any moment).

Yes, the question of the horrendously arch and Victorian locutions is rather a vexed one. I rather wish you had taken a censorious pencil and scribbled furiously under the offending locutions. The trouble is that although some may be errors of judgement on my part, in principle they are deliberate, and intended to reflect Leopardi's own practice. He had a passion for all things ancient, including vocabulary. In the very line you chose for stricture (being the first of its kind), he calls birds 'augelli', rather than 'uccelli' simply because it's the 'poetic' word. Birds are 'augelli' 12 times in the Canti, and how often does he call them 'uccelli'? Not once. But in the prose *Operette* they are 'uccelli', just as they were when he was telling the gardener to put out crumbs for them at Christmas.[6] It's because he was deliberately and with infinite care and craft writing in a different language, the language of poetry as he inherited it and understood it. His poetry is in the highest degree artificial, not only in vocabulary but in structure. Those enormously long and complex periods of his, where you hang there for a dozen or sixteen lines before landing on the main verb, have to be wrought as nearly as possible in the way he did it, words and ideas strategically placed to highlight the meaning, or indeed convey it at all.

What it all boils down to is that with certain exceptions the language of the Canti is consistently and purposefully *distanced* from that of common speech. It's therefore impossible [to] put them into the low, conversational idiom that appeals to the ear today because it sounds 'natural', when they themselves are so artificial, so utterly cured in the brine of tradition and antiquity (cor! what a metaphor). My attempt to render Leopardi as he actually is, rather than what he would be had he written on the contrary set of principles, may have led me into certain horrendousness of a positively horripilating nature, and I can try to moderate and compromise; but not abandon the attempt. For example, words such as hither, whence, wherefore, oftentimes etc. are absolutely intrinsic to my whole endeavour, serving as they do to distance the language of the poems from common speech. The same goes for echoes of other poets. They are a major feature of the Canti, an integral part of the Leopardi method. You'll find more than one echo of Milton in my version of 'la ginestra', and by all that's holy I believe them absolutely appropriate in that context.

Enough of that for the moment. What I'll do, if I may, is send you hard copies of the ones you've seen but I've revised, plus the ones you haven't seen at all.

Meanwhile I'll go to work on revising ones you have seen, bearing your strictures in mind and trying to weigh it all up. Because I also have to bear in mind what the poet himself said about translation: that the essential thing is to render the *style*; take away the style and you take away everything. It will be very sad if being faithful to him means being unacceptable.

Well, we'll see. In the meantime,

With all best wishes,
Patrick

P.S. Sorry to go on and on, but you know I rather liked 'blitheful rivalry'! The vowels have that rising sound that to my ear suggests flight. Moreover, I like the word 'blithe' in itself. It is perfect for Silvia in her poem, having that sense of carefree that other near-synonyms don't. And in XXX (On a bas-relief) I bet you hated the way I kicked off with 'Whither away?' To me it seems just right: sprightly and Shakespearean. To start with 'Where are you going?' may be literally correct, but it's out of the question to start such a passionate poem with such a pedestrianism. And three lines later, I have 'Alone, a-wander...' Archly Victorian? Perhaps, but more important for me was the effect of 'Alone, a-wander', like two footsteps one after the other, to express in sound the young girl's motion. Rather like saying pitter-patter (or however it's spelt). Also, it may be irrelevant to the result in English, and downright academic of me, but in the original line ('Sola, peregrinando, il patrio tetto') only the word 'sola' comes from the spoken language. The rest is as literary as 'Phyllis tripped it o'er the mead', or some such stuff.

I've added this postscript to show you, as if proof were needed, just how screwily my mind works. When I send the batch of Canti I'll include a few pieces of my own.

*

Patrick Creagh was one of those extraordinary writers who came and went, as it were. We had periods of sustained communication and then years of silence which seem to have coincided with fundamental changes in the poet's life. After a time he would remember that Carcanet was there and had a space for him. One of my regrets is that the great Leopardi project did not get off the ground. It was a serious and well-conceived plan, and in Creagh it had the vocational translator that was required. But even vocational translators have to eat, and drink, and Carcanet was unable to provide the necessary financial sustenance. His 'Epistularium' sequence remains one of the poetry high-points of the early years of *PN Review*.

NOTES

1. The obituary begins: 'John Patrick Brasier-Creagh (he later shortened his name because, he said, he did not want to be a double-barrelled poet)', *Daily Telegraph*, 2 November 2012.
2. Carcanet had already published two volumes by Giacomo Leopardi (1798–1837) translated by J.G. Nichols: *Moral Tales* (1993) and *The Canti* (1994). Nichols won the John Florio Prize for his translation of *The Colloquies* by Guido Gozzano (1987), and also published translations of Gabriele D'Annunzio and Francesco Petrarch with Carcanet.
3. 'Epistularium' headnote: 'After nine years without writing verse, Patrick Creagh, now living in Italy, was engaged in a verse correspondence by the painter George d'Almeida. These poems are Creagh's side of this correspondence. Parts 10 and 12 he composed in Spanish, and Michael Schmidt has provided translations' (*PN Review* 12, March–April 1980).
4. Creagh translated Claudo Magris's *Danube* (1989), for which he won the John Florio Prize in 1990. The obituarist again: '[H]e sometimes found that the professional association led to friendship: such was the case with the great Sicilian novelist Gesualdo Bufalino. Creagh's translation of Bufalino's *Blind*

Argus, for his patient and most regular editor Christopher MacLehose, at Harvill, won the John Florio prize in 1992.' By 2005 Creagh was living with his third partner (and collaborator) in Panzano, a small village in Chianti. Harvill Press, founded in 1946, was known for its translated fiction; although it remained independent after a management buyout in 1996, it was sold to Random House in 2002 and merged with Secker & Warburg in 2005.

5. Probably Gianrico Carofiglio's *Involuntary Witness*, published in 2005 by Bitter Lemon Press.

6. Creagh's translation of Leopardi's *Operette Morali, Moral Tales*, was published by Carcanet in 1983, and reviewed in *PN Review* 38 (May–June 1984) by Paul Carter, who concluded: 'It is scrupulously attentive to the nuances of tone and diction in Leopardi's many styles. In short, it maintains the high standard which *PNR* readers have come to expect from the translator of the *Canti*. Attractively printed and dust-jacketed, as the first of five volumes in which publisher and translator hope to give a "comprehensive selection" (*sic*) of Leopardi's writings, it bodes extremely well.' There was nothing from Creagh in *PN Review* after the 1980s.

THE YEAR IN BOOKS

Chinua Achebe, *Collected Poems*
John Ashbery, *Where Shall I Wander?*
Anthony Astbury (ed), *The Tenth Muse*
Iain Bamforth, *A Place in the World*
Eavan Boland, *New and Collected Poems*
John F. Deane, *The Instruments of Art*
Padraic Fallon, *The Vision of MacConglinne and Other Plays*
Kenneth Ferris, *Football: Terms and Teams*
Philip French, *Westerns: aspects of a movie genre*
Jorie Graham, *Overlord*
Robert Graves and Raphael Patai, *The Hebrew Myths*, edited by

Robert A. Davis

William Hazlitt, *Metropolitan Writings*, edited by Gregory Dart

John Heath-Stubbs, *Pigs Might Fly*

David Herd, *Mandelson! Mandelson! A Memoir*

Tim Kendall, *Strange Land*

David Kinloch, *In My Father's House*

Edward Lear, *Over the Land and Over the Sea: selected nonsense and travel writing*, edited by Peter Swaab

John Masefield, *Sea-Fever: selected poems*, edited by Philip Errington

Christopher Middleton, *The Anti-Basilisk*

Edwin Morgan, *The Play of Gilgamesh*

Sinéad Morrissey, *The State of the Prisons*

Les Murray (ed), *Hell and After: four early English language poets of Australia*

Lucy Newlyn, *Ginnel*

Charles Olson, *The Charles Olson Reader*, edited by Ralph Maud

Ovid, *Metamorphoses: a selection*, translated by Arthur Golding, edited by Peter Scupham

John Polidori, *The Vampyre and Other Writings*, edited by Franklin Bishop

Karen Press, *The Canary's Songbook*

Richard Price, *Lucky Day*

Laura Riding, *The Telling*, introduction by Michael Schmidt

Lynette Roberts, *Collected Poems*, edited by Patrick McGuinness

Anni Sumari (ed), *How to Address the Fog: XXV Finnish Poems 1978–2002*

István Turczi (ed), *At the End of the Broken Bridge: XXV Hungarian Poems 1978-2002*

Daniel Weissbort (ed), *An Anthology of Contemporary Russian Women Poets*

Jane Yeh, *Marabou*

2006

Alastair Fowler (b. 1930) graduated from the University of Edinburgh in 1952 and went to Oxford to study for his further degrees. MNS relished the essay Fowler submitted for *PN Review* about the Oxford tutorial system: 'I ran into abrasive banter, which put me off the stride I hadn't yet got into. The Merton men would resent being "farmed out" to a Scot scarcely older than themselves, who had no teaching room in college. I held tutorials in our tiny attic flat at 2A Church Walk, with nappies steaming away. Pupils would enter panting, "Do you have much trouble with the altitude up here, sir?" [...] A congenial tutorial allowed profoundly satisfying intellectual enquiry. [...] After fifteen years of tutorials, I was ready, and yet reluctant, to leave for a chair at Edinburgh, city of lectures.'[1] Fowler was Regius Professor of English Literature at the University of Edinburgh 1972–84, and published several volumes of poetry.

FROM ALASTAIR FOWLER
Edinburgh
2 February 2006

Dear Michael,

I've been enjoying *PNR* 167. That was a good obituary of Robert Woof.[2] A sweet man. He was kind to me when I went to Pembroke in 1952, introducing me to the Johnson Society, etc. I'm sorry I lost touch with him later when I moved to Queen's.

You're right in my view to be dubious about the Google deal.[3] It will in the end be bad for academic book publishing, which is already very sick. As for academic authors, universities are all too quick to sign away their rights. The committee of vice-chancellors even tried to chisel authors out of their photocopying royalties. That 200 million isn't all that much, either, when you divide it among the universities concerned.

The appreciation of Derry Jeffares started off many memories of him.[4] It was his tutorial on *Paradise Lost* in 1950 that first got me seriously interested in Milton's style. A strange man, of many gifts. Choosing houses with a pendulum wasn't the only paranormal practice he went in for. If you went to visit Derry and his wife you'd be liable to find them waiting with cold remedies, having dowsed the problem at long distance. And did you know about his passion for cars? He had an arrangement with a garage in Fife, to stand in as a driver (complete with uniform) and pick up people from the airport. But Derry is too large a topic for a letter.

With best wishes for 2006,
Yours ever
Alastair

FROM MICHAEL SCHMIDT
Manchester
5 April 2006

Dear Alastair,

I wonder if you are going back to Pembroke for the Thomas Gray celebrations? I know Brian Cox is going to be there.

My scheme for saving academic scholarship is to establish a proper means for publishing on the web scholarly editions of letters and manuscript trails. The AHRB awarded me an 'A' on my big proposal but found no funds to back it. So the revolution has been delayed!

I used to know Derry Jeffares quite well, visiting him first in Leeds and then in Scotland. Unfortunately my relations with him were soured when I backed the intolerable Ian Hamilton Finlay in some of his battles.[5] I also soured a warm relationship with Lord Balfour, a really kindly and good man.[6] I did not know about Derry's passion for cars! I loved his wife and her benign witchcraft.

All the very best,
Yours ever
Michael

FROM ALASTAIR FOWLER
Edinburgh
13 April 2006

Dear Michael,

No, I'll give the Gray celebrations a miss. My connections with Pembroke and Queen's have become more tenuous than with Brasenose. Incidentally, did you see the *Scotsman* photograph of Brian Cox mooning the spectators in New York?[7] A very different role from that of Lear.

AHRB has a way of withholding funds. Leverhulme might be a better bet. How would your scheme recompense the libraries? As things are at present, libraries have some control, although that may go when the Microsoft-Harvard scheme goes through. But a dark straw in the wind is the peanut dust that comes from the USA for photocopying of one's books and articles. With the abandonment of royalties, this means that earnings from publication approach zero. Indeed my last book, *Renaissance Realism*, cost me about £4,000 in reproduction rights, of which OUP paid only £250.

Yes, Finlay caused a lot of strife with his psychotic culture war. I too supported him, and in return he woke me up at dawn with an obscene phone call. My crime was membership of the SAC. I have come to think that the Arts Councils should have no direct dealings at all with artists and writers. They could do more by being unseen angels. De Marco was another who gave the long-suffering SAC awful grief.[8] [...] Balfour was a real saint – besides being the brightest man in the whole outfit.

All best,
Yours ever,
Alastair

*

Alastair Fowler, having been a tutor at Oxford, expressed in his *PN Review* essay precisely what constituted a good tutorial. It is not unlike what constitutes a good editorial session, in which the editor likes the work under review and is keen to make it better or understand it more deeply.

What Professor Fowler says about Ian Hamilton Finlay is also pertinent: Finlay was the extreme form of the artist as arrogant beggar, persuaded of his superiority, his integrity, and most of all, his entitlement. Every pound of public or private funding he received he translated into an affront, always performing his role as though he were a radical at war with the system. Like any extremist he knew that, eventually, his patron, benefactor, friend, would be unable to follow him further into his private arguments; as soon as an ally said 'no further', he became an object of denigration and attack. I went a long way with him, lost a number of valued friends, and in the end realised how he worked and how I had been used. His vendettas were, as Professor Fowler makes clear, cheap and self-degrading. My participation in the Battle of Little Sparta was immortalised in a *PN Review* supplement and Finlay was a prominent presence in the magazine in the 1980s, though he only contributed twice: some 'detached sentences on gardening in the manner of Shenstone' and an issue cover.

The restrained obituary of Finlay in *PNR* 169 (May–June 2006) notes, 'long-time readers will remember the *PN Review* supplement dedicated to the "Battle of Little Sparta", and the virulent attacks the poet later mounted against the journal and its editor in the *Times Literary Supplement* and elsewhere. Finlay's installations remain on display at Tate Britain and at the Serpentine Gallery, and his vision and collaborations survive at "Little Sparta", open to the public during the summer months.' It hardly hints at the amount of trouble he caused, or the degree of malicious rancour with which he pursued us.

NOTES

1. Alastair Fowler, 'Tutorials', *PN Review* 171 (September– October 2006).
2. *PN Review* 167 (January–February 2006) carried a brief appreciation of the scholar and curator Robert Woof (1931– 2005), the first Director of the Wordsworth Trust .
3. The News & Notes section of *PN Review* 167 commented: 'Harvard, the University of Michigan, Stanford, the New York Public Library and Oxford University have signed agreements with the search engine Google to create searchable digital copies of their library collections. This will entail Google scanning fifteen million books from the five leading research libraries. Supporters of the controversial project believe it will help to preserve academic material and make it accessible to the world. However, many authors and publishers protest that it violates copyright law; Google was sued in September by a group of authors, and in October by five major publishers.'

4. Alasdair Macrae's 'Professor Derry Jeffares: an appreciation', vividly evokes the Yeats scholar and 'kingmaker' of academic English departments A.N. Jeffares (1920–2005). Macrae wrote: 'I talked to Seamus Heaney about the gap left by his death, to which Heaney replied: "It is not a gap. The wind has stopped blowing."'

5. Ian Hamilton Finlay (1925–2006), the Scottish poet, writer and garden designer who was known for his combative stance towards anyone he identified with the Establishment, was in frequent correspondence with MNS in the 1980s. Despite *PN Review*'s championship of I.H.F.'s cause in 'The Battle of Little Sparta' (see *PNR* 32 in particular) and the editorial in *PN Review* 62 (July–August 1988) setting out the elements of the controversy over his work *Osso* in France with clear sympathy ('He is in a sense our greatest Naive, for despite the sophistication of his works, their impeccable finish, his wide learning, his verbal-visual puns and startling juxtapositions, his art is simple despite its scale, with the inexhaustible simplicity of its joyful convictions, its optimism and its sense of truth'), Finlay wrote public denigrations of the journal and its editor.

6. Lord Balfour of Burleigh (b. 1927) was Chair of the Scottish Arts Council 1971–80, after which he became Chair of the Edinburgh Book Festival, while serving as the Deputy Governor of the Bank of Scotland 1977–91.

7. A confusion over Coxes here: MNS was referring to Professor C.B. Cox, and Fowler to the Scottish actor Brian Cox, who played King Lear at the National Theatre.

8. Richard De Marco (b. 1930) is a Scottish artist and promoter of the visual and theatrical arts, with a particular interest in the European avant-garde.

THE YEAR IN BOOKS

Iain Bamforth, *The Good European: essays and arguments*

Djuna Barnes, *Ladies Almanack*, edited by Daniela Caselli

Caroline Bird, *Trouble Came to the Turnip*

Elizabeth Bishop, *Edgar Allan Poe and the Juke-Box: uncollected poems, drafts and fragments*, edited by Alice Quinn

Christine Brooke-Rose, *Life, End of*

J. Edward Chamberlin, *If This Is Your Land Where Are Your Stories? Finding Common Ground*

Linda Chase, *Extended Family*

John Clare, *The Shepherd's Calendar*, edited by Tim Chilcott, illustrations by Carry Akroyd

Donald Davie, *Purity of Diction in English Verse & Articulate Energy*

Greg Delanty, *Collected Poems 1986–2006*

Mark Ford (ed), *New York Poets II: an anthology*

Louise Glück, *Averno*

Lorna Goodison, *Goldengrove: new and selected poems*

Robert Graves, *King Jesus & My Head! My Head!*, edited by Robert A. Davis

Robert Graves and Alan Hodge, *The Long Weekend & The Reader Over Your Shoulder*

Robert Gray, *Nameless Earth*

Marilyn Hacker, *Essays on Departure: new and selected poems 1980–2005*

Horace, *Odes*, translated by Len Krisak

Gabriel Josipovici, *Everything Passes*

Gabriel Josipovici, *The Singer on the Shore: essays 1991–2004*

Marion Kaplan, *The Portuguese: the land and its people*

Thomas Kinsella, *Marginal Economy*

Thomas Kinsella, *Readings in Poetry*

Karen Leeder (ed), *After Brecht: A Celebration*

Grevel Lindop, *Playing with Fire*

Andrew McNeillie, *Slower*

Dunya Mikhail, *The War Works Hard*, translated by Elizabeth

Winslow

Mervyn Morris, *I Been There, Sort Of: new and selected poems*

Les Murray, *The Biplane Houses*

Togara Muzanenhamo, *Spirit Brides*

Mary O'Malley, *A Perfect V*

Frederic Raphael, *Cuts and Bruises: Personal Terms III*

Peter Sansom, *The Last Place on Earth*

Joachim Sartorius, *Ice Memory: selected poems,* edited by Richard
    Dove

Charles Tomlinson, *Cracks in the Universe*

Vernon Watkins, *New Selected Poems*, edited by Richard
    Ramsbotham

Robert Wells, *The Day and Other Poems*

Clive Wilmer, *The Mystery of Things*

Judith Willson (ed), *Out of My Borrowed Books: poems by Augusta
    Webster, Mathilde Blind and Amy Levy*

2007

Katharine Kilalea moved to London in 2005 to study for an MA in Creative Writing at the University of East Anglia. Her first book, *One Eye'd Leigh*, published by Carcanet in 2009, was shortlisted for the Costa Poetry Award and longlisted for the Dylan Thomas Prize for writers under thirty. Her poem 'Hennecker's Ditch' was published in *PN Review* in 2010. In conversation with Emily Berry, Kilalea said: 'The transition from poems to novels happened because I'd reached a dead end in poetry. "Hennecker's Ditch" used me up and when I tried to write poems afterwards I felt like a jobbing writer (and there's no worse crime, in my opinion, than writing something which doesn't need to be written). So I gave up on the poems and then, suddenly, I was writing a novel.'[1]

FROM MICHAEL SCHMIDT
Manchester
23 July 2007

Dear Kate Kilalea,

I am sorry to have been a little time writing to you about your poems. I have to tell you that I think they are wonderful and would like to retain all of them for *PN Review*.[2] I have a rather pressing question for you: have you completed a first collection? If so, who is publishing you? If not, do you think Carcanet might have a look at it? Your work really is quite remarkable and I would like to see more of it.

With kind regards,
Yours ever,
Michael Schmidt

FROM KATE KILALEA
26 July 2007

Dear Michael Schmidt,

Thanks for your letter. I was so happy to receive it. I was in Berlin over the weekend with an artist friend who told me that Karen Press (I was born in Cape Town too)[3] has a book with Carcanet and it got me thinking about the poems I submitted to *PN Review*.

Your enthusiasm is a great compliment – of course I'd love to show you more. And if you have time, I'd love to meet you. I'm not sure whether a first collection is quite complete. I did an MA at UEA last year and some of those poems might be a bit odd. I've also been working on a novel which has distracted me a bit, as has a project embroidering poetry on t-shirts...

I prefer the newer poems and suspect a collection would benefit from more of them. This kind of thinking, I've been warned, could mean it will never be finished!

Lastly, thank you for accepting the poems for *PN Review*. Would you mind if I sent something to replace 'Portrait of Our Death'? I'm sorry, it's just been published, everything happened so quickly... I hope this is OK.
[contact details]

Best from
Kate

*

The importance of *PN Review* as bait, and a filter for new work, was once again proven by Kate Kilalea. 'The Boy with a Fire in his Boot' still seems to me one of the more remarkable poems we have published, first in *PN Review* 178 and then in book form:

So there were two fires running,
neither pursuing, neither pursued
one on its own and the other in a boot.

They passed through the leaf-litter,
the grasses, the queued-up trees
and the moon passed through the smoky-clouds above

like being young, in transit,
which passes through us
as a finger moves through a candle,

unscathed. He was burning,
but he did not grow smaller,
like a cigarette.

He was breathing, but it hurt
to breathe
(but he was made to breathe). […]

Kate Kilalea's poems immediately appealed. They are news that stays news because they continue to surprise, they grow in urgency. I admire what the poet says about writing only what needs to be written. As an editor, the steadily rising tide of poems doggedly written in accordance with contemporary formularies of relevance and relatability, without much formal ambition and within the confines of the uncontentiously sayable, threatens to drown the instinctive love of poetry.

NOTES

1. Kilalea's debut novel, *OK, Mr. Field*, was published by Faber and Faber in 2018. See https://granta.com/katharine-kilalea-and-emily-berry-in-conversation/ (accessed 4 July 2019).

2. Four of Kilalea's poems were published in *PN Review* 178 (November–December 2007).

3. Karen Press (b. 1956) lives in Cape Town; she is a co-founder of the publishing collective Buchu Books. Carcanet has published three of her collections, most recently *Slowly, As If* (2012).

THE YEAR IN BOOKS

John Ash, *The Parthian Stations*

John Ashbery, *A Worldly Country*

John Ashbery, *Notes from the Air: selected later poems*

Eavan Boland, *Domestic Violence*

Moya Cannon, *Carrying the Songs*

Paul Celan, *Snow Part*, translated by Ian Fairley

Inger Christensen, *It*, translated by Susanna Nied

Sara Coleridge, *Collected Poems*, edited by Peter Swaab

David Constantine, Hermione Lee and Bernard O'Donoghue (eds), *Oxford Poets 2007: an anthology*

Brian Cox, *My Eightieth Year to Heaven*

Sasha Dugdale, *The Estate*

Elaine Feinstein, *Talking to the Dead*

Gerrie Fellows, *Window for a Small Blue Child*

Ford Madox Ford, *It was the Nightingale*, edited by John Coyle

Philip French, *Collected Reviews*

Iain Galbraith (ed), *The Night Begins with a Question: XXV Austrian poems 1978–2002*

Robert Graves, *Goodbye to All That*, edited by Steven Trout

Sophie Hannah, *Pessimism for Beginners*

Richard Howard, *Inner Voices: selected poems 1963–2003*

Mimi Khalvati, *The Meanest Flower*

Thomas Kinsella, *Selected Poems*

R.F. Langley, *The Face of It*

Jenny Lewis, *Fathom*

Dulce Maria Loynaz, *Against Heaven: selected poems*, edited by
    James O'Connor

Bill Manhire, *Lifted*

Friederike Mayrocker, *Raving Language: selected poems 1946–2005*,
    translated by Richard Dove

Peter McDonald, *The House of Clay*

Kei Miller, *There is an Anger That Moves*

Kei Miller (ed), *New Caribbean Poetry: an anthology*

Edwin Morgan, *The Book of Lives*

David Morley, *The Invisible Kings*

Gregory O'Brien, *News of the Swimmer Reaches Shore*

Iolanda Pelegri with Anna Crowe (eds), *Light off Water: XXV
    Catalan poems 1978–2002*

Richard Price, *Greenfields*

Raymond Queneau, *Elementary Morality*, translated by Philip Terry

Jody Allen Randolph (ed), *The Eavan Boland Sourcebook*

Henry Reed, *Collected Poems*, edited by Jon Stallworthy

Fiona Sampson, *Common Prayer*

Robert Saxton, *Local Honey*

Michael Schmidt, Stephen Proctor and Eleanor Crawforth (eds),
    New Poetries IV,

Robert Southwell, *The Collected Poems of S. Robert Southwell*, edited
    by Peter Davidson and Ann Sweeney

Edward Thomas, *Edward Thomas's Poets*, edited by Judy Kendall

Andrew Waterman, *The Captain's Swallow*

Gregory Woods, *Quidnunc*

2008

Carcanet Press has been supported for many years by Arts Council England. The nature of the relationship has changed from the more personal connection it was possible to have in the 1970s with the Literature Directors to the regionally devolved connection with ACE officers; and from fairly straightforward applications to the more comprehensive and demanding sets of papers that are now required – at least on a four-year basis, as Carcanet has been a Portfolio Organisation, with annual interim reports. An extract from Carcanet's narrative in one such report, in a year of worldwide financial upheaval, shows the impact of external factors on a small literary publisher, and its business concerns. There was plenty of material about Carcanet's successes in this report, but its stated anxieties, as quite a mature organisation, are revealing.

c) 2008/09 funding year and beyond

In addition, please summarise in **no more than 1,000 words**:

A. issues for 2008/09 programme
The chief issues facing us in 2008/09 relate to the uncertainty of the economy. Already fuel price rises are affecting the cost of paper; we have notice from our rep force that a £30 premium per month will need to be levied against the sheer rise in petrol prices; the steep rise in rents reported threatens the survival of many independent booksellers, a sector which

we have been cultivating and which once more delivers almost a third of our UK trade turnover. In these circumstances the improvements we have achieved in our margins may prove hard to sustain.

There is also a decline in anthology publication in the current year which is reflected in a decline in subsidiary rights income, a situation which may persist into the following year.

The continued very high rate of poetry production from the smaller presses eats into the market and into review and feature space. Only the quality of our books, and the general perception of that quality, will make it possible for us to remain in a position of strength and growth. We feel that editorially and in terms of staff we can weather what looks like being a difficult year or more.

As last year, we are concerned by the continued, accelerating erosion of copyright vis-à-vis traditional territories and also vis-à-vis the internet. The erosion of exclusive copyright areas has rendered Carcanet vulnerable. Given the position of sterling, US editions are cheaper worldwide, including in the UK, and US editions are increasingly finding their way into our exclusive markets damaging our sales here, especially when US editions appear before Carcanet editions. Scheduling, sharp pricing and alert policing are required. We must also continue strict control of output and constant attention to margins.

B. outline plans and objectives for 2009/10 and beyond including any plans to apply for Grants for the Arts. You should highlight any changes in your activity or operations that would affect your future programme

Primarily, we recognise that our chief ongoing challenge is to balance creative aspirations with commercial reality.

Our plans and objectives for 2009/10 onward are to continue with our excellent editorial programme, publish new writers from a wide range of backgrounds, and honour

our substantial commitment to the writers we are already nurturing. We intend as much as possible to maintain margins and to improve further our financial performance.

PN Review digitisation is being pursued and by the end of 2010 the whole run from 1972 to the present will be electronically archived and available to subscribers.

We are keeping pace, within our means and abilities, with the development of e-book technology and when expedient we will begin to create an income stream from this source.

Our website applications have improved and we intend at last to implement Onix [XML standard metadata formatting for the book trade] during the current year.

We will continue to produce *PN Review* for its strong committed subscribership and a steady sale through booksellers via Central Books. Its publication and gradual growth will continue, with special focus on new poets from a variety of cultures and on developing readership abroad.

We do not have any plans to apply for Grants for the Arts in the near future. The company has recognised, however, the need to continue upgrading and developing IT resources and will seek to do this through efficiency savings and increased earnings.

C. any other issues you wish to discuss with us

We would be very glad if, over this year, the reporting requirements and the terms of reports for all those clients in our sector could be harmonised so that significant statistics (anonymised if necessary) on stock turn and valuation, unit sales, turnover levels, pricing etc could be generally understood. At present we are not sure against what criteria we are to judge our own performance, and the sooner there is an agreed set of auditing protocols for reporting, the sooner we will understand the sector at large and our place within it.

THE YEAR IN BOOKS

Valentine Ackland, *Journey From Winter: selected poems*, edited by
  Frances Bingham

Sujata Bhatt, *Pure Lizard*

Alison Brackenbury, *Singing in the Dark*

Dan Burt, *Searched For Text*

Austin Clarke, *Collected Poems*, edited by R. Dardis Clarke

Gillian Clarke, *At the Source: a writer's year*

Peter Davidson, *The Palace of Oblivion*

John F. Deane, *A Little Book of Hours*

Elaine Feinstein, *The Russian Jerusalem: a novel*

John Gallas, *The Book with Twelve Tales*

Jon Glover, *Magnetic Resonance Imaging*

Grey Gowrie, *Third Day: new and selected poems*

Jorie Graham, *Sea Change*

Kelly Grovier, *A Lens in the Palm*

William Hazlitt, *Liber Amoris*, edited by Gregory Dart

Brigit Pegeen Kelly, *Poems: Song and The Orchard*

Frank Kuppner, *Arioflotga*

Pierre Martory, *The Landscapist: selected poems*, translated by John
  Ashbery

John Masefield, *Reynard the Fox*, edited by Philip Errington

Chris McCully, *Old English Poems and Riddles*

Gerry McGrath, *A to B*

Charlotte Mew, *Selected Poems*, edited by Eavan Boland

Christopher Middleton, *Collected Poems*

Robert Minhinnick, *King Driftwood*

Mervyn Peake, *Collected Poems*, edited by Robert Warner Maslen

Frederic Raphael, *Ticks and Crosses: Personal Terms IV*

John Redmond, *MUDe*

Lynette Roberts, *Diaries, Letters, and Recollections*, edited by Patrick
  McGuinness

Stephen Rodefer, *Call it Thought: selected poems*

Stephen Romer, *Yellow Studio*

James Sutherland Smith, *Popeye in Belgrade*
Jeffrey Wainwright, *Clarity or Death!*
Chris Wallace-Crabbe, *Telling a Hawk from a Handsaw*
Sylvia Townsend Warner, *New Collected Poems*, edited by Claire
    Harman

2009

Tom Raworth (1938–2017) was described by Geoff Ward in his obituary as a 'leading figure in the British poetry revival of the 1960s', who 'brought the radicalism of the Beat, New York and Black Mountain schools in postwar American poetry to bear on British writing. Ditching closed form and metre, capital letters and punctuation, he wrote with a quickfire lyricism that elevated snapshot and spontaneity over the grand projects of high modernism.'[1] He was known for the rapidity of his reading style, and the variety of the form of his books; he had taught himself to typeset and print in his early twenties, and with Barry Hall founded Goliard Press in 1965, publishing Charles Olson among others. His massive *Collected Poems* was issued by Carcanet in 2003, and a selection, *As When*, was edited by Miles Champion for Carcanet in 2013.

FROM: TOM RAWORTH
16 August 2009 at 07:43

Dear Judith, Dear Michael,

Back a couple of days from China and slowly getting over both jet-lag and culture-shock.[2] An interesting trip, both the festival (though that had its longueurs of speeches – one of the organisers is the Vice-Governor of the Province (and also a 'poet') so there was much repetition down the hierarchy of officialdom: he also wants the festival (this time with 42 foreign poets and 168 Chinese) to be the 'biggest in the world'.... and to 'establish the poetry brand for Qinghai Province': so you can imagine) and the trips in the region... to the ancient Ta'er Monastery.... to the Qinghai Lake (the largest and highest salt water lake.... relic of an ancient ocean now stranded at 4000 metres above sea level.... a sort of contradiction as of course it is ALSO 'sea level')... and to the Yellow River high above the new hydroelectric dam. As in any such large group there were congenial souls among the time-servers. Fred Wah, the Canadian who goes back as far as Olson and Buffalo; the German poet Ulf Stolterfoht; Miroslav Kirin from Croatia; Dora Ribeiro from Brazil; Karlis Verdins from Latvia; and my old friend the Chinese poet Huang Fan from Nanking. There were so many poets that readings took place at the same times in different venues so I missed the one possibly interesting moment when the woman Israeli poet complained that she couldn't read anywhere alcohol was being served; then that if they couldn't change that she must read first and leave; read; stayed; and then when the Lebanese poet read a piece based on the shooting of a Lebanese child by an Israeli soldier, stormed out complaining that poems like that should not be allowed and she would be writing to the Chinese and Israeli Governments. Again, because of the numbers of poets (and the Chinese poets, well-mannered, were always reading AFTER the foreign poets in the groups) people were asked to limit their reading to five minutes. Not difficult, one would imagine... I mean watches have been invented and are quite cheap. But you both, and I, know poets. So many times no Chinese poets got to read. I remember one evening when the Greek poet (one of those always posed on a chair with an invisible arrow pointing at him saying 'look how handsome I am') got up. A poem to Medea. I listened for five minutes, went and had a beer or two with a friend, came back half an hour later... and he was still going strong. And with the

Chinese translation to follow.

Well, enough. In this clip you can see me unveiling the 'poetry wall'. I am 'famous English poet Tom Raworth'.... to my right is 'famous Estonian poet Jaan Kaplinski'.[3]

And what I wanted to do was:

(a) send you our address at least for the next three months (below); and

(b) ask if two copies of the Collected could be sent to me here, set against any future income – as I gave my one remaining copy to the Brazilian poet and will need something to take to the US in mid-September to read from.

With good wishes to you both (and to the press); and apologies for going on and on... but the images are still fresh.

Tom

诗意弥漫大学校园
——高校诗歌朗诵会
在青海民族大学举行

FROM: MICHAEL SCHMIDT
27 August 2009 at 18:19

I love the photo of famous poet! China must have been a considerable shock to the system, in every sense.

So pleased about the book.

The academic term is about to begin again, a prospect that becomes more shadowy each year. At least I'll have a couple of days in New York, and I'll be seeing Miles Champion for the first time in twenty years.[4]

All best
Michael

FROM: TOM RAWORTH
27 August 2009 at 18:40

Dear Michael,

Good to hear from you. Yes, there was indeed a moment when, up by Qinghai lake, near the 4,000 metre mark, I realised I was at the exact edge of what I could physically do.... I was at the edge of the lake with Dora Ribeiro, a Brazilian poet living in Beijing... and we tried to play ducks and drakes... the two swings of my arm were exactly enough to tell me I couldn't do one more. It was that close.

I wonder (which would be a remarkable fortune) if you'll be in New York the week of September 28th to October 4th which is when I'll be staying (if it works out for Rachel) with Miles and her in Brooklyn. I expect we won't coincide... but enjoy the trip. Miles has been a good friend to me for many years and I'm delighted he's writing again. I think the years at the Poetry Project, dealing constantly with 'poets' and their egos, made him so glad not to be there that even poetry became (apart from his love of it, and constant reading) something to be approached with caution.

I'm a little weary, getting settled in to our first home (even though temporary) for more than a year. It is the first time I've lived anywhere directly in front of the ocean and I delight in long dawn bike rides along what one can of the edge.

warm regards,
Tom

*

A mong experimental writers, which is what Tom Raworth still seems to me to be, the kind who raises different questions of form and language each time you approach him, the way in is often laughter. He is among the best-loved poets we publish, with a wide following in the UK and abroad, and he toured and gave readings and remained one of the most penniless poets I know. There was continual concern, in the years when we published him, for his health and his material survival with Val, his wife, a dear companion. Much of my correspondence with him touches or centres on medical and material issues. In 2009 his emails had as postal address:

NO FIXED ABODE
UNTIL FURTHER NOTICE
AND NO LAND TELEPHONE

He provided an American and a British cell phone number, since he often went to the United States to give readings.

There were also issues of archaeology: Philip Terry unearthed translations Raworth had done of Vicente Huidobro and Hans Arp fifty years earlier. Professor Arthur Terry had been Raworth's external examiner when he completed his translation project at Essex. I had hoped he would like his work enough to let us feature it in *PN Review*, but he didn't. In fact his contributions to the magazine were only two: a tribute to his old friend Ed Dorn, which he read at the launch of the Dorn *Collected Poems* in London, and a single poem.

NOTES

1. Geoff Ward, *The Guardian*, 16 April 2017.
2. The email is also addressed to Judith Willson, Carcanet's editor and production manager 2002–12. She edited the *Selected Poems* of the late-eighteenth-century writer Charlotte Smith (Carcanet, 2003), and *Out of My Borrowed Books* (2006), a selection of poems by three late Victorian writers, Augusta Webster, Mathilde Blind and Amy Levy. Carcanet published Willson's first collection of poems, *Crossing the Mirror Line,* in 2017.
3. Jaan Kaplinski (b.1941), poet, essayist and novelist, is widely translated. His poetry is published in the UK by Bloodaxe, including a *Selected Poems* (2011) translated into English by Jaan Kaplinski with Sam Hamill, Hildi Hawkins, Fiona Sampson and Riina Tamm.
4. Miles Champion (b. 1968) was born in Nottingham and lives in New York. Carcanet has published two collections of his poems: *Compositional Bonbons Placate* (1996) and *A Full Cone* (2018).

THE YEAR IN BOOKS

John Ashbery, *Planisphere*
Caroline Bird, *Watering Can*
Thomas A. Clark, *The Hundred Thousand Places*
Gillian Clarke, *A Recipe for Water*
Fred D'Aguiar, *Continental Shelf*
Jane Draycott, *Over*
Anthony Dunn, *Bugs*
Padraic Fallon, *The Circles of Archimedes*

Ford Madox Ford, *Provence: from minstrels to the machine*, edited by
John Coyle

Mary Griffiths, *Pictures of War*, afterword by Stella Halkyard

Gwen Harwood, *Mappings of the Plane: new selected poems*, edited by
Chris Kratzmann and Chris Wallace-Crabbe

Andrew Johnston and Robyn Marsack (eds), *Twenty Contemporary
New Zealand Poets: an anthology*

Gabriel Josipovici, *After and Making Mistakes*

Venus Khoury-Ghata, *Alphabets of Sand: selected poems*, translated by
Marilyn Hacker

Katharine Kilalea, *One Eye'd Leigh*

Thomas Kinsella, *Prose Occasions: 1951–2006*, edited by Andrew
Fitzsimons

Chris McCully, *Polder*

Paula Meehan, *Painting Rain*

Sinéad Morrissey, *Through the Square Window*

Frank Ormsby, *Fireflies*

Jeremy Over, *Deceiving Wild Creatures*

Petronius, *Satyrica*, translated by Frederic Raphael

Peter Pindar, *Laughing at the King: selected poems*, edited by Fenella
Copplestone

Richard Price, *Rays*

Robert Rehder, *First Things When*

Fiona Sampson (ed), *A Century of Poetry Review*

Norm Sibum, *Smoke and Lilacs*

Muriel Spark, *Curriculum Vitae*

C.K. Stead, *Collected Poems: 1951–2006*

Charles Tomlinson, *New Collected Poems*

Marina Tsvetaeva, *Bride of Ice: new selected poems*, translated by
Elaine Feinstein

Arto Vaun, *Capillarity*

Robert Wells, *Collected Poems and Translations*

Matthew Welton, *'We needed coffee but…'*

2010

Kay Ryan (b. 1945) was born in California, where she has lived in Marin County since 1971, teaching at a community college. She was the USA's Poet Laureate 2008–10, and *The Best of It: New and Selected Poems* (2010) won the Pulitzer Prize for Poetry. When an interviewer asked about page vs stage, Ryan said, 'I really love the exchange with an audience. I love generating a kind of sense of rapport and a sense that we are understanding these things together, that we are doing these things together. I hate leaving an audience out or leaving them behind, just talking at them; I want to engage them. Of course, the paradox is that if a poem is an interesting poem it's not going to be gotten that way, you know? Some portion of it will be exchanged, but it is still going to remain a mysterious object and is still going to require or invite private contemplation. [...] I think that my main interest in poetry is that I read it silently. I mean I don't even like to go to poetry readings. I like to give them but not attend, because I like to read the work and I want the voice in my brain to do the work.'[1]

FROM: MICHAEL SCHMIDT
25 March 2010 at 10:41

Dear Kay

Your book arrived this morning (I am off home to Mexico for a fortnight tomorrow). It has played havoc with my busy preparations. I love it. Unfortunately my editor Judith Willson has commandeered it to read while I am away. We must think how we are going to do your British book. We very much want to bring your work out here.

Thank you for sending it! And for writing it, of course.

All best
Michael

Dear Michael,

Have a lovely time in Mexico, and I'm delighted with your enthusiasm for the work and eager to get thinking.

Best,
Kay

Dear Kay

I have been loving your book, and I have the Board's permission despite a very full 2011 to slot our Kay Ryan into August of next year. Judith Willson, who will be your editor, and I are certainly pleased about this.

We now need to determine how we will play a variation on THE BEST OF IT so as to differentiate it from the American edition and give you a bespoke British and European aspect.

I suggest that we consider adding an interview at the end and perhaps a preface/introduction by a poet you and we regard highly who is also well known on this side of the water. One name immediately comes to mind...

Let me know if you have another idea. And whom should we be writing to about rights and setting? Have you an editor at Grove for us to approach?

Please reply to me and to Judith at the same time and we will begin assembling the European You.

Kind regards
Michael

FROM: KAY RYAN
7 June 2010 at 16:16

Dear Michael and Judith (hello Judith),

This is great news. And I will really look forward to British publication. I'm very honored to think you have worked the book into your very full 2011 line-up. This is a good time for me to be thinking about a project like this, with the laureateship winding down this month. As I may or may not already have said, I have always cherished the hope that the people of the sceptered isle would like my poems. For so long they seemed so not quite American that I hoped maybe they were British.

Now, as to how to make this book distinctive. An introduction by someone distinguished would of course be wonderful. As to an interview, I can see how one might friendly-up the book, but I always feel so frustrated and trapped in them. An interview is so much less than the thing itself; I can feel myself dismantling the force of the work as I jabber away. One thing we might possibly consider is making the book shorter – The Best, Boiled. Or perhaps longer: The Best, Bloated.[2] Well, we can think seriously about these things soon, but I didn't want to wait any longer before telling you how happy I am that this is really going to happen.

Regarding rights, I haven't mentioned this to my American publisher Grove/Atlantic, and I have two names for you to contact there. The first is my own editor, Joan Bingham, Executive Editor, and the second is Eric Price, Executive

Vice President, Associate Publisher & COO, who deals with contracts.

I look forward to getting into all of this a lot more. And Judith, I certainly look forward to working with you.

Very best wishes,
Kay

*

PN Review published poems by Kay Ryan in 1984. Her book was over two decades away, conceived for a British readership, a selected poems with a substantial helping of new and previously uncollected poems. The poem 'Wash' – about hanging out laundry – answers Wordsworth's 'Immortality' ode: 'No Glory has passed / from the Earth, old man.' It concluded with a memorable image:

> I will begin you again
> Pin you by the beard and habits
> Pull ears out of your pockets.

NOTES

1. Interview by Devin O'Hara of the *Long River Review* at the University of Connecticut, April 2012. http://longriverreview.com/blog/2012/an-interview-with-kay-ryan/ (accessed 6 July 2019)

2. The Carcanet collection *Odd Blocks: selected and new poems* was published in 2011, without any introduction or interview. Ryan's essays for *Poetry* magazine are instructive: 'When I am writing, I feel that I have insinuated myself at the long, long desk of the gods of literature – more like a trestle table, actually […] and I want them to like me.'

THE YEAR IN BOOKS

Judith Aronson, *Likenesses: with notable sitters writing about each other*

John Ash, *In the Wake of the Day*

John Ashbery, *Collected Poems 1956–1987*

Anthony Astbury (ed), *A Field of Large Desires: a Greville Press anthology 1975–2010*

James K. Baxter, *Selected Poems*, edited by Paul Millar

Lucie Brock-Broido, *Soul Keeping Company*

Sarah Broom, *Tigers at Awhitu*

Dan Burt and Paul Hodgson, *Cold Eye*

David Constantine, Robyn Marsack and Bernard O'Donoghue (eds), *Oxford Poets 2010: an anthology*

Ernest Farres, *Edward Hopper*, translated by T. Lawrence Venuti

Elaine Feinstein, *Cities*

Ford Madox Ford, *Parade's End: Volume I: Some Do Not*, edited by Max Saunders

Nigel Forde, *The Choir Outing*

John Gallas, *Forty Lies*

Louise Glück, *A Village Life*

Robert Graves and Joshua Podro, *The Nazarene Gospel Restored*, edited by John Presley

Robert Graves, *Translating Rome*, edited by Robert Cummings

Edward Hirsch, *The Living Fire: new and selected poems 1975–2010*

Evan Jones and Todd Swift (eds), *Modern Canadian Poets: an anthology of poems in English*

Gabriel Josipovici, *Heart's Wings*

Patrick McGuinness, *Jilted City*

Andrew McNeillie, *In Mortal Memory*

Kei Miller, *A Light Song of Light*

David Morley, *Enchantment*

Les Murray, *Taller When Prone*

Jody Allen Randolph (ed), *Close to the Next Moment: Interviews from a Changing Ireland*

Tom Raworth, *Windmills in Flames: old and new poems*

Anthony Rudolf, *Zigzag*

Fiona Sampson, *Rough Music*

Peter Sansom, *Selected Poems*

Robert Saxton, *Hesiod's Calendar: a version of Hesiod, 'Theogony' and 'Works and Days'*

Philip Terry, *Shakespeare's Sonnets*

Emilio Rui Vilar (ed), *Environment at the Crossroads: aiming for a sustainable future*

John Whale, *Waterloo Teeth*

W.B. Yeats, *The First Years: poems by W.B. Yeats, 1889–1899*, edited by Edward Larrissy

2011

Carola Luther (b.1959) grew up in South Africa and moved to England in 1981, where she lives in the Pennines. *Walking the Animals* (Carcanet, 2004), was shortlisted for the Forward Prize for Best First Collection; her second collection, *Arguing with Malarchy*, was published in 2011. She was Writer in Residence at the Wordsworth Trust in 2012. Writing for *The Compass* on 'The Struggle with Form', Luther observed: 'For me there is usually a tension between imposed and natural pattern. I did not grow up in a city, and in a city my eyes are drawn to birds, parks, puddles, sky. I remain at greatest ease with looser forms and believe these facts are connected. [...] A poem that has found its true form is a potent thing.'[1]

FROM: CAROLA LUTHER
26 August 2011 at 15:29

Dear Michael,

[...] What an offer and how you worded it makes me think you may have meant an interview with me.

If you did mean that, I fear you will think I am throwing your kindness back in your face, and will be most irritated, but Michael, I am not – but would you mind awfully if I can I take a little time and think about it – an interview is my idea of purest terror, as I am one of those unhealthy paranoid people, who both distrusts and fears talking about themselves in a public arena, and yet perhaps hypocritically wants also to write poems that others read.

If you didn't mean that, I would of course love to interview someone else if you ever need that (anytime after September due to the libretto thing which has to be finished), and will write something about something anyway by the end of the year that you could look at and judge whether I am cut out for prose and critical thinking! I might well not be!

Love Carola x

PS The reason I didn't get straight back was chapter 2 in Tales from the Farmyard! Went down to check the chicken and the others were scratting about, and suddenly they all went ballistic. I looked up and there was a huge MINK staring at us! All the allotments have closed in their livestock now – Lockdown!!!

FROM: MICHAEL SCHMIDT
26 August 2011 at 16:36

Dear Carola

That's terrifying! Minks are fierce and best worn in stoles!

I did have in mind an interview with you. I know they can be scary: you could work out all sorts of strategies of evasion, or you could fictionalise yourself… Reflect… There may be someone you want to interview and that too is possible!

Much love
Michael

FROM: CAROLA LUTHER
02 September 2011 at 12:13

Dear Michael,

I said I'd get back to you about your thought about a possible interview in *PN Review*.

I have been reflecting as you suggested on this scary idea, and speaking to Sheila and friends and colleagues about it. And everyone is as clear as I am that it is a massive privilege to be offered this opportunity, but unlike me, can't see what I've been fussing about. Anyway if it is still open, I have concluded I will screw my courage to the sticking place and accept your offer graciously (if belatedly so!) – with the proviso of course, you still think it might be a good idea. If not, or the moment has passed, that is really really fine too of course! […]

Thirdly (in case you want follow-up!) Tales from the Farmyard III: The Mink was caught! Humane trap but then a rather hunky farmer dispatched it swiftly. Somehow, the mink was thrilling, SO vital and nasty and effective and sleek and so FURIOUS! It screamed with rage perfectly and so chillingly, it could have been the star in a vampire movie. It was also clever! It tried (and very nearly succeeded) lifting the complicated trap door before the bigger nastier equally effective but possibly not so clever farmer descended with his gun.

Well the chickens don't care about nastiness – they have brought out the bunting and relaxed visibly and are flouncing about and twitching their skirts in the sunshine as if it was another bank holiday! And the little hen is at about 70 percent now I'm glad to say, though still definitely not quite right. But we are so pleased she's picked up so well.

Hope all is well with you. Hope to see you at either Manchester or London *PN Review* celebration.

with love and thanks

Carola

*

Whenever Carola Luther comes to visit she brings eggs from her chickens. As I write, only two remain, one (she says) a voluptuous Marilyn Monroe of a chicken who lays ostentatiously large eggs and the other a petite white bird who lays petite white eggs. The eggs are always fresh and wonderful. The flock was larger but an earlier ferret, or perhaps the very mink described here, reduced it.

NOTES

1. http://www.thecompassmagazine.co.uk/carola-luther-poetics/ (accessed 18 September 2019)

THE YEAR IN BOOKS

Eavan Boland, *A Journey with Two Maps: Becoming a Woman Poet*

Dan Burt, *Certain Windows*

Moya Cannon, *Hands*

Linda Chase, *Not Many Love Poems*

Gillian Clarke, *Collected Poems*

John F. Deane, *The Eye of the Hare*

Jane Draycott, *Pearl*

Sasha Dugdale, *Red House*

Will Eaves, *Sound Houses*

Ford Madox Ford, *Parade's End: Volume II: No More Parades*, edited by Joseph Wiesenfarth

Ford Madox Ford, *Parade's End: Volume III: A Man Could Stand Up*, edited by Sara Haslam

Ford Madox Ford, *Parade's End: Volume IV: Last Post*, edited by Paul Skinner

Philip French, *I Found it at the Movies: reflections of a cinephile*

Natalia Gorbanevskaya, *Selected Poems*, translated by Daniel Weissbort

Kelly Grovier, *The Sleepwalker at Sea*

Fawzi Karim, *Plague Lands and other poems*, versions by Anthony Howell

Mimi Khalvati, *Child: new and selected poems 1991-2011*

David Kinloch, *Finger of a Frenchman*

Thomas Kinsella, *Fat Master*

Thomas Kinsella, *Love Joy Peace*

Tim Liardet, *The Storm House*

Carola Luther, *Arguing with Malarchy*

Sorley MacLean, *Collected Poems*, edited by Christopher Whyte and Emma Dymock

Olivia McCannon, *Exactly My Own Length*

Peter McCarey, *Collected Contraptions*

Chris McCully, *Selected Poems*

Peter McDonald, *Torchlight*

Hope Mirrlees, *Collected Poems*, edited by Sandeep Parmar

Eric Ormsby, *The Baboons of Hada*

Ian Pindar, *Emporium*

Mervyn Peake, *Complete Nonsense*, edited by Robert Warner Maslen and G. Peter Winnington

Frederic Raphael, *Ifs and Buts: Personal Terms V*

Peter Riley, *The Glacial Stairway*

Arthur Rimbaud, *Illuminations*, translated by John Ashbery

Kay Ryan, *Odd Blocks: new and selected poems*

Michael Schmidt and Eleanor Crawforth (eds), *New Poetries V*

Peter Scupham, *Borrowed Landscapes*

Iain Crichton Smith, *New Collected Poems*, edited by Matt McGuire

Toon Tellegen, *Raptors*, translated by Judith Wilkinson

David C. Ward, *Internal Difference*

Gregory Woods, *An Ordinary Dog*

Caroline Bird (b. 1986), poet and dramatist, published her first collection with Carcanet, *Looking through Letterboxes* (2002), when she was fifteen. *The Hat-Stand Union* was published in 2012, when she was one of five official poets at the London Olympics. Her fifth collection, *In These Days of Prohibition* (2017) was shortlisted for the T.S. Eliot Prize. In an interview, Bird remarked that in this book she had made a conscious decision to change one writing habit: 'Generally, if a poem felt painful to me, the penultimate line would have the emotion in it and the last line would be a look away or a punchline or a laugh or snigger, like the pendulum swinging off. With these poems, a lot of the time I decided to grab the pendulum while it was bang in the centre and end there and see what that did. I'm not saying that either way of writing is better, it was just new for me.'[1]

FROM: CAROLINE BIRD
28 May 2012 at 16:50

Dear Michael,

I've attached the second draft of my manuscript, with the re-writes you suggested. I have re-written the poem, 'Run,' into something more coherent in its wateriness. The poem about fairy godmothers – 'I'm Sorry This Poem Is So Painful' – I've turned into more of a 'moment' of a poem, rather than a narrative, which I think works better. And I've also edited and rearranged 'Thoughts Inside a Head Inside a Kennel Inside a Church' into something with a breathable structure. Plus all the other changes. See what you think anyway – as I'm happy to do more if needed.

I've also been playing around with title ideas. One title I keep coming back to is: '*The Hat-stand Union*'.

Reading through the book as a whole, I realise that a lot of the poems are about people trying and failing to communicate with each other, and fragmented groups of people. Maybe this is why I refer twice to mistaking hat-stands for people. So the title, 'The Hat-stand Union,' was sparked by that idea... that the 'tall dark and handsome hat-stands' have their own union, silently, but the people don't. Or, maybe, the union of hat-stands represent people not talking to each other. I just like the sound of the words anyway... and it's been growing on me. What do you think? It would be great to meet up soon, and discuss the final shape and order of the book.

Hope you're well and enjoying the sunshine.

All best, Caroline

FROM: MICHAEL SCHMIDT
28 May 2012 at 17:20

Dear Caroline

Thanks so much! Shall we plan another meeting to tie up the laces? I think the title may be good. My colleagues differ in their views. One is very pro and two are not anti, so we have a kind of plurality if not a majority. I am very glad about the hat stand which needs to be there.

Let me know whether there might be a meeting-slot in a couple of weeks' time, or are you off to a proper summer by the seaside?

Love, Michael

FROM: CAROLINE BIRD
28 May 2012 at 17:28

Dear Michael,

I agree the hat-stand is a must. And your colleagues seem to have the same reaction as my friends and family, either they immediately like it without question, or they say 'I kind of like it, but why?' Both reactions I quite enjoy. But I will carry on listing titles, and present you with some alternatives when we meet.

No I'm not heading off to the seaside just yet... so how about the week beginning 18th June? I can do any day at week, except Friday. Or I can do sometime during the first week in July. Are any of those dates good for you?

Best,
Caroline

*

Caroline Bird, when we accepted her for Carcanet publication, was the youngest poet we had ever published. Her work was recommended to me by Simon Armitage. He was struck by its many surprises and its formal precocity. Her work has changed and developed, so the early success did not spoil it. Performance has not spoiled it either, because she realised in good time that writing for audience effect was different from writing a poem. The audience needs to come to the poems on their terms.

NOTES

1. https://lunarpoetrypodcasts.files.wordpress.com/2018/02/ep110-caroline-bird-transcript.pdf (accessed 4 June 2019)

THE YEAR IN BOOKS

Fran Brearton and Edna Longley (eds), *Incorrigibly Plural: Louis MacNeice and his legacy*

Dan Burt, *We Look Like This*

Gillian Clarke, *Ice*

Andrew Crozier, *The Andrew Crozier Reader*, edited by Ian Brinton

John F. Deane, *Snow Falling on Chestnut Hill: new and selected poems*

Greg Delanty, *The Greek Anthology, Book XVII*

Ed Dorn, *Collected Poems*, edited by Jennifer Dunbar Dorn

Roy Fuller, *Selected Poems*, edited by John Fuller

John Gallas, *Fresh Air & The Story of Molecule*

Jon Glover, *Glass is Elastic*

Jorie Graham, *Place*

Oli Hazzard, *Between Two Windows*

David Herd, *All Just*

Julith Jedamus, *The Swerve*

Elizabeth Jennings, *The Collected Poems*, edited by Emma Mason

Evan Jones, *Paralogues*

Gabriel Josipovici, *Infinity: the story of a moment*

Frank Kuppner, *The Same Life Twice*

William Letford, *Bevel*

Pippa Little, *Overwintering*

Owen Lowery, *Otherwise Unchanged*

Peter McDonald, *Collected Poems*

Gerry McGrath, *Rooster*

Robert Minhinnick, *New Selected Poems*

Les Murray, *New Selected Poems*

Mary O'Malley, *Valparaiso*

Ian Pindar, *Constellations*

Neil Powell, *Proof of Identity*

Karen Press, *Slowly, As If*

Richard Price, *Small World*

Rodney Pybus, *Darkness Inside Out*

Gareth Reeves, *To Hell with Paradise: new and selected poems*

Margaret Tait, *Poems, Stories and Writings*, edited by Sarah Neely
Jeffrey Wainwright, *The Reasoner*
Clive Wilmer, *New and Collected Poems*
James Womack, *Misprint*
Jane Yeh, *Ninjas*

2013

Kei Miller (b.1978), born in Jamaica, came to MNS's attention when he was studying for his MA in Creative Writing at Manchester Metropolitan University. The book under discussion here, *The Cartographer Tries to Map a Way to Zion* (2014) won the Forward Prize for Best Collection, and few who were at the South Bank that evening will forget the huge audience's emotional and jubilant response when that award was announced. Interviewed for the Carcanet blog before the announcement, Miller commented, 'I think a lot of writing by black post-colonial subjects – in order to be taken seriously – has to hide their politics under subtlety. It makes us seem more savvy and rational and nuanced. But this book isn't so much interested in burying. Instead it bears witness. Sometimes it bares its teeth and its claws.'[1]

FROM: MICHAEL SCHMIDT
9 June 2013 at 18:55

Dear Kei

I like the book very much. I attach it with a number of comments, questions and suggestions from which you will see a pattern emerging. I hope that in certain places you can curb the elements dictated by performance rather than orality, a tendency to orotundity which is not quite earned, and a use of phrases which have a kind of Dylan Thomas abandon about them, often genitive constructions. There is also the burning issue of definite articles, and I hope you will review, whether to agree or not is up to you. There are some places where small adjustments are needed and others where I expect the problem is my ear for dialect.

The main thing I hope you can do is trust metaphor when it will bear your weight (avoiding seems and perhapses) and push yourself towards greater variation in syntactical patterning and also parataxis which will modulate and nuance your voice. You are such a good performer that sometimes that big beautiful voice dictates a poetry that is less tense and considered than it ought to be.

All that said, the ensemble is satisfying indeed. I am not sure (I am not sure that you are sure) that the basic trajectory is complete yet. I like the way it fits with the earlier books.[2]

Bravo, a good sabbatical then! Give me a bell this week or next for a palaver if you can.

Abrazos
Michael xx

FROM: KEI MILLER
9 June 2013 at 23:06

Thank you for such wonderful feedback! I apologize in particular for what I left as the bones of a villanelle 'The Day of the Watchman' to be filled in. In any case, I subsequently finished it, and then deleted it – as I did some other poems. I tried hard not to play my usual switcharoo game. Two words I worry about now that are almost fundamental Rastafari words – 'Sights' (which I wanted instead of cites), but more importantly 'Trods' – which is the only way a Rastafarian would talk about his journey. I think I have to keep it, but I want to signal that I am doing it purposely.[3]

It won't be long before I send you something revised

– maybe with a few new poems you haven't seen, and a new order – but much closer to what I want.

Thanks again!

K

FROM: KEI MILLER
29 June 2013 22:03

Dear Michael (and Helen),[4]

Here is the collection revised, and much closer to something I like. As said, the order is now quite different – a few poems have been removed, and about 10 poems have been added.

While I took on most of your suggestions, there are a couple I ignored for strong reasons, but some I ignored for less strong reasons and though I retain them now it's not that I'm unbudge-able. 'the crawling brawl of vines' for instance – the sound of which I love, or 'the dylan-esque' 'that pack the purple band of evening'. I tried these without but each time, after a week, I restored them. Do you feel strongly?

Kei

*

When Kei Miller applied for a place on the MA in Creative Writing at Manchester Metropolitan University, he had a fully funded place offered at another institution, but it was clear to me that he had to come to MMU: his submitted portfolio was extraordinary. He went on from Manchester to Glasgow – where I later taught – for his PhD. If you are lucky enough as a teacher, occasionally a student comes along who adjusts your way of seeing your discipline and its place in the world. Kei is a compelling performer of his poems and his lectures, the kind who makes readerly demands on his audience because his writing is so deeply invested in language and its various incarnations and weathers. He treated me less as a remote professor and more as a friend, so that there was a continual sense of exchange with him, and therefore of changed horizons. Unfortunately, we did not publish his first book of poems, *Kingdom of Empty Bellies* (Heaventree Press), an omission I regret. It appeared shortly before *The New Caribbean Poetry*, an anthology he edited, which was his first Carcanet book. The anthology signalled those changed horizons: the recent poets laureate of Jamaica – Mervyn Morris and Lorna Goodison – are on the Carcanet list, and the Caribbean has provided two of our most exciting younger authors this century.

NOTES

1. https://carcanetblog.blogspot.com/2014/07/spotlight-on-author-interview-with-kei.html (accessed 7 July 2019)

2. Carcanet published his second collection, *There is an Anger that Moves* (2007), and *A Light Song of Light* (2010); the latest, *In Nearby Bushes* came out in 2019. Miller has also published novels and short stories.

3. In the same interview, Miller observed that 'sometimes the way that language alienates is part of the poetic effect you want to achieve and obviously there are so many times in this book where I want to play with this effect of alienation by language. [...] Rastafari communities are often in disputes over land which governments have appropriated from them; what I don't want to do is to appropriate their language which is one of the last things they have.'

4. Helen Tookey (b. 1969) was editorial and production manager at Carcanet 2012–14. She now teaches creative writing at Liverpool John Moores University. Carcanet published her debut collection *Missel-Child* (2014); her second collection, *City of Departures* (2019) was shortlisted for the Forward Prize for Best Collection.

THE YEAR IN BOOKS

John Ashbery, *Quick Question*

Iain Bamforth, *The Crossing Fee*

Chris Beckett, *Ethiopia Boy*

Gottfried Benn, *Selected Poems and Prose*, translated by David Paisey

Tara Bergin, *This is Yarrow*

Sujata Bhatt, *Collected Poems*

Caroline Bird, *The Hat-Stand Union*

Eavan Boland, *New Selected Poems*

Alison Brackenbury, *Then*

Lucy Burnett, *Leaf Graffiti*

Richard Crashaw, *Selected Poems*, edited by Robin Holloway

Fred D'Aguiar, *The Rose of Toulouse*

Peter Davidson, *Distance and Memory*

Iain Galbraith and Robyn Marsack (eds), *Oxford Poets 2013: an anthology*

John Gallas, *52 Euros: Containing 26 Men and 26 Women in a Double A-Z of European Poets in Translation*

Lorna Goodison, *Oracabessa*

Rebecca Goss, *Her Birth*

Grey Gowrie, *The Italian Visitor*

Jorie Graham, *The Taken-Down God: selected poems 1997–2008*

John Greening, *To the War Poets*

Thomas Kinsella, *Late Poems*

David Morley, *The Gypsy and the Poet*

Sinéad Morrissey, *Parallax*

Stanley Moss, *No Tear is Commonplace*

Raymond Queneau, *Hitting the Streets*, translated by Rachel Galvin

Frederic Raphael, *There and Then: Personal Terms VI*

Gareth Reeves, *Nuncle Music*, with drawings by Barrie Ormsby

Michel Remy (ed), *On the Thirteenth Stroke of Midnight: surrealism in Britain*

Muriel Spark, *Mary Shelley*

Chris Wallace-Crabbe, *New and Selected Poems*

Rory Waterman, *Tonight the Summer's Over*

John Whale, *Frieze*

2014

Vahni Capildeo (b. 1973) was born in Port of Spain, Trinidad, and was awarded a DPhil from Oxford University for work in translation studies and Old Norse, and the Judith E. Wilson Poetry Fellowship at Cambridge 2014–15. *Measures of Expatriation* (2016) won the Forward Prize for Best Collection, and Capildeo's third volume from Carcanet, *Venus as a Bear*, was shortlisted for the same prize in 2018. Asked by the *TLS* what time and place to be a writer they might choose, the answer was: 'If I back-projected myself into my own ancestry, yes, I might be literate, most likely in Hindustani and perhaps Sanskrit. However, I would have belonged to an oppressor class. If I back-projected my smallish, brownish, XX-chromosome body into Europe (including Britain), considerable problems regarding possible, real and perceived literacy and authority might arise, at least until I hit the Roman period.'[1]

FROM: VAHNI CAPILDEO

22 May 2014 at 13:57

Dear Michael

I wonder what you think of Ashbery's instruction manual poem about imaginary Guadalajara?[2] Altieri's speaking on it tomorrow at UEA & I'm going to it –[3] but feel dubious about Ashbery on the whole and this poem in particular – no doubt I'm being very wrong...? Sth to do with the impossibility of imagining New York in a poem from Guadalajara and having anyone seminar it (if that's an ambition for a poem anyway)... also while I wish to defend the freedom to imagine, there's the fact of the bulking continent of Badly Imagined Foreignness Down There, and every time I try to lay the poem alongside other playful poems, instead it slips alongside the Bad Imaginings as a Good Imagining but still in a centre-periphery relation. Perh. shd go to seminar & write about it for next *PNR*. Sorry, I know you're too busy to be receiving these undergraduattey misgivings. No word from Judith E. as yet, btw; shall let you know. – Enjoying the magnificent Carcanet Ashbery French poetry (esp. for the French! quite in love with Supervielle again,[4] a love of my youth; and thinking of translating some Reverdy myself).

Vxxx

FROM: MICHAEL SCHMIDT
22 May 2014 at 17:06

It is wholly imaginary and I take it to be a tribute to Elizabeth Bishop.[5] It is one of my five favourite ashberies.

Supervielle is delicious. You are right!

Just returning to Manchester from Charleston festival. Met and liked dour Karl Ove Knausgaard![6]

Xxx
Michael

PS Altieri is a wilful subtilizer. I resist his academicising!

*

Vahni Capildeo is a wonderful anachronism. She speaks English with a correctness I relish, the shaping of phrases and sentences matters to her because they are part of the meaning, as is tone; and she has a habit of eloquent, wry or ironic silence when she disagrees about something, a silence in which she revolves the subject, determining whether it is worth replying to, and if so, how best, economically and effectively, to reply. Her sense of style, too, is that of a dancer or an actress. She has a personal elegance in all aspects, a kind of aristocratic bearing. And she is generously intelligent. I have learned an immense amount from working with her and seeing how much good she does and how readily some people misread or misunderstand her.

As to John Ashbery's poem, the poet himself wrote to me in 2015, 'I still haven't made it to Guadalajara, I'm sure it's disappointing.'

NOTES

1. *Times Literary Supplement*, 4 December 2017, at https://www.the-tls.co.uk/articles/public/twenty-questions-vahni-capildeo/ (accessed 3 June 2019)

2. John Ashbery's 'The Instruction Manual' is from *Some Trees* (1956). His *Collected French Translations: Poetry* was published by Carcanet in April 2014.

3. Professor Charles F. Altieri teaches in the English Department of the University of California, Berkeley. Among his many publications on American poetry is *The Art of 20th-Century American Poetry: Modernism and After* (2009).

4. Jules Supervielle (1884–1960) was born in Montevideo, educated in Paris, and spent his life between Uruguay and France. One of Ashbery's first translations when he arrived in France in 1955 was Supervielle's poem 'To Lautréamont'.

5. Elizabeth Bishop's 'Invitation to Miss Marianne Moore' (*Cold Spring*, 1955) has the refrain 'please come flying'. MNS did not list his other four Ashbery favourites in subsequent emails.
6. Karl Ove Knausgaard, a Norwegian writer whose six autobiographical novels, under the collective title *My Struggle*, have been very well-received in English translation.

THE YEAR IN BOOKS

John Ashbery, *Collected French Translations: Poetry*, edited by Rosanne Wasserman and Eugene Richie

John Ashbery, *Collected French Translations: Prose*, edited by Rosanne Wasserman and Eugene Richie

Edmund Blunden, *Fall In, Ghosts: selected war prose*, edited by Robyn Marsack

Eavan Boland, *A Woman Without a Country*

Gaius Valerius Catullus, *Carmina*, translated by Len Krisak

Thomas A. Clark, *Yellow & Blue*

Arthur Hugh Clough, *Mari Magno, Dipsychus, and Other Poems*, edited by Anthony Kenny

Tim Dooley and Martha Kapos (eds), *The Best of Poetry London: Poetry and Prose 1988–2013*

Louise Glück, *Faithful and Virtuous Night*

Kelly Grovier, *The Lantern Cage*

Caoilinn Hughes, *Gathering Evidence*

Gabriel Josipovici, *Hotel Andromeda*

P.J. Kavanagh, *New Selected Poems*, foreword by Derek Mahon

Mimi Khalvati, *The Weather Wheel*

Sarah Kirsch, *Ice Roses: selected poems*, translated by Anne Stokes

Marius Kociejowski, *God's Zoo: Artists, Exiles, Londoners*

Mikhail Lermontov, *After Lermontov: translations for the bicentenary*, edited by Peter France and Robyn Marsack

Gabriel Levin, *Coming Forth By Day*

Jenny Lewis, *Taking Mesopotamia*

Karen McCarthy Woolf, *An Aviary of Small Birds*

Andrew McNeillie, *Winter Moorings*

Bill Manhire, *Selected Poems*

Paula Meehan and Jodie Allen Randolph (eds), *Eavan Boland: A Poet's Dublin*, with photographs by Eavan Boland

Christopher Middleton, *Collected Later Poems*

Kei Miller, *The Cartographer Tries to Map a Way to Zion*

Togara Muzanenhamo, *Gumiguru*

Tom Pickard, *Hoyoot: collected poems and songs*

C.H. Sisson, *A C.H. Sisson Reader*, edited by Charlie Louth and Patrick McGuinness

Muriel Spark, *The Essence of the Brontës: a compilation with essays*

Muriel Spark, *The Golden Fleece: essays*, edited by Penelope Jardine

Jon Stallworthy, *War Poet*

Arthur Symons, *The Symbolist Movement in Literature*, edited by Matthew Creasy

Philip Terry, *Dante's Inferno*

Helen Tookey, *Missel-Child*

Lucy Tunstall, *The Republic of the Husband*

David C. Ward, *Call Waiting*

Rowan Williams, *The Other Mountain*

2015

Sasha Dugdale (b. 1974), poet, playwright and noted translator from Russian, later won the Forward Prize for Best Single Poem with 'Joy', which she offers so tentatively here. She was editor of *Modern Poetry in Translation* (the magazine founded by Ted Hughes and Daniel Weissbort in 1965) from 2012 to 2017. Interviewed by Jamie Osborn as her fourth collection *Joy* (2018) was nearing completion, she said: 'I am very occupied by this problem of how to integrate the two parts, the conscious intellectual thought process and the lyric impulse which seems best when (as Keats says) it doesn't "have a palpable design upon us". I wonder if the answer is that the enmeshing of these two elements happens at a pre-textual level, and then we write from that new position. I don't want to seem certain or prescriptive about this because I am feeling my way. I am reluctant to say anything about writing poetry which makes it sound any easier than it is.'[1]

FROM: ALEXANDRA DUGDALE
2 November 2015 at 21:35

Dear Michael

I hope you don't mind me writing out of the blue. It was very good to see you in Durham and I have been thinking and thinking about what to send you. I have got some poems, but they have on the whole already been published in magazines

– I must put them together as a collection and send you the beginnings of the collection. But I do have this monologue by William Blake's wife after his death and I wondered if there was anything to be done with it. I wrote it a while ago for a Russian exhibition of William Blake and it was translated and published in *Foreign Literature Magazine*, but never published in English. I think it is probably too long for *PN Review*, but it might be good for a collection – or perhaps I should forget about it.

It has been very hard to write while I've been editing *MPT*. I know you can probably sympathise with that! I need some space and time, and I simply don't have it. I also feel as if my poetics have changed and reshaped themselves. I want to write differently, but I can't yet see how it will be. All this work with poems and translations has changed me and my work, but I just need a little more patience and then I will find out how!

Good luck with it all. It was funny in Durham! […]

Best wishes
Sasha

FROM: MICHAEL SCHMIDT
5 November 2015 at 13:04

Dear Sasha

I am just hightailing it to New York, so this is a brief note to thank you for 'Joy' which I am delighted to have for the magazine. It is long, but I think it is sustained, and it has a rich historical as well as a contemporary aspect.

We are of course keen indeed to see your next book. I know how hard it can be to write and edit (and teach). One of them usually goes, and the one that usually goes is the writing. In my case, years without. I hope you escape from *MPT* in time to restore your creative equanimity! But not too soon, since you are doing a wonderful job with it.

[…] Let's meet up again soon, in a less public context.

All best!
Michael

FROM: ALEXANDRA DUGDALE
11 November 2015 at 14:57

Dear Michael

I am really overjoyed. And thank you for your lovely letter which restored me. Good luck with your own writing, I hope you are finding a space now.

Best wishes
Sasha

*

As editor of *PN Review*, my heart sinks when a covering letter begins, 'I enclose four poems for your consideration'. Four seems to be the preferred number, one short of a fist, and usually four discrete poems, whose only connection is the author's name. How much better it is to receive a single long poem, for example Sasha's 'Joy', something that challenges the magazine (editors and readers) as much as it has challenged the poet. Sasha Dugdale, with her experience of translation and as an editor, knows the importance of the series, the sequence and the single long poem. She is also brilliant at hearing across languages and across times the inflections of other women and men, finding them in the writing they have left, pictures, objects, landscapes. The poet as interpreter is also the poet as formalist at her most inventive, because the poem is not an act of accommodation but an unconditional surrender to the demands of its subject. Two years earlier, writing to her about her long poem 'The Canoe' (*PNR* 213), I said:

> the trouble with much that I love running in *PNR* is that people don't let themselves go with it, i.e., they resist reading it altogether. Irony makes them proof against the innocence a reader needs for the non-satirical, non-Modernist extended poem. The Victorians were the great innocents, weren't they, after the eighteenth century's buttons and braces. Are you and I (and Alison Brackenbury) the New Victorians? I hope not! What's wonderful about your *MPT* work is that it exposes you regularly to all that great work which is outside the radioactive field of contemporary British irony and correctness!

NOTES

1. *PN Review* 240 (March–April 2018).

THE YEAR IN BOOKS

John Ashbery, *Breezeway*
Iain Bamforth, *A Doctor's Dictionary: writings on culture and medicine*
Willis Barnstone, *Mexico in My Heart: selected poems*
Sheri Benning, *The Season's Vagrant Light: new and selected poems*
Sujata Bhatt, *Poppies in Translation*
Moya Cannon, *Keats Lives*
W. H. Davies, *The True Traveller: a reader*, edited by Rory
    Waterman
John F. Deane, *Semibreve*
John Dennison, *Otherwise*
Elaine Feinstein, *Portraits*
Sophie Hannah, *Marrying the Ugly Millionaire: new and collected*
    poems
Jee Leong Koh, *Steep Tea*
R.F. Langley, *Complete Poems*, edited by Jeremy Noel-Tod
Tim Liardet, *The World Before Snow*

Grevel Lindop, *Luna Park*

Rod Mengham, *Chance of a Storm*

Owen Lowery, *Rego Retold: poems in response to works by Paula Rego*

Kate Miller, *The Observances*

Edwin Morgan, *The Midnight Letterbox: selected correspondence 1950–2010*, edited by James McGonigal and John Coyle

David Morley, *The Invisible Gift: selected poems*

Les Murray, *Waiting for the Past*

Michael Schmidt and Helen Tookey (eds), *New Poetries VI*

Ezra Pound, *Posthumous Cantos*, edited by Massimo Bacigalupo

Tom Raworth, *As When: a selection*, edited by Miles Champion

Pierre Reverdy, *Haunted House*, translated by John Ashbery

Pierre de Ronsard, *Cassandra*, translated by Clive Lawrence

Peter Sansom, *Careful What You Wish For*

Jon Silkin, *Complete Poems*, edited by Jon Glover and Kathryn Jenner

Muriel Spark, *The Complete Poems*, afterword by Michael Schmidt

Algernon Charles Swinburne, *Selected Verse*, edited by Alex Wong

Shuntarō Tanikawa, *New Selected Poems*, translated by William I. Elliott

2016

Eavan Boland (b. 1944), currently Mabury Knapp Professor in the Humanities at Stanford University, California, is a pioneering figure in Irish poetry: 'I know now that I began writing in a country where the word *woman* and the word *poet* were almost magnetically opposed', she has written.[1] 'She wrapped her hands around the tree of Irish poetry and shook it to its foundations,' Paula Meehan declared of her fellow poet at the presentation of the Bob Hughes Lifetime Achievement Award at the 2017 Irish Book Awards.[2] For Boland, the woman poet is an emblematic figure, 'Not because she is awkward and daring and disruptive but because – like the modernist and romantic poets in their time – she internalizes the stresses and truths of poetry at a particular moment.'[3] Carcanet has published thirty of Boland's books, beginning with *The Journey and other poems* in 1987, and more recently *New Selected Poems* (2013) and *Woman without a Country* (2014).

FROM: EAVAN BOLAND
22 October 2016 at 15:57

Dear Michael,

Thank you so much for writing. One of the true bright spots of the last decade was that wonderful book of Brigit's you brought out – I always have it with me.[4]

She was intensely private and though she died – apparently

a few days ago in Illinois – of recurrent illness there was no chatter at all about it. Our Stegners keep in touch with many of the teachers and students of other programs.[5] But there was not a word of it.

I admired her so much. Occasionally I wished she were more in the world of publication/presence/exposure. I feared she wouldn't publish more and would become – and in a way she did –the hermetic figure which was always in her heart. I wish I could have one more conversation with her.

When I think of her work I like to think of 'Three Cows and the Moon' best – the poem at the end of *Song*. It has an expansive, pastoral ease in the world that isn't always in the more gothic poems. And it breathes with a sort of happiness I always felt she didn't have enough of.

Again, thanks for writing. I know you absolutely understood her work. She was a poet's poet's poet and I will miss her greatly.

Much love
Eavan

FROM: MICHAEL SCHMIDT
28 October 2016 at 11:12

Dear Eavan

In a way there is a sort of justice in the neglect of Brigit Pegeen Kelly's passing in the ephemeral media.[6] It puts her in a class of her own, which is where she seems to have wanted to be, as little as possible trammelled by contemporary fashion and fashion-making. I have been re-reading her with the same amazement I felt when you first put her work in my way. Remember the Scorpion poem in the *New Yorker* which you sent me as an attachment?

You have drawn a number of key poets to my and therefore

Carcanet's and *PNR*'s attention. Indeed, where would we have been without you, your poetry and essays, and without your generous counsels?

Tomorrow I have to lecture on the poetry of Elizabeth Jennings at an Oxford conference on her work. It seems on the face of it an unlikely subject for a conference, but it is over-subscribed… Returning to the poems after a long absence (she was a very close and very difficult friend for many years, and a tremendous challenge to edit) I realise that her copiousness conceals the real qualities that are there in the best poems. Colm Toibin on my Facebook page suggested that she'd written ten of the best poems of her time, but when I asked which ten they were he did not reply…

Much love, and thanks –
Michael

*

Without Eavan Boland Carcanet would be a very different operation. She has opened my ears to a number of writers, Irish and American.

What keeps readers and editors on their toes is that her viewpoints change, develop, in response the writing and the world. When her biography is written, a compelling feature will be the story of these changes: not standing still, in her poetry or in her critical writing. Of *Outside History*, she said:

> Here I was in a different ethical area. Writing about the lost, the voiceless, the silent. And exploring my relation to them. And – more dangerous still – feeling my ways into the powerlessness of an experience through the power of expressing it. This wasn't an area of artistic experiment. It was an area of ethical imagination, where you had to be sure, every step of the way – every word and every line – that it was good faith and good poetry. And it couldn't

be one without the other. There is very little technical experiment in *Outside History*.

The *ethical imagination* is what she admires in Adrienne Rich's work, of which she has been a critical advocate. Rich's poems 'began to open my mind to new ideas of who writes a poem and why. Truly important poets change two things and never one without the other: the interior of the poem and external perceptions of the identity of the poet.'

NOTES

1. 'Author's Preface' to *Object Lessons: the life of the woman and the poet in our time* (Carcanet, 1995), p.xi.
2. Quoted by Marjorie Brennan in the *Irish Examiner* , 14 August 2018: https://www.irishexaminer.com/breakingnews/ lifestyle/culture/poetry-has-always-changed-with-the-changing-world-eavan-boland-keen-for-poetry-to-move-with-digital-age-861943.html (accessed 4 June 2019)
3. 'Making the Difference', *Object Lessons*, p.235.
4. Brigit Pegeen Kelly (1951–2016), American poet; Carcanet published her second collection *Song* (BOA Editions, 1994) and her third *The Orchard* (BOA Editions, 2004) together as *Poems* in 2008. She taught on the creative writing programme of the University of Illinois at Urbana-Champaign. Boland's appreciation of her work in *Poetry Ireland Review* (issue 121) includes the assessment: 'In this context [of modern poetry], it often seemed to me she stood on the wrong side of the inheritance. With the rise and fall of modernism, the experiments in surrealism, the gestures towards interiority, it could be argued that poetry failed to build a convincing architecture of the inward life. The self-reflective life, certainly. But not the contemplative one that so many of Kelly's poems seem to yearn for.'

5. Wallace Stegner Fellowships at Stanford University are annually awarded to five poets and five fiction writers.

6. Poet and translator Beverley Bie Brahic (Carcanet published her collection *The Hotel Eden* in 2018) emailed MNS (13 February 2017), on reading Boland's appreciation in *PN Review* 233:

> I heard Kelly read and talk about her poetry a few years ago, at Stanford University, invited, I believe, by Eavan and the Creative Writing faculty. I was glad to put a body and face to a poet who, for me, too, belongs on a shelf alongside Moore and Bishop. But, saying this, I wonder: do I mean a great woman poet? And is this, in some way, to demean her work?
>
> I think not. I think I could as easily say alongside Coleridge, Hill...but there is a small, more exclusive shelf, in my room of my own, for Moore and Bishop, Woolf... where Kelly *also* belongs.

THE YEAR IN BOOKS

Abdellatif Laabi, *Beyond the Barbed Wire: selected poems*, translated by André Naffis-Sahely

Angela Leighton, *Spills*

William Letford, *Dirt*

Thomas McCarthy, *Pandemonium*

Chris McCully, *Serengeti Songs*

Peter McDonald, *Herne the Hunter*

Peter McDonald, *The Homeric Hymns*

Ian McMillan, *To Fold the Evening Star: new selected poems*

Vladimir Mayakovsky, *Vladimir Mayakovsky and Other Poems*, translated by James Womack

Stanley Moss, *It's About Time*

Les Murray, *On Bunyah*

Mary O'Malley, *Playing the Octopus*

Tom Pickard, *Winter Migrants*

John Redmond, *The Alexandra Sequence*

Håkan Sandell, *Dog Star Notations: selected poems 1999–2016*, translated by Bill Coyle

Muriel Spark, *John Masefield*

Sergey Stratanovsky, *Muddy River: selected poems*, translated by J. Kates

Philip Terry, *Quennets*

Jeffrey Wainwright, *What Must Happen*

Rebecca Watts, *The Met Office Advises Caution*

Matthew Welton, *The Number Poems*

Alex Wong, *Poems Without Irony*

2017

James Keery (b. 1958) taught English at Fred Longworth High School in Tyldesley (Wigan). Carcanet published a collection of his poems *That Stranger, The Blues* in 1996: 'It is funny, perhaps even unusual, but I've never been able to shake off the feeling that I've written my last poem. Often I find I *have,* for months at a time, and perhaps it's natural that a poem should be accompanied by a sense that a spring has run dry. I suppose it's because I tend to write from a present that's already past.'[1] Keery's interest in post-war British poetry, in mapping and making connections between poets, in close reading of their poetry, has been a steady feature of *PN Review* since 1985. Keery and MNS are discussing *Apocalypse!: an anthology*, a forthcoming project.

FROM: JIM KEERY
29 January 2017 at 21:57

Dear Michael,

Guess what? I've retired!

Took early retirement at Christmas, after thirty-five great years and one miserable one – ended happily, though, with a nice send-off.

I'm 59 in February, so the reduction isn't much, and though it's all a bit bewildering, I think I've done the right thing.

For the obvious reason, I've been cracking on with the anthology – more progress in a month than the last six

– January of all months, the Monday of the year – strange to be out of the workaday world, at least for the time being, but not complaining.

I've got over 320 pages of actual text already – I mean typed up – but with 12–20 poems each by the core Apocalyptics, there's plenty of scope for thinning it out if – as I hope to – I find many more poems amongst the 'undergrowth' as Larkin calls it – never happier than when tangled up in it – *Poetry Quarterly* in particular I just love, for some reason, partly because I've got *copies*, though I like my Kraus reprint of *Poetry London*, too. Finding 'Cain' by Burns Singer in a beautiful red copy in the UL – predating the earliest published poem I'd come across – is another reason.[2] Then, too, permissions may mean a cull – a Muriel Spark love poem to Howard Sergeant might be a no-no,[3] though Skelton printed a poem from *Far Cry* in *Poetry of the Forties*, so I may be wrong to fear the worst from the MacCaig estate, but I aim to have more than enough to replace any non-runners, for whatever reason. What about Kathleen Raine, for example? Scary: ['Invocation' follows].

She means every word of it – she always does. According to Kenneth Allott, 'she can express an apocalyptic element in feeling without inflation' – as he no doubt recalled from her thirties *New Verse* days – found this in *Now* – not in *Collected Poems*, though I find it was in *Stone and Flower*, the PL collection illustrated by Barbara Hepworth, which I haven't seen:

'FAR-DARTING APOLLO'

I saw the sun step like a gentleman
Dressed in black and proud as sin.
I saw the sun walk across London
Like a young M.P. risen to the occasion. [...]

The sun plays tennis in the court of Geneva
With the guts of Finn and the head of an Emperor,
The sun plays squash in a tomb of marble,
The horses of Apocalypse are in his stable.

The sun plays a game of darts in Spain,
Three by three in flight formation,
The invincible wheels of his yellow car
Are the discs that kindled the Chinese war. [...]

Spain and China – must be circa 1937 – one of only two or three modernist poets to use the word before the Apocalyptics reminted it ...

I know you won't want to be briefed on every raid, but anything you would like an update on, anything, do let me know.

If you want to hedge your bets, incidentally, you might commission Rob Jackaman to edit a rival anthology of *Apocalyptic Shockers* – get this:

'I've never met anybody in my years specialising in the poetry of this period who would argue with the opinion that the New Apocalypse (with the possible exception of some of Dylan Thomas's work, always assuming that it fits under the umbrella term) was anything but a pathetic failure'.

Bit harsh? [more quotations follow]

Nuts. I wouldn't mind, but his books are good value – New Zealander – one on Surrealism and this one, *A Study of Cultural Centres and Margins in British Poetry Since 1950: Poets and Publishers* (Edwin Mellen Press, 1995). You probably know it – you're in it – in fact you're the subject of a paragraph that would make a cat laugh, which I will share with you:

'Certainly in some respects Booth and Schmidt are working at separate ends of the spectrum. Booth remains the champion of the small press, the underdog, the outsider; whereas Schmidt seems to have been seduced into the big time, accepting the overdog, and moving towards the centre'.

Wait till he gets a load of *Overdogs of the Apocalypse*! I'll be in touch.

Love,
Jim

FROM: MICHAEL SCHMIDT
6 February 2017 at 18:17

Dear Jim

RETIRED??? You could knock me over with a feather! Why, you're only about 30…. I'm sure you have done the right thing so long as you have some way of being in touch with young heads.

We must meet around the anthology soon, in March? Let's make a date. And tell me please: would you be willing to put together a Julian Orde Abercrombie?[4] David Wright loved her work, and the few things we did in *Poetry Nation* really appealed to me…

More soon. I have to eat dinner or die. But congratulations on retiring and let's give a shape to your afterlife as soon as possible!

Love,
Michael

FROM: JIM KEERY
16 February 2017 at 01:19

Dear Michael,

There's a name – I came across several poems by Julian Orde in *Poetry Quarterly* – quirky, quicksilvery, all about wings – 'And into birds they were all startled' – and creatures of 'earth and river' - 'the athletic flesh' of fish is fine, I think, imagining a fish as a swimming muscle – with a constant sense of 'the force that through the green fuse drives the flower': [quotations] and ['The Awaiting Adventure', from *Poetry Quarterly*] is immediately followed, I was delighted to find, by 'The Day and Night Craftsmen' by Graham, who was her partner for a while in the forties – as Wrey Gardiner was no doubt aware. They all dedicated poems to each other, and even put each other in, which is half the scene and I hope an intriguing thread in the book. 'The Lonely Company' recalls Stevie Smith at her least skittish – and 'the day of wrath' seals her an Apocalyptic poet, if anyone were minded to quibble.[5] 'The Flying Child' is wonderful, so is 'In the Holidays', in fact all Wright's picks – even 'The White Sofa', more like Stevie Smith at her *most* skittish – are appealing, and he's right about 'Conjurors', too, which I take to be very late – I haven't seen the Greville Press pamphlet – I like the way the caterpillar 'In his carpet coat' takes flight on 'her early wings', after negotiating its metamorphosis in that ungainly adverb 'Unbalancedly' – even the capital letter adds to a lopsidedness that the rhythm then so beautifully redeems. The allegory of her own imago or ship of death – 'She walks like a boat on the beach/ Dragging her drying sails' – is so unforced as hardly to occur to you, but the 'indistinguishable' ending reminds of Muchafraid crossing the river singing, though 'none could hear what she sang'.

Rexroth put her in *The New British Poets* – almost as good an eye as Wright – 'The Changing Wind', the last poem in the book, as it happens, so she is a card-carrying, anthologised neo-romantic into the bargain, for adherents of the distinction – but bees in bonnet aside (I have incriminating credentials for every poet who put pen to paper during the forties with the exception of Betjeman and a handful of school-of-Auden burn-outs) – and though you can see what Geoffrey Hill was driving at – 'It's she/ The courage has' seems unaccountably clumsy in such a cobwebby, 'gossamer' poem – she's better than half the poets in *New Lines*![6] Or *The Crown and the Sickle*, to be fair – my great grief at the moment is that the Ulster contingent of the Apocalypse – John Gallen, Robert Greacen, Roy McFadden – they turned *The Northman* at Queens into an Apocalyptic rag, and McFadden edited *Rann* from Lisburn – *Lisburn*, where we spent every six-week summer holiday – are unanthologisably miserable.[7] McFadden and Gallen have their moments, but to get them to sustain even a short poem without disaster is going to be tricky.

Incidentally, her husband, Ralph Abercrombie, was a tart reviewer for *Time and Tide*, with little time for 'Mr Treece and the other horsemen of the Apocalypse', but 'Esyllt' is an excellent spot – a stone ginger for the anthology [quotations follow] 'Esyllt' is – with Lawrence – the inspiration of Larkin's marvellous 'Wedding Wind':

As he climbs down our hill, my kestrel rises,
Steering in silence up from empty fields,
A smooth sun brushed brown across his shoulders,
Floating in wide circles, his warm wings stiff.
Their shadows cut; in new soft orange hunting boots
My lover crashes through the snapping bracken.
The still gorse-hissing hill burns, brags gold broom's
Outcropping quartz; each touched bush spills dew.
Strangely last moment's parting was never sad,
Than this intense white silver snail calligraphy
Scrawled here in the sun between these stones.

Why have I often wanted to cry out
More against his going when he has left my flesh
Only for the night? When he has gone out

Hot from my mother's kitchen, and my combs
Were on the table under the lamp, and the wind
Was banging the doors of the shed in the yard.

'Snapping bracken' is lovely, I think, and so is 'Each touched
bush spills dew' – they don't if you are careful enough to keep
each word from touching another, as the consonants ensure
that you do – a brilliant lift from *In Parenthesis* – 'bright in
each drenched dew particle'.

   Eek – it's late – supply at Edmund Arrowsmith in Ashton
tomorrow – really enjoying it – but the anthology even more.

   I'll be in touch.

Love,
Jim

Dear Jim

Let's set a lunch date. Your letter has made me unaccountably
happy and young, all those known names from my own youth,
mainly poets I refused to have any truck with. I love your
enthusiasm and your unerring eye-ear.

   I really do want to see a Selected Julian Orde Abercrombie
edited by you for Carcanet.[8] Wherever would her papers be?

   So what about some day the week of 6 or 13 March – free I
have at this moment 7, 8, 10, 12 and 16. Any one of those, or
all of them if you like!

Un abrazo
Michael

*

James Keery is the most energetic and sure-eared reader I have ever encountered. His patience with the Apocalyptics is exemplary: he is a reader, not an academic; his interest is in bringing good and possibly useful poetry back to the table. Ever since we met in the 1980s he has been an important contributor to *PN Review*, and he has shared my enthusiasm for Julian Orde Abercrombie, Burns Singer, late George Barker and much else. We also both rate the editorial and anthologising work of David Wright very highly. His first critical contribution to *PN Review* (88, 1992) includes this about the fissured nature of the then contemporary poetry scene (and how much more fissured it may appear today, without the critical focus it had then):

> To read Prynne but not Larkin, or Davie but not Fisher, is to miss a dimension, not only of each poet, but of the true context of everything else that has been written since the war. So it's ironic, and frustrating, that *Thomas Hardy and British Poetry*, the most generous critical text of the period, to say nothing of its prescience, should be viewed from both camps as a procrustean device for the mutilation of diverse figures into Hardy (or Donald Davie) lookalikes!

NOTES

1. https://www.encyclopedia.com/arts/educational-magazines/ keery-james-1958 (accessed 8 July 2019)
2. Keery edited Burns Singer's *Collected Poems*, published by Carcanet in 2001. Singer (1928–64) was born in New York but brought up in Scotland, and lived in London in the last years of his life. In Cornwall he met W.S. Graham, who was a major influence on his poetry.
3. Muriel Spark (1918–2006) wrote in the foreword to *All the Poems* (Carcanet, 2004), 'Although most of my life has been devoted to fiction, I have always thought of myself as a poet.'

Carcanet published some of her non-fiction, her autobiography *Curriculum Vitae* (2009), and the *Complete Poems* (2015). Howard Sergeant (1914-87), with whom Spark was in love, was a poet, editor, and the publisher of *Outposts*, a long-running poetry magazine.

4. David Wright made a selection of the poems of Julian Orde Abercrombie (1917–74) for *PN Review* 2 (January–March 1978), accompanied by a personal memoir. He remarks that most of her poems of the 1940s seem flawed: 'The neo-romanticism of the 1940s infected nearly the whole generation that was born around the Great War in time for the next. Everybody had it, like measles; even those who are not now thought of as neo-romantics – Keith Douglas, Philip Larkin, Norman MacCaig for example – caught the infection to begin with.'
Orde had an affair with W.S. Graham in the forties; Wrey Gardiner (1901–81) was the editor of *Poetry Quarterly* from 1939. Julian Orde's husband was the son of Lascelles Abercrombie, who had been one of the Georgian poets.

5. Stevie Smith (1902–71), poet and novelist; David Wright, reviewing her 1957 volume *Not Waving but Drowning*, remarked that 'not only does she belong to no "school"—whether real or invented as they usually are—but her work is so completely different from anyone else's that it is all but impossible to discuss her poems in relation to those of her contemporaries.' https://www.poetryfoundation.org/poets/stevie-smith (accessed 8 July 2019).

6. Kenneth Rexroth (1905–82), American poet, translator and critic, edited *The New British Poets* anthology in 1949. Wright quotes in *PNR* a comment made to him by Geoffrey Hill: 'I'd say that someone as good as [Orde] had a duty to herself to be consistently better'. The *New Lines* (1956) anthology, edited by Robert Conquest, presented poets of 'The Movement', including Jennings (the only woman) and Donald Davie.

7. The poet Roy McFadden (1921–99) co-founded and co-edited the Northern Irish poetry magazine *Rann* (1948–52).

8. On 6 March 2017 MNS emailed John Ashbery:

> Ever since *Poetry Nation* VI (which must have been 1976) I have been intrigued by Julian Orde Abercrombie, maybe the daughter of Lascelles, or daughter/grand-daughter in law, whose 'The Conjurors' still seems to me one of the most peculiarly wonderful poems we have published. James Keery is working around in the 1940s and trying to put together an anthology for me, and he has exhumed this other poem of hers (only about twenty or so seem to be locatable) which I thought you might like:

> 'On Looking Out'   *PQ*, Summer, 1947 (p.95)
> A mushroom morning and a day for kites,
> And the ricksha boys bickering in China,
> And myself in the middle of the middle ring,
> (But everyone else thinks they are);
> And a skyscape just arrived, with quite
> Its best and inrepeatable design, a
> Water-land built solid out of nothing,
> And beautiful as my imagined China.

> (The apparent typos, ricksha and inrepeatable, are hers.)

> The 1940s seem to the ageing me much more beguiling than they did, and there is so much going on. Indeed the 1930s–1940s period was written off too easily and totally by the conspirators. Graham is being exhumed, but not yet Burns Singer who is so astonishing if curate's eggy. And as if to heighten the synergy Kate Gavron, my wonderful chairman, gave me a handsome Humphrey Jennings painting of a tractor and a purple sky that went exactly with the better poems of the period and edged me forward

on a perilous path for which, in fact, your poems have long prepared me.

THE YEAR IN BOOKS

Tara Bergin, *The Tragic Death of Eleanor Marx*

Caroline Bird, *In These Days of Prohibition*

Yves Bonnefoy, *The Poems*, translated by Anthony Rudolf, John Naughton, Stephen Romer

Miles Burrows, *Waiting for the Nightingale*

Thomas A. Clark, *A Farm by the Shore*

Gillian Clarke, *Zoology*

Joey Connolly, *Long Pass*

Bei Dao, *City Gate, Open Up: A Memoir*, translated by Jeffrey Yang

Dick Davis, *Love in Another Language: collected poems and selected translations*

James Davies, *Stack*

Sasha Dugdale, *Joy*

Elaine Feinstein, *The Clinic, Memory: new and selected poems*

John Gallas, *The Little Sublime Comedy*

Lorna Goodison, *Collected Poems*

Jorie Graham, *Fast*

Michael Hamburger, *A Michael Hamburger Reader*, edited by Dennis O'Driscoll

Peter Hughes, *Cavalcanty*

David Kinloch, *In Search of Dustie-Fute*

Eric Langley, *Raking Light*

Angela Leighton and Adrian Poole (eds), *Trinity Poets: an anthology of poems by members of Trinity College, Cambridge*

Drew Milne, *In Darkest Capital: collected poems*

Robert Minhinnick, *Diary of the Last Man*

David Morley, *The Magic of What's There*

Mervyn Morris, *Peelin Orange: collected poems*

Sinéad Morrissey, *On Balance*

Stanley Moss, *Almost Complete Poems*

Dennis O'Driscoll, *Collected Poems*
Neil Powell, *Was & Is: collected poems*
Richard Price, *Moon for Sale*
Salvatore Quasimodo, *Complete Poems*, edited by Jack Bevan
Stephen Romer, *Set Thy Love in Order: new and selected poems*
Anthony Rudolf, *European Hours: collected poems*
Claudine Toutoungi, *Smoothie*
Rory Waterman, *Sarajevo Roses*
David Wheatley, *The President of Planet Earth*
Judith Willson, *Crossing the Mirror Line*
James Womack, *On Trust: a book of lies*
Karen McCarthy Woolf, *Seasonal Disturbances*

2018

Iain Bamforth (b. 1959) grew up in Glasgow and graduated from its medical school. He has pursued a peripatetic career as a hospital doctor, general practitioner, translator, lecturer in comparative literature, and latterly public health consultant in several developing countries, principally in Asia. Carcanet published *Sons and Pioneers* in 1992, and his fourth collection, *The Crossing Fee*, in 2013; also his essay collection *The Good European* in 2006. He has been a regular contributor of reflective and erudite reports and articles to *PN Review* since the late 1980s. Reviewing *The Good Place* (2005), David Morley wrote: 'From his level place, Bamforth surveys the circles of European culture, searching for ethics and civil society within its changing order. His poetry brims with its pasts, potentialities and connections.'[1]

FROM: IAIN BAMFORTH
19 avril 2018 at 11:38

Dear Michael,

Good to hear from you. We were last in touch before Christmas, and now Easter has come and gone. Fugit inreparabile tempus. Much has happened in between, not least the death of my much admired ex-environmental journalist father-in-law Christian, who celebrated his 90th birthday in December in a frailer condition than I had seen him before, and then decided when faced with the prospect of renal dialysis in February that it was time to die. We provided the palliative care, and he died about ten days after making his decision, lying on the sofa-bed in his study, free of pain or anxiety, quoting Heine and Hamlet – a very moving occasion for all of us. Oddly enough, I was in Heidelberg only a few days later to study 'consultancy skills' for a fortnight at the university: it was where Christian had studied after the war listening to Gadamer and other professors who had made it one way or other through the Nazi years.[2]

I ought to tell you that the medical 'dream book' manuscript (Scattered Limbs) which you turned down in November 2016 has been picked up by Robert Hyde at Galileo: he is even coming over to meet me next month on his BMW bike.[3] I spent a lot of time looking at it from various angles as you suggested, but decided in the end that its scrapbook shape is the right one; I'll have to discuss with Robert whether we ought to bring some illustrations into the text (and who might be responsible for hunting them down). It's a relief that it has a house, even if Galileo is even more obscure than Carcanet (same distributor, he tells me!).

Meanwhile, I've been busy editing other material. I've put together a collection of essays (mainly freestanding stuff plus a few reviews that seem germane to the theme) which ventures into the engine room of culture and fuels it with this remarkable substance called zest. What I've sent is only about half of my planned contents: this has to be a bumper book, around 100-120,000 words in length, in order to justify its subtitle. Some of the key items to be added include a look back at my Brethren past (and how I survived it) and also a short account of emerging from the shipwreck of closing my practice twenty years ago. The notion of 'the art of living', philosophy in the practical sense or leisure in the Greek sense, will need expanding, and I would hope to do that in the introduction. I suspect you won't be thrilled by the notion of such a large work (although Craig Raine pulled it off with *Haydn and the Valve Trumpet*), but let me know what you think of the proposal

I also attach a little treat for *PNR*: I meant to review the new (German) film on Lou Andreas-Salomé which appeared in the cinema here last year but was so disappointed in it that I mention it only in the addendum.[4] The events of 1882 are of some interest though, not least owing to Nietzsche's very high-minded attempt to sweep the young Lou off her feet. She wasn't having any of it.

Regarding PNR, I didn't continue my subscription because the usual reminder slip never arrived in the post: I usually send on a cheque (old-fashioned, I know) every September. Perhaps somebody in the office can remind me how much it is.

I read Philip Terry's *Gilgamesh* at Christmas.[5] It is certainly a strikingly novel approach to the poem, but I had some reservations about the 'powerful and logical' assumptions governing the use of 'Globish': if anything, early languages tend to be far more complex than modern ones, and the notion that Globish is somehow a neutral vehicle has been disproved by Anna Wierzbicka among others.[6] I would certainly agree however that the fragmentary and jagged nature of the original is an integral aspect of its fascination, and that Terry's version is really startling. One name he might usefully have dropped in his talk is that of Viktor Shklovsky, whose ruminations on literary forms would certainly have provided some justification for his clipped idiom.[7] I could turn in a good review of the book when it appears.

I hope your own writing on the subject has advanced from Rilke's enthusiastic blowout in 1916.[8] I've been reading a dual biography of Rilke and Rodin called *You Must Change Your Life*: the more I read about Rilke in the early years of last century the more puzzled I am that such a neurotically dependent person (especially on Lou) could regard himself as a font of wisdom, handing down instructions on how to live more authentically to others (especially in the *Letters to a Young Poet*). Just look at that famous phrase which ends the archaic torso poem!

Warm regards,

Iain

FROM: IAIN BAMFORTH
3 May 2018 at 17:45

Michael?

FROM: MICHAEL SCHMIDT
3 May 2018 at 18.49

Dear Iain

Thank you for your really wonderful letter to which I want to reply in full. I cannot at present due to the pressure of work: writing another catalogue, editing *PNR* 242 (with you in it I hope!) and doing a great deal of editorial work.

Maybe over the coming weekend which is supposed to be extended.

What you wrote about your father-in-law was deeply moving.

All best, dear Iain

Michael

*

As a publisher and editor, I love the essay form as much as Herb Leibowitz, editor of *Parnassus*, does. *PN Review* is the place where essays can be published and where they will be read. Books of essays are quite another matter. It is possible to publish an excellent volume and to sell fewer than 300.

PN Review has been blessed since 1983 with the collaboration of Iain Bamforth, easily the most civilised and broadly read among friends roughly of my generation, and one of the best essayists we have. The essays that he writes are very hard to publish in book form. The one success we have had was with *A Doctor's Dictionary*, the title and alphabetical ordering enhancing – or masking – its true nature.

Of the books of essays we have published, Idris Parry's *Speak Silence*, Christopher Middleton's *Bolshevism in Art*, C.H. Sisson's *Anglican Essays* and *In Two Minds*, and Edgell Rickword's *Essays and Opinions* are among those of which I've been proudest. Most of them are out of print: there was no continuing demand. Iain Bamforth's *The Good European: Essays and Arguments* remains in print. Its themes remain news. This profoundly European (because Scottish?) intelligence, whose letters have instructed and delighted me with their insights, merits a wider readership. But his readers must be readers: we find him in the midst of thoughts, theories and arguments, and he is not a remedial teacher.

Iain Bamforth is a physician, a man of action and of the world, and not an academic, not a writer in residence or a career poet. He sees things whole. He is one of the last of the letter-writers. His emails are carefully written, as if long-hand with a fountain pen, rich with completed thought and pertinent questioning. There is nothing old-fashioned about him, but there is a broad living culture still informing everything he says and does.

NOTES

1. https://www.theguardian.com/books/2005/jun/04/ featuresreviews.guardianreview21 (accessed 8 July 2019)
2. The German philosopher Hans-Georg Gadamer (1900-2002) took up his position at the University of Heidelberg in 1949, and published his most famous work, *Truth and Method*, in 1960.
3. *Scattered Limbs: a medical dream-book* was published by Galileo Publishers (Cambridge) in 2019.

4. 'Lou and Fritz: sensible shoes meets starstruck', *PN Review* 242 (July–August 2018).

5. Philip Terry's *Dictator* (Carcanet Classic, 2018) recreates the Akkadian epic *Gilgamesh* using Jean-Paul Nerrière's 1,500-word vocabulary of Globish. Terry has published four volumes of poetry with Carcanet, reworking Shakespeare's sonnets and Dante's *Inferno*, developing a form based on Raymond Queneau's sonnet-like poems, and translating Queneau's last book, *Elementary Morality*. He is currently Director of the Centre for Creative Writing at the University of Essex.

6. Anna Wierzbicka (b. 1938) is a distinguished Polish linguist and Emerita Professor at the Australian National University, Canberra. Her book *Semantic Primitives* (1972) launched her influential theory of Natural Semantic Metalanguage.

7. Victor Shklovsky (1893–1984), who coined the term 'defamiliarisation' (*ostranenie*) in 1917, was one of the major Russian formalists, a theorist, critic and writer.

8. Bamforth is referring to MNS's work on *Gilgamesh: the life of a poem*, published by Princeton University Press in 2019. Several emails in 2017 relate to the poem, particularly Rilke's reaction to it, which Bamforth was able to trace through correspondence for MNS He then mentions Rachel Corbett's *You Must Change Your Life: the story of Rainer Maria Rilke and Auguste Rodin* (W.W. Norton, 2017).

THE YEAR IN BOOKS

John Ashbery, *Collected Poems: 1991–2000*, edited by Mark Ford and David Kermani

Nina Bogin, *Thousandfold*

Beverley Bie Brahic, *The Hotel Eden*

Edmund Blunden, *Selected Poems*, edited by Robyn Marsack (new edition)

Anthony Burgess, *The Ink Trade: selected journalism 1961–1993*, edited by Will Carr

Vahni Capildeo, *Venus as a Bear*

Gaius Valerius Catullus, *The Books of Catullus*, translated by Simon
  Smith

Miles Champion, *A Full Cone*

Fred D'Aguiar, *Translations from Memory*

John F. Deane, *Dear Pilgrims*

Ned Denny, *Unearthly Toys: poems and masks*

Martina Evans, *Now We Can Talk Openly About Men*

Philip French, *Notes from the Dream House: selected film reviews
  1963-2013*

Harry Gilonis, *Rough Breathing: selected poems*

James Harpur, *The White Silhouette: new and selected poems*

John Heath-Stubbs, *Selected Poems*, edited by John Clegg

Oli Hazzard, *Blotter*

A.C. Jacobs, *Nameless Country: selected poems*, edited by Merle
  Bachman and Anthony Rudolf

Gabriel Josipovici, *The Cemetery in Barnes: a novel*

Fawzi Karim, *Incomprehensible Lesson*, versions by Anthony Howell

Frank Kuppner, *The Third Mandarin*

Jenny Lewis, *Gilgamesh Retold*

Tim Liardet, *Arcimboldo's Bulldog: new and selected poems*

Gabriel Levin, *Errant*

Christine Marendon, *Heroines from Abroad*, translated by Ken
  Cockburn

Chris McCully, *Beowulf*, translated by Chris McCully

Rod Mengham, *Grimspound and Inhabiting Art*

Leonard Nolens, *An English Anthology*

Walter Pater, *Selected Essays*, edited by Alex Wong

Phoebe Power, *Shrines of Upper Austria*

Sextus Propertius, *Poems*, translated by Patrick Worsnip

Frederic Raphael, *Against the Stream: Personal Terms VII*

Evelyn Schlag, *All Under One Roof: poems*, translated by Karen
  Leeder

Michael Schmidt (ed), *New Poetries VII*

Philip Terry, *Dictator*
Charles Tomlinson, *Swimming Chenango Lake: selected poems*, edited
   by David Morley
Julian Turner, *Desolate Market*
Chris Wallace-Crabbe, *Rondo*
Andrew Wynn Owen, *The Multiverse*

ACKNOWLEDGEMENTS

I am grateful to all those who have helped in the making of this book, especially to generous authors and executors, whose response was so encouraging. I appreciated the work done by Eleanor Crawforth (Carcanet's Marketing Manager 2005– 13) in assembling texts for an earlier, different version of this book. My warmest thanks to those who went out of their way to identify and help contact copyright holders; and especially to Stuart Airlie, who has (re)lived the Carcanet experience alongside me.

I am grateful to Jessica Smith, Creative Arts Archivist at the John Rylands Library, for all her help and that of the assiduous team in the Reading Room in locating material held in the Carcanet Press Archive; and to Sarah Hepworth for identifying the Edwin Morgan letters held in the Special Collection of the Glasgow University Library. Thanks to the Archives and Special Collections, University of Glasgow Library, and to the University of Manchester Library for allowing the use of correspondence held in their collections.

The publisher and editor are very grateful to all those authors and executors who gave permission to print the copyright letters in this volume. Some letters are covered by permissions gained for their first publication in *Letters to an Editor*, edited by Mark Fisher (Carcanet, 1989).

David Arkell, by permission of Michael Schmidt (Executor); John Ashbery © 2019, all rights reserved - used by arrangement with Georges Borchardt Inc for the Estate of John Ashbery; James Atlas, by permission of the author; Sujata Bhatt, by permission of the author; Iain Bamforth,

INDEX OF NAMES

'The Year in Books' listings have not been included in the index.
Numbers in bold indicate the main correspondence with an author.